POW

POW

Allied Prisoners in Europe, 1939–1945

ADRIAN GILBERT

JOHN MURRAY

© Adrian Gilbert 2006

First published in Great Britain in 2006 by John Murray (Publishers)
A division of Hodder Headline

The right of Adrian Gilbert to be identified as the Author of the Work has been asserted by him
in accordance with the Copyright, Designs and Patents Act 1988.

I

A CIP catalogue record for this title is available from the British Library

Hardback ISBN-13 978-0-7195-6128-3
Hardback ISBN-10 0-7195-6128-0
Trade paperback ISBN-13 978-0-7195-6129-0
Trade paperback ISBN-10 0-7195-6129-9

Typeset in 11.5/14 Monotype Bembo by Servis Filmsetting Ltd, Manchester

Printed and bound in Great Britain by William Clowes Ltd, Beccles, Suffolk

Hodder Headline policy is to use papers that are natural, renewable and recyclable products and
made from wood grown in sustainable forests. The logging and manufacturing processes are
expected to conform to the environmental regulations of the country of origin.

John Murray (Publishers)
338 Euston Road
London NW1 3BH

To Louis, and to Rosie and Freya

Contents

Illustrations

Photographic credits: 1, Sipho; 2, US Air Force Academy McDermott Library; 3, J. H. Witte; 4, 11, Mary Tagg; 5, Marc and Francesca Vietor; 6, Linda and Rob Prouse; 7, B. A. James; 8, Mrs LeFevre; 9, 10, 16, 18, 19, 25, 26, 28, 29, 32, 34, Imperial War Museum; 12, 14, 27, H. C. M. Jarvis; 13, 15, 21, 30, Museum & Archive, British Red Cross Society; 17, author's collection; 20, C. Whitcombe; 22, 23, Jonathan Goodliffe; 24, W. Stephens; 31 American Red Cross; 33, PNA.

Preface

APPROXIMATELY 295,000 BRITISH and American servicemen were captured by the Axis forces of Germany and Italy during the Second World War. A precise number for British, Commonwealth and Empire POWs in Europe seems impossible to obtain; estimates for the three armed forces and the merchant marine range from 170,000 to 200,000 men, although the higher figure seems most likely. POW figures for the United States are more certain, however: around 95,000 soldiers and airmen were imprisoned by the Axis. Whereas most American prisoners were captured relatively late in the war – the majority entering captivity in 1944 – the British suffered several major defeats in the first half of the conflict, with the bulk of their prisoners being captured between 1940 and 1942. Consequently, the British were the long-stay detainees who tended to set the tone of the Anglo-American POW experience.

British and American prisoners enjoyed a special status within the prison camps of Germany and Italy. Their homelands had not been overrun by the Axis – unlike those of many other Allied prisoners – and, as the war progressed, Britain and the United States accumulated ever-increasing numbers of enemy prisoners; the Germans and Italians were aware that the fate of their own men in captivity was largely dependent on the care of the British and American prisoners under their control.

But if the treatment of British and American prisoners was better than that experienced by other POWs, captivity was still a wretched business. The gung-ho escape narratives that came to define prison life in the post-war years give a false gloss to the drab realities of existence behind barbed wire: poor living conditions, chronic – sometimes acute – hunger, deadening monotony, and the misery of being beholden to the will of the enemy with no release date in sight.

Despite the fundamentally negative nature of POW life, there were positive aspects that sprang from the prisoners' own determination to make the most of their otherwise poor lot. Escape and sabotage were obvious ways of fighting back against the enemy, but there were other, more oblique, means adopted by prisoners to maintain a sense of purpose and dignity. Imprisonment provided men with an opportunity to develop their artistic and intellectual potential. One enterprising music-lover even commissioned the composer Benjamin Britten to write a choral piece for a prison-camp music festival. Others continued their education, with several thousand taking academic and professional examinations that were set and marked in Britain and the United States.

Scattered like islands across Greater Germany and Italy, POW camps were small havens of civilization and democracy within a totalitarian sea. In most camps men were elected by ballot to positions of authority and responsibility; free speech was taken for granted; books prohibited beyond the wire were read by those within, and for the first time in years the music of a banned composer like Mendelssohn could be heard in Germany. Prisoners of war displayed an inspirational fortitude in enduring – and sometimes overcoming – their circumstances.

For the sake of convenience I have used the term 'British' to include British, Commonwealth and Empire forces, except where a distinction needs to be made. And I have followed the POWs' practice of calling Soviet prisoners 'Russians', although many came from different nationalities within the Soviet Union. Also for convenience's sake I have used the general expression 'other ranks' to include both NCO and private ranks.

In a book that reflects the diversity of experiences of captivity in Germany and Italy, I have had the good fortune to be able to draw upon an array of source material and information held in institutions and supplied by individuals. In Great Britain I must acknowledge the invaluable help provided by the Imperial War Museum, with its treasure trove of documentary and audio materials, and the National Archive (Public Records Office) at Kew. Also of great help were the National Ex-Prisoner of War Association, the London Library, the

British Library, the Second World War Experience in Leeds, the Monte San Marino Trust, and the libraries of the Wiener Institute and University College London. In Australia I would like to thank the Australian War Memorial for its help. In the United States I am grateful for the assistance provided by the US Military History Institute at Carlisle, Pennsylvania, and the US Air Force Academy Library, Colorado, and to the American Ex-Prisoners of War (AXPOW) organization.

Among the individuals who helped me in my researches are A. D. Azios, Bill Bunbury, Professor Lewis H. Carlson, Cheryl Cerbone, Dr Arthur A. Durand, Dr Jerry Flack, Peter Hart, Professor Milan Hauner, Joseph O'Donnell, William O'Neill (and Jean Sax), John Reis, Pina Saccone, Brigadier S. C. Sharma (Military Adviser, High Commission of India), Peter Stanley, Martin Sugarman and Patricia Wadley. My thanks to them all.

I owe a special thanks to the copyright holders of the unpublished first-hand narratives that appear in this book. They include the Australian War Memorial (Douglas LeFevre), Squadron Leader B. A. James, A. C. Howard, Linda and Rob Prouse (A. Robert Prouse), William and Sebastian Stephens (W. L. Stephens), Mary Tagg (Revd R. G. McDowall), Francesca and Marc Vietor (John A. Vietor) and J. H. Witte.

Every effort has been made to clear permissions. If permission has not been granted please contact the publisher, who will include a credit in subsequent printings and editions.

I am grateful to the following authors, publishers and agents for allowing me permission to quote from the following works: *We Were Each Other's Prisoners* by Lewis H. Carlson (Basic Books); *The Anti-Warrior: A Memoir* by Milt Felsen (University of Iowa Press), *A Crowd is Not Company* by Robert Kee (Sphere, 1989), represented by David Higham Associates; *A Terrier Goes to War* by Jim Robert (Minerva); *Wars and Rumors of Wars* by Roger L. Shinn (Abingdon Press).

My thanks also to my agent, Andrew Lownie, who made this project happen, to Roland Philipps and Rowan Yapp at John Murray, and to Bob Davenport and Martin Collins.

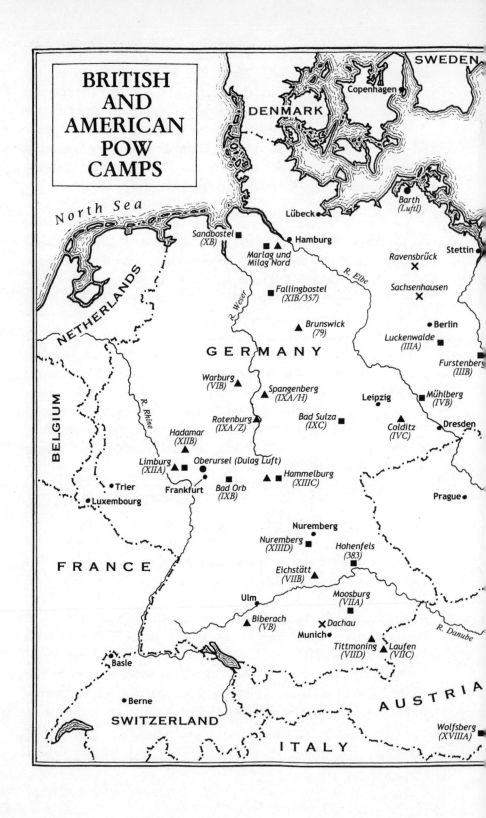

BRITISH AND AMERICAN POW CAMPS

SWEDEN

Copenhagen

DENMARK

North Sea

Lübeck

Barth
(LuftI)

Stettin

Sandbostel
(XB)

Hamburg

Marlag und
Milag Nord

Ravensbrück

R. Elbe

Sachsenhausen

Fallingbostel
(XIB/357)

R. Weser

Brunswick
(79)

Berlin

Luckenwalde
(IIIA)

GERMANY

Furstenberg
(IIIB)

NETHERLANDS

R. Rhine

Warburg
(VIB)

Spangenberg
(IXA/H)

Leipzig

Mühlberg
(IVB)

Rotenburg
(IXA/Z)

Bad Sulza
(IXC)

Colditz
(IVC)

Dresden

Hadamar
(XIIB)

BELGIUM

Limburg
(XIIA)

Oberursel (Dulag Luft)

Hammelburg
(XIIIC)

Prague

Trier

Frankfurt

Bad Orb
(IXB)

Luxembourg

Nuremberg

Nuremberg
(XIIID)

Hohenfels
(383)

FRANCE

Eichstätt
(VIIB)

Moosburg
(VIIA)

Ulm

R. Danube

Biberach
(VB)

Dachau

Munich

Tittmoning
(VIID)

Laufen
(VIIC)

Basle

AUSTRIA

Berne

SWITZERLAND

Wolfsberg
(XVIIIA)

ITALY

BRITISH POW CAMPS

I

Battlefield Surrender

Lieutenant H. C. F. 'Bertie' Harwood remembered the morning of 20 May 1940 as particularly sunny and peaceful; it would have been idyllic, he thought, except for the tramp of French refugees streaming behind him, clogging up the road from Arras to Doullens. Harwood was an officer in C Company, 5th Battalion the Buffs, and his company had been ordered to defend the village of Pommera a few miles north-east of the market town of Doullens.

As the morning wore on, Harwood and his fellow officers became increasingly worried. They had been told a German force was somewhere in the vicinity but its size, whereabouts and line of advance were unknown. Even on this clear spring morning the fog of war blanketed all around. The refugees had no useful information to give the Buffs, and to Harwood's disgust the column contained growing numbers of French soldiers fleeing from the front. Most had thrown away their arms without any sign of a fight, and some even smirked as they passed the British infantrymen holding the line.

The anxiety felt by the officers was compounded by the knowledge that their battalion was unprepared for the task ahead. The 5th Buffs was part of 12th (Eastern) Division, one of three second-line Territorial formations that had been shipped over to France in April for training and labour duties. When the great German offensive in the west was launched on 10 May the division was engaged in building work well away from the front line. The Buffs' regimental historian wrote of the 5th Battalion at Doullens, 'No troops were in support, and the battalion possessed but three Bren guns, three anti-tank rifles and one 2-in mortar per company, the latter without ammunition.'

At 32, Harwood was considerably older than his fellow junior officers, having been recalled to the colours after several years in civilian life. On arrival in France, his CO – aware of his former involvement in the Cambridge Footlights – had asked him to take charge of the battalion concert party. After mornings supervising training, he spent much of the remainder of the day recruiting theatrical talent from the battalion and among local civilians. Despite the war it was a pleasant time for him: 'Those few weeks with the 5th Battalion the Buffs, in France, were some of the happiest in my whole experience in the Army.'

On 18 May the war rudely elbowed its way into Harwood's peaceful existence. The Buffs and the 6th Royal West Kent Regiment – both part of 36th Infantry Brigade – were ordered north to Doullens. When they arrived, the following day, they found the town almost deserted. A sense of impending doom hung in the air. The proprietor of the Café d'Arras told Harwood to help himself to the wine cellar; anything, he said, was better than letting the Boche get hold of his stock. Harwood and another officer accepted a couple of bottles of champagne before marching up the Arras road to their battle positions.

On the morning of the 20th an intelligence report informed the Buffs that 'a few light tanks and AFVs [Armoured Fighting Vehicles] had broken through.' Harwood subsequently recounted that 'the story of the "few light tanks and AFVs" was now a standing joke to all those who stayed behind to witness this diabolical misrepresentation of the true facts.' The two battalions of the 36th Brigade were, in fact, about to face the German 6th Panzer Division, an elite all-arms formation whose soldiers had first seen action in Poland in 1939 and were now flushed with the success of smashing through the French lines on the Meuse.

Around noon Harwood heard the first signs of enemy activity – the drone of German aircraft, and distant artillery fire. The noise quickly grew louder, and at 12.30 p.m. German armour was sighted pressing towards and around Pommera. The men of C Company did what they could to stem the German tide, but the position was soon untenable. Their obsolescent Boyes anti-tank rifles knocked out a few light armoured vehicles and forced others to withdraw, but these were isolated successes.

Within the space of thirty minutes the forward companies of the Buffs were overrun and cut off from battalion HQ and the rest of the brigade, under attack from aircraft, artillery, mortars, machine-gun fire and armoured fighting vehicles. Harwood and his company commander, Captain David Hilton, were forced to accept that Pommera was lost, and their only hope lay in getting as many men away to safety as possible. During a lull in the fighting, what remained of C Company slipped away, boarded a 30-cwt truck, and drove towards a previously agreed rendezvous point at Saint-Pol, using back roads and farm tracks to avoid the Germans, who were now pushing westward on the main highways. They experienced further setbacks, as their truck stuck fast in a muddy lane, despite frantic pushing. Abandoning it, the men carried on by foot. As dusk began to fall they looked down from a rise towards Saint-Pol – and the sight of the 8th Panzer Division streaming through the town. Demoralized and exhausted, they sheltered for the night in a hilltop wood before deciding to return southward in the morning.

In the gently rolling downland around Doullens concealment was difficult, and the evading British soldiers were spotted by German troops, who opened fire. The Buffs dashed for the shelter of a nearby copse. They began to take casualties, and, having used up their remaining ammunition, waited for the end. Harwood described the final moments of C Company:

> A voice shouted from outside the wood: 'Surrender, or we all of you will shoot.' I looked at David and made a gesture conveying the futility of the whole business. And so, beckoning to the remainder of the men scattered around us, we chucked away our rifles and advanced towards an opening in the trees. As I came out from the cover of the undergrowth into the open I saw a German officer or NCO (I couldn't tell the difference) approaching me and brandishing a pistol in a lamentably reckless fashion. He was young and powerfully built with a fair moustache and very light blue eyes. When the last man had emerged from the wood, we were lined up and thoroughly searched. Having satisfied themselves that we had no arms or ammunition on us, we were marched off. I stumbled along with my hands above my head. All I knew was that I was now a prisoner in German hands and God only knew what was going to happen to me and to the other poor wretches with me.

As the Buffs were led away, their German captor declared, 'For you the war is over' – a phrase the Germans seemed to believe de rigueur when capturing Allied troops. The British soldiers were escorted to the divisional headquarters, where Harwood and Hilton were separated from their men. A short, desultory interrogation followed, in which the two officers gave only name, rank and number.

That Lieutenant Harwood was offered a surrender his captors honoured owed much to the Buffs' ceasing fire before the Germans entered the wood: troops who carried on fighting to the end were rarely given the opportunity to surrender. In such cases the victors, whether Allied or Axis, routinely killed the vanquished. This phenomenon was described in an attack led by Lance Sergeant Weir of the Irish Guards against a well-defended German position in Italy in 1943: 'He led his men full tilt into the Germans and they killed those who delayed their surrender with the traditional comment, "Too late, chum".'

Front-line soldiers accepted the brutal morality of killing those who surrendered 'too late'. In the First World War, Charles Carrington, a British officer, proposed that 'No soldier can claim a right to "quarter" if he fights to the extremity.' Ernst Junger, from the other side of no man's land, agreed: 'The defending force, after driving their bullets into the attacking one at five paces' distance, must take the consequences. A man cannot change his feelings again during the last rush of blood before his eyes. He does not want to take prisoners but to kill.'

That this bloodlust could not be turned on and off at will was commented upon by many officers who saw their men shoot or bayonet enemy soldiers attempting to surrender. Although such killings were in breach of the conventions of warfare, they were a reality of close-quarters combat. Another such deadly reality was the swift dispatch of soldiers captured with weapons the ordinary infantryman considered beyond the pale. Machine-gunners and mortar teams could find themselves in mortal danger if caught close to recently fired weapons; soldiers equipped with flame-throwers were also vulnerable, although the most hated were snipers – they were killed without a second thought if captured.

More controversial was the shooting of men who had formally surrendered, especially when some time had elapsed between capture and homicide. In a civilian context this would be straightforward murder;

in the confusion of battle the deaths of one or two men being led to the rear went unnoticed and largely unrecorded.

Such killings were not motivated only by continuing bloodlust: they were often a consequence of simple battlefield expediency. Officers and senior NCOs were invariably reluctant to lose men from their company to escort prisoners back to the rear. A British lieutenant fighting in France in 1944 admitted that German prisoners were shot 'because I couldn't spare the men to take them to a prisoner of war cage'.

The ambivalent attitude of front-line soldiers to the offering of surrenders was at variance with general military policy. Despite their administrative and logistical nuisance, prisoners remained a desirable commodity. They were a valuable propaganda tool: newsreels of enemy soldiers marching into captivity were a visual 'proof' of military success. Prisoners could be used as hostages at some point in the future, and, crucially, they acted as a bargaining counter to ensure reciprocal good behaviour for one's own troops captured by the enemy. They were also a source of intelligence and, subsequently, a form of cheap labour.

Stunning military victories – not least those of the Germans against France in 1940 and against the Soviet Union in 1941– were won not by simply killing the enemy, but by overrunning his forces and taking them prisoner. It made good military sense to encourage the enemy to surrender. In the west, both Allied and Axis military propaganda promised good treatment to captured soldiers, and it was important that these promises had some basis in reality – at least in the short term. And another reason to persuade the enemy to give up the fight was one that found favour with combat-hardened infantrymen: it saved their lives by discouraging the enemy from making last-ditch stands. But on the battlefield there was always an unresolved tension between the policy of promoting surrenders and that of 'taking no prisoners'.

When larger numbers of prisoners were killed – and where there were surviving witnesses – attempts were made to bring those responsible to trial. As usual, the vanquished had little access to justice, so that after 1945 it was Axis soldiers who were tried and judged by Allied military courts for war crimes. The Allies did make some effort to bring to justice their own soldiers who had committed major misdemeanours against civilians or prisoners, but such trials remained rare, and the sentences for those convicted were minimal.

Two mass killings took place just a week after Lieutenant Harwood's surrender, when British troops were slaughtered at Le Paradis and Wormhoudt during rearguard actions to protect the Dunkirk evacuation.

On 27 May 1940 the remnants of 2nd Battalion the Norfolk Regiment conducted a tenacious defence of a large farmhouse at Le Paradis against the 2nd Infantry Regiment of the SS 'Totenkopf' Division. When the Norfolks eventually surrendered, they realized their captors were in an ugly mood: as they were lined up outside the farmhouse, the British soldiers were kicked and hit with rifle butts. This menacing atmosphere continued as they marched into a nearby field. Facing them were two German machine-gun teams, who opened fire without warning. The men collapsed in a heap. Those showing signs of life were finished off with bayonet thrusts or single shots to the head. After the Germans had departed, two badly wounded survivors climbed out from underneath the pile of bodies, and subsequently testified against the officer leading the SS unit.

The massacre at Wormhoudt on 28 May followed a similar pattern. Advancing SS troops – from the 'Leibstandarte Adolf Hitler' – were held up by soldiers from the 2nd Battalion the Royal Warwickshire Regiment, who inflicted heavy casualties on the Germans. When Wormhoudt was taken, the captured Warwicks were led away through the town to a nearby barn. The Germans threw grenades into the building, and fired their sub-machine guns at the mass of struggling men inside. Despite the ferocity of the assault, fifteen men managed to get out alive. They were given medical assist-ance by a passing German Army unit and subsequently sent to prisoner-of-war camps.

While some Waffen SS formations behaved honourably towards Anglo-American POWs – notably the 9th and 10th SS Panzer Divisions after the Battle of Arnhem in 1944 – it was no coincidence that the major atrocities committed against prisoners in western Europe were conducted by the Waffen SS. As the military vanguard of National Socialism, they revelled in their ruthlessness. And moral sensibilities were progressively anaesthetized as the war went on. This was clearly evident in the fighting in western Europe in 1944, with the Waffen SS again prominent in the killing of Allied prisoners. During the Normandy campaign at least 106 prisoners (103 Canadians, 2 British and 1 American) were killed by troops from the 12th SS Panzer Division 'Hitlerjugend'. An Allied post-war court of inquiry came to the conclusion 'that it was understood throughout the ["Hitlerjugend"] division that a policy of denying quarter or executing prisoners after interrogation was openly approved'.

One particularly infamous SS atrocity against Allied prisoners in the west occurred during the Ardennes offensive. A battle group from the 'Leibstandarte', under the leadership of Lieutenant Colonel (SS-Obersturmbannführer) Joachim Peiper, was responsible for the massacre of eight-six US Army prisoners of war just outside the Belgian town of Malmédy on 16 December 1944. A column of American troops had been surprised and overrun by the SS battle group. Some men were put into trucks and driven away into captivity, but others were herded into a field and mown down by machine-gun fire. Approximately thirty men – many badly wounded – survived the attack, and as darkness fell a group made a dash for cover. Some were shot as they struggled across the field, but others managed to escape to US lines and tell their horrifying story.

The killing of the Americans at Malmédy was an example of the arbitrary nature of a prisoner's fate: some of the captured GIs were marched away to captivity, while others were gunned down in cold blood. The prime motive for the slaughter lay in the simple but unpalatable truth that the officers and men of the 'Leibstandarte' – brutalized by years of combat and atrocity – killed because killing had become their stock response to such a situation. Some would have enjoyed the experience.

The massacres that took place at Le Paradis, Wormhoudt and Malmédy were shocking, reflecting men's behaviour at its bestial worst. At the same time, it is also worth pointing out that atrocities were committed by all sides during the Second World War. In what was the worst such war crime committed by Allied troops, seventy-four Italian and two German prisoners were shot by men of the US 45th Infantry Division at Biscari in Sicily on 14 July 1943. The fact remains, however, that Waffen SS troops were more likely to commit atrocities against prisoners of war and civilians than other fighting organizations. But these were extreme forms of conduct. Most British and American troops who put up their hands in surrender were not shot out of hand, leaving approximately 295,000 of them to march into captivity in Germany and Italy.

The campaigns fought in North Africa were noted for the soldierly restraint displayed by both sides. The harsh climate and terrain, the virtual absence of civilians on the battlefield, and the war's geographical isolation from the main European conflict gave it a character of its own. Soldiers often described the war as having been fought with a sense of chivalry: the wounded were well cared for, and surrenders were honoured. There were exceptions, but these were rare. One such incident that threatened to get out of hand involved New Zealand prisoners captured during their division's breakout from Minqar Qaim, shortly after the fall of Tobruk in June 1942. The Germans lined up the New Zealanders, saying they were to be shot, having accused them of bayoneting German wounded and prisoners during the breakout. The order was eventually rescinded – possibly on the intervention of a German-speaking British officer – although the New Zealanders were forced to stand for hours in the hot sun, deprived of water.

The desert war – with its rapid and far-ranging armoured thrusts overwhelming slow-moving infantry formations and fixed defences – made significant captures almost inevitable. The war's first major operation, the British and Commonwealth advance in December 1940, netted 130,000 Italian POWs within a few weeks. On the Allied side, British and American troops repeatedly suffered at the hands of the Germans, from the Afrika Korps's opening offensive of March 1941 to the Battle of Kasserine Pass in February 1943.

One of the first Allied soldiers to encounter the Afrika Korps was 21-year-old Gunner James Witte. After initial successes against the Italians in North Africa in the winter of 1940–41, the British lost many of their best formations to other theatres of war. General Erwin Rommel, the charismatic commander of the Afrika Korps, was not slow to grasp this fact, and on 24 March 1941 he launched a preliminary attack against the now dangerously overextended British.

Jim Witte had joined the Territorials in 1936 as a gunner in 414th Battery, the Essex Yeomanry. An old cavalry regiment, the Essex Yeomanry had been converted to artillery after the First World War, although it kept many traditions – including a uniform of breeches, boots and spurs. Witte, commuting to work in London from his home outside Southend, found the glamour of the Yeomanry irresistible.

In January 1940 the Essex Yeomanry set sail for the Middle East, where, newly equipped with 25-pounder gun-howitzers, it trained for the coming offensive against the Italians. While there, Witte secured a transfer to headquarters as the driver responsible for the regimental water truck. In the desert, the man who controlled access to water, no matter what his rank, had real influence, and this new posting allowed Witte to exercise his budding entrepreneurial skills to the full, providing extra water to senior NCOs in exchange for useful favours.

Attached to the support services of the battery's B echelon, Witte did not see action in the offensive against the Italians, but this would dramatically change as Rommel's panzers overran British positions in Cyrenaica during March–April 1941. Widely dispersed and unprepared for action, the British fell back in disarray. The regimental history of the Essex Yeomanry described the disaster in this measured but telling sentence: 'Even an orderly withdrawal is a depressing affair: when control is lost and retreat becomes precipitate the ensuing confusion lowers morale to dangerous depths at the time and leaves bitter memories in the minds of all caught up in the maelstrom.'

Witte certainly had bitter memories – most a consequence of the actions of a newly arrived officer in command of the B-echelon vehicles. In the confusion of the retreat, they had taken a wrong turning and become separated from the battery. The officer, nicknamed Snurdge by the men, insisted that they drive due south, while the other ranks, represented by the experienced Sergeant Johnson, suggested that they should join the main stream of retreating traffic heading north-east towards Tobruk. Immune to Johnson's pleas, the subaltern effectively ordered B echelon to head towards lead elements of the Afrika Korps.

After a day's fruitless driving had failed to reunite B echelon with the rest of the battery they halted for the night. Witte described the events leading up to capture:

Next morning it was quiet, too quiet for comfort. Suddenly there was a burst of shellfire a few miles to the rear. Soon afterwards a 15-cwt truck with an anti-tank gun mounted on the back dashed into our bivouac. It belonged to the 3rd RHA [Royal Horse Artillery] who were apparently fighting a desperate rearguard action against Rommel's tanks. The sergeant yelled at us to get out of it quickly. 'What the fucking hell are you fucking idiots doing here? Get going before it's too late!'

The chief 'fucking idiot' appeared and started to question the sergeant. But he didn't stop to argue; his driver put his foot down and disappeared in a cloud of dust. It then dawned on our commander we had better do as the RHA sergeant had said. We withdrew hurriedly and went back the way we came. But instead of fanning out in desert formation Snurdge kept us in column of route, a dangerous practice when the Germans were so near.

By mid-afternoon we began to believe that we would escape the tightening Panzer ring. But suddenly a fusillade of shots ripped through the canvas of our three tonner. We stopped abruptly behind the vehicle in front and dived beneath our own. For a few minutes nothing happened. We crept out and there a few yards away was a solitary German half-track. Its occupants had captured the entire column without us making a single move to escape. A German soldier marched briskly down the line of vehicles shouting *raus* (out), a word we were to hear a lot of in the months to come. We were lined up and counted and put back into one of our own vehicles but this time driven by a member of the Afrika Korps. Meanwhile the cause of our capture had disappeared, to where we didn't know. All we knew was that the Germans always quickly separated officers from the men.

The capture of 414th Battery's B echelon was an ignominious affair, an example of confusion and incompetence in the British retreat, although the remainder of the battery retired in good order to Tobruk.

Witte and his comrades were driven to a prisoner-collection point, a large circle of stones that contained some 2,000 British troops. Witte's anger at the nature of his capture existed side by side with the sheer surprise that it had happened at all. 'When I signed on the dotted line way back in 1936,' he wrote, 'I never believed for one moment that I would ever become a prisoner of war. I imagined that when you went out into action you could get wounded or even killed. Anyway the unbelievable happened and I found myself in the bag.'

Witte prided himself on his resourcefulness, and, putting aside feelings of despondency, he looked for an opportunity to improve his lot. German sentries guarded the circle, beyond which were several British trucks loaded with clothing. Hiding his field cap, Witte persuaded a sentry to allow him to board one of the trucks to get a cap. Once in the truck he stuffed all the clothes he could find into his pack, although his great discovery was a carton of 200 cigarettes – pure gold in a community of tobacco-starved smokers. Witte summed up his stroke of good fortune: 'I was launched on a racketeering career which lasted for four years. I was determined to make things as easy as I could for myself.'

Witte's attitude would have found little favour with Major the Very Revd R. G. McDowall, a chaplain attached to the 7th Anti-Tank Regiment of the New Zealand Infantry Division. A Presbyterian minister from the farming community of Riverton, in the far south of New Zealand's South Island, McDowall had been brought up to respect honesty and hard work, and to avoid the evils of 'drink, moral turpitude, sex, Catholicism and a very real devil who often appeared under the guise of "modern ideas"'.

McDowall – 42 at the time of his capture – was not an easy-going man. What he saw as the shortcomings of others caused him much upset, and his critical tone could make him unpopular, especially in the close confines of a prisoner-of-war camp. But he was equally self-critical, and he did not spare himself in his diary of captivity. McDowall was also somewhat physically awkward, a victim of many self-inflicted mishaps – the diary opens with him crashing his car into a wayside desert cairn. But his sense of duty overrode criticism and ridicule. He was also physically and morally brave, and for this he won the respect of the ordinary soldier.

Rommel's first offensive had driven the British back into Egypt, leaving the port of Tobruk besieged by the Germans. Operation Crusader was the British attempt to relieve Tobruk and drive the Axis forces out of Cyrenaica. The New Zealand Division was allotted a major role in the attack: to advance directly towards Tobruk on the northern flank with the support of armoured forces on the open southern flank. In what was the most complicated and confused action of the desert war, the New Zealand Division found itself alone, facing powerful German armoured units for critical periods in the battle.

During the fighting that swirled around the main New Zealand positions near Sidi Rezegh, Bob McDowall was asked to help tend the wounded in the division's three main dressing stations (MDS). Padres traditionally worked closely with medical officers and their staff; they provided spiritual comfort to the severely wounded and the dying, and as well as conducting burial services they helped collect the personal effects of those who had been killed.

On 26–7 November 1941, the 4th, 5th and 6th MDS were combined with a mobile surgical unit and field ambulances, plus some British and South African medical units, to create a vast medical encampment. On the morning of the 28th the division's commanding officer, Major General B. C. Freyberg, VC, visited the MDS to confidently inform staff and patients that the road to Tobruk would be cleared to allow the evacuation of the wounded. In the late afternoon, however, German armoured units arrived out of nowhere and captured the entire camp.

The Germans took full possession of the MDS, allowing the medical staff to carry on their work unmolested – a standard practice in North Africa. But the German presence around the MDS brought down shell, mortar and machine-gun fire from British and Commonwealth positions. This was the first time McDowall had come under fire – a testing moment for him as for others. 'I was always afraid I might be afraid under gunfire,' he wrote, 'but I was almost overcome with thankfulness to find I was not frightened. Tried to help the wounded by moving about among them. I did not go to the trenches.'

The battle raged for several days, with staff, patients and guards being hit by shell splinters. For the severely wounded, unable to crawl into the slit trenches that had been hastily dug around the MDS, it was a hellish experience. Except when the shelling was at its worst, McDowall tended the wounded. 'Took all food and water over to common fund,' he wrote. 'Went round men with cigarettes and matches two or three times a day, making them spin out. Some were hoarding, others had nothing. Some had badly shattered nerves with gunfire.'

The wounded men had believed they would soon be rescued, but by 1 December it was clear that this would not happen in the near future. The main battle had moved westward, leaving the MDS in German and Italian hands for the time being. For their part, the Axis commanders knew that they could not hold the position indefinitely and decided to evacuate walking-wounded and fit prisoners to their rear lines.

McDowall was one of six chaplains from different Christian denominations working in the MDS (a seventh was wounded). The proposed Axis withdrawal posed an intriguing ethical dilemma. As non-combatants, there was no compulsion for them to make this move, and no pressure was placed upon them by German or Italian officers. If they remained at the MDS they would, in all likelihood, be freed in a matter of days. If they chose to go with the men they would enter captivity, possibly for the duration of the war. And yet if all the chaplains stayed behind, the several hundred evacuees – medical staff and lightly wounded – would be without pastoral care.

On the morning of 2 December a meeting of the chaplains was convened by Presbyterian minister Frank Green to resolve the dilemma. McDowall's diary entry was blunt: 'Green and the others did not want to go, we decided two should go, so [Father W.] Sheely and I went.' In McDowall's mind he had a responsibility to the men, and if he had to make the hard choice of entering captivity by his own volition, then so be it. The other chaplain to voluntarily accept imprisonment was a Roman Catholic priest, but whatever their theological differences the padres' courageous decision was welcomed by the wounded prisoners. Four days later the MDS was relieved by British forces, the ordeal of the sick and wounded finally over.

One of the last mass captures of British and Commonwealth troops in the desert war took place on Ruin Ridge on 26/27 July 1942, when a battalion of Australian infantry was virtually wiped out after a doomed night assault. The 2/28th Battalion of the 9th Australian Infantry Division was assigned the task of securing Ruin Ridge, supported by the British 69th Infantry Brigade and 2nd Armoured Brigade. Initially the assault went well. Despite coming under heavy fire from German guns, mortars and machine guns, the Australians got through the minefields and advanced on to their objective. The Germans fought with their customary tenacity, but were unable to halt

the attack. At 1.10 am, just seventy minutes after the troops crossed
the start line, the 2/28th were on Ruin Ridge.

Lance Corporal Douglas LeFevre was on the right flank in C
Company. A small, wiry individual, LeFevre had experienced a harsh
upbringing. Born in the Channel Islands in 1917, he soon moved with
his family to England, where, rejected by his mother and stepfather,
he was sent to a Barnado's home. At the age of 10, without any say in
the matter, he was put aboard the SS *Ballarat* and sent to Western
Australia, where he received a rudimentary education before starting
work as a teamster looking after horses. Already in a militia unit, the
10th Light Horse, LeFevre joined up on the outbreak of war in 1939
and after basic training was shipped to North Africa.

Once in position on Ruin Ridge, LeFevre and his fellow Australians
began to dig in, but even though they used some German prisoners as
ad-hoc labourers (in flagrant disregard of the Geneva Convention) the
ground was so hard that only scrapes and shallow trenches could be
excavated. The Australians knew they would be counter-attacked by
German tanks, but expected to receive support from the British. This
was not to be. The two battalions of the 69th Infantry Brigade had
been caught in a minefield and, exposed to withering German fire
had been forced to retreat. The British armour suffered a similar fate:
over thirty tanks were knocked out for no gain. The 2/28th was on its
own.

A veteran who had fought with the 9th Australian Division during
the celebrated 1941 defence of Tobruk, LeFevre nonetheless found
the German night barrage against the Ruin Ridge position an
unnerving experience: 'Our officer lost his eye, two men lost legs and
I was badly frightened.' To make matters worse, battalion headquarters was out of communication with the rest of the division, and
ammunition was running low.

As dawn broke, the Germans moved in. LeFevre found it an
awesome sight: 'First light found us facing what looked to be a
million German tanks, armoured fighting vehicles, half tracks and all
sorts of vehicles, and they were in an ominous semi-circle around
us.' The Australians had a few 6-pounder anti-tank guns but their
ammunition was quickly expended, leaving the infantry – armed
only with rifles and Bren light machine guns – effectively defence-
less against the German armour. The 2/28th fought on until just

after 10 a.m., when Lieutenant Colonel Lew McCarter, the battalion commander, decided further resistance was futile and signalled his men to surrender. 'We may as well have been shooting at the moon,' remembered LeFevre, 'because they just kept coming on and on, and one-by-one they picked us off and one-by-one they took us prisoner.'

LeFevre's C Company was the last to surrender. He promptly put his wristwatch into a tobacco tin and buried it in the sand, to prevent the Germans from looting a treasured possession given him by his wife, Eileen. (They had married just before he sailed for North Africa.) In the confusion of the last moments of battle, LeFevre attempted to evade capture by hiding in one of the shallow slit trenches. As he was burrowing into the trench, he heard an Australian voice shout, 'Get out, you silly bastard!' He did so seconds before a German tank drove over the trench, caving it in with a slur of its tracks.

The 2/28th had committed some 600 men to the attack, and had lost 65 dead and 490 captured, many of them wounded (including LeFevre, who picked up a flesh wound in the arm). The battalion history records the dejection of the survivors: 'Many of the men of the 2/28th were in tears as they were formed up into a column and marched off into captivity. The bitterness of the moment was aggravated when the column trudged into the [British] artillery concentrations which were still being fired, and more casualties were suffered.'

After the defeat of the Axis forces in North Africa, the focus of strategic action turned to Europe, first towards Italy and then to northern France – the long-awaited Second Front. An amphibious assault against well-defended positions is generally considered to be the hardest of all military operations, and this judgement was borne out by the disastrous attack against Dieppe on 19 August 1942, a forerunner to the successful Normandy landings of June 1944.

A Canadian force was ordered to land on the beaches of the resort town, capture it, and then retire in good order. But the planners had failed to provide sufficient fire support to suppress the German defences, which were anyway far stronger than anticipated. Although the flank attacks to the east and west of Dieppe achieved some success, the main assault was halted on the beaches with heavy Allied casualties. Just under 5,000 Canadians took part in the battle, and 3,367 were killed, wounded or captured – of whom 2,195 entered German POW camps.

The outbreak of war in Europe on 1 September 1939 was thousands of miles and a world away from the farm in Quebec where Bob Prouse was helping out his brother-in-law, but it still acted as a summons to the adventurous Canadian. Prouse was, however, deterred from joining up by his wife, who took a 'dim view' of her newly married husband realizing his 'childhood dreams of battle and glory'. But the call of action eventually proved too strong, and in 1940 Prouse enlisted in the Canadian Provost Corps.

Among the many jobs undertaken by Prouse in pre-war years had been that of private investigator, and the Provost Corps needed men with investigative experience to join the Canadian Expeditionary Force in Britain. After two years in Britain, Corporal Prouse was about to be sent on an officers training course when his CO asked if he would like to participate in a 'special manoeuvre' instead. Increasingly bored by his day-to-day policing duties, Prouse immediately volunteered, and a few days later the 30-year-old was onboard Landing Craft Tank (LCT) No. 5 en route to Dieppe.

As the landing craft neared the shoreline, the Germans opened fire with artillery, mortars and machine guns, supported by Stuka dive-bombers. The fire was so heavy and accurate that when Prouse's landing craft crashed on the shingle the troops were unable to advance up the beach. Impatiently, Prouse pushed forward and jumped into the surf. 'I was up to my thighs in water,' he wrote, 'and still didn't know how I got ashore without being hit. I threw my body onto the coarse gravel beach and squirmed my way to the concrete sea wall. I had to get through a mess of barbed wire already strewn with bodies and finally pulled myself up to the wall where a soldier lay dead, draped over the barbed wire that ran along the top.'

The intense German fire forced Prouse back to the comparative safety of a knocked-out scout car. A nearby mortar-burst tore a chunk out of his steel helmet, and shell splinters cut into his leg. Although British tanks attempted to provide fire support, most were unable to get over the sea wall and instead milled around on the beach, their churning tracks a fatal danger to wounded soldiers.

The Canadian advance had stalled before it had begun. Prouse wormed his way back to the LCT, which had now swung sideways to the beach and provided the only real protection from German fire. In the process he was again hit in the leg by shell splinters. The Royal Navy attempted to get men off the beach, but the landing craft trying to evacuate the men near Prouse was hit and began to burn. German machine-gun fire riddled the water with bullets, and he abandoned any hopes of swimming to safety. Prouse, who underwent what would later be described as an 'out-of-body' experience, recalled the final grim moments before the end, as dead bodies washed against him in the ebb and flow of the tide:

> I felt no fear because I wasn't there at that moment. I was detached from the whole bloody scene, watching the tragedy from afar. I was a silent spectator at a mass sea burial. This state of mind seemed to last for some time, as I floated above it all, taking in every minute detail. I came back to reality with a shudder. I gazed down at the dead soldier who was bumping against my legs. His face was up and his lids were rolled back, showing only the whites of his eyes. I thought these lids were fluttering, trying to tell me something, but all I could do was stare in a dreadful fascination.

As the firing began to die down, the Canadian beachmaster shouted an order to throw all weapons into the sea and destroy any means of identification. A short while later a German voice called on Prouse and the men sheltering in the lee of the landing craft to come out and surrender.

German troops began to move along the beach. One Canadian reported seeing two German officers shooting the most severely wounded on the shoreline as a form of rough-and-ready battlefield euthanasia. And yet the majority of Canadians considered the Germans to have been correct in their treatment of prisoners, both wounded and unwounded. A few Germans showed acts of kindness: one spoon-fed a badly wounded Canadian with his own soup; another handed out bottles of beer.

Such treatment was not, however, accorded to the captured commandos, whose units had been engaged in silencing the batteries that flanked Dieppe. The German Army believed that the cloak-and-dagger tactics employed in commando raids – where guards might

17

have their throats slit – placed commandos and other similar special-forces units outside the protection of the Geneva Convention. A few of the Dieppe commandos were shot out of hand; others were subjected to mock executions, being lined up against a wall and reprieved only at the last minute. This hostility was subsequently codified by Hitler in his Commando Order (*Kommandobefehl*) of 18 October 1942, which stated that all such troops, whether wearing uniform or not, caught operating behind the front line were 'to be slaughtered to the last man'. The order was not always carried out to the letter – local commanders exercised their own discretion – but over 200 British and American special forces soldiers captured behind enemy lines were shot under its terms.

The Canadian prisoners were marched through the town to assembly points for the wounded and non-wounded. Despite the damage done to the town, the local French population gave V for Victory signs to the prisoners, and brought out pitchers of water for the thirsty. The Germans were in a forbearing mood and allowed a limited degree of fraternization, although they arrested a Frenchman who hurled his own shoes to a barefoot prisoner. Bob Prouse received first aid for his wounds at a hospital in Rouen, and was then put on a train for Germany.

If Dieppe was a military disaster for the Allies, then D-Day was a triumph – a victory for the integration of air, sea and land forces, and for the co-operation between the British and American armies. The breakout from the Normandy bridgehead led to the collapse of German forces in France, and to many at the time it seemed possible that the war really would be over by Christmas. But towards the end of 1944 the Allied advance came to a virtual standstill, a consequence of logistic failure and increased German resistance. Hitler – ever the gambler – decided to deploy his strategic reserves in one last offensive in the west, intended to cut the Allies in two. The wooded and hilly Ardennes region was chosen for the German breakthrough. It was only lightly defended by American forces: just four divisions covered a front 75 miles long.

The US 9th Armored Division was one of those formations, and the 60th Armored Infantry Battalion – detached from the division – would find itself holding the southern shoulder of what became the

Battle of the Bulge. Captain Roger L. Shinn, aged 27, commanded Company C, and though it held a battalion-level length of front he was not unduly concerned, having been assured by his superiors that the Germans opposite were even more thinly spread. An introspective man – a student of philosophy and theology – Shinn was also a competent and experienced infantry officer, who had trained and led his men from the division's formation in the United States in July 1942.

Shinn recorded that 15 December had been a quiet day like any other in this sector, but the following day 'was like no other, before or since. I woke early with plaster falling on my face. The C.P. [Command Post] was shaking. Shells crashed fast and furiously; our bewildered senses could not estimate their directions or numbers. Everyone was awake, and the headquarters crew went into action.' Company C's three rifle platoons and anti-tank platoon were sited directly ahead of Shinn's CP, but were too few to prevent the advancing Germans from infiltrating the American positions. Yet throughout the day the men of Company C held the line. The following morning Shinn moved his CP back to the Hotel Meyer, a large stone building which would provide better protection against German artillery fire and act as a rallying point for the company. During the day the barrage increased in intensity, and by evening the hotel was surrounded by German infantry.

Shinn and his headquarters prepared for the coming attack. Although they might be trapped, the Americans were well stocked with ammunition and had a good cover. As darkness fell, Shinn described the battle: 'This fight was exciting. It was not like absorbing artillery. We could fight back, match wits and strength with the enemy. Our men were exhilarated and fought brilliantly. We were killing Germans, so far at low cost to ourselves. In years gone by I had wondered with some moral agony how I would feel about killing men. Now I wasn't thinking about that.'

During the fighting, telephone and radio contact with the forward infantry had been lost, and Shinn received permission from his battalion commander to send out a patrol to guide his men back to the main US lines. Shinn decided a two-man patrol would be most effective: Sergeant Ziringer and himself. 'While daylight remained,' he wrote, 'we pored over the map and picked our route. We ate a K ration meal. I was weak from lack of food, but excitement kept me from noticing it. We gulped a few Benzedrine pills and put chocolate rations in our pockets.'

In the darkness they slipped past the German front line, but they were exhausted and progress was slow. Shinn decided they should abandon their cautious approach march:

> So we moved ahead. Now we covered ground faster, and we were encouraged. Then there was a grunt that sounded something like a 'Halt'. In the split second that I had to make a decision, I could not tell whether it was an American or German voice. So I simply halted. My eyes struggled to see. There was a rifle barrel sticking out of a hole in the ground. Another grunt, and other men came running towards us. Closing in from the sides, they grabbed our weapons and quickly searched us. Then they marched us off into the darkness. We were prisoners of war.

Captain Shinn was one of approximately 23,000 American soldiers to be captured in the initial German advance through the Ardennes. But German success was short-lived. Allied resistance stiffened, the panzers began to run out of fuel, and the foggy weather cleared, allowing the Allied air forces to wreak havoc against the long and vulnerable German columns. By early January 1945 the Germans were in retreat: Hitler's gamble to win the war in the west had failed. But the American prisoners would endure a grim winter before any prospect of liberation.

Despite the many privations that Allied prisoners faced at the hands of their Axis captors, they had good grounds to expect to survive their time in captivity. In international law they had the safeguard of the Geneva Convention, and, while its terms were regularly broken in minor ways, major violations – such as at Le Paradis, Wormhoudt and Malmédy – were rare. But a group that remained unambiguously outside the protection of the Convention was the British Special Operations Executive (SOE), raised to spread subversion and create mayhem across German-occupied Europe through clandestine military action. To the Germans, SOE agents were saboteurs, and those caught were to be handed over to the Gestapo. If captured, the SOE agent typically faced the stark prospect of brutal interrogation followed by a sentence of death.

The operational role of SOE agents in France was to help organ-ize local resistance movements, supply them with arms and equip-ment, and encourage them to fight the Germans. It was soon discovered that women were well suited for certain kinds of under-cover work, especially acting as couriers. They were able to move around the country with greater ease than men, and generally aroused less suspicion, whether from Germans or from the pro-Nazi French authorities. And the British could draw upon a large pool of women whose native language was French. Among these was Odette Sansom, a Frenchwoman who had married an Englishman and moved to Britain in 1931.

Odette took the collapse of France in 1940 as an almost personal affront, a disgrace to her own and her nation's honour. Aged 28, with three young children, she was determined to help her country. Her original intention had been to use her language skills in a clerical capacity, but SOE put it to her that she could be more effective in an active role, and suggested she train to become an undercover agent. This placed her in a quandary: whether to put first her responsibility as a mother or her duty towards the liberation of her country. At first Odette declined the SOE invitation, but nagging doubts plagued her while living as a housewife in the West Country. As she described her feelings after the war, 'Am I going to be satisfied to accept the safety of beautiful Somerset [when] other people are going to suffer, get killed, die because of this war, trying to get freedom for my own chil-dren. Am I supposed to accept all this sacrifice that other people are making without lifting a finger in any way?' Her steely resolve to act rather than stand on the sidelines led her to contact SOE again. She joined the First Aid Nursing Yeomanry (FANY), a precondition before induction into SOE. During her training some doubts were placed on her temperament, but she did well enough to convince her SOE superiors that she was suitable for clandestine work in France.

Odette sailed from Gibraltar in a small boat and made a night landing in Antibes on 31 October 1942. There she joined a circuit organized by SOE agent Peter Churchill, and immediately proved her worth not only as a courier but in organizing the network. She seemed to have a sixth sense for danger that was invaluable in secret operations. The relationship between Churchill and Odette developed into something that was more than just professional, and in their intensely pressured world they became lovers (and subsequently married after the war).

Peter Churchill was negotiating with an organization set up by a French Resistance member, code-named Carte. The network turned out to be largely fictitious, and quarrels within the Carte organization became sufficiently worrying for Churchill, Odette and their radio operator to move to what they considered the relative safety of the mountain resort of Saint-Jorioz in the French Alps, then under fascist Italian administration. Peter Churchill returned to London to discuss the deteriorating situation with his superiors in SOE. While he was in England, Odette was mysteriously approached by a man calling himself 'Colonel Henri'. He claimed to be a disillusioned German intelligence officer who wanted to work with the Allies against the Nazis. Odette was not convinced by his story, but in order to gain time she told him she would meet him again in a few days.

Odette was right to be suspicious of 'Colonel Henri', who was in fact Sergeant Hugo Bleicher of the Abwehr (German military intelligence/counter-intelligence). He would be instrumental in breaking several Resistance networks during the course of the war. Other members of 'Carte' were less astute and were taken in by 'Colonel Henri', divulging names of fellow members, including those of Odette and Churchill.

On the night of 14/15 April 1943 Churchill parachuted back into France and was met by Odette at a mountain dropping point above Saint-Jorioz. Realizing that the network had been fatally compromised, they agreed to flee the area the following day. But they were too late. That evening Bleicher and a detachment of Italian soldiers surrounded the hotel that the two agents were using in Saint-Jorioz. Just after 11 p.m. Odette was woken by a knock on the door from the proprietor; he told her there was a visitor to see her with an urgent message. Thinking this might be one of her couriers, she rushed down to the hotel reception only to discover Bleicher pointing an automatic pistol at her. Bleicher and his agents forced their way past her to the bedroom, finding Churchill asleep. There was no hope of escape. Odette and Churchill were led away to a waiting car to begin the journey that would lead to Paris and the dread process of interrogation by the Gestapo.

★

The capture of the two SOE agents was a police arrest rather than a military action – not unusual given the clandestine nature of SOE's war. Bleicher used his advantages of surprise and superior numbers and firepower to achieve his objective of capturing Odette and Peter Churchill alive.

Lieutenant Bertie Harwood, by contrast, had been offered the choice of surrender or of continuing to fight to the death. Harwood and his company commander accepted the offer of surrender. This was the sensible option: they were outnumbered, surrounded and apparently without ammunition. If they had refused the German terms they would have almost certainly been killed. And yet at the same time soldiers – especially officers – were expected to fight on, regardless of what was sensible.

From the time of the ancient Greeks and the last stand of the Spartans at Thermopylae, soldiers who died in battle earned admiration while those who broke ranks or surrendered became objects of contempt. But in many instances of surrender both officers and other ranks had no choice in the matter: they were ordered – as were Bob Prouse and Doug LeFevre – to give up the fight. Other soldiers were captured through ambush: Jim Witte and Roger Shinn had only a second or two at most to make any sort of decision whether to surrender or not, and would have almost certainly been killed if they had resisted their captors.

To complicate matters further, an officer or senior NCO had an added responsibility, to his men. He might have wished to carry on fighting for his own reasons – personal glory or hatred of the enemy, for example – but his soldiers' well-being would have weighed heavily in his decision to surrender. On occasion, British and American soldiers were criticized by the Germans for surrendering too readily, although this criticism was based on perceived Allied incompetence and soft-heartedness rather than being an accusation of cowardice. The democracies of Britain and America – and their armies – placed a premium on human life that the armies of totalitarian states found hard to comprehend.

Comparison of the armies of Britain and the United States in the war against Germany and Italy shows that the British had far higher numbers taken prisoner. Army statistics indicate well over 170,000 British soldiers captured to 62,000 Americans. Considering prisoners and missing as a percentage of overall casualties, the British figure was 38.1 per cent, the American just 10.9 per cent. This was not because the British were more prone to giving up the fight than their American comrades, but because in the early phases of the war the British experienced severe defeats – Dunkirk, Greece, Crete, Tobruk – on a scale encountered only once by the US Army, during the Battle of the Bulge.

These British disasters did, however, lead Winston Churchill to request the Army Council in December 1942 to consider whether Army regulations were allowing men to surrender too easily. The Council decided against making changes to the regulations, preferring instead to encourage a more positive approach to morale and discipline. And from 1943 onward – with the Allies on the offensive – proportional prisoner losses among the Anglo-American armies were broadly similar. Overall, British and US soldiers did not become captives easily, and the only significant surrenders occurred when large formations were overrun or surrounded by the enemy. While the Germans were generally more skilful and tenacious than their Anglo-American opponents, they too surrendered when the situation seemed to them hopeless. Only the armed forces of Japan differed significantly when it came to surrender. Field Marshal Lord Slim, who spent three years in Burma fighting the Japanese, succinctly remarked, 'We talk a lot about holding a position to the last man and the last round. The Japanese actually do it.'

One common means of assessing the moral acceptability of surrender was whether a soldier had the means to continue the struggle: in effect, did he have weapons and ammunition? As Slim suggested, to fight to 'the last man and the last round' might have been a soldierly ideal, but honour was served if that last bullet had been fired. Many POW narratives are careful to explain that ammunition was running low before surrender was contemplated; Harwood, for example, made it clear that his men 'fired off their remaining ammunition in the general direction of the enemy' before laying down their arms. Without ammunition a soldier had lost his military effectiveness, and if he could not retreat or evade his captor then surrender was an admissible choice.

In these situations the probability was that further fighting would cause the enemy minimal casualties at best, to be set against the slaughter of one's own side. This 'reasonable' attitude might not have appealed to King Leonidas at Thermopylae or to the samurai spirit of the Japanese armed forces, but it allowed hundreds of thousands of Allied soldiers to enter captivity and survive the war.

2

Capture from Air and Sea

FOR MANY AIRMEN, the carrying of charms or the wearing of lucky scarves or other pieces of clothing was seen as essential to safeguard their return from a bombing mission. Other rituals might include the order in which the men would clamber aboard their aircraft, and, in the case of Number 9 Squadron RAF, how they radioed in to the control tower as they taxied on to the runway before take-off. The tradition in 9 Squadron was for the pilot to say 'Au revoir' or 'Cheerio', or even 'See you for eggs and bacon when I come back' – anything but 'Goodbye'. With this in mind, Pilot Officer B. A. 'Jimmy' James, a Wellington bomber co-pilot, was a little disconcerted when his new pilot, Squadron Leader George Peacock, DFC, called out 'Goodbye' on take-off – he had never done that before. An hour later he was dead.

Number 9 Squadron had been attempting to slow the German blitzkrieg through France and the Low Countries by flying interdiction missions against bridges, rail stations and other communication links. The target that night was the river docks at Duisburg. On the evening of 5 June 1940 the heavily laden Wellington slowly gained height over the North Sea, and looking out of his perspex window the 24-year-old James could still see the fires burning in Dunkirk.

Once over the Dutch coast the Wellington was suddenly caught in a searchlight cone. Four flak batteries opened up almost immediately, hitting the aircraft. The port engine caught fire, and with flames and smoke beginning to race towards the cockpit the order was given to bale out. James, along with the navigator and front gunner, leapt into the darkness through the forward escape hatch. Seconds later the Wellington blew up in a massive explosion, its remains plunging to the ground below. 'I pulled the rip cord,' recalled James, 'and waited rather tensely. Suddenly there was a tremendous jerk, which seemed to pull me apart, and I was floating silently in the night sky in what seemed perfect peace.'

While in the air James began devising a plan of action: to walk towards the coast and commandeer a boat to sail back to England. During the final seconds of the descent the ground seemed to rush towards him and, miscalculating his landing – height being difficult to gauge at night – he hit the ground with a thump, spraining his ankle. Gathering up his parachute in the dark, he saw large figures looming up across the field. Fearing they were Germans he prepared for the worst, only to discover their true identity from several loud moos. 'Reassured by these familiar farm noises,' recalled James, 'I relaxed, found a gate onto a road, and started to limp along it in a westerly direction.'

Evasion – the attempt to reach friendly lines without being captured – was in its infancy in 1940. Later in the war, aircrew were routinely issued with escape kits – containing foreign currencies, miniature button compasses, silk maps hidden in jacket linings, and flexible hacksaw blades – as well as being taught how to move unobtrusively through occupied territory. And the most vital element of all, a system of organized assistance from local people, had yet to be established. In 1940 a downed airman was very isolated: in James's words, 'The evader was on his own in a shadowy and unreal world with every man's hand against him.' Slight in height and build, James was a determined and resourceful individual; to him anything was possible given sufficient application and a bit of luck.

After finding a boat to row across a waterway, James encountered a village. Attempts to get around it were thwarted by a profusion of canals and dykes. Although it was now getting light, he decided to chance walking through the village, pretending to be a German pilot. A Dutch farmer passing on a bicycle was not fooled, and immediately asked him if he was English. He then motioned James to get on the pannier of his cycle and took him to a nearby barn, where he gave him food and maps of the locality.

Although the Germans had occupied the Netherlands for less than a month, the local people knew the dangers of harbouring a British flyer. The farmer's brother, who apparently owned the barn, took a negative view of the British airman's presence. James was summoned to the farmhouse to join the family for breakfast. He was unable to make much of the discussion that ranged around him, except for the word *Burgomeister*. Maybe he would help, James wondered hopefully. He then spotted German troops outside the farm, which with his sprained ankle ended any vague hopes he had had of making a dash for it.

Soon afterwards Dutch police arrived and James was escorted to the town hall, where he was formally met by the burgomaster and his officials. Neither side knew the other's language; they drank coffee, making 'polite noises and deprecatory signs, and it was quite evident that this meeting was intended as an official apology for their inability to help'. By now James's presence in the area was known, and a large crowd gathered to gawp at the strange sight of an Allied airman on Dutch soil.

James accepted his misfortune philosophically: he had been unlucky in whom he had met – although, he mused, if the friendly farmer on the bicycle had won the argument his fate might have been different. Another police car arrived to take him away to the Luftwaffe headquarters in Rotterdam. A smartly turned-out officer was standing on the steps of the building to greet the new arrival with the well-worn phrase 'For you the war is over.' Pilot Officer James was among the first of what would amount to around 13,000 British and Commonwealth air-force captives in Axis Europe.

Pilot Officer James had faced the dilemma that almost all evaders experienced: whether to try to go it alone or to seek help. A few intrepid servicemen managed to travel on their own and reach a neutral haven, but most realized that their best hope lay in gaining the help of friendly civilians. The problem was whom to trust, a quandary that could never be fully resolved: collaborators and members of the Resistance were indistinguishable to British and American flyers. The evader had to go by instinct.

As the war progressed, so airmen became better versed in the tactics of evasion. Allied secret organizations – MI9 and MIS-X – set up escape lines that gathered up evaders in the Netherlands, Belgium and France and bundled them to safety either via Spain or directly across the Channel from France by boat. Airey Neave, the Colditz escaper and MI9 officer, estimated that approximately 4,600 British and

American soldiers and airmen escaped or evaded capture in north-west Europe during the war.

It was in the German-occupied lands of western Europe – the Netherlands, Belgium, France and post-armistice Italy – that the evader could operate most successfully. Airmen downed in the German Reich seldom lasted more than a few days as free men; only those who landed close to the border had any real chance of getting away. After the first great raid on the Schweinfurt ball-bearing works (17 August 1943) almost 400 Americans found themselves in enemy-controlled territory, having parachuted or crash-landed in a great swathe stretching through the Netherlands, Belgium, France, Germany, Switzerland and Italy. Most were swiftly picked up. Some managed to stay on the run for a little longer, and thirty-eight successfully evaded capture. Of these, thirty-five landed in the Netherlands, Belgium and France. Of the others, two landed in the German Eifel mountains and walked across the border into nearby Belgium to join an escape line; the last man landed in Italy and was sheltered by partisans until liberation.

Captured evaders found themselves in a grey area that the Germans exploited to their advantage. As they were often apprehended without a recognized uniform, the Germans argued that they were spies or saboteurs pretending to claim POW status. Evaders had not been officially processed as prisoners of war and were unknown to the International Red Cross and the Protecting Power (a neutral country whose inspectors acted on behalf of POWs – the United States initially represented British prisoners, but after America's entry into the war, in December 1941, Switzerland was responsible for both British and US POWs). As a result, the evaders were vulnerable when interrogated. The majority had been helped by civilians in the occupied countries, and the Germans were understandably determined to arrest those who had aided the evaders. The levels of persuasion used on the prisoners ranged from poor prison conditions and undefined threats to beatings and torture. Once interrogations were over and the identity of the evader as an Allied serviceman was established he would normally be sent to a POW camp. Others, especially those who failed to co-operate, could find themselves on their way to a concentration camp.

Captain Roland L. Sargent had been on the first Schweinfurt raid, and he and his crew were forced to bale out on their return flight to

Britain. Sargent landed heavily in woods outside the Belgian city of Liège, where he and some other American flyers were picked up by local people and handed over to a Resistance organization that gave them civilian clothes and took them to Brussels. From there, a group of ten American and British evaders were given a guide and put on a train to Paris. All went well until a check by French police at the border raised suspicions, and when the train arrived in Paris the guide was bundled off by the police, never to be seen again. The perplexed Allied evaders were then led away by a teenage boy, who took them to a small hotel where they were promptly arrested. Sargent was never able to find out what had gone wrong, but he was now in the hands of the Gestapo.

Sargent was accused of being a spy, and without uniform or identity discs it seemed impossible to prove to the Germans that he was an American airman on the run. Taken to the dreaded Fresnes prison in Paris, he was jailed with two other American evaders. While conditions were bad, the trio were not physically mistreated during their many interrogations. After several anxious weeks Sargent and his companions managed to persuade a visiting Luftwaffe officer of their proper status; they were then dispatched to the interrogation centre at 'Dulag Luft', near Frankfurt, out of the hands of the Gestapo and into the POW system.

Warrant Officer Stan Hope was heartbreakingly close to freedom when caught on 15 January 1943 as he prepared to cross the Pyrenees into Spain. Hope's RAF Mosquito had been shot down over Belgium several weeks earlier, and following discovery by the local Resistance he had been spirited through occupied Belgium and France along the famous Comet line. After capture he too was taken to Fresnes prison, but his treatment was more severe. Hope was subjected to repeated beatings by the Gestapo, who were eventually able to extract some information from him. He endured a four-month starvation diet in solitary confinement, before being sent to the Stalag Luft VI POW camp at Heydekrug.

Other evaders were shot, some at capture and others after interrogation. Three airmen – a Briton, an Australian and a Canadian – were hiding in the house of a Dutchwoman when the Gestapo banged on the door early on 9 July 1944. The airmen, correctly fearing the nature of the summons, ran out of the back of the house, but were gunned down by a Gestapo agent with a sub-machine gun. Two Canadian crewmen shot down over France on the night of 28/29 June 1944 managed to stay on the run for two weeks until captured in civilian clothing. They were held by German security forces for three weeks before being taken to nearby woods and killed.

Members of the Resistance and other helpers of Allied evaders lacked any form of legal protection when captured by the Germans. Almost inevitably they suffered most, and one source estimates that for every Allied airman who reached safety a helper lost his or her life. It was a high price to pay.

On 12 August 1943, five days before the first Schweinfurt raid, the 91st Bomb Group, US Army Air Force, was ordered to attack Gelsenkirchen in the industrial Ruhr region. One of the B-17 bombers on the mission included a high-ranking passenger, Colonel Delmar T. Spivey, commander of a flexible-gunnery school in Florida. The American daylight-bombing campaign relied on its heavy bombers flying in close formation to provide mutual fire support, but by early 1943 it was apparent that the unescorted bombers were suffering unacceptable losses to German fighters. Spivey and several other high-ranking officers were given permission to fly on combat missions to make an assessment of what was going wrong and to improve the bombers' machine-gun defences.

Spivey, a West Point graduate who had transferred from the Army to the fledgling Army Air Corps in 1928, welcomed the chance to fly an operational mission – and not just for purely professional reasons: no officer could expect to gain the full respect of his juniors unless he too had experienced combat. The mission of 12 August – three days after Spivey's thirty-eighth birthday – would be an opportunity to fly deep into enemy territory.

The unescorted B-17s flew across the Low Countries and then into Germany – and to inevitable attack from German interceptors. Spivey immediately noticed a lack of fire discipline among the American gunners as they opened up on the enemy at too great a range, failing to use their gunsights in the recommended manner. The attack was soon over, however, the German fighters returning to base, their ammunition expended. The B-17s were left to encounter the flak defences ringing Gelsenkirchen. Spivey described his fateful bomb run:

As I watched the stick of demolition bombs falling away, keeping up with us in their forward motion, a burst of Flak racked the whole plane. The armor plate on which I was kneeling smashed up against my knees. The impact knocked off my steel helmet and sent the ammunition boxes flying. My nose gun came to rest at a crazy angle. The cowling of the two inboard engines flew off. Both engines stopped and the right one caught fire. I saw the two wing bombers beside us quickly leave us behind. And there we were, at 30,000 feet, shot up and feeling naked, all our friends disappearing in the distance.

The B-17 struggled back towards England but began to lose altitude, its starboard wing red hot and soon on the point of disintegration. The order was given to prepare for a crash landing. At that moment Spivey was in the bomb bay, and his parachute harness snagged on one of the bomb racks. Reaching the cabin door he found it shut fast, and he had to pound on it to be let in and avoid an almost certain fatal landing if he remained where he was:

The door opened. I squeezed in just in time to flop down in a sitting posture and receive the full impact of the head of the man in front of me as it snapped back when the plane plunged through telephone wires and crashed to the ground. My dental bridge was broken and several teeth were swimming in a bath of blood and saliva. The old airplane churned to halt in a wheat field. I'm not quite sure what happened next. I only know that there was a mad rush to get out before the plane exploded. We did get out, and none of us seemed to be too badly wounded.

The B-17 had come down on the Dutch–German border, and while the aircrew scattered in all directions the alarm had already been raised. The airmen had all been trained in the basic techniques of evasion and hoped to eventually make contact with the Dutch underground, but Spivey was soon cornered by a brawny farmer armed with a hunting rifle and pitchfork. Spivey felt a hot surge of anger and humiliation as the farmer held his arm in a vice-like grip to search him. He was led back to a nearby farmhouse, where he was given some breakfast and coffee before being taken to a police station in the nearby village. During the day the remainder of the crew were rounded up. They would become part of the 33,000-strong contingent of US airmen held in Germany as POWs during the Second World War.

★

B-24 pilot Captain John A. Vietor Jr had no hope of getting back to friendly territory as he hung from his parachute and slowly descended through the cold winter air into the heart of the Bavarian countryside. His main concern was trying to guide his parachute away from the river Danube, which loomed below him and seemed uncomfortably wide.

As he finally hit the snow, a safe distance from the icy waters, Vietor ruefully realized that this was his second time on German soil. Before the war, as part of the US Diplomatic Service, he had been sent to the new German Reich. It had been a fascinating if increasingly disturbing posting, which eventually convinced him that war was inevitable. On his return to America in 1939 Vietor applied to join the US Army Air Corps, and was accepted as a cadet the following year. After flying anti-submarine patrols and acting as an instructor on B-26 and B-24 bombers, he joined the 98th Bomb Group in Italy in December 1943.

On 25 February 1944 the 29-year-old Vietor and his B-24 crew had been assigned to bomb the Messerschmitt aircraft factory outside Regensburg. They opened the bomb-bay doors in preparation for the run-in to the target, but were hit by a burst of flak. Although the damage was potentially critical, they decided to press on and make the bombing run. As the B-24 turned away from the target it was pounced on by a wave of Bf 109 fighters. Unable to manoeuvre effectively, the aircraft was easy meat for the Germans: two engines were shot out, and the right wing tip and right rudder were ripped off. With the intercom and oxygen also out of commission, Vietor shouted to his crew to bail out:

> As soon as the rest of the crew were successfully away, I took over what was left of the controls while Lieutenant Bowman put on his chute; I held her as best as I could until she started to spin. I felt a sharp sting in my right leg . . . a .30 calibre bullet. I crawled back towards the bomb bay. I hastily adjusted my chute, taking off my gloves to fasten it more securely. The pressure of the centrifugal force of the spin made it difficult for me to reach the bomb bays and I had a moment of terror and panic, not from fear of jumping, but from the fear that I might be trapped and unable to pull myself out. Somehow I managed to pull myself clear, almost unconscious from lack of oxygen. It was only by the most tremendous exertion of will power and concentration that I remembered to pull the rip cord.

Within minutes of landing Vietor saw figures running across the snow towards him. He waited calmly for arrest:

When the leader was fifty yards away he shouted to me, but I couldn't hear him. A bullet whistled over my head. I had seen enough war movies to know what to do now. Repressing a momentary impulse to laugh, I stuck my hands up over my head and yelled 'Kamerad!' – an action that seemed ludicrous and unreal. In the approved melodramatic manner, a pistol was thrust into my back, and I was searched. Hoping for the best, I announced in my best German, *'Ich bin Amerikanische Offizier!'* This didn't seem to impress my captors one way or the other. They seemed uniformly taciturn and surly. With a man on each side holding an arm, one man leading, and the rest following watchfully behind with their squirrel guns, I was firmly escorted to the village. I was a Prisoner of War.

Vietor was held in the village *Gasthaus* until the arrival of a Luftwaffe officer and two guards. Announcing 'For you the war is over', the officer accompanied Vietor to a truck with barred windows and a locked door. A short while later the truck door was unbolted to let in other crew members, although three men remained missing. As the crew was assembled, Vietor was surprised how little interest the villagers took in their arrival: looking out of the window he saw that they 'were absorbed in the more familiar difficulties of a woman in the middle of the street, single-handedly attempting to "service" a moody and reluctant cow with a sleepy bull'. When the Luftwaffe had completed its search of the area, the truck drove off to the local airbase.

John Vietor was fortunate in the reception he received from the local population. As the strategic air offensive against Germany gained momentum, so hostility against Allied airmen increased, and by early 1944 it was commonplace for downed flyers to be beaten, and on some occasions even lynched, by civilians. When the first Allied airmen fell into German hands they were objects of curiosity and even sympathy, but from 1943 onward, as the Allies systematically laid waste to Germany, attitudes turned to anger.

But, reflecting the often arbitrary nature of the POW experience, there were exceptions. One US prisoner wrote to his wife on 19

February 1944, 'War is a crazy game. The very people who are sup-posed to be your enemies do everything to save your life. I came down near a farm and the old lady was as good to me and as sympathetic as a mother would have been.' It was certainly safer for an airman to land in rural districts, where bombing was limited. Had Vietor landed near his target of Regensburg then it is likely that he would have encountered more than the stolid indifference of a farming commu-nity. A couple of days later, while in transit on a station platform in Munich, he described how he and his crew 'heard muttering around us. Several women spat at us and we heard growls of *"Terror Flieger"*, child murderers, gangsters etc. This was the first time we had encoun-tered hatred and bitterness against Allied flyers.'

Germans' hostility towards the people who had bombed them out of their homes and killed their families and friends was hardly sur-prising. By the war's end the air offensive had killed at least 600,000 Germans, most of whom were civilians. The Nazi Party inflamed the situation by publicly condoning acts of violence against Allied airmen. On 27 May 1944, in a front-page editorial in the Nazi mouthpiece the *Völkischer Beobachter*, Goebbels declared, 'Only with the aid of arms is it possible to secure the lives of enemy pilots shot down during such attacks, for they would otherwise be killed by a sorely tried pop-ulation . . . It seems to us hardly possible and tolerable to use German police and soldiers against the German people when it treats murder-ers of children as they deserve.'

Police and other government officials were positively encouraged not to intervene when Allied airmen were attacked by civilians. On 25 February 1945 Albert Hoffman, Gauleiter of South Westphalia, issued an order that confirmed Nazi policy in unambiguous terms: 'Fighter-bomber pilots who have been shot down are in principle not to be protected against the fury of the people. I expect all police officers to refuse to lend their protection to such gangsters. Authorities acting in contradiction to the popular sentiment will have to answer to me. All police and gendarmerie officials are to be informed immediately of my views.'

Most officials, police or otherwise, did not follow these Nazi out-bursts, however, and the majority of British and American airmen entered captivity having suffered little more than bad language and threats from the civilian population. One organization acting in the airmen's favour was, perhaps ironically, the Wehrmacht – the German armed forces – itself. Once an Allied airman was in the proper custody of the German Army or Air Force his protection was usually guaranteed.

The murders of Allied airmen in Germany were analogous to the killing of certain categories of soldier such as snipers or flame-thrower operators: the victims' methods of waging war were deemed too terrible for them to expect mercy. But, in other respects, surrenders from the air were different from those on land. There were none of the mass captures in which thousands of men could find themselves taken prisoner without firing a shot. And, while the actual surrender of airmen might be relatively peaceable – as experienced by James and by Vietor – the loss of their aircraft was traumatic. Every captured airman could genuinely consider himself a survivor; few passed through the ordeal without harm to themselves or witnessing the injury or death of fellow crewmen.

Airmen also considered themselves an elite. Unlike the Army, the Air Force was able to draw upon a relatively small pool of well-educated, highly motivated volunteers for service as aircrew. And the men who survived to enter POW camps were front-line servicemen: there were no supporting arms among them – no cooks and bottle-washers and, with a handful of exceptions, no doctors and clergymen.

The soldier's dilemma – when could an offer of surrender be made to the enemy? – was largely avoided by the airman. The matter was taken out of the pilot's hands by mechanical failure or enemy action disabling his aircraft. In a badly damaged aircraft a decision might be taken to return to base or to bale out, but without hindsight either choice was as fraught with danger as the other. Once on the ground, the unarmed airman had little alternative but to surrender when faced by his armed captor.

Like airmen, sailors had limited choice when it came to surrender. In the navies of Britain and the United States, the abject surrender of a vessel was unthinkable. A ship might run from a superior opponent, but it would not strike its colours until it was sinking or disabled as a fighting vessel. Merchant seaman also showed a remarkable tenacity in refusing to give way to the enemy.

Once in the water or drifting in a small boat, sailors were more rescued than captured. The 'cruel sea' bonded opponents in a way not encountered on land, and sailors made great efforts to save stricken opponents where they could. The numbers of POWs from the British navy and merchant marine were relatively small: approximately 5,500 Royal Navy POWs and roughly the same number of merchant seaman.

Most sailors from the merchant marine were captured in the Atlantic during the early stages of the war, victims of German commerce raiders. Naval prisoners came mainly from the North Atlantic and Mediterranean, although by mid-1943 onward – with the domination of European waters by the Allied navies – their numbers dwindled. One reason for the relative paucity of prisoners captured by both sides lay in the nature of maritime warfare: unless help was close at hand, stricken ships went under, taking their crews with them. And in major naval engagements fatal casualties could be massive. Perhaps the most extreme example occurred during the hunt for the *Bismarck* in May 1941: HMS *Hood* exploded leaving just 3 survivors from a complement of 1,419 men, and only 115 sailors from a 2,222-strong crew were picked out of the water following the sinking of *Bismarck*.

The raid on the docks of Saint-Nazaire on 27/28 March 1942 was one of the most audacious amphibious operations of the war, intended to prevent the German battleship *Tirpitz* from using the port's dry-dock facilities and hence prevent it from operating against Allied convoys in the Atlantic. The assault would be spearheaded by HMS *Campbeltown*, an old American Lend-Lease destroyer packed with explosives. The destroyer would ram the main lock gates, its massive explosive charge timed to explode some hours later. A force of commandos would accompany *Campbeltown* in fifteen motor launches and, on landing, would support the main attack and destroy Saint-Nazaire's other dock installations.

In charge of the motor launches was Lieutenant Commander W. L. 'Billie' Stephens of the 20th Motor Launch Flotilla. Tall, fair-haired, with piercing blue eyes, the 30-year-old Stephens was a keen sailor who had joined the Royal Naval Volunteer Reserve before the war. His buccaneering spirit made him an ideal coastal-forces leader.

The British flotilla, with *Campbeltown* followed by two columns of light craft, sailed up the Loire estuary towards the heavily defended docks of Saint-Nazaire. For a while the raiders managed to bluff the defenders into thinking they were a returning German convoy. But with the British craft still well over a mile from their target the German defences delivered a barrage of fire from massed 40-mm and 20-mm guns. 'We opened fire too,' recalled Stephens, 'and the ensuing display was quite unbelievable – no fireworks I have ever seen equalled it.'

As one of boats nearest *Campbeltown*, Stephens's wooden-hulled Fairmile-B was attracting a heavy volume of fire: shots missing the destroyer were striking the motor launch. A few hundred yards from their target, disaster struck. The launch was hit twice by shells from heavy guns: both engines and the steering were knocked out, and the hull was holed under the waterline. Worse still, fires had started and were raging close to the auxiliary petrol tanks on deck. Stephens had no alternative but to abandon ship. While some men were able to use the few Carley floats, others had to swim ashore. In keeping with naval tradition, Stephens oversaw the abandonment and waited to be last man off the boat:

> There was practically no firing at us by this time, it being only too obvious to the enemy that we had already 'had it', and they were concentrating on other targets. I stood right up in the bows and whilst getting out my flask for a 'quick one' I looked around me. The scene was indescribable. We were burning furiously as were two other boats astern of us a little further out in the river; it was a very sad sight. Tracer was still flying in all directions and the whole scene was brilliantly illuminated by searchlights. After a very long pull at my flask (little did I realize when I should next taste whisky), I slid over the bows on a line into the water, and, my God, it was cold!
>
> I started to swim quite slowly and casually because it was only sixty or seventy yards to the shore, then harder as I suddenly realized the current was carrying me fast downstream and away from the only possible landing place. I kicked off my flying boots – something I was to regret bitterly later – and swam as I've never swum before. I had to fight to stop myself panicking. Slowly I began to make headway, the time seemed interminable, but I suppose I had only been in the water seven or eight minutes when I reached a small slipway and having arrived at

it I just lay there half in and half out of the water and quite exhausted. At that moment I didn't really care much what happened to me; however, someone, I think it was my First Lieutenant, pulled me clear and after a minute or two I became more or less normal.

Stephens and a group of seven or eight survivors from the motor launch began to edge their way from the sea wall towards the darkness of the dock buildings in the hope of evading the Germans and meeting up with the commandos already ashore. But they were soon spotted by an enemy patrol that gave chase. 'It was just a question of minutes', Stephens wrote, 'until we were rounded up and made to understand that we must hold our hands up; and so at 2.30 a.m. on 28 March 1942 I became a prisoner of war.'

The British sailors were lined up and force-marched through the town to the submarine pens. It was a painful march for the barefoot Stephens, but the guards' rifle butts kept them all moving. Once there they 'were herded down below into what was evidently an air-raid shelter and here we stayed for the rest of the night, cold, wet and miserable, and with our Nazi friends coming in from time to time to jeer at us and even refusing water for our wounded'.

Campbeltown exploded later in the morning, destroying the dry dock and killing several senior German officers inspecting the ship. (It also killed two commando-officer prisoners, who knew of the explosive charges but heroically kept quiet.) Stephens and his fellow prisoners did not hear the blast, however: they were on their way to a transit camp near Rennes, the first step on the road to imprisonment in Germany.

3

The Road to the Camps

A NY RELIEF A prisoner may have felt in surviving the ordeal of capture was short-lived. He now faced a new, profoundly unsettling, experience over which he had little or no control: the transit from battlefield to permanent prisoner-of war camp. This would be a long, difficult and, for some, terrible journey. When the numbing effect caused by the shock of capture had worn off, the prisoner was forced to take stock of his new situation. He would undergo many, often conflicting, emotions.

After his capture in northern France in 1940, Lieutenant Bertie Harwood was sent by foot and truck towards Germany. 'I sat on the side of the road,' he wrote, during a brief stop, 'inhaling the cool fresh air, my mind a jumble of hope and despair mingled with resignation.' Captain John A. Vietor Jr railed against his misfortune: 'I felt angry and frustrated and bitched at the lousy luck that singled us out to be knocked down. If the controls hadn't been hit by Flak, I would have been back at the Villa [in Lecce, Italy], eating fried chicken and drinking red wine with two attractive signorines.' For aircrew, the switch from the pampered conditions enjoyed at an airbase to those of a prison camp was painfully abrupt.

Lance Corporal Doug LeFevre and Corporal Bob Prouse both felt the misery of depression as they were marched away from their respective battlefields at Ruin Ridge and Dieppe. LeFevre experienced the 'terrible feeling of being a prisoner. The nearest I can describe it is having a good kick in the pants. The whole world had collapsed. After all our efforts, all our mates' efforts, all the loss of life, we had achieved nothing.' Prouse was 'deeply disappointed that in only a few hours of hell and frustration all of my boyhood dreams of reliving Ypres, Mons and other great battles had been wiped out in one fell swoop'. Captain Roger L. Shinn was similarly burdened as he crossed the river Sauer on to German soil after the Battle of the Bulge: 'Now I was depressed. Now for the first time I felt like a prisoner. A terrible weight came with that feeling. So far I had worried – about those surrounded platoons, about what the Colonel was thinking when I didn't show up, about plans for escape. But I was now in Hitler's Germany. Every inch was foreign ground. There was a river between us and my duty. I felt helpless.'

Officers were used to giving orders and assuming responsibility. After surrender their role was reversed: they accepted orders and became the responsibility of others. This loss of function and associated prestige was a hard blow, a form of reduction to the ranks. And there were always nagging questions to be answered: how had they acquitted themselves in combat, and had their surrender been honourable? They might reason that what had seemed appropriate behaviour at the time of surrender would subsequently be construed by others as a failure of duty. Once in a camp, the prisoner was among men who had been through a similar experience and understood the complex emotions that surrender occasioned. But the outside world tended not to understand, and this was a source of concern to prisoners. The apocryphal 'Dear John' letters, with their attendant accusations of cowardice, were a reflection of those worries.

One American infantry officer – who had himself become a captive of the Germans on the orders of a superior officer – wrote, just after his release, of the semantic embarrassment caused by surrender:

> The general attitude toward our own men who surrendered is vague and indefinite. Everyone, including the ex-captives themselves, studiously avoids the word 'surrender'. Instead they were captured, caught, picked up, bagged and so on, as though it were possible to be captured without surrendering. Many ground force officers in Germany began saying 'When did you go down?' in imitation of the Air Force officer prisoners. Once, in Paris, I wearied of all this beating around the bush and told a rear echelon major that I wasn't 'picked up' as he put it. 'I surrendered – unconditionally!'

Feelings of shame were not the sole preserve of officers. Those NCOs and privates who made the decision to surrender suffered similar pangs of conscience, but the majority of other ranks were ordered to surrender, thereby taking away much of the burden of guilt. For those told to lay down their arms a common emotion was one of anger, of having been let down by their superiors.

In some cases this resentment may have been justified. One such instance was the surrender forced upon Gunner Jim Witte and B echelon of the Essex Yeomanry, captured by the Afrika Korps in early April 1941. The reason for their capture, Witte maintained, was the almost wilful incompetence of an officer who refused to heed the common-sense suggestions of his senior NCO. Witte and his Yeomanry comrades subsequently found themselves corralled inside a wretched Italian transit camp when their former commanding officer – nicknamed Snurdge – arrived accompanied by an Italian officer. Witte recalled their anger:

> He made a bee-line for us so we sat down on the deck deliberately, knowing full well that you had to stand when addressed by an officer. Snurdge looked a bit annoyed, but he got more annoyed when someone said, 'If it hadn't been for you, you cunt, we wouldn't be here now!' Snurdge departed hurriedly with an amazed Italian officer who couldn't believe his eyes at the sight of common soldiers who laid around when they were addressed by a superior.

Whatever the differing emotions men felt about their capture, one thing was obvious to most: they were no longer fighting men. A few prisoners refused to accept this redundancy, however, and regarded their time in captivity as a war to be fought by other means. This was the approach of committed escapers, and in the likes of Pilot Officer Jimmy James and Lieutenant Commander Billie Stephens it had real meaning: their total commitment to escape was a constant thorn in the German side. But for most men the comment made by one US prisoner probably rang more true: 'You suddenly realize that by passing from the right side of the front to the wrong you have become a nonentity in the huge business of war.'

A week after capture Shinn was placed in solitary confinement. This gave him time to analyse his feelings: 'In this lonely cell the transformation from soldier to prisoner became complete. Here *nothing happened*. I had moved all the way from battle – where activity was feverish and men drove themselves to the limit of human possibilities – to solitary confinement – where a man was alone and did nothing . . . The dominant impression was the *lifting of responsibility*.'

Capture also severed the ties a man had with family and friends. Even though such links might be stretched over thousands of miles, they were a tangible connection to a civilized, non-military world. With capture those links had gone, and in the anxious prisoner's mind might never be re-established. For those with wives and children it was particularly difficult. Some thirty-six hours after his capture by a farmer on the German–Dutch border, Colonel Delmar T. Spivey was left to spend the night in a local Luftwaffe-station cell. Alone for the first time, and with nothing to distract him, Spivey's thoughts turned to his wife and young son: 'My throat closed so tightly I had trouble breathing or swallowing, and I could find no handkerchief to blow my nose. I buried my face in my old winter flying helmet and fell asleep.'

Shot down in August 1943, Spivey could at least console himself with the knowledge that his family was safe from harm, and that inevitable Allied victory would eventually secure his release. For those British servicemen captured in the first couple of years of hostilities – when the tide of war flowed with the Axis – the outlook was bleak. In 1940, German guards gleefully reminded prisoners of Dunkirk and prophesied Britain's imminent defeat: the phrase 'England in sechs Wochen' – 'England in six weeks' – kept recurring, as did taunts of how the Germans would avail themselves of the prisoners' wives, sisters and daughters. Harwood summed up the despair felt by those early captives:

> I thought of England. I thought of the war. I thought of everyone who mattered to me and imagined that the chances of seeing them again in this life were slender. England was tottering on her knees and the future was too uncertain to contemplate. Although none of us would have admitted it to each other, we must all of us have had the same thought at the back of our minds: what would happen to our families and ourselves if we lost the war. I heard others telling jokes and, although I have never felt less amused in my life, I forced myself to tell a story, longing with all my heart that time would blunt my sensibilities; I knew full well that the others must be feeling the same as I did because I noticed that their laughter was tinged with nervous hysteria. Anything was better than thinking.

The transit from battlefield to permanent camp would typically begin with the enemy helping themselves to the personal possessions of the newly captured. Bob Prouse and his fellow Canadians handed over watches and lighters, Doug LeFevre lost a leather belt decorated with Australian cap badges, and Jack Vietor had his wristwatch confiscated. In the submarine pens at Saint-Nazaire, Billie Stephens and the rest of his crew were searched: 'This wasn't a very thorough search and it was simply done in order that the Hun could get a little loot. Everything we possessed, wallets, letters, photos, cigarette cases, money, disappeared into a sack, never to be seen or heard of again.' Although illegal, such plunder counted among the spoils of war, and prisoners were in no position to complain. Yet in the random world of the POW other prisoners did not suffer this indignity, and some even managed to hold on to personal possessions throughout captivity.

From their point of capture by the Germans, soldiers would be moved to one or more temporary collecting centres (*Frontstalags*) and then to a Dulag (an abbreviation of *Durchgangslager*, or transit camp), where they were evaluated before transfer to a permanent POW camp. There were two types of permanent camp: a Stalag (*Stammlager*) for other ranks and an Oflag (*Offizierlager*) for officers. The Italian Army had a similar system of transit camps, permanent camps, and separation of officers from other ranks. Allied airmen shot down over German-occupied Europe were sent to the nearest Luftwaffe station and then to Dulag Luft (*Durchgangslager Luftwaffe*) near Frankfurt for interrogation. Stalag XB at Sandbostel housed naval and merchant-marine prisoners in a special compound, although from early 1942 onward this Army-administered camp was replaced by Marlag und Milag Nord (*Marinelager und Marineinterierenlager*, or naval camp and merchant-navy internment camp) under the control of the Kriegsmarine – the German Navy. Some officers and naval specialists might be sent for interrogation at German naval headquarters in Wilhelmshaven.

Once in a Dulag, men were officially registered as POWs. Their names were given to the Red Cross, who would notify their governments and through them their next of kin. Red Cross post-cards could also be sent by prisoners directly to their families. This was an important service for prisoners, who were invariably anxious to let families know that they had not been killed on the battlefield. Bob Prouse turned down an offer of escape during transit in part so he could be registered and notify his wife of his where-abouts.

How men fared in their journey to permanent camps depended on many circumstances. Perhaps not surprisingly, officers had an easier time than NCOs and private soldiers, but even here there were wide variations in Axis treatment of prisoners.

British soldiers captured in France in 1940 suffered real hardship. Although the Germans were unprepared for the size and scale of their victory – and the concomitant numbers of prisoners – this is insufficient to explain away their treatment of the British. Many pris-oners thought German behaviour was a deliberate attempt to break their physical and mental resolve, to make them more compliant and easier to guard. Others saw the Germans acting in the traditionally ascribed role of the arrogant bully, a view subsequently reinforced by a change to a more accommodating attitude when the war turned in the Allies' favour.

The men and some officers were force-marched across France, Belgium and the Netherlands towards transit camps in Germany. Already weakened by their exertions in battle, the prisoners were deliberately deprived of food and water. Attempts by French civil-ians to help were prohibited by the Germans: thirst-racked prison-ers recall how buckets of water left out for them were kicked over by their guards. In one instance, near Maastricht, nuns had placed sandwiches on a table by the road. A hungry prisoner remembered how, 'to our helpless disgust, the guards forced us at rifle-point to pass by on the other side of the road while they loaded up on "our" sandwiches'.

Although the prisoners were gratified by the kindness of the French people, relations between French and British soldiers reached their nadir in the summer of 1940. British POWs noticed how their French counterparts seemed prepared for captivity – well clothed, and with reserves of food. The British, by contrast, had little more than the clothes they stood in. A famished and bitter Bertie Harwood recorded his feelings towards his erstwhile ally:

The Germans, determined to sow the seeds of hatred and discord between the French and ourselves, allowed the French officers and men to send out and buy food from the town and even gave them chickens and meat on the strict understanding that they did not share anything whatever with the British. I have often been told that starvation brings forth all that is lowest and worst in man, and I only hope that I never again experience the same downright hatred that I felt for those Frenchmen guzzling away, quite impervious to us or our needs. Yes, the Germans certainly succeeded in their object.

The Germans provided just enough food and water to prevent the men from actually dying, but the prisoners' desperation was enough to make them break ranks and grab food growing by the roadside. If caught in the act they were liable to be shot out of hand. Rifle butts and bayonets kept the long columns moving. Private James Goulden of the East Lancs Regiment recalled being told by the Germans that anyone escaping would be shot dead, and any stragglers shot in the leg. 'Whilst on the march,' he claimed, 'I saw at least six men shot in the legs for this "offence". They were picked up by lorries.'

At the German border prisoners were shoved into cattle wagons, and when disembarked at a transit camp they faced a hostile civilian population. Jim Roberts, a Territorial in the Queen Victoria Rifles, recounted his arrival in the Rhineland city of Trier: 'Leaving the railway yards we were marched through the town (fortunately I was in the middle of the column) when suddenly we were being showered with stones thrown at us by German civilians, mostly women who were lining the pavements. Some unfortunate prisoners closest to the pavement took the full brunt of the missile attack and the spittle aimed at them by the violent women.'

Although conditions improved marginally once in German transit camps, the respite was temporary. The other ranks were soon ordered back into cattle wagons – many of them French and marked '*Hommes 40 et Chevaux 8*' – for the journey across Germany to camps along the former Polish border. The prisoners were not allowed out of the wagons, and in a trek that could last three days or more, with many men suffering from diarrhoea, conditions were grim. Regimental Quartermaster Sergeant G. E. Lyons of the Royal West Kents found himself among sixty men forced into one such wagon at bayonet point. 'The train stopped only once,' Lyons recalled, 'when we were given a drink of ersatz coffee (less sugar and milk). No sanitary arrangements at all, so one can visualize the state of the wagons and the spirits of the men. Three men in my wagon died and this was only discovered when we arrived in Szubin in Poland. I feel this journey was the worst period of our captivity.'

British officers transported to camps in Bavaria endured unpleasant if less terrible conditions. From the Dulag at Mainz, Harwood went by wagon to Munich, then, via Salzburg, to Oflag VIIC at Laufen.

The next great influx of prisoners into Germany came as a consequence of the Allied disasters in Greece and Crete during April–May 1941. British, Australian and New Zealand troops made up the vast majority of these POWs. In Greece the men were herded into two main camps, Corinth in the south and Salonica to the north. Salonica – designated Frontstalag 183 – became the main staging post for all British and Commonwealth troops on their way to permanent camps in Austria and Germany, and it earned an unwholesome reputation for inadequate food and poor sanitation.

The German front-line soldiers – spearheaded by elite parachute, alpine and Waffen SS troops – generally behaved well towards their prisoners, especially the wounded. The looting of personal effects was rare, and some German guards helped in the trade between the prisoners and Greek hawkers on the other side of the wire. On Crete, however, relations between the two sides went through a difficult phase when the Germans discovered mutilated bodies of their comrades, who they mistakenly believed had been victims of the British. Threats were made to the British on Crete (complete with mock executions), and the already meagre rations were cut in both Greece and Crete until the matter was resolved and the British were absolved of blame.

While the German authorities were mainly, in their word, *korrekt* in their dealings with the British, they were largely indifferent to their prisoners' long-term welfare. Food remained in short supply – so much so that men suffered from blackouts, fainting if they stood up too quickly (a common occurrence in camps short of food). To make matters worse, the scale of the German victory led to massive overcrowding. Diseases caused by dirty water and malnutrition were rife, and medical supplies were never sufficient to meet the scale of the problem. Only the perseverance of the Greek Red Cross and the generosity of the Greek people saved matters from getting even worse.

The Germans were slow in transporting their Balkan prisoners to permanent camps, which had better facilities and where men would eventually have access to life-saving Red Cross parcels. The railway line running through Greece and Yugoslavia was often single gauge and interrupted in places, while rolling stock had been diverted for Hitler's invasion of the Soviet Union. The first POWs began to move north in the summer of 1941, the final batch leaving Salonica as late as April 1942.

As was the usual practice, prisoners were loaded into cattle trucks for a journey that could take between five and ten days. For some the ordeal was as terrible as that suffered by the prisoners crossing Germany in 1940, but in many cases the Germans did allow men out of the wagons once or even twice a day, when they might receive food from local Greek and Serb civilians. Howard Greville, a British wireless operator in the Royal Corps of Signals, was greatly moved by Greek generosity at these impromptu stops, which, he recalled, were

> seemingly known in advance to the women of nearby Greek villages. They would approach the train from the opposite side from that on which the prisoners had disembarked, and throw pieces of dried bread over the trucks for the starving prisoners to catch in mid-air if they could. The guards tried with shouts and sometimes even shots to discourage this show of sympathy for prisoners. Undaunted, the women always came with their bread which the hungry men devoured like wolves.

The war in North Africa comprised a series of campaigns and battles that effectively lasted from December 1940 to May 1943 and became the main theatre of operation for the British Army. Allied prisoners were rounded up into transit camps and then escorted to a nearby port for transport to Italy. A few high-value prisoners were either flown over the Mediterranean or crossed it underwater in a submarine. The long distances, harsh terrain and climate were all factors that could make the prisoners' progress particularly arduous. The Germans captured the vast bulk of Allied prisoners, but once behind the front line the POWs were handed over to the Italians.

Gunner Jim Witte was among the first large batch of prisoners to be captured by the Axis in North Africa. To the Italian transit camp in Derna he brought some 'M&V' (meat and vegetables) tins and a good haul of cigarettes, the standard currency within POW camps. Witte teamed up with a similarly entrepreneurial type called Hill, who had a store of tobacco, and as a two-man combine they set about trading for more food to supplement the Italian rations of 'weak macaroni stew and square biscuits as hard as roof tiles'. Keeping watch over their supplies was, as they saw it, an onerous responsibility – one which their comrades, albeit semi-starving, did not have to shoulder. 'We had to guard these precious commodities,' explained Witte, 'so we couldn't leave our bed spaces and little bits of kit unattended for a minute. Tobacco barons had hard lives in POW camps, lives of tension, unable to trust anyone.'

At the end of April 1941, Derna, Witte and a large contingent of prisoners were taken to Tripoli – a four-day journey of spectacular monotony relieved only by insults and stones thrown at them by Italian colonists, who, according to Witte, 'were well imbued with the fascist spirit'. From Tripoli the prisoners faced the short but perilous dash across the Mediterranean to the relative safety of the Strait of Messina. British submarines operating out of Malta were a constant danger, and Witte was relieved to see that his convoy had a full escort of destroyers with a cruiser in reserve. They arrived in Naples after an uneventful crossing; prisoners were allowed on deck, and the food was good and plentiful. From Naples they were taken to another transit camp at Capua and then on to their permanent camp, *Campo concentramento di prigionieri di guerra* (PG) 78 at Sulmona, where Witte would spend the next twenty-eight months.

The Revd Bob McDowall was sent to a transit camp at Benghazi, to await a crossing to Italy. He just missed being in the batch of 2,100 men transported in the *Jason* on 8 December 1941. The following afternoon, a mile or so off the Greek Peloponnese coast, the ship was hit by a torpedo from the British submarine *Porpoise*. The Italian captain and his crew promptly took to the two remaining lifeboats, but a German naval engineer onboard the ship took command. With help from the prisoners he managed to beach the *Jason* on an open stretch of coastline within swimming distance of the shore. Thanks to the engineer's courageous and decisive action many lives were saved, although approximately a third of the complement of prisoners were killed in the initial explosion or by drowning while trying to get ashore.

McDowall was assigned to the next shipment, on 11 December, aboard the light cruiser *Luigi Cadorna*. He was among the seventy officers crowded into a small hold, which soon became thick with cigarette smoke and foul air. McDowall began to feel ill as the ship sailed into the night, and was forced to race over to the lavatory chute to be sick. But here disaster struck: the top half of his false teeth shot out and disappeared down the chute – 'a severe loss', he later recorded. The following morning the officers were allowed greater freedom of movement and were well looked after by the Italians. McDowall, however, thought the British officers abused their good fortune. 'Had fair meals next day,' he wrote. 'Some men unbelievably greedy. One had six glasses of wine. Many also stole glasses when leaving ship.'

The prisoners felt bitterly cold as they disembarked at Brindisi; most were poorly clad, some with just shirts and shorts. From there they travelled by train and on foot to the big transit camp at Bari, PG 75. McDowall felt wretched, still physically ill and desperately homesick for his wife Pat and young daughter Mary. He was also having difficulty coming to terms with his fellow prisoners, whom he considered crude and boorish as they drank, swore and gambled around him. 'I felt lonely among them today' was his diary entry for 20 December.

Jim Witte and Bob McDowall had experienced decent conditions in their transits to Italy. Others were not so lucky: conditions worsened over time, both in the camps and aboard ship. The poor treatment meted out by the Italians is described in numerous testimonies from British prisoners in North Africa. It would seem that Italian attitudes towards Allied prisoners were undoubtedly malicious at times, although the prime cause of the POWs' suffering remained straightforward neglect – which inevitably caused hardship.

Doug LeFevre's view of the Italians was that they had an inferiority complex, and on the occasions when they held the whip hand they were keen 'to let you know who was boss'. After capture at Ruin Ridge he went via Tobruk to the transit camp at Benghazi, known as the Palms. Like other camps in North Africa, it was grossly overcrowded, with no working sanitation and limited and irregular food supplies. Inevitably, the Palms developed into a breeding ground for dysentery, beriberi and desert sores, the prisoners' health being made worse by septic lice and flea bites.

Conditions on the transport ships ranged from poor to abominable. LeFevre was packed into a hold with 500 other prisoners, although he had some respite when allowed to go on deck to have his wounded arm inspected by an Italian doctor. Bertram Martin, an artillery signaller captured at Tobruk, described a fairly standard crossing for other ranks:

> We were taken to the ship and battened down in our hundreds. There were no toilet facilities at all. It was absolutely atrocious; three or four days of sheer hell. In the boat it was completely dark and it was so crowded that if you moved your leg you found someone else's leg. It was the done thing to urinate in your boot, there was nowhere else to go. When we eventually got off the boat in Naples we only just had strength to walk.

Shortly before LeFevre's departure from North Africa on 17 August 1942, the Italians divided the prisoners into two batches to travel in separate ships. According to LeFevre, those with surnames beginning with A to L boarded the *Sestriere*, M to Zs travelled in the *Nino Bixio*. While on the deck of the *Sestriere*, LeFevre found himself a witness to a maritime tragedy. 'I was standing under the bridge,' he recalled, 'and I noticed the German gun crew on the gun in the bow of the vessel seemed agitated and they were putting on lifebelts. I looked across and I saw this white streak go across our bows and I thought, "I didn't know there were flying fish in the Mediterranean," and all of a sudden the other vessel [the *Nino Bixio*] exploded – this was a torpedo!'

The torpedo had been fired by the British submarine *Turbulent*. A second was fired and also hit the *Nino Bixio*. Many prisoners in the holds were killed and wounded by the explosions, but under the able direction of its Italian captain the ship stayed afloat and was taken in tow by a destroyer to the Greek port of Navarino. A total of 432 men were killed in the attack. The sinkings of the *Jason* and the *Nino Bixio* made the Mediterranean crossing a fearful business for British and Commonwealth POWs.

Doug LeFevre had had a lucky escape, saved by his surname. His wounded arm was giving him increasing trouble, however, and when the *Sestriere* docked at Brindisi he was transferred to a local hospital before being sent north to Bergamo to convalesce. From there he was transferred to PG 73 at Carpi, and then to the new Anzac camp, PG 57 at Gruppignano.

Lieutenant Commander Billie Stephens stepped down at Bremervörde station en route to the naval compound in Stalag XB at Sandbostel. Stephens experienced a relatively smooth journey, although initially he didn't realize it when put aboard a battered coach near his transit camp in France: 'I remember well how furious we were at having to travel third class.' On later realizing his good fortune, a chastened Stephens wrote, 'Actually we were very lucky because it was the Hun custom to send all prisoners in cattle trucks.'

Stephens had been escorted to a transit camp near Rennes in France – with the usual poor food and atrocious sanitation – before dispatch to a French hospital, where an escape attempt was planned. A day before the scheduled breakout, the escapers were informed of their move to Sandbostel with only half an hour's notice. 'I shan't attempt to describe our disappointment,' Stephens wrote. Once again French civilians raised spirits: 'Rations for the journey were issued and here the French were very good to us, giving us a lot of extra tinned meat and biscuits which I suppose they must have stolen from somewhere. We were then put into a lorry and driven to the station under an enormous armed guard, with motor cyclists ahead and astern of us, and the French cheering as we went past. It was all rather impressive.'

The opening of the Second Front in June 1944 saw a new stream of Anglo-American prisoners on their way to German POW camps. Although the net flow of prisoners was now going in their favour, the Allies still suffered local reverses and major defeats at Arnhem (6,000 British POWs) and in the opening phase of the German Ardennnes offensive (23,000 US POWs). The Americans captured in the Battle of the Bulge had to endure more than most. The well-equipped and warmly clad Americans were an irresistible target for German front-line troops, and the long columns of prisoners marching eastward through the snow towards Germany were stripped of such vital items as greatcoats, jackets and rubber overboots. The winter of 1944–5 was particularly severe, and hypothermia and frostbite were common for those men without decent clothing.

Added to the cold, the insufficient food and the inadequate sanitation was an increasing threat of Allied air attack. Not only were the prisoners liable to be attacked by heavy bombers, when in transit they were also subject to attack by Allied fighter-bombers, which roamed the battlefield at will in clear weather.

On his way to a transit camp for US prisoners in Stalag XIIA at Limburg, Roger Shinn remembered, his guards were very edgy at the sound of aircraft. On arrival at Limburg, Shinn discovered that the camp had been bombed by the RAF the previous night, with sixty American officers killed. On another occasion he noticed a couple of planes flying overhead: 'We winced, then saw the swastikas on them and with some astonishment felt safe. I realized that we needed a new set of conditioned reflexes in Germany. We were quickly learning to dread the American air force.'

Interrogation was an ordeal that some prisoners had to undergo before they could enter the relative safety of their permanent camps. Most POWs slipped through the net, however. In mass captures, such as at Tobruk in 1942 and in the Ardennes in 1944, there were just too many prisoners to process. And the ordinary soldier generally knew less about what was happening on his own side than an enemy intelligence officer. Interrogation was usually reserved for officers and NCOs with specialist or technical knowledge. Chance too played a part in who was interrogated, and to what level of intensity.

Interrogators were always keen to play up their role, both to impress superiors and to overawe captives. But interrogation was only one part of a wider intelligence-gathering process that included wireless intercepts and the capture of enemy documents and other physical objects, as well as strategic intelligence gained from embassies, spies and the analysis of the enemy's media.

Axis interrogation of captured Army prisoners – both officers and other ranks – tended to be of a perfunctory nature. In a typical interrogation session, once the Allied soldier had given his name, rank and service number, the interrogator would probe for more information and if this was refused would threaten the prisoner with harsher treatment, usually at the hands of the Gestapo. If these threats failed to elicit a favourable response, the interrogator would lose interest and try anew with another prisoner. Harwood's experience was fairly typical of the process. A day or so after capture he was taken to a chateau commandeered by the Germans:

> I was shown into a room where a German officer with spectacles was sitting behind a large table littered with maps and papers. He asked me to sit down. He had a broad American accent and discoursed for some time on America, the friends he had in England and every topic which he considered would put me at my ease and, incidentally, off my guard. Then he began some tentative questioning. What was my regiment? What was the number of my battalion? Where was I captured? I pointed out to him that he could easily get the answer to the last question by asking the fellow who captured me. After about twenty minutes of futile sparring he announced in a very unpleasant voice that I had not answered enough of his questions. I replied that I had told him as much as I was allowed to say and would he have given any more information had the positions been reversed? This seemed to shut him up; he became quite pleasant again, offered me a cigarette and told me I could go.

Although Billie Stephens was professionally interrogated at the naval base of Wilhelmshaven – 'a prolonged process cleverly done' – he also underwent a strange, though not violent, interrogation in his transit camp at Rennes. Hitler's personal interpreter, Paul Schmidt, arrived at the camp to interview Stephens and other British officers. Schmidt was interested in broader strategic matters, including such things as the state of Allied civilian morale and the intentions of Allied leaders – not usually foremost in the minds of junior and field officers. Among other questions, Stephens was asked whether Britain would accept peace terms, was the country turning communist, and what was the British public's opinion of Stafford Cripps? When this largely farcical interview ended, Stephens was only annoyed with himself for not having spun it out longer to cadge more cigarettes from Schmidt.

The Luftwaffe prided itself on the quality of its interrogation service. The relatively small numbers of captured airmen and their levels of technical and operational knowledge made detailed interrogations both feasible and desirable. Initially, however, interrogation and general intelligence-gathering were ad hoc and inefficient.

Pilot Officer Jimmy James found his interrogation in Rotterdam 'a mixture of sweet and sour – a favourite Gestapo recipe'. He was faced by six Luftwaffe officers and a civilian interpreter whom James believed was from the Gestapo. James was shouted at and threatened when he refused to give more than name, rank and number. When this failed to work, James was sent to Luftwaffe headquarters at the Carlton Hotel in Amsterdam. There he was softened up with beer and cigars and a friendly conversation with a Luftwaffe major who spoke perfect English. Midway through the conversation the officer tried to trick James into providing technical information about his aircraft. But it was all rather obvious, and James had no problem in skipping past these clumsy ambushes. The major then left, the beer and cigars were whisked away, and James was escorted to the orderly room before his journey to Dulag Luft at Oberursel, a few miles north-west of Frankfurt.

The *Durchgangslager Luftwaffe* (air-force transit camp) was initially, as its name implied, a holding camp where Allied aircrew were assembled before dispatch to a permanent POW camp. Downed airmen – captured individually or by the handful – were sent to Dulag Luft directly after capture, escorted by one or two guards on the road or rail network. When James arrived at Dulag Luft in June 1940 the interrogation facility had yet to be developed, and he spent only a few days there before being sent to Stalag Luft I at Barth on the Baltic coast. The Germans were, however, beginning to realize that their intelligence-gathering was being undermined by poor interrogation methods and the looting of souvenirs from both the airmen and their aircraft. A new Luftwaffe directive ordered the swift removal of airmen from the crash site and their holding in solitary confinement before a prompt transit to Dulag Luft for interrogation. Crashed aircraft were to be guarded before inspection by qualified personnel, and relevant documents and equipment were to be forwarded to Dulag Luft.

On arrival, prisoners were held in solitary confinement in preparation for interrogation. Once that was complete the prisoner was sent to join the other prisoners in the main part of the camp, generously supplied with Red Cross parcels. Adjoining the camp was a hospital for the lightly wounded or injured. Its main purpose was to gain further information from potentially vulnerable prisoners; the level of actual medical care was considered only adequate, but patients were put at their ease and well fed and cared for. Female nurses had been instructed to elicit information from their patients, but the level and quality of information was found to be disappointing and they were replaced by male orderlies. Through the good treatment afforded them in the transit camp the Luftwaffe hoped to lower the prisoners' guard and make them more amenable to German persuasion.

A small permanent POW staff was appointed – at first British and then Anglo-American – to help the incoming prisoners prepare for the rigours of camp life. Many RAF men passing through Dulag Luft had deep suspicions about the loyalty of the permanent staff, however, and believed that they were helping themselves to Red Cross parcels. These misgivings arose because of the good conditions to be found in the camp and the natural suspicion aroused among men who had just endured long and difficult interrogations. In Britain, airmen had been warned against stool pigeons and against Germans masquerading as RAF officers, and the permanent staff's close relationship with the Germans was construed by some as collusion.

The first senior British officer (SBO) at Dulag Luft was the formidable Wing Commander H. M. A. 'Wings' Day. Awarded the Albert Medal (forerunner of the George Cross) as a Royal Marine during the First World War, he transferred to the RAF and became one of its star pilots. At the outbreak of war in 1939, Day insisted on leading his squadron into battle – a 1914–18 tradition – but on his first mission over Germany in October his Blenheim reconnaissance aircraft was shot down by German fighters. He led the first mass breakout from Dulag Luft in June 1941, and along with Jimmy James was one of the few survivors of the Great Escape – the mass breakout from Stalag Luft III in March 1944. But Day's co-operation with the Germans unjustly earned him the suspicion and contempt of some RAF prisoners, and at one point he was accused of taking Red Cross parcels for his own use. This distrust lingered, and was only partially rectified by the knowledge of his escape from Dulag Luft.

Day's successor, Squadron Leader E. D. Elliott, also suffered similar accusations, although in Elliott's case there was little doubt that he maintained very cordial relations with the Germans and discouraged escape attempts. Elliott's defence was that newly arrived prisoners needed good treatment, and that antagonizing the Germans might have led to the withdrawal of Red Cross parcels and other privileges.

As a result of the mass escape from Dulag Luft and disappointment with intelligence results, the camp underwent a reorganization in November 1941 under a new commander, Lieutenant Colonel Erich Killinger. The camp expanded and was redesignated *Auswertestelle West* (Evaluation Centre West). There was also a general toughening-up of interrogation procedures that stretched the Geneva Convention to its limit.

As part of a disorientation process, the newly arrived prisoner was held in one of 200 small, sparsely furnished cells, and kept there in solitary confinement. There were virtually no washing facilities, and food was poor and limited, although lice and fleas were there in abundance. Within the cells – and elsewhere in the camp – hidden microphones relayed inadvertent comments made by the prisoners, which were written down in shorthand for subsequent use by the interrogators. There was no natural light in the cells, and strong artificial lights were kept on for long periods to make sleep difficult. A further discomfort were the radiators, which could be turned on and off only by the guards and sometimes generated fierce levels of heat. According to one witness, on a warm day the heated cell temperature could reach 129°F.

Colonel Spivey experienced only two days in solitary confinement, possibly because of respect for his rank and because the cells were beginning to fill up with men captured after the ill-fated Schweinfurt raid. He was subsequently taken to the hospital, where he received some treatment for his damaged leg and wounds to his mouth. And, more important for Spivey, he was also able to clean himself up, enjoy good Red Cross food, and sleep on a proper mattress with sheets and blankets – a real luxury for any POW. While in the hospital he received a bogus Red Cross form from a Luftwaffe reception officer. As well as name, rank and number, it included spaces for family addresses and for some basic operational detail of the man's unit and where it was stationed. The idea of the form was not just to gain information, but also to see whether the prisoner was prepared to cross the line from a 'name, rank and number' response. While encouraging the prisoner to complete the form, the reception officer also made an evaluation of the likelihood of him providing useful information at his main interrogation.

When Spivey refused to complete the form, the reception officer surprised him with detailed knowledge of both his operational and his personal life: 'He told me about the group I had been flying with and the names of the members of my crew; that I had a wife and child whose birthday would come two days later; where I had been during my service life.' The quality and detail of the information presented to the surprised prisoner was a valuable tool in breaking down resistance. The implication given was that German intelligence was so good that it would make little or no difference if a few more details were added. And to further weaken resolve the Germans implied that the information had come from fellow flyers.

After his efforts to coax him into filling out the form, the reception officer eventually decided Spivey would be too stubborn to merit further interrogation, and he was released from hospital into the transit camp. There he was briefed by Squadron Leader Elliott and 'served the most heavenly tea, cookies, and jam I had ever tasted'.

Jack Vietor had a more testing time than Spivey, spending several days in solitary before a visit by the reception officer with the bogus Red Cross form. Vietor did not receive the 'sweat-box' treatment, and the radiator remained off throughout his solitary. The cold weather outside was considered a useful enough softening-up tool, as was the lack of medical treatment for the wound in his leg, which was now infected and giving him some pain. Two or three days after the departure of the reception officer he was called out to a large, well-heated office where he was formally interrogated by a Luftwaffe major.

Vietor had not worn identify tags on the day of the raid, and his interrogator used the standard approach for prisoners caught without them. He told Vietor he would have to assume that the American was a saboteur unless he could provide some corroborative detail, such as the number of his squadron. The threat of the Gestapo was raised when Vietor again refused to go beyond name, rank and number. He was then dismissed to think things over.

The second interrogation, a couple of days later, was intended to dazzle Vietor with the interrogator's knowledge of him and his unit. While impressed with the detail of the Luftwaffe's information, Vietor was pleased to hear a number of mistakes within the confident account given him by the major, although Vietor made no attempt to correct him. When Vietor failed to provide any information he was again threatened with the Gestapo. But this marked the end of his formal interrogation, although the major made one last attempt to gather information.

On this third occasion Vietor was invited to dinner in a well-furnished room. Whisky and cigars were produced after the meal, and the major turned the conversation to general war aims. As the drink flowed, Vietor was relieved to discover that his interrogator seemed mainly interested in delivering a political justification for Nazism and reminiscing about his time as a fighter pilot in the First World War. With the whisky finished, Vietor was escorted back to his cell. The following day he was discharged into the transit camp.

Although it would seem that the Luftwaffe major got little or nothing from Vietor, the interrogation centre was an effective intelligence-gathering tool. From the files in Dulag Luft it was clear that Allied airmen did give away information, sometimes without knowing they were doing so. And the best interrogators, such as Hanns Joachim Scharff, made a deep impression on many POWs. They used their skills to create a mystique of their having almost supernatural powers. And yet much of the information garnered from POWs was low grade and served only to supplement other, better, intelligence sources, such as wireless intercepts and material gathered from downed aircraft. Scharff noted the surprise of POWs when informed that 'that every word they had uttered over the radio was down in our books'. Allied aircrew were also careless in what they carried with them on operations, and documents and letters were not only sources of information but useful interrogation tools.

Colonel Hubert Zemke, the renowned US fighter commander, went through the various stages of interrogation in November 1944. He considered Scharff a dangerous opponent: 'I suspected that the man could easily charm an unwary prisoner into divulging the information required.' But wary prisoners could withstand such probing without undue difficulty. And the Allies, aware of what was happening at Dulag Luft, instructed aircrews in how best to counter their interrogators. At the conclusion of his interrogation Zemke was taken by Scharff to meet high-ranking general-staff officers who attempted to persuade him to lead a renegade air force to fight on the Eastern Front. He was also asked to provide 'technical assistance' for a documentary on Allied air power. 'Declining,' wrote Zemke, 'I realized that the basic purpose of this get-together was to try and ensnare a US officer into something that could be used for propaganda purposes by the Nazis. Even so, I was astounded at the apparent naivety of these men in trying to turn me traitor and concluded that the attempt revealed how desperate the Nazi situation must be.'

No matter how tough the interrogations at Dulag Luft, they were conducted broadly within the framework of the Geneva Convention. Some prisoners elsewhere were not so fortunate. The governments of both Allied and Axis nations had no compunction in executing spies and saboteurs caught without uniform on home soil. Hitler's Commando Order went further, however, by depriving uniformed special-forces troops of the protection of the Geneva Convention. While most who fell foul of this order were shot without delay, a few were taken for brutal interrogation and, if they survived, were sent to concentration camps.

Operating behind the lines in plain clothes, the men and women of the SOE had few illusions about their fate if captured by the Germans. Cyanide pills were handed out to agents as they prepared to leave for occupied territory. But when Odette Sansom and Peter Churchill were captured by Abwehr Sergeant Hugo Bleicher on 15 April 1943 they clung on to hope, no matter how illusory. The seizure of the two SOE agents had been a hurried business, and instead of being separated immediately after arrest they were left together. They agreed that they should claim to be married and also claim kinship with the British prime minister. This decision would ultimately save their lives.

They were taken to Fresnes jail in Paris, the main French prison holding enemies of the German state. Odette was thrown into solitary confinement. She was still under German Army jurisdiction, and Bleicher conducted several interrogations. He tried to insinuate himself into her confidence with promises of lenient treatment. If she refused to co-operate, he told her, he would reluctantly have to hand her over to the Gestapo. But these were not the hollow threats that had been levelled at Jimmy James and Jack Vietor: when Odette rejected Bleicher's blandishments she was sent to 84 Avenue Foch, the Gestapo's interrogation centre.

The Gestapo adopted a softly-softly approach in their first session, but this got them nowhere. On the second interrogation the torture began. Odette was made to sit down in a room containing the interrogator from the previous session and another man, who stood behind her. The German interrogator demanded to know the whereabouts of Odette's radio operator, code-named Arnaud, and another SOE agent. When she again refused to answer, a red-hot poker was pressed against her spine just below her neck.

'Where's Arnaud?' demanded her interrogator.

Through her pain, she replied, 'I have nothing to say.'

In a level voice the interrogator then informed Odette that if she did not answer the question his assistant would pull out the nail of the small toe of her left foot. He would carry on asking the same question, and every time she refused another nail would be removed. He asked the question ten times, and still received no answer.

Looking down, Odette saw her bloodied feet. Waves of nausea swept over her, but she remained resolute. She recalled her feelings: 'I know there must be a time when you cannot [continue] no matter how much you want to, nature is stronger than you. But if I accept that it will not be my decision if they kill me, they will kill me physically but that's all. They won't win anything; they'll have a dead body, useless to them. But they will not have me, because I won't let them have me.'

Odette believed a sense of duty instilled at an early age and the experience of childhood illnesses helped prepare her for this ordeal:

I had been blind as a little girl. I was blind for three-and-a-half years so I had that experience. I also had polio and I was paralysed for more than a year. I suffered quite a lot. I had a very wonderful grandfather who did not accept weaklings very easily, so one had to learn to put up with pain. And this feeling in my family that we all, boy or girl, had to do our duty, not only to our country but our father [killed in the First World War], was with me.

Amid her agony Odette felt a sense of elation. She had not talked. In this, at least, she had defeated them. But her resolve was to be tested again. Her interrogator told her that her fingernails were to be next. Before the torture could continue, however, the interrogator was interrupted by a superior, who had apparently decided that they were wasting their time with her. As she hobbled out of the room to be taken back to Fresnes prison, she was shocked to discover that her torturer was French.

Odette tended her wounds as best she could, tearing up strips of prison cloth to make bandages to wrap round her feet. A few days later she was again summoned to Avenue Foch. She was made to wait in an anteroom, until a soldier bellowed, 'Frau Churchill!' She was led into a richly decorated room, where an officer told her she was condemned to death. She had been expecting the sentence, and felt a strange relief that alternated with a cold fear that she would be taken away to face the firing squad. But the Germans were not finished with her yet. Her name held a certain fascination: a Churchill might be a useful bargaining chip for the future.

More Gestapo interrogations followed, although without torture. Again they gained nothing. Hugo Bleicher also returned:

> He used to have me taken out of my cell and taken to an interrogation room in Fresnes and he would talk and say: 'I went to a beautiful concert last night. I thought of you, you would have loved it.' He was very clever, he used to try and break you down that way. One day he came and said: 'I've decided tomorrow I am coming to fetch you very early in the morning, take you to Paris for the day, bring you back about ten o'clock. You can have a bath, a good meal, you can wash your hair.' I said: 'I will not go to Paris with you, not to friends or anything. I will have no contact with anybody. I will not go.'

Bleicher reluctantly accepted Odette's refusal. She was determined not to compromise with her interrogators: 'I wasn't going to accept anything [extra], not a drop of water or crust of bread, nothing. That was the only way.' By August 1943 both the Gestapo and Bleicher had given up on Odette. She was to spend more than a year in Fresnes, the threat of execution ever present.

Before entering a permanent POW camp, the ordinary prisoners had to undergo the rituals of delousing and registration. Lice were carriers of typhus and typhoid fever, and the German authorities had an almost pathological fear of the spread of these diseases. Delousing involved the prisoner stripping off his clothes – which were put into an industrial dry-cleaning machine where poison killed the lice – and the shaving of his hair. Bob Prouse described the latter process, which took place at a hospital where he was recovering from wounds sustained at Dieppe:

We were shaved from head to foot, and I mean that literally. No hair escaped the hospital barber and, when my turn came, I almost panicked, not from his shaving my head but from what followed. He held my penis gently between thumb and forefinger and with quick and expert movements of his straight razor quickly denuded me of all pubic hair. I held my breath during the whole operation, expecting any minute for him to cut off my pride and joy and leave me with a giggle. When he finished there was a loud sigh of relief, not only from me, but from the other prisoners who had jumped out of bed to watch, knowing their turn was coming.

While Prouse adopted a fairly phlegmatic view towards the whole business, others resented what they considered another method to dehumanize and humiliate them. This was certainly Bertie Harwood's view: 'I was told to go to the arrival yard where I would have my head shaved. In some curious and tortuous way it was supposed to prove to the Germans that they were the lords of creation and that we were so much dirt.' Jim Witte – who, with his thick blond curls, fancied himself as something of a lady's man – was even more distressed when told what was to happen on entering PG 78 at Sulmona. 'One event almost shattered us,' he wrote.

We had to have our hair off. I don't think that there is anything quite so demoralizing as losing your hair. It made us look like convicts, real villains in fact. To crown it all we were obliged to have our picture taken for record purposes. Once your hair is shaven it takes almost nine months to get it back to normal. The next few months were very troubling for the Don Juans as they struggled to comb their bristles.

Registration involved the taking of the prisoner's photograph, fingerprints and some basic information on his physical appearance, home address and next of kin.

Deloused, shorn and registered, the prisoners entered their permanent camps. In Germany, POWs were termed *Kriegsgefangenen*, a name they took as their own, shortening it to 'Kriegie'. All were relieved that the ordeals of transit were over, and for most there was the hope that life would improve. But there was also anxiety about what lay ahead.

4

Camps and Captors

To a victorious army, prisoners were a tangible sign of military success, a potential economic resource, and a means of depriving the enemy of vital manpower. But at the same time prisoners were an irksome administrative problem, especially as no army could foresee how many men would be captured. As Germany geared up for war in the late 1930s, provision was made for the containment of POWs, but the numbers taken in the early stages of the war exceeded all but the most optimistic estimates.

After the campaigns against Poland in 1939 and in the west in 1940, the German Army captured more than 2 million enemy soldiers. The conquest of Yugoslavia and Greece and the invasion of the Soviet Union in 1941 produced an even bigger haul: on the Eastern Front almost 3 million soldiers from the Red Army were netted in the first four months of fighting. In September 1943, when Italy dropped out of the war, the Germans overpowered their former ally and sent 600,000 captured Italian servicemen to POW camps in Germany, along with over 50,000 British and American prisoners. These unpredictable surges of captive manpower tested German organization to the full. Prisoners suffered terrible overcrowding as a consequence, although Anglo-American POWs, given their status at the top of the Axis POW hierarchy, suffered less than most.

Germany was divided into military districts (*Wehrkreise*) that were responsible for POW camps in their area and had the authority to requisition buildings and construct camps where necessary. Each camp was assigned a Roman numeral corresponding to the particular *Wehrkreis* with a letter or letters added to distinguish the particular camp, so that, for example, camps in the Bavarian Wehrkreis VII included those at Eichstätt (Oflag VIIB) and Laufen (Oflag VIIC/H – the letter H, for *Hauptlager*, indicated a main camp; Z, for *Zweiglager*,

indicated a subsidiary camp). During the war new camps were sometimes designated with Arabic numerals, without reference to the local
Wehrkreis.

In October 1939 Germany possessed 31 POW camps, a figure that
by the end of the war would increase to 248, of which 134 housed
British and American prisoners. Due to changes in policy and sudden
increases in POW numbers, the system was always in a state of flux,
with camps opening and closing or altering their function. For the
prisoners this could entail repeated switches of location, especially for
those captured early in the war.

The camp system was run by the *Oberkommando der Wehrmacht*
(OKW) – Armed Forces High Command – on behalf of the three
armed forces, albeit using guards from the Army. In 1940 the
Luftwaffe and the Kriegsmarine each decided to build and run camps
for prisoners of its own service. The Luftwaffe, however, underesti-
mated the size of the Allied bomber offensive, and its prison-building
programme was never able to keep up with the numbers of British
and American flyers captured in Germany and occupied Europe. As
a result, groups of Allied airmen were scattered across Army camps,
and in some – such as Stalag VIIIB at Lamsdorf and Stalag IVB at
Mühlberg – there were separate and sizeable RAF compounds. Large
contingents of USAAF personnel were held in Stalag VIIA at
Moosburg and in Stalag XVIIB at Gneixendorf.

In North Africa the Germans handed most of their prisoners over
to the Italians, and by September 1943 nearly 80,000 Allied POWs
were held in some 72 camps spread across Italy in 6 districts (*posta
militare*). British and Commonwealth troops made up the bulk of the
POW population in Italy (just over 68,000 men), with contingents
of Free French, Yugoslavs, Greeks and Americans – the latter mainly
airmen.

Officers were separated from NCOs and private soldiers, either in
different camps or in separate compounds. Some efforts were made to
distinguish between Commonwealth and British troops, but they
tended not to work when an influx of prisoners threatened to overwhelm the system. PG 57 at Gruppignano was built to hold
Australians and New Zealanders, but they were subsequently joined
by South African, British and Indian POWs (although the Indians

were kept in their own compound). In contrast to the Germans, the Italian authorities did not attempt to segregate the three services, especially as the vast majority of prisoners were soldiers, with only a few airmen and sailors.

A POW camp was run by the commandant and his staff of officers and senior NCOs, below whom were the guards – soldiers unfit or too old for front-line service. In Germany commandants had a certain degree of latitude in the implementation of policy, and in a number of cases they ignored or at least ameliorated some of the harsher orders received from higher authority. By the same token, however, an unpleasant commandant could impose a particularly severe regime on his camp. In Italy the organizational system was similar, although commandants seemed to have had less freedom of action than their German counterparts.

The commandant would typically have a deputy and a number of camp officers to undertake general administrative duties. Slightly separate from the other members of the camp staff was the security officer, responsible for preventing escapes and other acts of resistance and sabotage. In Germany security officers were drawn from the Abwehr, and each officer had his own team of guards, most of whom spoke good English. Unarmed and dressed in overalls to protect their uniforms, they would roam around the camp and through barrack blocks looking for anything suspicious. Their habit of crawling under the blocks to locate tunnel entrances and lurking among POWs to overhear 'careless talk' earned them the title of 'ferrets'. In Italy security officers came from the ranks of the *Carabinieri Real*, a paramilitary police force which had a reputation for thoroughness that POWs interpreted as fascist zealotry. The Italian security guards were more prosaically named 'snoopers', and were similarly dressed in overalls and equipped with screwdrivers and steel rods to probe mattresses and other bulky items of POW property.

The ordinary prisoner rarely had much to do with camp officers; his contact with his captors came through the guards, whose behaviour and attitude towards POWs differed widely. In the post-Dunkirk period the guards were especially overbearing and often brutal. Kicks and blows from rifle butts were not uncommon, and prisoners' legitimate requests were often ignored; one American remembered guards retorting 'Scheisse am Schweitz' ('Shit on Switzerland') when POWs demanded their rights under the Geneva Convention.

Another unwelcome characteristic was a tendency towards hysteria. Shortly after arriving at his first camp, Bertie Harwood noted how 'the Germans, contrary to general belief, are quite the most excitable and hysterical race when they get worked up; and it takes mighty little to send them into a mad frenzy.' This view was confirmed by other POWs, including Bob Prouse, who recalled that 'very few of the guards or officers could give an order quietly. They had to scream their instructions, a continuous repetition of *"Raus"* (short for *heraus*) and *"Schnell machen"*, literally, "Get out and make it fast".' Prisoners preferred older guards, especially those who had seen front-line service: they were believed to have greater sympathy for prisoners than their younger counterparts – and they shouted less. Captain A. N. L. Munby, captured at Calais in 1940, considered that from 'the older Germans, past veterans of the last war, we had a reasonable degree of courtesy and consideration, while it was the younger, inexperienced, excitable NCOs of the second line troops who caused the trouble'.

Over time, prisoners tended to get the measure of the guards and were able to exploit their weaknesses, especially when supplies of Red Cross parcels gave the POWS tools for trading and bribery. The venality of the guards was much remarked upon, and the one described by Jack Vietor at Stalag Luft I would have had his equivalent in other camps: 'Tisch was a gnarled gnome of about forty with a cocky, bustling manner; he spoke excellent English. He was always willing to smuggle watches and other scarce items into the camp for the prisoners. He made no secret of the fact that his job was a sinecure and delighted in telling us how lucky he was not to be sent to the front because of his age, children and value in the camp.'

As calls on German manpower grew, so the quality of the guards decreased. This became a cause of concern to OKW, which feared that the Army's honour might be compromised in the Oflags by men of a low grade. As early as 1 September 1941 an OKW directive noted:

Complaints have been repeatedly made that guards who are entirely unfit for their task by reason of physical disabilities (club-foot, impaired hearing, marked near-sightedness, etc.) or low intelligence are being used for surveillance of prisoner-of-war officers. For the sake of the prestige of the German Wehrmacht, officers' camps are to use only such personnel as are physically and mentally unobjectionable and who are thus not liable to produce an unfavourable impression on the prisoner-of-war officers. An appropriate exchange of personnel within the guard battalions is to be undertaken immediately.

In the event, the snobbery of OKW was overridden by the demands of the front line, and it was the old and the infirm who guarded the camps, especially in the final stages of the war.

Although there was no set pattern for the construction of POW camps, both German and Italian camps tended towards two distinct styles. The first was based around a large existing building, such as a castle, barracks, school, convent or orphanage. Such camps usually housed Army officers and might be best represented in the popular imagination by Oflag IVC at Colditz, a forbidding castle that had been a lunatic asylum before assuming its more famous role as a prison. Other well-known camps of this type included PG 49 at Fontanellato in Italy's Emilia-Romagna region (a newly built orphanage reassigned to hold British prisoners in 1943) and Oflag 64 at Schubin in Poland (a former girls' school used to house American officers). As the numbers of POWs increased, the accommodation provided by the main building was progressively augmented by huts and other temporary structures.

The second and more numerous type was the barrack-hut-and-barbed-wire camp, which included the Luftwaffe-run Stalag Luft III at Sagan – the model for the camp in the film *The Great Escape*. These purpose-built camps were larger in size, and were usually divided into compounds; as prisoner numbers increased, so new compounds were added. In addition to the main prisoner compounds was the *Vorlager* – a wired-off area containing storerooms for food, fuel and Red Cross parcels, as well as showers, a dispensary and a cookhouse – and the *Kommandantur*, which contained accommodation and offices for the German camp staff and guards.

The barrack huts were constructed of brick, concrete or wood (the better wood-built huts were of double thickness, providing insulation in winter). In the more escape-prone camps the huts were raised off the ground on brick piles to help the guards spot tunnelling activity.

Over the course of time the huts deteriorated, and by 1944–5 those in the older camps, such as Stalag IVB at Mühlberg and Stalag Luft I at Barth, were in poor condition: windows lacked glass and were patched with board, roofs leaked, and rain and snow blew through cracks in the walls.

The camp's location and immediate surroundings had a striking psychological influence on the prisoner. Many camps in Italy and in southern Germany were sited in remote and hilly regions, with fine views of the surrounding countryside. PG 78 at Sulmona was perched on high ground in the wild Abruzzi region. Imprisoned there for over two years, Gunner James Witte had a rather jaundiced view of the camp as a whole, but he did admit that it was 'a truly beautiful place, set amidst a mountain range with snow-capped peaks'. A few miles to the east the prisoners in PG 21 also had panoramic views, with the added bonus of being able to observe the goings-on in the nearby town of Chieti. Further north at PG 29 at Veano the Revd Bob McDowall looked out over the Lombardy plain and on a clear day could see the Swiss Alps. On the other side of the Alps, in Oflag VB at Biberach in Bavaria, Bertie Harwood wistfully enjoyed similar views: 'Day after day I would look over the hills and valleys; in the distance on a clear evening I could plainly see the Alps about fifty miles away – Switzerland and freedom.'

In marked contrast, the camps situated on the flat and largely featureless North European Plain – in northern and eastern Germany and along the former Polish corridor – had little to offer the eye. POWs at Stalag Luft III in Silesia found the surrounding pine forest positively oppressive, and one British officer, on being sent from Bavaria to a camp in Poland, exclaimed, only half jokingly, 'Good God, do you mean to say this is the place we're fighting the world war over!'

Regardless of location, all prison camps shared the same prime function of keeping people within their perimeters. Security measures in most camps were simple yet effective. In a few cases, high walls and plunging vertical drops were used as barriers to escape, but barbed wire was the main constraining device. A typical camp was surrounded by a perimeter fence comprising two parallel barbed-wire fences, typically 6 feet apart and 10 to 12 feet high, with coils of razor wire in between. Wooden towers were sited along the perimeter, manned by guards equipped with machine guns and searchlights and with clear fields of fire to detect and shoot prisoners attempting to climb over or cut through the barbed wire. A knee-high warning wire ran a few feet inside the perimeter fence; any prisoner crossing it was liable to be shot. Some guards would shout a warning; others did not.

Armed guards patrolled both within the camp and immediately outside, the latter looking into the camp to observe unusual behaviour not readily visible from inside the wire. Ferocious guard dogs – usually on leads – also patrolled the camp interior, and at night were let loose to ensure that the prisoners obeyed the night curfew. In some German camps where the risk of escape was considered high, microphones were hidden in huts and seismographs were buried around the perimeter to pick up the sounds of digging.

Levels of security varied between the camps, with the greatest resources being devoted to those containing high-value prisoners, persistent escapers, and other troublesome individuals. At Colditz and its Italian equivalent, PG 5 at Gavi, the number of guards was greatly increased from the average of one to every seven to ten prisoners for the Army and one to four for the Air Force. The 230 Allied prisoners held at Gavi were guarded by 254 Italian soldiers, and guards similarly outnumbered prisoners at Colditz.

Within the Axis POW system there was a hierarchy of relative comfort. Standing at the top were the high-ranking officers under Italian jurisdiction. Rommel's first offensive in North Africa in April 1941 netted the two most senior officers captured during the war, Lieutenant Generals Sir Philip Neame and Sir Richard O'Connor. A handful of major generals and brigadiers soon joined them. They were housed in the Villa Medici at Sulmona – on the map a short distance from Jim Witte in PG 78, but in other respects miles apart.

For those in the Villa Medici imprisonment effectively took the form of a long stay in a pleasant country hotel. The officers had their own rooms and batmen, and, although the house was tightly guarded, the Italians were solicitous of the needs of their guests. Major General Adrian Carton de Wiart – who had gained a VC and lost an eye and

71

hand in the First World War – arrived in Sulmona at the end of April 1941. He described life at the Villa:

> Sulmona offered us certain privileges which we did not appreciate fully until we had lost them. The country around us was very beautiful, and we were allowed to go on long walks and even picnics lasting the whole day with only one officer as an escort. We were permitted to go shopping in the town, which was lucky from my point of view, for I possessed nothing at all except my bamboo stick and I had to replenish my wardrobe from the beginning. The quality of all my purchases was excellent, most of my clothes coming from the Union Militaire, the equivalent of our N.A.A.F.I. Money was arranged through government channels; we were allowed a certain amount of our pay which helped towards buying food extras; wine, cheese, fruit, etc. These were the days before Italy ran short of food herself and several months before the regular stream of Red Cross parcels.

In October the inmates of the Villa Medici were moved northward to PG 12, the Castello di Vincigliata near Florence. Conditions there were a little more severe, with increased security and less food, although each officer had his own room, baths every other day, and access to parole walks. Despite this easy lifestyle the prisoners did not become soft or idle. The prospect of returning to duty remained uppermost in their minds, and while at PG 12 the generals planned and executed one of the finest escapes of the war (see Chapter 14).

The Italians had a greater respect for officer welfare than most other combatant nations, and Allied officers of all ranks were generally well treated, although overcrowding increased and food supplies diminished as the war progressed. In the summer months, if the weather was good and food supplies sufficient, it was generally agreed by officer prisoners that, confinement apart, life was tolerable.

The main camp at Sulmona had separate compounds holding officers and other ranks. In the upper part of the officers' compound, each room held just two men. In the early stages of the war, at least, POW officers had their own mess with armchairs and tableware, as well as a gym and a games room. The men lived a far more Spartan existence, with up to eighty to a block. The officers also had better food than the other ranks, who, especially in winter, when Italian rations declined, relied heavily on their Red Cross parcels. When the supply of Red Cross parcels dried up in the winter of 1941–2 the other ranks experienced real hunger. The visibly better conditions enjoyed by the officers was, according to a visit by the US Protecting Power in May 1941, a cause of resentment among the other ranks, many of whom held a poor opinion of their officer neighbours. Jim Witte regarded them as a slovenly lot, 'lounging around in deckchairs'.

PG 49 at Fontanellato held around 540 mainly British officers. The prisoners were housed in a four-storey brick-and-marble building, the *Orfanotrofio Nazionale* (National Orphanage), which had been taken over by the Italian authorities and reassigned for use as a POW camp. Although it was designed to be an imposing example of fascist architecture, the prisoners though it jerry-built. While somewhat overcrowded and lacking in space for recreation, PG 49 was considered by an inspector from the Swiss Legation in Rome to be one of the best camps he had visited. Food was adequate, tobacco plentiful, and each man was allowed a glass of wine and of vermouth each day. Sanitation was considerably better than the communal earth closets of an other ranks' camp, although the toilets were a little rough and ready according to one prisoner: 'They were of the kind in which you squatted over a dark hole in the floor and at unpredictable intervals a huge head of water like the Severn Bore came swirling up and filled your boots.'

The commandant of PG 49, Colonel Eugenio Vicedomini, a First World War veteran who had fought with the British in 1917–18, was considered by the POWs to be a gentleman of the old school. He controlled a staff of six officers, a sergeant major and some sixty guards, who got on reasonably well with the British officers. Even escapes, which usually soured relations between captor and captives, did not seem to perturb Vicedomini. A *carabiniere* caught Lieutenant Jack Comyn trying to slip out of the camp dressed as an Italian workman. He was brought before the commandant.

> I was still in my disguise, and at first the Colonel refused to believe it was me. When convinced his consternation was amazing. 'But Tenente Comyn,' he exclaimed, 'my sentries on the wire might have shot you – and then what would your mother have said?' As I had not been expecting this question I was uncertain how to reply, but his concern touched me and I received with equanimity the statutory sentence of twenty-eight days in solitary confinement which he awarded.

The solicitous and, as it was to turn out, steadfast commandant of PG 49 may have been exceptional, but most Italians were reasonably well disposed towards Allied POWs – although until the signing of the armistice in September 1943 Italy's armed forces and civilians were mindful that Allied prisoners were still their enemies. A smaller number of Italians were, however, actively hostile.

The commandant of PG 57 at Gruppignano – which housed both Bob McDowall and, for a brief period, Doug LeFevre – was Colonel Calcatera, a *carabinieri* officer obsessed with discipline and security. According to camp folklore, Calcatera had a notice in his office which read, 'English are accursed but more accursed are the Italians that treat them well.' Whatever the truth of this statement, infractions of the commandant's code of discipline were dealt with harshly. LeFevre described the atmosphere in the camp: 'You could be punished for anything. You could be punished for failing to salute a corporal. You could be punished for smiling or laughing. The Italians didn't like to be laughed at and they would dream up all sorts of punishments, such as making you stand out in the cold, or sending you to the boob [solitary confinement] or cutting your hair off – any little thing that would annoy you.' Calcatera was nonetheless an efficient administrator, and with supervision from Commonwealth NCOs the camp – which held 4,500 other ranks in three compounds by March 1943 – was generally well run, although shortages of food, fuel and blankets made the winter of 1942–3 a difficult time.

Calcatera was a dominating presence in PG 57. In other camps, however, the commandant was often a more distant figure, with subordinates – such as the security staff or the camp officer – taking a more active role in POW affairs. In PG 21 at Chieti, Captain Croce – a *carabinieri* camp officer and interpreter – made a lasting impression on the prisoners. He was always immaculately turned out, with a well-cut uniform, highly polished boots, and a carefully trimmed moustache and beard. One POW described him as looking 'every bit the perfect villain in a Hollywood movie. We suspected he cultivated the image deliberately. His English had only a slight, and to us sinister, accent.' Croce made clear his contempt for the prisoners, who loathed him in return.

Such ardent anti-British fascists as Calcatera and Croce were in a minority, but the stereotypical image assigned to Italians as good-natured incompetents was seldom the case in prisoner-of-war camps. Although individual guards may have been friendly, the system was run from Rome on rigorous and inflexible lines, and until the armistice escapers had a better chance of getting out of Germany than Italy.

When Pilot Officer Jimmy James was sent to Stalag Luft I at Barth in the summer of 1940 it was a small camp with two barrack huts for officers and six for NCOs. The camp was situated on a narrow, sandy peninsula jutting into the Baltic Sea. Morale among the prisoners was low, especially in the light of recent British defeats in France and chronic food shortages. The prisoners at Barth also had a long-running grievance against the permanent staff at Dulag Luft for their access to Red Cross parcels and for what was seen as an overly friendly relationship with the Germans. Otherwise depressed, James found new hope in a campaign of escape activities that began in earnest with the arrival of sixty RAF officers from the Army camp at Spangenberg (Oflag IXA).

Jack Vietor arrived at Stalag Luft I in March 1944, and like James he found the camp a dispiriting place:

> Cold damp fogs rolled in from the Baltic alternating with bleak, chilling winds. During the summer it was light until almost midnight and daybreak was early but in winter it would become dark as early as three o'clock in the afternoon and stayed dark until nine the following morning. Tall, gloomy pines hedged us in at the north; directly adjoining the camp was a Flak School where German soldiers studied anti-aircraft procedures. Windswept, sandy and desolate, the peninsula was an isolated cul-de-sac of the war.

But by the time of Vietor's incarceration Stalag Luft I had been transformed. James and most of the other RAF officers had been transferred to Stalag Luft III, and the NCOs, by a roundabout route, to Stalag Luft VI at Heydekrug. Stalag Luft I was to expand enormously to accommodate the influx of American airmen during 1944, and by February 1945 it comprised four compounds with over 8,346 officers and orderlies.

Increasing numbers of RAF prisoners led to the opening of a new camp in April 1942 – Stalag Luft III, located deep in Silesia near the town of Sagan and far from any friendly or neutral border. Security measures were improved: there were more seismographs, and barrack blocks were situated further from the wire to make tunnelling more difficult. Ostensibly intended as a show camp, Stalag Luft III was in fact similar in most details to its predecessor at Barth, although until late 1944 there was little overcrowding and ample space for outdoor recreation. Initially Stalag Luft III had two compounds: East for officers and Centre for NCOs. Constant pressure from new prisoner arrivals led to the reorganization of Stalag Luft III as an officers-only camp, and the construction of three more compounds. As had happened at Stalag Luft I, the camp took on an increasingly American character: East and North Compounds housed RAF prisoners, while the old Centre compound was turned over to US officers (under the leadership of Colonel Delmar T. Spivey), with two new compounds – South and West – also holding Americans. By early 1945 there were over 10,000 officers and orderlies imprisoned in Stalag Luft III and its nearby satellite camp of Belaria, over two-thirds of them from the US Army Air Force.

As the numbers of prisoners increased in Stalag Luft III, so did the prison staff, which reached a total of 2,000 officers and guards. The POWs were fortunate in their camp commandant, Colonel Friedrich von Lindeiner, an English-speaking officer who did much to help the prisoners in difficult circumstances and earned their respect and even affection. The tone set by Lindeiner was followed by other members of the camp staff, and relations between them and the POWs were probably better than anywhere else in the German POW system. Staff Sergeant Glemnitz, one of the compound officers, was especially admired as a worthy adversary – highly intelligent, but with a sense of humour. 'All in all,' wrote RAF airman John Dominy, 'Sagan was a remarkable camp, for it contained men who were the best of their respective warring races.'

The new camp for NCOs – Stalag Luft VI at Heydekrug – opened in June 1943, and was sited in the sandy wastes of East Prussia, almost on the border with Lithuania. The camp had been a former military barracks, and the POWs were pleased to find well-constructed brick-built accommodation blocks that were equipped with 'Russian-type, flat-topped brick stoves which burned a minimum of fuel and gave a maximum of heat'. The camp was divided into three compounds:

one for the British, one for Americans, and the third for both nationalities. The brick blocks were supplemented by wooden huts, which provided an overall capacity for just over 6,000 men, but by the time of the camp's closure in July 1944 – due to the proximity of the Red Army – numbers were exceeding the formal limit.

Stalag Luft VI enjoyed decent facilities, including a library with 6,000 books, and an adequate supply of Red Cross parcels. Morale among the prisoners was generally high, with a determined escape committee and an excellent educational set-up that earned the camp the title the Barbed-Wire University. The presence of Colonel von Hoerbach, the commandant in 1944, was also beneficial. The American camp leader, Technical Sergeant Frank S. Paules, said of him, 'He did everything he could to treat us as soldiers, according to the rules and regulations of the Geneva Convention. I believe von Hoerbach treated us well to the best of his ability.' Unfortunately for the prisoners, other camp officers were less respectful of the Geneva Convention, and the camp security officer, Major Peschell, did nothing to rein in his trigger-happy guards, so that, for example, prisoners were shot and killed after surrendering during escape attempts.

On the closure of Stalag Luft VI in the summer of 1944 the prisoners were dispatched to other camps further to the west. Many were sent to Stalag Luft IV at Gross Tychow in a terrible journey that included the infamous 'run up the hill' in which POWs were made to run at the double to the camp while being set upon by dogs and by guards' rifle butts and fixed bayonets. At least 228 men suffered from bayonet thrusts or dog bites, and one man had 60 separate wounds.

Stalag Luft IV was divided into four compounds, and was soon filled to overflowing with predominantly USAAF NCOs. By the time of the camp's evacuation in February 1945 it held over 10,000 prisoners, some living in regular barrack blocks while others were forced ten at a time into six-man wooden huts known as 'dog kennels'. The camp staff maintained a deeply antagonistic attitude towards their charges. The commandant, Lieutenant Colonel Aribert Bombach, was particularly unpleasant and, fearful of a mass breakout of the type that had occurred at Stalag Luft III, was obsessed with security at the expense of prisoners' welfare. According to Staff Sergeant Bill Krebs, POWs were 'treated harshly and their wishes or desires were given little or no consideration'. When the prisoners arrived at the camp they were roughly searched and valuables were stolen. Food was in short supply, and Red Cross parcels were routinely pilfered. 'The Germans', wrote Krebbs, 'ate the best of the food while we were on extremely short rations and almost allowed to starve.'

The last Luftwaffe camp constructed for NCOs was Stalag Luft VII at Bankau, holding just over 1,350 RAF prisoners. Conditions were generally good, with facilities that included a regular water supply – sometimes with hot water – and, for such a short-lived camp (June 1944–January 1945) surprisingly good recreational amenities, so that, for example, plays and revues were produced by the prisoners. In contrast to the regime of Stalag Luft IV, Bankau had a reasonable commandant and decent camp staff, although Major Peschell – the infamous security officer transferred from Stalag Luft VI – was condemned by the British camp leader Flight Lieutenant Peter Thomson as 'a bastard of the first water'.

The naval camp at Westertimke was divided into two compounds: Marlag (O) for officers and Marlag (M) for petty officers and senior ratings. Royal Navy prisoners had originally been allotted a compound in Stalag XB at Sandbostel, but prisoner increases in 1940–41 encouraged the Kriegsmarine to build its own camp, so that during the spring and summer of 1942 naval prisoners were gradually transferred to nearby Westertimke. As with other barrack-block camps built on the featureless North European Plain, Marlag had a forbidding appearance, but it possessed those key elements that combined to make a reasonable POW camp: adequate facilities, minimal overcrowding, and a commandant and staff generally well disposed towards the POWs. Marlag was one of the smaller camps in Germany; even after new arrivals had been absorbed from Italy in late 1943 there were only 306 POWs in the officers' (O) compound and 508 in the other ranks' (M) compound. (Junior ratings were sent to Army work camps, where they remained for the rest of the war.)

The larger camp for merchant seamen, Milag, was built a few hundred yards away and comprised a main compound – which by 1944 was packed to overflowing with 2,800 officers and men of 41 different nationalities – and a separate Inder Lager, which housed over 500 Indian and South-East Asian sailors. Milag was a distinct entity from the naval camp, although new arrivals could find themselves mixed up for short periods until reassessed by the Germans. Milag was not built to the same standards as Marlag: water and lighting compared poorly, and over the course of time the huts began to show increasing signs of wear and tear.

The first POW camp in Germany to house British prisoners from the Army was opened in October 1939 in an old castle near Spangenberg, which by the end of the year had been designated Oflag IXA/H (although during the Phoney War most British prisoners there were in fact aircrew). Spangenberg – like Oflag IVC at Colditz – was dramatically situated high on a crag, and encircled by a 30-foot-deep dry moat it had something of the appearance of a castle from a Grimm Brothers' tale. Closed for a time, it was reopened as a prison for older, senior officers, although persistent escapers were also sent to Spangenberg, because its thick walls and rock foundations were considered a deterrent to tunnelling.

The Allied disasters in France in 1940 produced an influx of over 40,000 British POWs into Germany. Most officer prisoners were confined at Oflag VIIC at Laufen and Oflag VIID at Tittmoning – both camps situated in scenic locations on the Bavarian border with Austria. Severe overcrowding – combined with the absence of Red Cross parcels – made life miserable for the new POWs, although at Tittmoning the commandant was respected by the British. By contrast, the vehemently anti-British commandant at Laufen, Colonel von Frey, was loathed. Bertie Harwood and his fellow officers refused to take him seriously, ostentatiously talking through his foam-flecked parade-ground harangues on British ill discipline. Von Frey instituted a hard, obstructive regime, from which most other camp staff took their lead.

Conditions improved somewhat when substantial numbers of officers were transferred to Oflag VB at Biberach, a smaller, less crowded camp. This move eventually included Harwood, but before arriving at Biberach he and a group of other officers were sent to Stalag XXID at Posen, as a retaliatory punishment for the alleged mistreatment of German POWs in Canada. Posen, like Stalag XXA at Thorn, was an old fortress built to defend Germany from possible Russian attack in the nineteenth century. Both these camps comprised a central fortress, much of it subterranean, surrounded by satellite forts that also housed prisoners. The buildings were distinguished by their dirt, decay and dampness. Harwood's interlude at Posen taught him to appreciate the improved conditions at Biberach, where the accommodation consisted of well-built concrete barrack blocks. He considered Biberach's commandant to be 'very old and doddery', but found his deputy to be 'quite friendly and keen to do anything to make us as comfortable as conditions permitted'. One incident etched into Harwood's memory was the sudden arrival of the German general officer responsible for Allied POWs:

> He was blind drunk when he arrived and his face was a mottled purple. Nevertheless, it was to our advantage that he was stinking because he suddenly got it into his sodden brain that the British should learn something of German *Kultur*. He stomped into our room and with a lavish wave of the arm proclaimed loudly in German to the Kommandant: 'Flowers! That's what they need! Flowers! Window boxes filled with flowers! And beautiful pictures on the walls!' There was an influx of window boxes and flowers, which of course had to be paid for; but we didn't mind that as there was little else on which to spend our money. The most dreadful pictures arrived, a sort of German equivalent of the *The Stag at Bay*. A few people with a sense of humour bought these monstrosities for amusement's sake.

Harwood's stay in Biberach was short-lived, and the camp was closed in August 1941, with the prisoners being transferred to a larger camp, Oflag VIB at Warburg. The Germans decided that it would be better to house as many British officers as possible in one super-camp, and approximately 3,000 officers (including some from the RAF) were crammed into Warburg – a camp condemned by all forced to live there. Warburg was also repeatedly criticized in inspections by the International Committee of the Red Cross, which considered it 'much the worst we have seen in Germany'. The buildings were infested with vermin and poorly constructed, and the roofs leaked. (The roof on Harwood's hut collapsed during a heavy storm on his first night at the camp.) Cooking and latrine facilities were grossly inadequate, and in winter the whole site turned into a quagmire, into which sewage overflowed.

In early 1942 the Germans began to wind down the camp and sent most of the senior officers to a reopened Oflag IXA at Spangenberg. When Warburg closed, in September 1942, the RAF contingent had been transferred to Oflag XXIB at Schubin or to Luftwaffe-run camps, and the remainder of the Army officers to Oflag IXA/Z at Rotenburg (a branch camp of Spangenberg) or Oflag VIIB at Eichstätt – the latter camp taking Harwood and 1,800 more junior officers.

A former cavalry barracks, Eichstätt was set 'in a beautiful Bavarian countryside of meadow, trees and hills', and divided into an upper camp, containing the original three-storey stone barracks, and a lower camp of newly constructed barrack blocks. For the POWs the idyllic location was spoiled by overcrowding and by the damp, marshy conditions in the lower camp. Another bugbear was the security-conscious commandant, Colonel Bletterbauer, who instituted a severe regime that restricted many otherwise harmless activities within the camp. A further negative feature of Eichstätt's early days was the shackling of selected prisoners as retaliation for alleged Allied misde-meanours at Dieppe and during a subsequent commando raid in the Channel Islands. Over time conditions improved and more space was found after the departure of officers to other camps. Recreational facilities were good, with playing fields (converted to an ice rink in winter), active music and theatre groups, and a good library – much of it brought over from Warburg – that would eventually hold 15,000 volumes.

Apart from Colonel Bletterbauer, relations were good with most of the camp staff. One keen escaper, Captain Terence Prittie, even had kind words to say of the camp security officer, Captain Klau: 'A keen soldier, he inspired a degree of respect, not only because he did his job well, but because his dealings with British officers showed him to be an entirely straightforward and honourable opponent.' Escapes continued as before, and culminated in a mass breakout in July 1943 when sixty-five officers successfully tunnelled out of the camp, although all were subsequently recaptured. They were sent to other camps for determined escapers – most to Colditz, a few to Spangenberg – which fortunately provided more space for the remaining Eichstätt POWs.

The most famous of all POW camps was Oflag IVC at Colditz. Oflag IVC was a *Sonderlager* or special camp, and held persistent escap-ers and those considered to be *Deutschefeindlich* (hostile to Germans). It also contained prisoners the Germans believed had some particular importance – *Prominente* – who might be used as hostages at a future date. Another distinguishing feature of the camp in its early years was its multinational nature: it included large contingents of Poles, French and Dutch, as well as British. Colditz was intended to intimidate the prisoner, and on first acquaintance it normally did so. Billie Stephens was sent to Colditz after repeated escape attempts from Marlag, Stalag VIIIB at Lamsdorf and various places en route. 'We walked up through the town,' he wrote, 'and as we got nearer the castle my spirits sank appreciably. It looked very grim and forbidding.' But once inside Stephens found the accommodation better than expected and was cheered by the high morale of his fellow POWs, 'most with one purpose – to escape'.

Oflag 64 at Schubin in the old Polish Corridor was assigned to US Army officers, although smaller numbers were scattered amid the British Oflags or were held for long periods in transit camps such as Stalag XIIA at Limburg. The new camp had originally been designated Oflag XXIB and had contained many escape-minded RAF officers, including Jimmy James. As a consequence of a mass breakout the camp was closed to the British in April 1943 and subsequently reopened as Oflag 64 in August. By 1 June 1944 there were 500 American officers in the camp, and numbers rose slowly until early 1945, when a sudden influx as a result of the Battle of the Bulge took numbers to almost 1,500.

Oflag 64 compared favourably with the best of the British Oflags, and possessed good facilities and a reasonable German commandant and staff. A former country house and then school, the camp was centred around a group of substantial structures, including a stone-built chapel and the main administrative building known as the White House, with several barrack blocks for accommodation purposes. When Captain Roger L. Shinn arrived in the camp in January 1945 he found it a welcome haven from the miseries of Limburg. It was a well run by the prisoners, with high morale.

POW camps for privates and NCOs were very different from those reserved for officers. The Stalags were much larger and typically consisted of a central camp and its many subsidiary camps for work parties (*Arbeitskommandos*). The central camp housed non-working NCOs, and was also used as a transit camp for working prisoners. Some men

came and went from the main camp on a regular basis, while others –
such as Jim Witte, attached to Stalag IVB at Mühlberg – remained in
work camps for the duration of the war, oblivious of the goings-on
in the wider prison world.

Conditions in Stalags were generally worse than those in Oflags.
While the officer camps shared in the general POW privations of
overcrowding, poor buildings, bad sanitation and shortages of food
and heating, these problems were usually of a lesser nature. In addition, the Germans, like their Italian allies, had a higher regard for
officers than was usual in the British and US armed forces.

Stalag IVB at Mühlberg opened in 1939 to house Polish prisoners,
although by 1940 it had expanded rapidly to include 23,000 French
and Belgians. By mid-1940 the camp had sixty barrack blocks: forty
for living quarters, the remainder for administration and storage purposes. More nationalities began to arrive at the camp, including large
contingents of British and Russians, and from late 1944 onward
American ground-force troops. By then the camp was divided into
five large compounds. Estimates of the size of Mühlberg varied:
German figures claimed at least 30,000 POWs of all nationalities by
the end of 1943, rising to between 50,000 and 90,000 by early 1945.

The Revd Bob McDowall and Gunner Jim Witte arrived at Stalag
IVB in September 1943, when the camp served as a transit camp for
15,000 British and Commonwealth POWs transferred from Italy.
While the majority of officers and other ranks went elsewhere – as
did Witte, to work camps at nearby Chemnitz and Leipzig –
McDowall stayed behind to act as a senior chaplain. McDowall found
Mühlberg a decent camp, although he experienced somewhat better
conditions than the men, sharing a room with a few of his fellow
padres and having the option of taking parole walks in the locality. He
certainly regarded his temporary posting to the more pleasant Oflag
VIIB at Eichstätt in 1944 as an irritation and longed to get back to
Mühlberg.

The largest camp holding British prisoners was Stalag VIIIB at
Lamsdorf. At its peak in early 1944 it contained 10,000 British prisoners, with a further 9,000 in the 235 work camps attached to the
main site. Lamsdorf had been a POW camp during the 1914–18
conflict, and a few unfortunates served time there in both world wars.
When the first British prisoners arrived in 1940 it was a dilapidated

place with no recreational or sporting facilities, and men found its vast size and location amid the industrial, coal-mining region of Silesia a depressing experience. German discipline was also tough, the guards displaying their post-Dunkirk arrogance to the full. The British part of the camp was eventually divided into eleven compounds, which included separate compounds for contingents of RAF, Indians and Canadians, as well as a punishment compound (*Straflager*) and compounds for kitchen and medical staff, for POWs in transit to and from work camps, and for those awaiting repatriation. Prisoners could usually walk freely between many of the compounds, providing them with a chance to meet up with old friends or at least get away from the confines of their own section of the camp.

The arrival of Red Cross parcels and a new, more sympathetic, commandant in 1941 improved conditions at Lamsdorf, as did the imposition of order by energetic British camp leadership. Within the camp there was a reservoir of talent – theatrical, artistic and educational – which the Germans encouraged. And yet the buildings and other facilities were so run-down that Lamsdorf continued to have a reputation as the 'prison camp from hell'.

In camps such as Lamsdorf, where basic services – accommodation, sanitation, clothing and blankets – were poor, the chronic problem of overcrowding, which could be absorbed to a greater degree in better camps, became painfully acute. In 1942 overcrowding at Lamsdorf began to cause problems, and by the autumn of 1943 – when the camp was absorbing British and Italian prisoners transported from Italy – crisis point was reached. Men were without blankets, with many forced to sleep on concrete floors; supplies of running water became increasingly irregular, and the camp's sanitation was so poor that medical officers feared an epidemic of dysentery. And the threat of a mass outbreak of typhus began to loom large.

Protests were made by the British camp leaders and by representatives from the Swiss Protecting Power. In the past such protests had usually fallen on deaf ears, but in this case the Germans rectified the situation with unusual haste (quite probably because of the danger of a typhus epidemic). A new, more dynamic, commandant, Lieutenant Colonel Messner, was installed in November 1943, and was described as 'a man of deeds rather than a man of words'. The camp was divided in two early in 1944: Lamsdorf was renamed Stalag 344, and many prisoners were transferred to a new camp at Teschen, which became Stalag VIIIB. Camp facilities at Lamsdorf improved, but the underlying problems of poor building construction and sanitation were never properly resolved.

Lamsdorf was a rough, wild camp – the author of the New Zealand official POW history described it as a place 'where a profusion of the world's languages were spoken and where prisoners seemed able to get away with almost anything provided they did not make it too blatant. It seems to have had something of the atmosphere of a European seaport city, with a good deal of the spit-and-polish of the regular British Army superimposed.' Although Sergeant John Dominy was never held there, he was well aware of its reputation: 'To have belonged to a tough camp like Lamsdorf had a certain cachet like being an Old Etonian.'

Of the other ranks' camps the most unusual was Stalag 383 at Hohenfels in Bavaria. Despite the many and often brutal attempts to force British NCOs to work, the determination of British opposition towards compulsory work caused the Germans to rethink their policy and send the non-working NCOs to their own camp – the former Oflag IIIC, redesignated Stalag 383. Although non-working NCOs remained within the working Stalags, the Germans believed the removal of a hard core of opposition would make life easier for them. The NCOs – who included a few privates and lance corporals with 'prison-camp promotions' – were told that they were to be sent to a punishment camp or even a concentration camp, but despite these threats Stalag 383 turned out to be one of the better camps in Germany, comparable to most Oflags. The first prisoners, drawn from camps throughout the country, arrived in September 1942, and by the end of the year the camp had a strength of over 3,000 POWs, which would rise to 5,000 by early 1944.

Stalag 383 was situated in a fold among wooded, hilly countryside. Facilities were good – a reflection of the sterling work performed by the Red Cross and the YMCA (with co-operation from the commandant) – and until the end of 1944 food was adequate and overcrowding never a problem. In contrast to the vast barrack rooms of most Stalags, accommodation in Hohenfels comprised approximately 400 small huts which held no more than 14 men each, with two-tier bunks, stools and a table. The huts were made of wood, but were of double thickness and insulated with fibreglass which, with a good stove, provided 'snug billets'.

The commandant was well regarded by the prisoners, and Staff Sergeant James McGee went so far as to call him 'first class, fair, impartial and with a good sense of humour'. McGee wrote that the commandant's well-developed humour 'was noticeable when sentencing recaptured escapers. The further afield before recapture the less the punishment; those taken locally usually ended up with a month or more in the bunker.'

Of Stalag 383, Les Foskett remarked, 'After the best part of two years in various camps or working parties, I can only describe Hohenfels 383 as a holiday camp.' One of the indexes of a good camp was whether it had its own covert radio, which implied resourcefulness and the economic muscle and confidence for bribing guards to supply contraband electrical materials. Hohenfels had many radios.

Not all POWs came within the jurisdiction of the German armed forces: some were imprisoned by the SS. No matter how bad conditions might be in a Wehrmacht camp, prisoners were at least registered with the Protecting Power and enjoyed most if not all of the safeguards of the Geneva Convention. Prisoners in SS hands had no such protection: they could be starved, tortured or killed at will, safe from the prying eyes of international humanitarian organizations. Even those individuals who were being relatively well treated by the SS knew that they could be eliminated at a moment's notice.

In the circles of hell that constituted a concentration camp there was no equality of suffering. A privileged few – usually *Prominente* – were housed in special compounds (*Sonderlager*), where conditions could be surprisingly good. After his recapture following the Great Escape in March 1944 Jimmy James was sent to Sonderlager A in Sachsenhausen concentration camp, where he rejoined three fellow escapers from Stalag Luft III: 'Wings' Day, Johnny Dodge and Sydney Dowse. They shared a block with a mix of Russians, Poles and Irishmen who the Germans had hoped might join the Nazi cause. Also present were two Churchills: Peter Churchill, SOE agent and 'husband' of Odette, and Lieutenant Colonel Jack Churchill, a commando captured in the Balkans. Both were able to trade on the Germans' steadfast yet erroneous belief that people with the name

Churchill were inevitably related to the British prime minister, enabling them to acquire the status of a *Prominent*. (The American-born Dodge, however, *was* a distant relation of Winston Churchill.)

The eighteen or so men in the barrack hut had plenty of room, weekly showers, and the use of two highly proficient Italian orderlies. Access to adequate food gave the British prisoners the strength to respond in their usual way to the commandant's boast that Sachsenhausen was 'escape-proof'. Despite the threat of death for further escapes, James and his comrades were unwavering in their commitment to continuing their war against Nazi Germany. A tunnel was begun shortly after their arrival.

After the British-sponsored assassination of SS leader Reinhard Heydrich in Prague, the Germans had a great fear of escaping POWs liaising with elements of the Czech resistance. POWs recaptured in Czechoslovakia experienced a particularly difficult time, and from 1944 onward were liable to be imprisoned in the concentration camp at Theresienstadt. After capture by the Czech police during an escape attempt in February 1945, Lance Bombardier Edward Stirling was questioned by the Gestapo and then sent to Theresienstadt. Beaten by German guards during transit, Stirling was thrown into a compound that included over eighty other British POWs. Conditions were abominable, but, being British, Stirling and his comrades did not suffer the terrible conditions of Russian and Jewish prisoners. In early April they were unexpectedly dispatched to a POW Stalag and liberated while en route.

In August 1944, as US forces advanced on Paris, 168 Allied airmen (86 British and Commonwealth, 82 American) were transferred from Fresnes prison in Paris to Buchenwald concentration camp. After a five-day cattle-wagon journey to Buchenwald the airmen were sent to the Small Compound, a wired-off area without shelter but packed with prisoners from all over Europe, slowly starving to death or succumbing to related diseases. The airmen's uniforms and footwear were taken in exchange for a shirt and a pair of trousers, but no shoes.

The Germans and the privileged prisoners (*Kapos*), who were armed with clubs and acted as sadistic warders, created a climate of fear that demoralized all but the hardest of prisoners. One of the Allied airmen, Canadian Ed Carter-Edwards, recalled some of the psychological consequences of existence in Buchenwald:

This constant shattering of human dignity and this total disrespect for a fellow human-being is probably one of the elements that scarred my memory and that of many others who were in the camp. I feel what was responsible for the mental breakdown of many of the people in these camps was the realization that there was no avenue of escape; no future; death by disease; death by starvation or being transported to work in areas being bombed. No matter which way you turned, death faced you. It was a landscape devoid of grass, trees, shrubs – no birds – nothing but suffering, starvation, diseased bodies all around you day and night. There was also the constant threat of being shot. Day or night, your life didn't matter one hoot.

The Allied airmen had the advantage of military training, and under the leadership of the New Zealand squadron leader Phil Lamson they worked as a team as best they could. 'We respected each other,' remembered Carter-Edwards, 'and we needed each other. This was why we were able to survive. The other people in the camp only thought as individuals, thinking of themselves and not worried about the other guy.' The airmen were also exceptionally fortunate in being helped by a group of SOE agents already in the camp, including the legendary 'White Rabbit', Wing Commander 'Tommy' Yeo-Thomas, who was organizing a resistance movement among the camp inmates. In September 1944 orders were received to kill the SOE contingent. Yeo-Thomas and six others managed to survive by going into hiding within the camp or by impersonating other prisoners suffering from typhus, but the remaining thirty agents were slowly strangled to death on piano-wire nooses.

One of the SOE survivors, Christopher Burney, acted as a camp interpreter, and through his contacts within Buchenwald he was able to send out a message to Luftwaffe officers at a nearby airfield, alerting them to the presence of the illegally held airmen – who were now under sentence of death. The Luftwaffe acted swiftly to secure the men's release into its custody. During October–November 1944 they were transferred to Stalag Luft III, although two men had already died in the concentration camp. Their stories of conditions at Buchenwald were greeted with disbelief by the other POWs.

The concentration camps also held some of those who had fallen foul of Hitler's Commando Order of 18 October 1942. They included seven commandos captured after attacking industrial sites in

Norway (Operation Musketoon). They were briefly held in Oflag IVC at Colditz, but were then transferred to Sachsenhausen on 22 October. The following morning each commando was killed with a shot to the back of the neck and their bodies cremated. Others survived. Edgar Hargreaves, a former commando, was a member of the British military mission to the Chetniks in Yugoslavia. Captured by the Germans, he was tortured before being sent to Buchenwald, where he spent long periods in solitary confinement. Resigned to death, Hargreaves was surprised to be handed over to the Wehrmacht, and saw out the rest of the war in Oflag VIIIF at Märisch-Trübau and then Colditz.

The fate of the SOE agents in Buchenwald demonstrates how tenuous life was for those imprisoned in concentration camps. And from late 1944 onward, as the Allies advanced on both fronts towards the Reich, the Nazis began to tie up loose ends in an orgy of killing. A few SOE operatives escaped death, sometimes by their own actions, sometimes by chance, but also in a few instances by the design of their captors. The idea of holding valuable individuals as potential hostages appealed to the gangster-like minds of the Nazis, and this was the reason for the survival of Odette 'Churchill', first at Fresnes and later at Ravensbrück concentration camp for women.

By August 1943 Odette's interrogations had petered out to the odd visit from Hugo Bleicher, the Abwehr sergeant who had arrested her the previous April. When he abandoned any hope of prising information from her, she was left in solitary confinement in the Third Division of Fresnes. A remarkably self-contained woman, Odette was able to endure solitary better than most, but the poor food and increasing cold – as autumn drew on – took its toll on her health. By the end of October she was seriously ill. The division captain decided that her condition was life-threatening and moved her to a warmer cell with three other women. She was also allowed her first bath since capture. The better living conditions contributed to a slow improvement during the winter of 1943–4. But, as ever, the sentence of death hung over her, underscored by the cries of those being led away to execution.

On 12 May 1944 Odette was told she was to be transferred to Germany within the hour, along with six other female French Section SOE members. Of the seven women, only Odette would survive the war. At Karlsruhe she was separated from her companions and sent to a transit camp at Halle, where for once her illustrious assumed surname worked against her. Imprisoned in a cell with forty Ukrainian women, she heard a voice calling for her. Confirming her name to a burly guard at the cell door, he smashed his fist into her face: 'I give you that for Winston Churchill – with my compliments.'

From Halle, Odette was transferred to Ravensbrück. The commandant, Lieutenant Colonel (Obersturmbannführer) Fritz Sühren, gave orders that she be placed in solitary confinement in the Bunker – the camp's prison cells – without privileges. Odette spent three months alone and, except during visits by warders, in complete darkness, Gripped by dysentery and suffering from scurvy, her health began to fail again. Sühren insisted that she be kept alive, and in September she was transferred to the camp hospital for basic treatment. There she received slightly better food, and more of it, and she was eventually assigned to a cell with a window; it was too high to see out, but ash, cinders and even burning hair from the crematorium chimneys blew into the room.

During the winter of 1944–5, the camp authorities stepped up the killings, and when orders were issued from Berlin to eliminate the Bunker inmates Odette's fate seemed sealed. Sühren, however, considered her a possible insurance policy, and stayed the executioner's hand.

5

The Fabric of Daily Life

As Captain John A. Vietor Jr prepared to enter the *Vorlager* in Stalag Luft I at Barth for delousing and registration, he could see a large crowd of prisoners on the other side of the wire. 'Being shot down', wrote Vietor, 'had seemed a unique experience and it was surprising that it should happen to so many other people as well. Each of us somehow felt to become a prisoner was something that happened to someone else, an unreal experience.'

A prisoner's first few days in camp were not easy. Although the shock of capture had worn off, the new inmate had to come to terms with the strange and unfamiliar life of long-term imprisonment. In a good camp the staff and fellow prisoners helped with the practicalities of life behind barbed wire. When there was sufficient food it was customary to give the new prisoner a Red Cross meal, after which the rules and regulations – of both captors and prisoners – were explained. Accommodation was sorted out, and in Air Force and Army officer camps a vetting procedure begun – POWs remained fearful that their captors might attempt to infiltrate a stool pigeon among them.

The prisoner was assigned to a barrack hut or room. Officers were generally given a degree of privacy and space, although Vietor considered himself lucky to be assigned a room that held just six men. In a camp for other ranks conditions were more daunting: a fairly typical hut or block in a Stalag was approximately 15 yards wide and between 60 and 80 yards long, and contained upwards of 200 men. The block was divided in the middle by a washroom with a few cold taps; in many camps the water supply was erratic, and in dry or freezing weather it could fail altogether. Latrine buckets were provided at both ends of the block, to be used at night when the POWs were locked inside the huts.

Side-by-side bunks (two or, more usually, three tiers in height) were packed into the building; they were often arranged into groups to create partially separate areas within the block. The beds were made from simple wooden frames with wooden slats (progressively removed for fuel or for shoring up escape tunnels) over which was laid a palliasse stuffed with straw or wood chippings. The only other pieces of furniture were a number of long tables running down the centre of the building and some benches – insufficient for the numbers in the block, so that many men had to sit or lie on their beds. When all the prisoners were packed in, the hut was an oppressive place, made worse in wet weather by lines of laundry hanging up to dry.

To walk into a crowded barrack block for the first time was to endure an assault on the senses. New prisoners were overwhelmed by the smell from unwashed bodies and night latrines, although they soon adapted, as one veteran noted: 'We had always commented about how everybody's room but ours stank.' Staff Sergeant Mike Harkovich in Stalag Luft I recorded this lament: 'Layed awake for a few hours and listened to the snores and farts of the other jokers. What a way to spend an evening.'

Edward Ward, a BBC journalist imprisoned in PG 78 at Sulmona, spent time in both the officers' and the other ranks' compounds. Although he preferred the company in the latter, the noise in an other rank's block was a challenge:

> The Italians put the lights out at about 11 o'clock. But this was anything but a signal for quiet. It was precisely the reverse. All card-playing, attempts at reading and other comparatively quiet pursuits stopped and singing, whistling and talking began. Interminable and pointless arguments in loud voices dragged on for hours. The din in those troops' rooms had to be experienced to be believed. For the first few weeks I thought it would drive me mad.

Heating was provided by a few stoves, which seemed designed to give out as little warmth as possible. The fuel ration – usually briquettes made from coal dust – was never enough except in mild weather, when it was withdrawn. Wood was scrounged from the camp where possible, and at times the commandant might allow prisoners out on parole to forage for branches and sticks in fields surrounding the camp. Lighting was provided by some 20- or 40-watt bulbs, throwing a dim glow insufficient for reading except when directly under the light.

Poor sanitation was a recurring problem. There were never enough latrines, especially with so many prisoners suffering from gastro-intestinal problems, and they were often badly sited and constructed. Privacy was a memory of the past as men sat alongside each other in 'forty-holers'. At its most basic, a latrine or *Abort* consisted of a long pit with a pole slung along it; men would balance on the pole hoping not to fall in the excrement below – a calamity not unknown. Some latrines had seats with lids, although these were primarily to prevent rats from swarming out of the holes.

The unpleasantness of inadequate sanitation was conveyed in Sergeant Milt Felsen's account of first coming across the latrines in the American compound of Stalag IIB at Hammerstein in the winter of 1943–4. The weather was particularly cold, and the previous night a group of POWs had stolen the doors and window frames from the latrines for firewood. 'I reached the entrance,' Felsen wrote. 'GIs lined both sides. They crouched as high as they could, and each one had a stick or implement with which they pounded the platform beneath them to keep the rats from jumping up and biting their testicles. Freezing snow blew in from where the doors and windows had been. Faces were contorted with the cold and the snow that attacked bare bottoms. The scene was horrendous and comic at the same time.'

The excrement in the latrines was periodically removed for use as a fertilizer by a civilian contractor using a device nicknamed a honey wagon or Smellie Nellie. Usually pulled by a horse, this was a large wheeled cylinder to which a flexible hose was attached. The hose was placed into the latrine, and gas in the cylinder was ignited – creating a vacuum which sucked up the excrement. 'When the gas explodes', wrote American airman Joseph O'Donnell, 'it sounds like flak. Everyone in the camp usually jumps.'

The smallest social unit within a POW camp was the combine, made up of anything from two to twelve men. It acted as a surrogate family: its members pooled their resources – Red Cross and personal parcels – and shared out domestic duties such as collecting food, cooking and cleaning. If a man was in trouble he would look to his combine for help. When Bob Prouse was too ill to work, the men from his combine covered for him, and when he was in the cooler they smuggled cigarettes and food into his cell.

Comradeship was a powerful binding force, but within the close confines of the camp the virtues of forbearance and tolerance were regularly called upon, as Jack Vietor explained:

> You were compelled to live with men who in the ordinary way you might not like. Since everyone was aware of this there was seldom any friction. No matter how controversial the subject or how irritating a man's personality, tempers were controlled. There were occasional flare-ups, usually over trivial matters. Two fighter pilots became most argumentative over the pronunciation of the word 'recipe'. One claimed it was 'receet' and the other asserted it was pronounced 'receipee'. I almost came to blows with Myers when I suggested that the German infantry soldier was better trained than the American soldier. But instances such as these were rare.

Lieutenant Bertie Harwood moved rooms in Oflag VIB at Warburg: 'I had seen many friendships broken up through petty squabbling which inevitably arises from constant proximity.' This 'constant proximity' placed great strain on prisoners. It was no coincidence that Jean-Paul Sartre's heartfelt line 'Hell is other people' was written shortly after his release from a German POW camp. Vietor also wrote tellingly of the predicament:

> Rarely in life does a man find himself in the position of compulsory intimacy with others. There is always an opportunity for an occasional respite. In our circumstances there was none. Regardless of an individual's tastes or inclinations he was forced to live, eat and sleep in daily association with a heterogeneous group of individuals. As the camp was constituted there was no isolated nook where a man might spend an hour in seclusion.

Jim Witte, a fellow prisoner with Edward Ward at Sulmona, welcomed the only chance of some solitude through a short spell in solitary confinement. This was a common occurrence in many camps, and in Oflag IVC at Colditz there was competition to be sent to the cooler – Edgar Hargreaves remembered that 'we had a roster of who was to insult the Germans next so we would get a turn in the jail.'

★

Clubs and societies were popular in POW camps. As well as the obvious hobby-based clubs for sports and pastimes such as chess and debating, men grouped together in associations based on their origins: county and city clubs for the English; Caledonian societies for Scots; state clubs for Americans. Freemasons had their own lodges in the larger camps. These were all ways of recreating a comforting pre-war civilian world. They also served a useful function in encouraging men to move from the often claustrophobic environment of their combines and barrack huts to engage in the wider world of the camp as a whole. In Vietor's room it only took six weeks for him and his companions to have 'drained each other dry searching for new conversational refreshment'.

The tolerance required to get on with one's fellows was hard even for the most easy-going, but for a man like the Revd Bob McDowall – with unwavering religious and moral principles, not to say prejudices – it was doubly difficult. His initial period of captivity in Italy was spent with a group of tough, largely irreligious British and Commonwealth officers. Swearing and bawdy songs were staples of Army life, and in a crowded POW camp McDowall could find no relief from what was undeniably coarse behaviour. Other padres might have shrugged this off, but for McDowall it was a torment he was unable to contain – as he recorded in his diary: 'Men with [a] little wine singing lewd songs in next room, could not read and at about 8.30 I could no longer stand the filth. Went in and said, "I say chaps, I don't like your songs, I think they are no credit to you or to the company," and walked out.' Unsurprisingly, this outburst failed to reform the singers, who carried on as before. A troubled McDowall concluded, 'I had thought these men above anything so dirty. Did not sleep well.'

As a chaplain, often working on his own, McDowall was in a difficult position, somewhat cut off from his fellow prisoners. The press of humanity in the camp made his isolation seem even greater, and on a number of occasions he came to regret his decision to voluntarily enter captivity. Even in March 1943, when he was well established as the padre of PG 57 at Gruppignano, he could still write, 'I felt inexpressibly lonely today.' The sense of being alone among many was common to most prisoners: Robert Kee's POW memoir *A Crowd is Not Company* was aptly titled.

Social harmony was affected by the emergence of factions within camps. This was especially marked following purges, the POW expression for the moving of a large number of prisoners from one camp to another. Oflag VIB at Warburg came into being as a consequence of several purges from other camps. Harwood noticed how 'officers from one camp rarely mixed with those from another' but instead 'split up into separate camps, in which there were cliquey little sets each imagining themselves superior to the others'.

In British officer camps, at least, class was ever present. Many commentators observed how similar the camps were to public schools and how easily the POWs seemed to fit into their new environment, with the more privileged groups usually in the ascendant. In PG 49 at Fontanellato, Eric Newby noted that 'upper-class officers set the style', forming a distinct group within the camp. 'Everyone else they ignored completely,' wrote Newby, 'unless they owned something worth buying, or had some skill which they could make use of to increase their comfort. It was not that they consigned these unfortunates to outer darkness; they simply never invited them out of it.' These views were echoed by J. Ellison Platt, a Methodist padre at Colditz, who encountered several Old Etonians: 'They ate together; paced the exercise ground in twos, threes or fours; attended the same lectures; and went to the *Abort* together.'

As well as class, there were other divisive factors at work. Regulars tended to look down on duration-only and Territorial servicemen; senior officers found junior officers difficult and rebellious, while junior officers believed their seniors to be hidebound and lacking in initiative; long-serving prisoners found new arrivals brash. The antipathy that many old hands reserved for new prisoners was summed up by Bertie Harwood:

> They spoke a completely different language and seemed so alive and alert that they got on our nerves. These late arrivals would refer to new weapons quite casually, weapons which the old POW had never heard of. A number of these men were only just going to school when the majority of us were captured, and for some reason we resented this. Perhaps it was because these youngsters, some of them majors, were senior in rank to a lot of regular army officers who were years senior in age.

The individual and factional squabbles that went on among the prisoners were indicative not only of overcrowding and poor physical conditions, but of the POWs' lack of control over their own lives. The everyday responsibilities and worries they had faced as servicemen and, above all, as civilians had largely been removed from them. Sergeant Milt Felsen in Stalag IIB noted how his comrades' pre-war conversations had been of 'debts and mortgages, of lousy, low-paying, dead-end jobs, of misbehaving kids and dull routine. Well, all that had been lifted from their shoulders. They had no more personal responsibilities. Instead, they had the luxury of not having to think for themselves what to do, of being, however badly, fed, housed and clothed. In a way it was a return to childhood.' This view was endorsed by other observers of prison-camp life, including Australian airman Calton Younger, who wrote that 'there were men for whom the barbed wire was a symbol of security . . . You neither looked for your food nor paid for it. You could read, paint, act or play the trombone, sleep for long hours and eat when you felt like it . . . Laws and regulations were not multifarious and complex, but rigid and easy to understand.'

Within the prisoner-of-war world the absence of food was constant. For POWs, hunger was not the vaguely unpleasant sensation of a missed meal and a grumbling stomach. Their hunger was an ache that dominated thought and conversation; over a period of months and years it wore prisoners down psychologically and physically. Even in the better camps, with benevolent commandants and good food stocks, there was only ever just enough to go round; in other camps men experienced chronic malnutrition and in the worst times outright starvation.

Under Article 11 of the 1929 Geneva Convention, the Detaining Power was responsible for the provision of 'sufficient drinking water' and food 'equivalent in quantity and quality to that of depot troops'. Neither Germany or Italy fulfilled those obligations: water provision was variable, and food supplies were inadequate and of poor quality. During times of famine, prisoners were too weak to perform any type of exercise and the sight of men fainting at roll call was not unusual. Climbing a staircase became a slow and painful operation. Diarrhoea and other gastrointestinal problems attendant on poor food and water were also common.

The rations doled out to Pilot Officer Jimmy James at Stalag Luft I at Barth were fairly typical for officers and men in German captivity:

A cup of Ersatz coffee, made from acorns, in the morning, a bowl of soup, usually Sauerkraut, with a few potatoes at midday, and one fifth of a loaf of black bread with a pat of margarine and a small piece of sausage or cheese in the evening, supplied on a room basis and divided up by the room stooge for the day – very accurately as he always had to wait until the others had chosen their portions! These rations amounted to barely 800 calories per day, less than half the optimum required for an adult human being. The pangs of hunger were ever present.

The black rye loaves, adulterated with sawdust, came as an unpleasant shock to men used to white bread. 'The sour taste at first offended the palate,' explained James, 'but there was little else to eat, and it could be improved by toasting when there was fuel.' Potatoes, the other food staple, were nutritious but due to poor storage were sometimes rotten. The midday issue of soup sometimes contained bits of meat, provenance unknown. A form of barley soup was issued to the POWs from time to time: 'It was always lukewarm, chunky and insufficiently cooked,' wrote Vietor. 'Since it had the consistency of glue, we used it as glue to make model aeroplanes. I liked the barley, even with the little white bugs that went with it. By mixing it with corned beef and covering it with sugar, a revolting combination to think about it now, it was quite palatable. Besides, barley bugs were supposed to contain vitamins.'

In Italian camps, macaroni (or rice in the north) replaced potatoes; otherwise food comprised bread and weak vegetable soups, occasionally with bits of meat or fish. There was sometimes access to fruit and vegetables when in season. Bob McDowall described the Italian rations at the transit camp PG 75 at Bari: 'Dinner: cabbage and pea soup very watery, and fish – small helping; same at night with cabbage and fish. Full of wind all the time.' The watery soups that were such a staple of POW food in Italy and Germany were a major cause of flatulence, which for McDowall had unfortunate if somewhat comic consequences.

After eating a quantity of cabbage during the evening meal, McDowall was forced to dash to the latrines but chose a route that had recently been banned. 'Had urgent call of nature,' he wrote, 'and in haste forgot prohibition and ran down side of hut. When near other end a guard challenged me, turned me back. As I turned – an immense quantity of wind came away involuntarily. Guard must have thought act done purposely.' McDowall was correct: the outraged guard unslung his rifle and fired shots after the retreating cleric – who had safely turned the corner. The alarm was raised – 'guards running in all directions, shouting, calling excitedly' – and McDowall was apprehended and roughly dragged off to the cooler. He spent the night in the cells for insulting the honour of the Italian Army, but was released the following day, the prisoners being ordered to prepare to leave for a permanent camp.

The more the POWs were without food the more they thought, dreamed and, above all, talked about it. There was a belief that any conversation, no matter how lofty, would turn in a matter of minutes to the topic of food. 'Nothing could rival food as a subject for talk,' wrote Captain Roger L. Shinn in Oflag 64 at Schubin. 'Sometimes I felt unacculturated since I seemed to be the only man in the barracks who did not plan to become a restaurant operator or a farmer someday.' The long westward march from Oflag 64 in January–February 1945 only increased the food obsession: 'Hour after hour on the march we talked of food. We thought with envy of soup lines in America's Depression. We made imaginary visits to grocery stores and spent imaginary budgets of twenty-five cents or a dollar, always starting with bread.' The culmination of all food conversations was the mythic feast that would be eaten on return to the civilian world: vast multi-course banquets with no expense spared – steak, salmon and lobster the most popular main courses, sometimes to be eaten together.

Fortunately, British and American POWs did not have to rely solely on the Axis – or their own imaginations – for sustenance, having access to food from and via the Red Cross and from their own sources: vegetable gardens, 'pets', and exchanges with guards or civilians.

As the prisoners were the first to acknowledge, starvation was kept at bay through the work of the Red Cross – there are few POW accounts that do not pay it profuse tribute. Humanitarian relief was a vast operation: overall, nearly 20 million parcels were sent from Britain alone. In the early months of the war the few British prisoners in Germany were reasonably well supplied, parcels being shipped from Britain to Germany via Belgium. The blitzkrieg of May 1940 severed this supply route, and the sudden influx of more than 40,000 British prisoners exhausted any remaining reserves. From the summer of 1940 until the spring of 1941, when a new supply route was established via Lisbon–Marseilles/Toulon–Geneva, British POWs slowly starved. The invasion of southern France in 1944 and repeated bombing attacks on the German rail system also disrupted Red Cross food supplies, the prisoners again suffering severe food shortages. And, even during the middle years of the war, local difficulties could prevent the supply of parcels to specific camps. Prisoners were aware that nothing could be taken for granted. In Italy the supply of Red Cross and other parcels tended to be even more irregular, especially to camps in the remoter regions during winter.

For men who had undergone extended periods surviving on Axis rations, the arrival of their first Red Cross parcel produced an ecstatic reaction. 'When the parcels did arrive, it was heaven,' enthused Bob Prouse, and American journalist Edward Beattie wrote, 'I received a whole Red Cross package this morning, and haven't had such a thrill since I found an electric train under the tree one Christmas.'

Not only providing essential nutrition, the parcels – or more accurately cardboard boxes – also included familiar, enjoyable foodstuffs. Each parcel weighed 10–11 lb, and the contents varied slightly from one to another. A British Red Cross parcel might contain tins of biscuits, cheese, chocolate, salmon, jam, butter, meat, bacon, condensed milk, vegetables, cocoa, dried eggs, rolled oats, and packets of dried fruit, tea, sugar and salt. In 1941 the Canadian Red Cross began to send parcels which were distinguished by their tins of powdered milk, appropriately called klim ('milk' spelled backwards); the empty tins were found to be very useful for a variety of purposes. New Zealand also began to pack and send a limited number of parcels, prized for their meat, cheese, milk and honey. A special parcel was developed for Indian troops, which dispensed with meat and included portions of atta, curry powder, dhal and rice. American POWs received British Red Cross parcels until the establishment of a steady flow from the United States towards the end of 1943.

American parcels contained highly valued instant coffee, along with packs of cigarettes, orange-juice concentrates and liver paté. When possible, Christmas parcels were sent to POW camps, featuring seasonal delicacies such as turkey, plum puddings, nuts, fudge and other sweets.

The parcels from different countries were fairly well jumbled, providing POWs with an opportunity to sample different foods. Canadian parcels were generally the most popular, although those from Britain and America had their adherents. The rarity of New Zealand parcels gave them an extra appeal, but for American flyer David Westheimer it was their contents that provided the edge: 'canned creamery butter, outstanding jams, canned bacon and rabbit, thick, sweet coffee essence, a box of dried peas and British army-ration chocolate in flat tins highly prized for cigarette cases.'

The Red Cross had intended that each prisoners should receive one parcel a week, but even in good times this was more usually reduced to one between two. As the war progressed the need for parcels grew. During 1941 the Germans cynically cut the food ration by up to a third, confident that the Red Cross would make up the shortfall. The Italians also instituted a cut in Allied POW rations in 1942, although in this case the reduction was a consequence of genuine food shortages within the Italian economy.

The tin cans that contained the Red Cross produce became a source of dispute between the German authorities and the POWs. The Germans were justifiably concerned that prisoners stockpiled tins for escape attempts, as well as using old tins for tunnelling purposes. In order to prevent hoarding, a common practice was for tins to be punctured on issue. This was extremely irritating for the POWs, who found it difficult to prevent tins of meat from going off in hot weather. A more extreme measure was the refusal by the Germans to let tins enter the camp at all. In some cases this allowed sadistic guards to empty out tins of fish, oatmeal and coffee into the sole container owned by the POW. More usually, however, the puncturing of tin cans was considered sufficient by the commandant.

In addition to Red Cross parcels, quarterly personal (or next-of-kin) parcels were allowed to be sent directly from private individuals to named prisoners. These were seen as an invaluable link between the prisoner and his family and friends. In Britain the parcels were sent to the Prisoner of War Organization, which repacked them, checking their contents for suitability. The only food allowed in British parcels was chocolate (as food was so crucial to a POW, it was considered potentially divisive if some men received more from private sources than others). Cigarettes were ordered and paid for by the relative or friend, and then sent directly from the manufacturer in separate parcels. Over a million next-of-kin parcels were posted from Britain, with chocolate, clothes and soap the most popular items included.

Food was allowed in American personal parcels, which, according to Jack Vietor, 'usually contained powdered eggs, soups, extra chocolate, nuts, cake mixes, and other delicacies'. During the great famine at Stalag Luft I in early 1945, Vietor was delighted to receive a personal parcel: 'I hustled excitedly back to my room to open it up with my room-mates. To my consternation instead of food it was a jigsaw puzzle. Added irony was the fact that the puzzle was a copy of a Breughel painting, showing men eating and drinking heartily in a country tavern. What a blow for a hungry man.'

The Germans and Italians allowed POWs to tend vegetable gardens where there was space. The prisoners either received seeds from the Red Cross or bought them from their captors. To be successful the POW gardeners needed decent soil, and in many camps this was hard to find. In Stalag Luft III Delmar Spivey did his best to encourage his officers to garden, but the sandy soil was not productive and they required large amounts of horse manure – procured ad hoc from the Germans – to achieve any real success. 'In my own garden,' wrote Spivey, 'the general [Brigadier General Arthur W. Vanaman] and the five colonels of my combine carried water by hand in small buckets day after day to water our tomatoes, onions, carrots and spinach.' In PG 29 at Veano, Bob McDowall had some success growing tomatoes, and during September 1942 he was able to harvest three separate crops for the camp kitchen.

Although impressive at first sight, the initiatives of Spivey and McDowall in growing fresh vegetables were too small-scale to influence the overall diet of the camp. Only Oflag 64 came close to providing its prisoners with a regular supply of vegetables. Under the inspired direction of Lieutenant John L. Creech, a horticulturist in civilian life, the POWs were able to take over an old greenhouse in the camp and 2½ acres of land. Creech oversaw the planting of 6,000 tomato plants and several thousand other plants, including beet, lettuces, leeks and onions. But J. Frank Diggs, a fellow prisoner and historian of the camp, was forced to admit that, no matter how good the vegetables were in providing a more balanced diet, men continued to lose weight.

In addition to garden vegetables were the camps' animals. In order to keep down rats and mice, POWs were allowed to keep cats. They made good pets, but in times of famine they could also become food. During the 1945 shortages in Stalag Luft I, Jack Vietor's combine looked after a pregnant cat which gave birth to five kittens – Ike, Winnie, Franklin, Joe and Monty – four of whom were raffled to other huts. The combine kept Joe, renamed Stew in anticipation of his eventual fate. 'Fattening the kittens for eventual consumption would have scandalized cat leagues everywhere,' wrote Vietor, 'but we were hungry, and really hungry men, no matter how humanitarian in usual circumstances, no longer look upon animals as companions but only as possible nourishment.' Unfortunately for Vietor's combine, Stew was kidnapped and consumed by men from another hut. The other cats in the camp also disappeared – a precursor to a massive expansion of the rat population. Using improvised klim-tin traps the rats were kept at bay, but despite their hunger the prisoners of Stalag Luft I could not bring themselves to eat the rodents.

Some camps – both German and Italian – allowed POWs to keep rabbits (for fur and food), and in Stalag 383 at Hohenfels the well-disposed commandant permitted egg-laying chickens as well as rabbits. Sparrows and other small birds were trapped and eaten during famine periods, although the keeping of pigeons – a far better food resource – was banned in case they were used for communication purposes.

The preparation and cooking of food supplied by the captors was carried out by POWs under the supervision of guards in the camp's main cookhouse. Other sources of food were left to the prisoners to do with as they wished. In Oflag 64, for example, meat items were taken out of the Red Cross parcels and sent to the cookhouse, where they were added to the German soup rations; the remainder of the food went to the POWs. In PG 49 all cookable food was removed to the kitchens, although in Stalag Luft III's Center compound Red Cross food was kept and cooked by individual combines.

Though combine members would usually share what food they received – from Red Cross and personal parcels – items like chocolate and cigarettes might be kept by individuals. Each man would be assigned cooking duties on a rota basis – an onerous responsibility. POWs who could cook were highly esteemed. Roger Shinn's combine in Oflag 64 'included one lieutenant who had formerly managed a Howard Johnson restaurant. He quickly became a man of invincible status, an oracle and counselor to all.' Men who failed as cooks were swiftly reassigned to washing-up and cleaning.

The main kitchens were used to boil water, otherwise personal cooking was done on barrack stoves or on improvised heaters. The basic heater, known as a smokey, was manufactured from two large klim tins joined together, with one tin acting as the stove and the other as the boiling receptacle. Fuel comprised twigs, shavings from bed boards and bunks, or small pieces of coal. Slightly more elaborate was the smokeless heater, which achieved its effect through an 'intricate system of air intakes' – although it was also dubbed the heatless smoker. The next level of development came with the blower: a pulley-operated fan-wheel was attached to a smokey, allowing a blast of air to be directed into the bottom of the stove. The blower was a highly efficient means of getting water to boil quickly with a minimum of fuel; according to one source, two pints of water could be boiled in around one minute. POWs took great pride in their inventions, and in PG 52 at Chiavari blower competitions were held to see who could boil water the fastest.

For special occasions – notably Christmas – the prisoners would save food from their parcels for a grand formal dinner: a clean sheet would be thrown over the table and place cards would be written out for the 'guests', who would arrive in their best uniforms. Menus were sometimes elaborately written out in French, the rather basic fare linguistically enhanced for the occasion. These meals briefly shut out the monotony of camp life, providing a sense of plenty and comradeship amid a world that was otherwise generally mean and miserable.

The chronic shortage of food had a tendency to make POWs acutely aware of those they considered greedy. Minor faults became major irritations. In Stalag IVB at Mühlberg, Bob McDowall shared a room with several other padres, one of whom, McDowall believed, was taking more than his share. 'He eats about half of our jam allowance himself,' McDowall complained. 'He has never had to do without anything.' During famine periods, tensions increased. At Stalag Luft III, Robert Kee remembered a time when there had been no Red Cross parcels for some weeks:

> People began to arrive early at meals so that they could size up and take the largest of the scrupulously rationed helpings of potatoes, or the thickest of the apparently identical slices of bread. Though the differences were minute they were capable of calling forth the highest passions: great content if you did well, or jealousy and despair if you did badly. You loathed it when you saw other people behaving like this and yet you could no more control it in yourself than you could any other automatic physical reflex. And it was small compensation to be able to loathe yourself.

Second only to shortages of food came those of clothing. At the point of surrender, few men were adequately equipped for life in a POW camp, and those rescued from the sea or captured in shorts and shirts in North Africa found themselves in a desperate position with the onset of winter. According to the Geneva Convention, the Detaining Power was responsible for providing clothing and footwear for prisoners. Although a well-intentioned ruling, this caused problems for prisoners on both sides – especially those in Axis hands. Both the Germans and the Italians were short of adequate clothing, and were not prepared to divert resources for the benefit of their prisoners. The Germans had cut food rations to force the Allies to supply the shortfall via the Red Cross. They did the same with clothes, footwear and blankets. It would have been better had the Geneva Convention sanctioned and facilitated the clothing of prisoners by their own side.

During 1940–41, British POWs requiring more clothes were obliged to wear cast-offs from other armies who had recently surrendered to the Germans. This produced some bizarre outfits. One of the more outlandish belonged to Joseph Pryce, a survivor of HMS *Gloucester*, sunk off Crete in May 1941. Arriving virtually naked at his main camp, Stalag XVIIIA at Wolfsberg, he was given a nightshirt and brown knee breeches, a blue French Army coat, a red Yugoslav forage cap with yellow tassel, British Army socks, and a pair of wooden clogs.

A supply of British greatcoats had been held in reserve by the Red Cross in Geneva from the outset of the war, but this was insufficient to meet prisoner needs, especially after Dunkirk. The British government attempted to get the Axis powers to accept their responsibilities, but faced by the prospect of British POWs living in rags it reluctantly accepted the cost of sending clothing and related articles (including toothbrushes, toothpaste and shaving gear). Friends and relations were also encouraged to send clothes in next-of-kin parcels.

The conflict over who was to assume responsibility for clothing continued throughout the war, made worse by the Germans' refusal to provide protective clothing for working POWs and their removal of German-issue blankets if prisoners had been given additional blankets by the Red Cross. Leaders in British work camps had asked for second sets of battledress, so that working POWs could have separate work and walking-out uniforms. This caused the War Office 'alarm', but the request was eventually granted; new uniforms raised prisoner morale, as well as having a negative effect on the German population who saw smartly turned-out men from a nation apparently on the verge of defeat. In a letter home, a British sergeant described their appearance: 'We have all had the Red Cross and St John complete woollen underwear, battle suits, boots, pullovers, socks, and shirts. The lads look smart. Sundays, we all go for a walk with a guard, and the smartness of the blokes really opens people's eyes.'

Until the end of 1943 American prisoners had to rely on the British for much of their clothing requirements, so that, for example, Delmar Spivey took command of Center compound in September 1943 wearing a British battledress tunic. Initially the Germans had refused to allow American POWs to wear US uniforms at all, believing them to be too civilian in appearance, but in early 1943 the ban had been lifted. Spivey successfully fought the Germans to ensure his men had a change of clothing, an overcoat and sufficient blankets. 'By the summer of that year [1944],' he reported, 'everyone had a change of everything. The camp fairly shone at Saturday inspections!'

After shelter, food and clothing, prisoners wanted cigarettes. The vast majority of servicemen smoked during this period, and supplying them with nicotine was seen as necessary in all armed forces. But, until prisoners reached an established camp, the chain of supply was broken. Captors might provide the odd cigarette, but for the most part men did without or smoked substitutes. Such was the demand for something to smoke that almost anything combustible was used. Held in the miserable transit camp at Salonica, Joseph Pryce observed that 'dried mint leaves, shredded and wrapped in strips of newspaper, was an innovation from which a great number of men derived a certain amount of enjoyment.' Other tobacco substitutes included grass, leaves of all kinds, coffee grounds, even manure.

While in Salonica, Pryce – a sixty-a-day man – decided to give up smoking. 'I realized that my decision to cut out smoking altogether was going to prove a very unpleasant ordeal', he wrote. 'It was more than just that. It was sheer hell. Even after six months of abstinence I still cast envious glances in the direction of anyone contentedly puffing away at a cigarette or joyfully sucking away at a pipe.' Long-term health benefits apart, Pryce's decision was a wise one. Such were the cravings for nicotine that smokers found themselves in demeaning situations – following guards around to snatch up discarded butts, or volunteering to clean out their ashtrays. Worse still, in times of shortage the most desperate smokers traded vital food for cigarettes, even though suffering from malnutrition.

Fortunately for POW smokers, the British and American governments sent vast quantities of tobacco and cigarettes to Germany and Italy. While the Americans included cigarettes in their Red Cross parcels, the British discontinued this practice in August 1940 and paid for shipments by tobacco companies to Geneva for distribution by the Red Cross. From the beginning of 1941 to March 1945, the Prisoner of War Organization sent over 6 million ounces of tobacco and nearly 1.5 billion cigarettes to camps in Germany and Italy. The aim was to provide a regular supply of cigarettes to each prisoner, but the tendency was for 'feast or famine' – a situation far from ideal for the committed smoker. In larger camps, leaders built up reserve stocks to cover lean periods and for trading purposes. These reserves could be substantial: when Center compound was evacuated at the end of January 1945 Delmar Spivey and his executive officers had built up a store of approximately 3 million cigarettes. Prisoners also received individual parcels of cigarettes, via tobacco companies, from family, friends, military units or former workplaces.

Cigarettes – along with chocolate, coffee and soap – were much more than simple consumer items. They were invaluable tools for bribing guards and civilian overseers to perform favours, overlook minor infractions of camp discipline, or supply contraband articles. They were also the basis for all trade, both within and outside the camp. When prisoners were well supplied with these scarce luxury items, they had a degree of economic power over their captors that made life much easier.

The Germans issued a form of camp money called *Lagergeld* for buying articles from the camp canteen, but apart from (irregular) supplies of toothpaste and razor blades the canteens had little of value for prisoners. As a consequence, cigarettes became the POW's currency of choice, and the prices of saleable objects would be quoted in cigarettes. The economist R. A. Radford was imprisoned in Italy and Germany, and as a way of passing the time he made a study of the economic organization within his POW camps. Cigarettes, he observed, bore more than a passing resemblance to conventional currency. 'They were homogeneous,' he wrote, 'reasonably durable and of convenient size for the smallest or, in packets, for the largest transactions.' Radford also noted a resemblance to money of an earlier age: 'They could be clipped or sweated by rolling them between the fingers so that tobacco fell out.'

But, unlike coins and notes, cigarettes were commodities in their own right, and during periods of shortage they would literally disappear in a puff of smoke. Their consequent scarcity would lead prices of other goods to fall, and in really lean times cigarettes would be withdrawn from the system, trade being then reduced to simple barter. Conversely in times of plenty – following the arrival of a large Red Cross shipment – prices would rise and a new surge of economic activity would begin.

The POW economy played its part in determining the structure of camp society, with groups or individuals performing particular functions. These might involve a marketable skill – such as tailoring, barbering or the drawing of portraits – although the most popular service was washing laundry. In Stalag IIB, POWs bribed the Germans in the camp kitchen to provide hot water, and with soap from Red Cross parcels they touted for business with handwritten price lists. Radford observed the development of more advanced services involving a degree of entrepreneurial risk: 'There was a coffee-stall owner who sold tea, coffee or cocoa at two cigarettes a cup, buying his raw materials at market prices and hiring labour to gather fuel and to stoke; he actually enjoyed the services of a chartered accountant at one stage. After a great period of prosperity he overreached himself and failed disastrously for several hundred cigarettes.'

The real entrepreneurs were the traders. For a few, trading became an obsession – trading for trading's sake. For others it was logical means to maximize their resources. Almost all POWs were involved in some sort of trading activity, even if there was little enthusiasm for the idea of making a quick buck. 'Partly because there was nothing else to do,' wrote Roger Shinn in Stalag XIIA at Limburg, 'bargaining went on all day. I bought a mirror with cigarettes.' Successful trading was often based on a shrewd appreciation of future need. In the spring of 1944, Jack Vietor spent sixty cigarettes on 'a pair of gloves from an optimistic American who was convinced that the war would be over by the summer of 1944. The gloves were a godsend during the raw winter of 1945.'

In officers' and non-working other ranks' camps, there was a fairly distinct separation between trade with fellow prisoners and trade with guards, the latter being subject to strict regulation. The more far-sighted British and American camp leaders realized that unregulated trade with the Germans would work against the POWs. Although the Germans were strictly forbidden to trade with the prisoners, as the war progressed increasing numbers were prepared to swap foodstuffs such as eggs and bread for Red Cross luxury goods, especially the trinity of cigarettes, chocolate and decent soap. The Allied camp administration tried to limit this trading to a few experienced German-speaking dealers who would be able to maximize the POWs' bargaining power. Such illicit bargaining – along with bribery – was an important part of an overall plan of corrupting the guards to make them more amenable to POW demands, with the threat of blackmail ever present in the background.

The conflict between individual rights and the greater good of the community was one of the unresolvable battles fought in most areas of camp life. In the economic sphere it centred on trade and its regulation. The camp leaders and staff – supported by a large if variable group of prisoners – favoured an orderly approach, with prices being fixed and profits limited. Not surprisingly, traders spurned regulation, arguing that prices should be set by the market to allow enterprise its just reward.

Markets tended to operate more freely in the Stalags than elsewhere. Large camps, such as those at Lamsdorf (Stalag VIIIB/344) and Hohenfels (Stalag 383) had well-established markets in which men set out stalls to buy and sell products. By the standards of the outside world what was on offer was limited, but in the POW world it was sufficient to draw men to trade. Vernon Cooper, in Stalag 383, explained their appeal: 'You never knew what you might find offered for sale on these stalls. You might find a pair of gym shoes or a balaclava, a book, or a pair of socks, or a wrist watch or a leather belt, or a tin of sardines or bully beef.' The more important sales, however, were made covertly with the German guards after dark. Staff Sergeant Raymond Ryan observed this trade in the same camp: 'The stall owners go round the fence at night and contact each guard in case he has something to exchange. At one part there were 12 of our chaps waiting to speak to him. The guards in the watchtowers co-operate by not shining searchlights along the fence until business is finished.'

Professional traders tended not to discuss their operations with outsiders. Despite his best efforts, Radford knew 'little of the workings of these people . . . [who] were largely of a retiring disposition'. Jim Witte was hardly of a retiring disposition, but he was an astute trader who worked tirelessly to improve his lot. As with all successful entrepreneurs, his first allegiance was to himself, but his activities also helped those around him. As a private soldier from a modest background he had no special privileges, apart from a loving mother and a generous former employer who between them provided him with the working capital to set himself up in business.

His mother sent regular clothing parcels. These were dispatched via Red Cross packing centres in Britain, and if the clothes were under the maximum 11-lb weight the Red Cross made up the shortfall in chocolate. On one occasion Witte was delighted to find a massive 8-lb slab of chocolate wrapped in a shirt. This was a marvellous treasure at a time when chocolate had all but disappeared from Continental Europe. But cigarettes were Witte's favoured trading resource. Before his call up Witte had worked for the newly formed Anglo-Dutch conglomerate Unilever (his father had been born in the

Netherlands). The company prided itself on its progressive employment practices, and a Miss Edwards sent cigarette parcels containing
the highly popular Churchman's No. 1 to Witte in Italy and
Germany. This regular supplement to Red Cross supplies helped him
to exploit the famine periods that were so painful for the ordinary
smoker.

From the chance discovery of a carton of 200 cigarettes just after
his capture in North Africa, Jim Witte had decided to use his trading
skills to minimize the discomforts of POW life. At his prison camp in
Italy he paid others a few cigarettes a time to perform various manual
tasks allotted him. Although his transfer to Germany entailed labouring in a locomotive repair workshop, the work camps opened new
doors for entrepreneurial activity:

> I built up a system of contacts and having a flair for languages soon
> learned colloquial German. I was fortunate in being well supplied from
> home with cigarette parcels. In short I became a tobacco baron and
> leader of the black market. I bought off the local Gestapo agent, Herr
> Schuster, whose allegiance to Hitler swiftly changed when confronted
> by a Churchman's No. 1, England's premier fag. They got me a good
> job replacing broken cab windows. My HQ was my bed space; beneath
> by bed was my *Kisten* (suitcase) filled with comestibles, Schnapps
> (a vicious 100 per cent firewater) and English cigarettes. My hoard had
> to be guarded, a job I gave to Taffy, an elderly South Wales Borderer
> who kept our lager [compound] clean. His salary was twenty
> Churchmans. The *Feldwebel* [staff sergeant] in charge received twenty
> cigarettes because it was important to keep him sweet. Others who
> helped me out got the odd English cigarette now and again.

There was always a degree of ambivalence among the wider camp
population towards the professional trader. Although he acted as
conduit for the flow of scarce supplies – from which many benefited –
there was also a general feeling that he was doing well out of others'
misfortune. And in times of shortage those who seemed to place
themselves outside or above the community became a focus for hostility. This was especially true when it was thought that traders had
secured some form of monopoly, which in a POW camp was considered fundamentally unfair. Radford noted one such example, where
a POW used his knowledge of Urdu to secure meat from vegetarian

Sikh prisoners in the Indian compound in exchange for butter and jam, selling the meat on for a tidy profit.

Bob McDowall discouraged trade in food, believing it made the weak vulnerable to the unscrupulous. Observing a bartering session in Stalag IVB at Mühlberg, McDowall wrote, 'The prices asked were very high. I very much dislike it anyway – it seems fearful to squeeze articles from men on the basis of hunger.' Roger Shinn agreed: 'It was immoral to buy food from a fellow American with cigarettes. That would be exploiting his weakness and hurting him.' Although Shinn and other more morally upright POWs may have refrained from such activity, trading in food – whether for cigarettes or barter – was a constant of camp life. And in times of famine – when the camp's medical officer might try to prevent the selling of food for the good of prisoners' health – there were always men who would be prepared to trade anything for a smoke.

With trade came fraud. McDowall recorded several instances of sharp practice that to him showed how food-trading undermined the POW community. At PG 57 he recorded how prisoners took the wrappers off less popular tins and replaced them with those from tins that sold well. At Mühlberg fraudulent practices were even more common: 'The Germans now puncture all tins. Some men shake out the milk powder through the hole, put [in] sand or dirt, then milk powder on the top third and sell! Others melt the butter, pour it out, fill the tins five-sixths full of wax, which can be bought cheaply, the last 6th with butter and sell as butter!'

Most prisoners favoured some form of regulated trade for both moral and practical reasons, and in the smaller and more homogeneous officer camps this normally occurred. Radford described its development in his Italian camp:

> In the permanent camp people started by wandering through the bungalows [huts] calling their offers – 'cheese for seven' (cigarettes) – and the hours after parcel issue were Bedlam. The inconveniences of this system soon led to its replacement by an Exchange and Mart notice board in every bungalow, where under the heading 'name', 'room number', 'wanted', and 'offered' sales and wants were advertised. When a deal went through it was crossed off the board. The public and semi-permanent records of transactions led to cigarette prices being well known and thus tending to equality throughout the camp.

Wounded Canadian soldiers surrender to the Germans following the landings at Dieppe, 19 August 1942

Delmar T. Spivey, the vigorous and thoughtful senior American officer of Center compound, Stalag Luft III

Jim Witte in PG 78 at Sulmona: 'I was determined to make things as easy as I could for myself.'

The Revd Bob McDowall in New Zealand, 1940. Captivity would transform a buttoned-up Presbyterian cleric into an inspirational padre

The urbane and unflappable American aviator Jack Vietor – a sketch by a POW in Stalag Luft I

Above: Bob Prouse shortly after joining up in Canada. Determined to 'do his bit' he was captured at Dieppe

Above right: Jimmy James, a survivor of the Great Escape; he also tunnelled out of Sachsenhausen concentration camp

Right: Doug LeFevre on the run in northern Italy. Helped by Italian peasants, he eventually made his way to Switzerland

Left: Oflag IXA/H at Spangenberg – a 'castle' POW camp surrounded by a deep, dry moat that made escape especially difficult

Below: A miserable-looking German guard surveys a snow-bound Stalag Luft III

Above: The entrance to Stalag IVB at Mühlberg, one of the larger Allied POW camps

Right: An RAF POW in Stalag VIIIB at Lamsdorf, a victim of the German shackling order

Wash day at a British POW work camp somewhere in Germany

Latrine contents are pumped into a 'honey wagon', Stalag VIIIB at Lamsdorf

American air-force officers in their barracks at Stalag Luft I

Two Indian POWs of a German work detachment

Kitted out with a German uniform, a Sikh lieutenant of the Free Indian Legion

In some German camps Exchange and Marts developed into a more advanced system called Foodacco. Pioneered by two enterprising officers in Oflag VIB at Warburg, it comprised a 'shop' where goods for sale by a prisoner were given an agreed price (in cigarettes, or in points based on cigarettes); when the goods were sold, the shopkeepers kept a small percentage of the sale price. Foodacco proved highly successful, and spread through the camp system. In Stalag Luft III's North compound the venture was 'nationalized' by Wings Day, with profits being channelled into a communal fund (which included cigarettes set aside for the bribery of German guards). This 'mixed-economy' approach to buying and selling was also adopted in Center compound, with most items accepted for sale. Clothing was an exception, however: the battle to get two sets of clothing for each man had been too hard fought to allow it to be jeopardized by indiscriminate trading.

While the Red Cross provided the essentials for life, it drew the line at supplying alcohol. Excessive alcoholic consumption was discouraged by both the Axis and Allied camp administrations, but there was a certain degree of tolerance of light use and on special occasions. The Italians allowed officers a small daily ration of wine and vermouth, as well as sporadically providing beer for other ranks. Italian guards could sometimes be persuaded to supply drink for celebrations. During the early part of the war the Germans sold weak beer and, very occasionally, wine. This was greatly appreciated by the POWs, and the alcohol was often stored up for a major 'bash' as a way of blotting out the tedium of imprisonment.

Not all POWs had access to legally supplied alcohol, and for those that did supplies were limited. Prisoners had therefore to look to other methods – bribing guards or home production. The supply from guards was also limited, especially where trade was regulated for communal purposes. Consequently the making of hooch was carried out in most camps, developing into a cottage industry in some.

The first stage of home-brewing was fermentation. The dried fruit in Red Cross parcels – raisins or prunes – was placed with sugar into a container and covered with water. The container was sealed and left in a warm place if possible. Yeast – bought from the guards, or stolen – might be used to speed up the process, but natural fermentation was normally sufficient to produce some sort of alcoholic beverage. To provide a drink with more kick, the next stage was distillation, which required the construction of an improvised condenser made from pieces of tubing – for those with access to musical instruments the slide from a trombone was found to be highly effective.

The brewers in some camps had chemical knowledge or practical experience from working in the drinks industry, and were able to produce 'effective' hooch from the outset. Others, however, had to start from scratch. The apprentices at Milag initially produced raisin wine – 'very cloudy and yellowish' – and prune beer – 'dark brown in colour, and one drank it with bits of prunes in one's mug'. For the Christmas of 1942 a still had been built in the camp to produce the more powerful 'alki', so that by the end of the following year 'wine had gone out of fashion and alki was the drink of the day.' In virtually all camps hooch was made to celebrate Christmas and the New Year, although in a few camps brewing and drinking went on throughout the year. One merchant seaman described the parties that were a feature of the captive sailors' weekends at Milag:

> Everybody sat around and in one corner was a large barrel and a fellow dishing out the wine in mugfulls. In another corner would be the band bellowing away on its instruments. Between drinking mugfulls of wine, the alki bottle was brought around and a tot was given at frequent intervals. [At] the beginning of the party all hands were yarning and drinking quietly, but in the end all hands were drunk, including the band, and everybody was dancing or fighting, which depended on the way the party ended.

The most intense celebrations took on a mythical quality, to be remembered years afterwards. The North compound of Stalag Luft III was the scene of some memorable events, not least the 1943 Fourth of July celebration. The compound at that time contained both British and US POWs, and, unknown to the British, the Americans began a raucous dawn march through the camp, fortified by copious amounts of alcohol. To the surprise of the Germans, the British joined in with equal enthusiasm, and the day ended with senior officers – including Wings Day and Colonel Charles Goodrich – being slung into the small firefighting reservoir.

Christmas was the usual focus for alcoholic and gastronomic festivity, although POWs also found this time a painful reminder of family and home far away. Although a welcome relief in the short term, copious amounts of alcohol tended to make things worse. There were also practical difficulties in consuming hooch: it was a vile concoction, and on stomachs not used to alcohol the results were predictable. Jack Vietor's account of the 1944 Christmas drinking celebrations at Stalag Luft I was far from atypical: 'Three drinks and you felt a mild, pleasant glow. Four drinks and you were spraying your Spam, barley and lumpy potatoes all over the barracks floor. It was difficult to get drunk on "Kriegie brew". As soon as you began to feel a pleasant glow, the next drink would cause the suffering stomach to revolt.'

Even the best hooch was tough: there were innumerable tales of it taking the enamel off mugs or eating holes in galvanized buckets. The worst sorts of hooch could be positively dangerous. Desperate drinkers would do anything for intoxication, including heating up tins of shoe polish and skimming off the spirit that had risen to the surface. Increasingly concerned at the drinking practices of some of the men at Milag, the camp medical officer, Major R. C. L. Harvey, issued a warning:

> In the past few weeks the following cases have been admitted to hospital: 1 case of paralysis of the right arm and leg. This man will never walk again. 7 cases of D.T.s. 2 cases of cut throat, both of whom narrowly escaped death. 1 case of insanity. Meanwhile 2 cases of permanent blindness have been reported from another camp. All these and many less severe cases are directly due to the drinking of hooch. It is undoubtedly undermining the health of many men in the camp. All those who brew hooch and especially those who sell it are morally responsible for these catastrophes.

Harvey attempted to stamp out its production, but the camp was resistant to an outright ban. 'In a meeting of hut captains,' wrote one seaman, 'it was decided not to stop brewing for party purposes, but only to stop the selling of it to regular boozers.' Harvey did not push his case further, and instead suggested the introduction of safer distilling practices to make alki less dangerous.

Bob McDowall was not completely opposed to drink, but abhorred the traditional way in which British and Commonwealth men consumed alcohol: drinking to get drunk. While in Italy he experienced something of a revelation, transforming his formerly strict teetotalism. For the first time he came across 'Continental' attitudes towards the drinking of alcohol, as exemplified by some Serb POWs also held in the camp. During the 1942 Christmas festivities he was invited to attend a Serb party: 'These chaps can have an afternoon and evening with wine [for] seven hours, never dull, never wild, at times hilarious, always pleasant, entertaining, and never coarse. What a lot we English have to learn!' McDowall was even persuaded to have a glass of wine. This more relaxed attitude towards alcohol continued in Germany, so that he might sometimes enjoy a drink of beer while on a parole walk.

Delmar Spivey shared McDowall's attitude towards alcohol: moderate drinking was acceptable, but unregulated hooch consumption – with its attendant health and order problems – was not. Once in command of Center compound he was determined to end 'Kriegie brews'. 'The determination was realized,' he wrote; 'only sporadic brewing took place, always without my knowledge and always well hidden from the Germans. When the boys made a brew and I found out about it, I had a cup of it with them and asked them not to make any more.'

Spivey's aversion to heavy drinking would have not have been helped by the party held by the British in North compound in honour of the Americans and their forthcoming departure to other compounds. A bar had been set up, complete with a few officers dressed as barmaids. Things started well enough, Spivey recorded: 'There was much conviviality and some close harmony [singing], a few bawdy songs by Wings Day and others, and farewell speeches by hosts and others.' After a couple of drinks Spivey felt a little queasy and sat outside – but under a window, to continue hearing the singing. 'This was a mistake,' he wrote, 'because I had no more gotten comfortably seated when one of the boys on the inside became violently ill and regurgitated the brews and cookies all over my rather bald head.'

While his temper at the time cannot have been of the best, it says a lot for Spivey that he was able to tell the story against himself. But it was the event as a whole that caused him most disquiet:

> My reaction to the party was, for the most part, one of revulsion. Some of the older POWs became maudlin, wept, and then disappeared to sleep off the effects of drunkenness. Others wanted to fight. There was

also much horseplay around the barmaids, which did not sit too well
at the time. My overall impression of the drunkenness was that it was
a reaction to many frustrations and that the alcohol acted to release
pent-up feeling the men had been carefully concealing.

If drinking was a contentious issue, then so was sex. Only men in
working camps had any possibility of heterosexual relations; for officers
and non-working NCOs the choice lay between abstinence and
homosexuality. But a by-product of POWs' chronic hunger was a
marked diminution in sexual appetite. American POW George
J. Davis was one of many POWs who described this change, albeit with
a degree of comic exaggeration: 'The sex organ will become quite
kaputt. Erotic thoughts, erections and wet dreams will become events
of the past. Ten naked beauties could saunter into a room full of
Kriegies, and if they arrive without snacks they would go unnoticed.'

The fear of homosexuality was a part of life in a POW camp. For
some men who had been incarcerated for long periods there was a
nagging anxiety that they might become homosexual. Bob Prouse,
imprisoned in an all-male work camp attached to Stalag IXC at Bad
Sulza, explained this worry: 'A few soldiers wouldn't wait for freedom
and indulged in homosexuality. Fortunately, they were a very small
minority but disturbing all the same when you realized that some were
otherwise tough soldiers. It made you wonder if you, too, could be
affected someday if the war went on endlessly.'

Homosexuality was then a criminal offence, and considered an aber-
ration by most people. Consequently it was a matter of concern for
camp leaders and those responsible for POWs' physical and moral
welfare. Spivey was worried that 'homosexual tendencies would appear
from time to time', and even requested his block commanders to 'keep
a special lookout'. He was greatly relieved that they found no instances
of homosexuality in Center compound, and proudly concluded, 'It is
to the everlasting credit of the American officers that they were men at
all times while POWs and acted in a rational manner concerning
matters of sex.' The Revd J. Ellison Platt worked himself up into lather
over what he suspected were unseemly goings on in Colditz. 'Homosexualism', he reported, 'has occupied an increasingly large place in
contemporary prison humour.' He also added, 'Jocular references to
masturbation, too, are freer than is usual among healthy minded adults.'

The actual prevalence of homosexuality within the camp system is hard to discern. In officer and other non-working camps homosexual activity seems to have been minimal, and a number of chroniclers confidently asserted that there were no instances of homosexuality in their camp (although as heterosexuals they may have been unaware of what was usually a very covert activity). According to Eric Newby, in PG 49 at Fontanellato overcrowding and a general lack of privacy ensured that 'whatever loves there were between prisoners could only be expressed by looks and words or perhaps a surreptitious pressure of the hand'. It was in PG 49 that the only POW work to consider homosexuality from a homosexual viewpoint was written, although its two authors felt unable to be explicit about 'the love that dare not speak its name' and instead described an intense friendship between its two main protagonists.

In the larger other ranks' camps there were instances of quite overt homosexual behaviour. Many prisoners seem not to have been particularly concerned, and if some were censorious others were tolerant. Ballroom dancing and theatrical activities became a focus for homosexual interest. Private Geoffrey Ellwood, a Canadian soldier in Stalag VIIIB at Lamsdorf, described homosexual behaviour on the dance floor:

> This is where you'd see the odd queer show up. I mean, it was one thing for guys to dance together because there's nobody else to dance with. But when they start dancing together and likin' it, and start snugglin' up, it became very, very obvious, you know. This went on, but nobody seemed to take it as serious. They'd look at it, and discuss it among themselves, and that was it. It was accepted that some people are that way.

The general level of toleration expressed towards homosexuality in Lamsdorf was echoed by South African Ike Rosmarin: 'Practitioners could be recognized because they tried to dress alike, wearing the same hairstyle and walking hand-in-hand through the camp.'

In Jim Witte's recollection, 'homosexuality was rife' in PG 78 at Sulmona, though once again sexual interest was determined by the quantity of food available to the prisoners. 'In winter,' he wrote, 'when Italian rations were poor and the issue of Red Cross parcels irregular, love took a back seat. But when summer arrived Cupid came into his own again.' In Sulmona, prisoners playing female roles in the theatre became objects of lust:

> Dutiful swains used to wait outside the theatre for the girls to appear after the show. They couldn't take them to dinner so they took them, instead, to quiet places in the compound. The trouble was, though, that there was very little privacy for love affairs of this nature. The boy friends used to get very jealous if you so much glanced at their girl friends. There was a corporal in the Military Police who was violently in love with one of the actresses called Jerry. Both were missing during a roll call and were found snuggled down under a blanket in a corner of another compound. This amused the Italians, who put them in solitary together for a week. They weren't so keen on one another after that.

Overcrowding and lack of privacy made even masturbation a tricky business. 'To perform the operation while lying cheek by jowl with twenty-six other people in a room illuminated by search-lights,' wrote Eric Newby, 'required a degree of stealth which had deserted most of us since leaving school. Nevertheless, some of the more vigorous among us revived these ancient skills.' In Sulmona there were those with less inhibition, but, wrote Witte, 'they earned the contempt of their fellows in their huts which manifested itself in descriptive epithets like "bishop bashers", "mutton floggers" and "wire-pullers".'

POWs were occasionally subject to female sexual provocation from the other side of the wire. At its simplest were the evening promenades by girls from the town of Fontanellato, enjoying their effect on the men staring down from the windows of PG 49. Stalag Luft III contained the Luftwaffe's POW mail-censoring service, and some of the 200 or so female censoring staff would deliberately walk past the perimeter wire, and on one occasion a women ostentatiously sun-bathed to a large Center-compound audience of gawping prisoners. Canadian airman Kingsley Brown recalled a female secretary who worked in the camp's *Vorlager* and who, from an office window, 'staged an elaborate and provocative tableau' for the watching airman. He concluded, 'Vorlager Fanny is a fond and happy memory.'

In Stalag IIB the provocation turned into taunting. Milt Felsen remembered how German soldiers from a nearby depot 'would bring women close to the outer ring of barbed wire and fornicate, all the while laughing gleefully'. According to Felsen, the American reaction was at best muted, with many having sympathy for the women lying on the hard cobblestones. A slightly different twist occurred at Oflag VIIB at Eichstätt, where, according to Harwood, the wife of one of the guards would 'come to a window and make as if to display her ample Bavarian bosom. If a tin of Red Cross cocoa was held up to her (at a distance of not less than fifty yards) she would bare one breast for a fleeting moment. A tin of bully-beef brought her garments down to her waistline. Her rewards were delivered to her through a tame guard in the camp, whom I rather suspect was her husband.'

POWs working among the civilian population had the opportunity to engage in full romantic and sexual relations with women, although such unions were not without danger. OKW issued several directives prohibiting POWs from having sexual relations with German women on pain of long prison sentences or, in certain cases, death (although it seems that no Anglo-American prisoners were ever executed for this offence). German women also faced severe punishment for any such liaison. Some POWs must have taken this prohibition seriously, but sexual relations between German women and Allied prisoners of all nationalities did take place. Considerable numbers of women from Austria – then part of the German Reich – seemed to be susceptible to the charms of British and Commonwealth POWs. The absence of young men throughout civilian life in German-occupied Europe provided many opportunities for smartly turned-out POWs equipped with soap, chocolate and cigarettes. And in Germany there were millions of female foreign workers displaced from their homelands, many of whom would have had no ideological objections to a relationship with an Allied prisoner.

Following his transfer from Italy to Germany, Jim Witte was sent to labour in locomotive repair works, first at Chemnitz and then near Leipzig, where he worked alongside men and women from all over Europe. 'To POWs who had spent two-and-a-half years without sight of a woman it was most refreshing,' he wrote. 'Our favourite in the works was a Dolly who operated the overhead gantry crane.' Although German, Dolly was sufficiently enamoured of Witte to invite him up to her cab for sex. For once Witte was overcome by the occasion and, to his chagrin, was unable to perform. This proved to be just a temporary setback, however, and he later began an affair with a buxom

Belgian worker called Adrienne, which ended only when an unsympathetic guard spotted them together outside their compound. This breach of camp rules led to a month's transfer to a punishment camp. Following his return, Adrienne and the Belgian contingent were transferred elsewhere. 'I was not particularly worried,' recalled Witte, 'as I had a nice little thing going with Vera, a comely well-stacked Russian girl who ably administered to my needs!'

Jim Witte was always prepared to make the most of his POW experience, and even in the unlikely circumstances of a rough, noisy factory in the heart of Germany he forged a life that was, if nothing else, materially tolerable, as he himself wrote: 'I was twenty-five, virile, well nourished with good food courtesy of the Red Cross, with white bread (unobtainable for ordinary Germans), washed down with 100 per cent proof Schnapps.'

6

Leadership and Discipline

POW CAMPS WERE communities – despite their unnatural form and nature – and if they were to prosper they required leadership and discipline. The generally upbeat narratives of POW life have tended to obscure the fact that not all prisoners had reliably sunny temperaments and permanently resolute characters. Even the strongest went through periods of depression and doubt. POWs needed a comradely yet disciplined structure to their lives. At a basic level this was drawn from the combine, and extended through the barrack block to the community of the camp as a whole. And, while it curbed the interests of the individual, a strongly communitarian society protected the vulnerable.

A disciplined POW community was also able to put up a united front against its captors. This not only was a way to restore pride and dignity – which had inevitably taken a battering on capture – but acted as a means to improve conditions within the camp. While the captors wanted their prisoners to be docile and manageable – to accept their lot without complaint – at the same time they admired military discipline, and those men exhibiting this quality secured better treatment than the apathetic and broken.

For the smooth running of the camp, the Axis authorities worked with and issued orders through the camp leaders. The system benefited both sides: the POWs were able to organize their own affairs with minimal outside interference, and the captors saved on manpower. Anglo-American POW camps were for the most part run by the prisoners themselves, and apart from at roll calls (two or three times a day) the ordinary POW seldom had direct dealings with Germans or Italians.

Leadership was not an easy business, however. The tight bonds of discipline that existed in an army – between men of all ranks – were loosened after capture. A few POWs were openly resentful of their superiors, believing that military authority had been discredited in the actions leading up to surrender. Allied leaders were certainly aware that they did not have the traditional support of military regulations and sanctions to impose authority. And it was fairly obvious that ultimate power lay not with the British or American leadership but in the hands of the Axis.

The camp leader's prime duty was to act as an intermediary between prisoners and jailer, gaining the confidence of both sides. Each required rather different strategies. To his men, a good leader was someone who divided and allocated scarce resources fairly, regulated disputes, and advanced their interests to the captors. Towards the commandant and his staff he had to play a confident hand with indifferent cards. Outright defiance would get him nowhere – except perhaps a spell in solitary confinement – but he required the moral authority to stand up to the Axis authorities and demand what was lawfully the prisoners' by virtue of the Geneva Convention. Those men who succeeded best with the Germans and Italians employed a combination of charm and guile with military professionalism.

Styles of leadership and discipline were never constant, reflecting the temperaments of individual leaders as well as more structural differences, especially those between officers and other ranks. The recognized practice in officers' prison camps was for the highest-ranking officer to assume command, as either the SBO (senior British officer) or the SAO (senior American officer). For other ranks the situation was more complex. In some camps the highest-ranking NCO might take command, but in others the leader was chosen by the men themselves, either informally or through election from several candidates by secret ballot. In Germany the NCO camp leader was often known as the Man of Confidence or *Vertrauensman* (a literal translation of the French *homme de confiance* used in the definitive text of the 1929 Geneva Convention), although in some camps there were two separate positions: the camp leader was supported by a German-speaking Man of Confidence who liaised directly with the Germans.

The Germans occasionally made attempts to influence the choices of camp leader. They had greater power in the Stalags, rejecting men they felt inappropriate for the job. At a punishment camp at Matalal in Austria the commandant got rid of the existing camp leader, a sergeant in the Black Watch, for incompetence and possible corruption, and simply replaced him with the prisoner with the longest years of service as a POW. In Stalag IIB at Hammerstein the Germans refused to have dealings with camp leader Private Harry Galler when they discovered he was a Jew, and forced the American prisoners to find another leader.

One pressing dilemma faced by all leaders was escape, and its consequences for the camp. A good leader promoted stability and harmony and discouraged disruptive actions. At the same time he was supposed to encourage his men to escape – but escapes were also the most disruptive activity that could take place in a POW camp. After a successful getaway the guards ransacked huts; privileges were withdrawn from the remaining prisoners and, despite being contrary to the Geneva Convention, some form of collective punishment was often enacted. And relations between the Axis authorities and the camp leadership would often be strained for some time afterwards. The problem remained unresolvable.

An interesting comparison between attitudes towards escape – and leadership – can be found in the POW careers of two prominent leaders who spent much of their time in Stalag Luft III at Sagan: Wing Commander 'Wings' Day, effectively SBO in East and then North compound, and Colonel Delmar T. Spivey, SAO of Center compound. Both were first-rate leaders, admired by the men under their command. Kingsley Brown, a Canadian airman in North compound, described Day's qualities: 'He was a man of the most magical and irresistible kind of charm, which was the strongest facet of his capacity for leadership.' Eugene L. Daniel, the American Presbyterian chaplain to Stalag Luft III, considered Spivey 'a superb natural leader whose courage, talent, and humanitarian character contributed greatly to our well-being and safety'.

The two men met briefly in 1943, when Day showed Spivey around North compound as part of the American's introduction to POW life. Spivey considered Day 'one of the finest Englishmen I have ever met. Wings was blessed with a totally charming personality.' Charm was indeed an integral part of Day's character, but beneath the charm was a steely determination to carry on fighting the Germans by any means possible. Throughout his POW 'commands' – Dulag Luft, Stalag Luft I, Oflag XXIB, Stalag Luft III and Sachsenhausen concentration camp – he was either engaged in escapes or organizing them. It was through escape – and other acts of resistance – that Day believed he and his fellow prisoners could refute the German notion that 'for you the war is over'. His dedication to escape was also a symptom of his deep frustration at being knocked out of the war in October 1939: a promising career had been blighted, but he was determined to stay 'operational'. And even if escapes were not ultimately successful, Day argued that they diverted German resources away from the front line.

By contrast, Spivey saw his prime mission as looking after his men, getting them back to the United States in good mental and physical condition. In this he succeeded admirably: a POW who died of pneumonia in the camp hospital in 1943 was the only fatality in Center compound during his tenure of command. Spivey was not averse to escapes – the compound had its own escape organization – but he did not pursue the matter with the urgency of Wings Day.

Shortly after his arrival at Stalag Luft III in September 1943, Spivey accepted the offer to become SAO of Center compound: 'I had been accustomed to working twelve to sixteen hours a day and I wanted something to occupy my mind.' The compound, formerly home to RAF NCOs, had been left in a poor condition, as Spivey recalled: 'Windows [were] broken, wiring torn out, beds and other German property strewn all over the place, latrines half dismantled to furnish shoring for tunnels and fuel for fires.'

More problematic than the physical dilapidation of the compound was the uncertain human element, whose slovenliness shocked Spivey on his arrival. The men under his command comprised a motley collection of disorganized American officers and a few British and Commonwealth NCOs and officers (whose tenure was only temporary). Knowing they were to be moved elsewhere, the British had limited interest in improving conditions in the camp, and instead devoted their energies to various escape plans. Spivey and his staff of a dozen or so senior officers left the British to themselves and concentrated on their own airmen.

Gathering the American aviators together, Spivey informed them of his intention to organize the compound along military lines. His remarks initially received a poor reception, and some of his staff recommended a tough approach as being the only way to get all the POWs onside. Spivey, however, adopted a middle course, 'giving orders and demanding that they be carried out. Our approach was firm but geared to an understanding of the situation. We determined to lead, guide, direct, and encourage instead of being arbitrary. I do not know what I would have done if the group had refused to co-operate.'

Spivey described his strategy: it began with 'a general clean-up of the compound and a gradual improvement in personal appearance. The process worked beautifully; by the spring of 1944 I was actually proud of the men and their surroundings. Our Saturday morning inspections would have done credit to a first-class military unit back in the United States.' However, a few men rejected both the new regime and Spivey's authority: 'Some believed they owed no allegiance to the will of the camp as a whole, nor did they care to consider what inconvenience the camp suffered as a result of their individualist actions.' The conflict between individual rights and the community was a constant dilemma of POW life. Spivey, a convinced communitarian, was determined to bring over the waverers, even if it meant putting in place some tough disciplinary procedures.

A few hundred yards away, the RAF staff of North compound adopted a more informal attitude to discipline: personal appearance and the niceties of military etiquette took second place to escape and frustrating the Germans. Despite this latitude, basic standards of personal behaviour were expected of all POWs, and most made some contribution to camp life. Those men who refused to engage in the community – called the 'irreconcilables' by Day – were placed in their own hut where they could, said Jimmy James, 'drive each other "round the bend"'.

A similarly relaxed attitude to military discipline was also adopted in most British Army officer camps. This outlook was often expressed in sartorial terms. British officers in Germany suffered from shortages of the correct uniform, especially in the early part of the war, and were obliged to wear cast-offs from other armies, which produced some bizarre outfits. In part this was a German policy intended to humiliate the British, but it backfired when the officers began to wear their odds and ends with relish to provoke the guards. In many camps – Colditz in particular – slovenly dress and casual behaviour at roll calls became a device for prisoners to demonstrate their contempt for the Germans.

From time to time attempts were made to tighten up discipline. The officer camps in Italy reflected the informal style of the Eighth Army in North Africa. Accordingly, the officers in PG 49 at Fontanellato were a little disconcerted at the arrival of their new SBO, Lieutenant Colonel Hugo de Burgh, in August 1943. He immediately began to remilitarize what had become a rather sedentary camp. The journalist Edward Ward spent over twenty months in Italy before transfer to Germany and imprisonment at Oflag XIIB at Hademar. Ward disliked the new camp, not least because of its more rigorous regime: 'There was a tendency on the part of some of the senior officers to enforce a degree of military discipline which a good many of us found somewhat distasteful after the free-and-easy days of Italy. This was supposed to maintain "morale". Personally – and I know many of my fellow POWs felt the same – I was quite capable of looking after my morale myself.' The arrival of Major General Victor Fortune and other senior officers early in 1945 only increased Ward's frustration: 'Under the new regime the camp smartened up outwardly, but it did not become a pleasanter place to live in, particularly for those of us who thought that extreme discipline may be a fine thing in its proper place, but not in a POW camp.'

Fortune, who had been captured with his 51st (Highland) Division at Saint-Valéry in 1940, remained the senior Allied officer in German captivity throughout the war. Despite Ward's strictures, he was widely respected by his fellow prisoners. Terence Prittie recalled that 'Fortune had made a great difference to almost everybody in the camp. The "General" was an inspiring personality, completely unwavering at all times and lending some of his own overbrimming confidence to those of us who had become slack physically and war-weary in mind.'

Another inspirational leader was Colonel Paul Goode, SAO of Oflag 64 in 1945. He came into his own during the evacuation of the camp, when the men were ordered to march 350 miles westward in desperate weather conditions. Captain Roger L. Shinn was one of the marchers who got to know Goode:

We admired Col. Goode because he was efficient and had courage. He stood up to Oberst [Colonel] Schneider [the commandant] in demanding our rights, and whenever given a chance, he ran things well, as he had done at Oflag 64. We admired him for the way he kept discipline among us. Morale and respect for rank grow low among prisoners, but Col. Goode demanded that we salute and address him respectfully. I remember seeing a junior officer shrink when he said, 'That's not the way a lieutenant talks to a colonel.' He insisted that we shave and clean up as often as there was opportunity. And though we complained, because shaving was painful in that weather, we respected him for it. He was old, and the trip was hard on him. We wondered how he kept up when so many younger could not. He was an inspiring sight, striding out at the head of the column each day, carrying under his arm, of all things, a set of bagpipes – reportedly a gift of the YMCA.

But discipline and inspirational leadership were only a part of a senior officer's work: most of his time was spent in administrative matters, negotiating with the Axis authorities and dealing with outside agencies that included representatives from the Protecting Power, the Red Cross and the YMCA. Spivey had his hands full with such various and often mundane matters as settling in new POWs and allocating them to barrack huts, censoring the compound newspapers, tracking down supplies of scarce toilet paper, and trying to dissuade the men from retailoring their uniforms – of the latter Spivey commented, 'The camp reminded me of a girls' school when it came to altering clothes to suit an occasion or the time of year.'

Spivey was able to develop a good working relationship with Colonel von Lindeiner, the commandant of Stalag Luft III. Both were reasonable men who had respect for each other, but Lindeiner controlled limited resources and was constrained by an increasingly hostile attitude from his superiors towards Anglo-American POWs. Spivey certainly felt frustrated at German intransigence: 'It was a constant battle to get them to give us anything, much less the things we needed for survival in reasonably good physical and mental health.' But, wisely, Spivey did not vent his frustration directly at the Germans as some other senior officers did – sometimes to their cost.

When Wings Day was temporarily sent from Stalag Luft III to Oflag XXIB at Schubin he encountered an arrogant commandant from the German Army, very different from the courteous Lindeiner. At their initial meeting both men became engaged in a shouting match and, while the 6 foot 4 inch former Royal Marine bawled out the commandant, relations were fatally soured – any subsequent requests made by the POWs met with a firm refusal. (Day had the last laugh, however: the mass escape from Schubin in March 1943 led to the commandant's removal and the closure of the camp to British POWs.)

A more serious breakdown in prisoner–captor relations took place in Stalag Luft I in November 1944. Colonel Henry R. Spicer, the popular SAO of North 2 compound, made a strong impression on his men, as one recalled: 'Colonel Spicer was an excellent example of a good commander – one who kept morale high by challenging the Germans on every occasion.' Spicer was involved in an ongoing dispute with the German compound officer over the length of time taken to conduct roll calls. On a particularly cold day, the normal fifteen-minute roll call was extended to two hours, at which point an infuriated Spicer ordered his men to return to their huts despite German protest. Spicer then assembled his men and condemned the Germans, concluding an incendiary speech by saying, 'They are a bunch of murderous, no-good liars and if we have to stay here for 15 years to see all the Germans killed, then it will be worth it.' The applause of the POWs further enraged the Germans, some of whom had listened in to Spicer. He was hauled before the commandant and charged with 'defaming the German character' and 'inciting prisoners to riot'. Spicer was placed in solitary confinement for six months pending a court martial, at which one of the penalties was death. Fortunately the camp was liberated the day before he completed his time in the cooler.

The comradeship of POWs and a natural antagonism towards their captors was normally enough to stymie any German efforts to play a divide-and-rule game. But one area of contention within POW ranks that the Germans exploited with some, albeit limited, success was the relationship between orderlies and officers. The practice of officers employing orderlies or batmen as their personal servants was considered quite normal by almost all officers during this period, and the system was replicated in POW camps. Approximately 10 per cent of an Oflag population was made up of orderlies – usually private soldiers who preferred the lighter work of cleaning and tidying to labouring for the Germans in factories or coal mines.

In the British armed forces orderlies were normally a part of the regimental 'family', where officer and batman had a long association. In prison camps, however, orderlies were assigned en masse without this relationship, and some began to resent their undeniably servile status. And the fact that the officer prisoners were, in effect, doing nothing seemed only to underline the inequality. In Oflag VIIC at Laufen relations between officers and orderlies – some of whom were interned civilians – were at best mixed. Captain A. N. L. Munby noted in his diary that the orderlies were 'a pretty tough lot and not amenable to any sort of discipline – heard one telling the colonel to fuck off'. Captain Terence Prittie believed that the Germans were deliberately encouraging the orderlies to be insolent towards the officers and refuse to do the work allotted them, although he maintained those orderlies who did so were in a small minority.

Relations between orderlies and officers at Oflag IVC at Colditz reached a low point in 1941 when the orderlies effectively went on strike, their position being tacitly supported by the Germans. Some of the orderlies were subsequently replaced and more harmonious relations were established. But one example – undoubtedly extreme – of how things could go wrong came in an encounter between Douglas Bader and his orderly, Alec Ross. Bader was a notoriously abrasive and egotistical character, and, even allowing for his disability (he had lost both legs), he made heavy demands on Ross. As a medical orderly, Ross was due for repatriation in 1943. He described how he heard the news of his repatriation and Bader's intervention: 'Hauptmann [Captain] Püpcke came into the courtyard and called me down. "Good news, Ross," he says. "You're going home." Douglas Bader happened to be there, and he said, "No he's bloody not. He came here as my lackey and he'll stay as my lackey." Püpcke looked at me and shrugged his shoulders. And so I had to stay for another two bloody years when I could have gone home with the rest of my mates.'

American POW officers had a more ambivalent attitude towards orderlies, preferring in the main to carry out household duties themselves. As a busy executive officer, Spivey had been assigned a British orderly on arriving at Center compound. Although impressed with his own man, he noted that the 'British orderlies did a minimum amount of work and controlled most of the rackets within the camp.' When the British were replaced by American orderlies, Spivey ordered that they be given just a few general duties – working in the cookhouse and sweeping the barrack-hut hallways and latrines. Spivey's prime motivation in employing orderlies was to remove them from the tougher conditions of a work camp and to deprive the German economy of their labour.

Leaders in German and Italian other ranks' camps faced greater difficulties than their officer counterparts. Physical conditions were generally inferior to those found in officers' camps, and the NCO camp leaders tended to be at a disadvantage when dealing with the rank-bound Axis authorities. But the biggest difficulty faced by NCO leaders, at least in working camps, was the size of the camps and the transient nature of their populations. In a camp or compound of around 2,000 POWs – such as Oflag VIIB at Eichstätt or Stalag Luft III's Center compound – a camp leader could get to know his men, but in vast working camps with thousands of prisoners coming and going, such as at Stalag VIIIB at Lamsdorf, this was impossible. As a consequence, leadership tended to lose its focus and discipline became harder to enforce.

Differences in discipline and styles of leadership were quite marked between Air Force and Army camps. The vast majority of British and all US non-officer aircrew POWs were sergeants of one level or another, and rank lacked the defining aspect it did in the Army: the three stripes on their sleeves came not from years of dutiful service but from technical ability. Without the presence of spit-and-polish sergeant majors, discipline was more easy-going and leadership less dictatorial. Length of time served as a POW seemed to count as much in terms of seniority as rank itself.

In British Army camps, sergeants and other senior NCOs zealously guarded their distinctions of rank. When escape-minded RAF POWs offered to trade places with soldiers on work details, they were seldom short of takers. Staff Sergeant Raymond Ryan, an Australian soldier captured in Crete and held at Lamsdorf, benefited from such an exchange: 'We soon became accustomed to our blue uniforms and found life with the "boys in blue" much more pleasant than in the army compounds. The barrack leaders and the others did not have the domineering manners of the British WOs [warrant officers] and best of all there were no rackets. Everything was shared equally between all members of the compound.'

Lamsdorf was a camp where theft and extortion were not uncommon; its sheer size allowed men to swap or lose identities and effectively go underground, unknown to both the British and the German authorities. Despite this, the camp possessed a highly capable leader in Regimental Sergeant Major Sidney Sherriff, a Dunkirk veteran, who did his best to preserve order and to protect the POWs from the Germans and from predatory prisoners. He earned the respect of the Germans, and his work was praised by the representatives of the Protecting Power and the prisoners themselves. Ike Rosmarin, a South African POW, said of Sherriff, 'His strong character and the confidence he generated with the Nazis gained us unheard of concessions.' Julius Green, a dental officer attached to a Lamsdorf work camp, considered him 'a remarkable man. I think there are a number of men alive today who owe their continued existence to RSM Sherriff.'

Although Stalag IVB at Mühlberg lacked the Wild West atmosphere of Lamsdorf, it was also a large, unruly, multi-compound camp. Its Man of Confidence was Warrant Officer Jack Meyers of the Royal Canadian Air Force – better known by his nickname Snowshoes or Snowy. His tenure of command was a troubled one, however, with complaints being made against him for not cracking down on corrupt practices within the camp. In January 1944 he stood down as camp leader, to allow other candidates to come forward and challenge him for the post. Camp elections were held on 28 February with seven candidates. Meyers had the support of the camp and secured 3,866 votes against 812 for his nearest rival.

Meyers's victory did not bring the matter to a close, however, and in November 1944 further elections were called for compound leaders as well as for overall camp leader. Meyers won again, but some compound leaders were replaced. In his diary entry for the 29th, the Revd Bob McDowall noted, 'The trouble in the camp is straightening out. New R.C. [Red Cross] Reps. have to be appointed. New compound leaders have already been appointed for two compounds.

So the men who have been doing the engineering [corruption] are now out. A mighty lot of dirty linen has been hung out. Snowy, by a miracle, has come out of the struggle with all honours.' It would seem that the main opposition to Meyers stemmed from disgruntled Army NCOs who resented the top position going to an RAF man and from a group of escapers who believed that Meyers was obstructing their escape plans.

The calling of elections as a means of resolving festering camp disputes was not uncommon, and nor was the decision by a camp leader, confident of his popularity, to use an election as a means of reaffirming his mandate. In Stalag 383 at Hohenfels the respected camp leader, Squadron Quartermaster Sergeant David MacKenzie, decided to use the tactic to resolve an ongoing dispute with several other senior members in the camp. In the ensuing referendum, only 300 out of a 4,500-strong electorate asked for a change of leader.

Given the many shortages that existed in the camps – especially of food and cigarettes – those who had access to such vital items were in a powerful position. The best jobs in a camp involved the distribution of Red Cross parcels and other foodstuffs, and many of these went to the senior NCOs who were in overall charge. There can be little doubt that some of these men were engaged in corruption, siphoning off food and cigarettes with the connivance of bribed German guards.

These rackets caused bitterness among the ordinary ranks. Held in Stalag XXA at Thorn, Rifleman Sam Kydd railed against what he saw as the dishonest practices of the British cookhouse staff: 'Two Sergeant cooks and two Corporal helpers got themselves installed in the cookhouse. The spud bashing as usual was done by the other ranks. Sergeants and Sergeant Majors were detailed off to collect the bread and margarine rations and dole them out – they practically had a platoon of them to do it! They were guilty in many cases of cheating the soldiers to whom they were supposed to set an example.' In his Italian camps, Bob McDowall despaired at the actions of some of his fellow prisoners. 'NZ chaps in from other camp', he wrote, 'report much interference with parcels by our own men, many parcels being denuded of much of their content. Such action is fearful.'

In fairness to the NCOs responsible for distributing parcels, it was almost inevitable that others would impute corrupt practices to them. Good leaders minimized discontent by making the distribution of resources as open as possible and confronting accusers and accused when there were disputes. Even in the well-run Center compound, Colonel Spivey recalled that 'there were on many occasions a cry of "rackets", but investigations by our inspectors, in company with the accusing individual, revealed no case of cheating as far as food was concerned.' However, he admitted that 'some individuals were sharper than others and managed in one way or another to eat better than their fellow prisoners.'

That justice be seen to be done was one of the watchwords of John Lord, the RSM of the 1st Battalion, the Parachute Regiment, and before that a sergeant major in the Grenadier Guards. Wounded and captured at Arnhem, Lord was sent with 450 other injured men to Stalag XIB at Fallingbostel. Lord made a deep impression on all who met him, including Bombardier Stonard, who never forgot the RSM's parade-ground roar at their first morning roll call: 'My name is Lord! J. C. Lord. Jesus Christ Lord, the only holy man in the British Army, and don't you forget it!'

Lord was much more than a parade-ground martinet, however. He possessed an astute understanding of human psychology and an ability to motivate the most dispirited men. One of his first tasks on assuming command (he felt there was no need for elections) was to make it clear to the men that there would be no rackets in the camp, and that scarce items such as food and wood 'would be seen to be fairly divided out and seen to be fairly distributed'. By so doing he reduced the suspicions of corruption that were so corrosive to morale. When, at the beginning, it was found that the rations party was returning with short rations, Lord dispatched a separate supervisory party to ensure there would be no further pilfering.

RSM Lord found himself in a miserable multinational camp holding thousands of POWs. The British contingent was only a few hundred strong in September 1944, but new arrivals would push the figure up to 4,500 by the time of Stalag XIB's liberation. The Germans were deliberately obstructive, withholding medical aid to the wounded and in Lord's opinion attempting to 'degrade the British soldier'. Lord was determined not to let this happen, but he had to admit that the morale of fellow paratroopers was at a low ebb and would need much work to 'ensure that the Germans saw the British soldier as I knew him to be'.

Lord was able to draw upon a small staff of Airborne warrant officers to begin the process of sorting out the British POWs. He began with himself: 'I made sure that my personal turn-out was as good as I could make it. Every evening before the lights went out I cleaned my boots and put my trousers down to crease and then slept on them on the [bed] boards, and I wiped my web belt with the German soap, which made extremely good blanco.' Lord and his NCOs cleaned out their own hut, and demanded that all other POWs do likewise. 'The stench in the huts at night was beyond imagination,' he recalled. 'There were no cleaning materials; we had to use twigs to sweep the floors. I insisted that every man make his bed properly and be clean and tidy. I also insisted that in the morning all windows be opened, and that every man jack who could walk at all went out for exercise around the compound. It was vital to their health.'

He persuaded the Germans to let him command the roll calls, 'to show the POWs that it was a British NCO taking charge of their affairs, and not a German'. This also made the roll calls much swifter, which in turn was of benefit to the men, many of whom were wounded or convalescing from their wounds. Another device to provide a military atmosphere was employed when Lord secured an old Belgian trumpet. Bugle calls were written out, and Lord had his batman sound them around the camp at the appropriate times of the day. Although conditions remained poor – with increasing over-crowding, food and fuel shortages, and lack of blankets – Lord and his staff turned around the British compound, and eventually took over control of the entire camp five days before the British Army arrived in April 1945.

There were many good leaders in the Allied POW camps, but perhaps the most exceptional was the usually soft-spoken Scotsman Flight Sergeant (later Warrant Officer) James Deans, often known by his nick-name Dixie (after the pre-war Everton centre forward of the same surname). An RAF regular, Deans was shot down on 10 September 1940 and, following interrogation at Dulag Luft, was sent to the NCOs' compound in Stalag Luft I at Barth. On his arrival he discovered growing dissatisfaction with the camp leader, a warrant officer who many believed was running things for his own benefit. An election was called, and Deans was voted in as leader; he remained the RAF NCOs' Man of Confidence until the end of the war in a succession of camps – Stalag Luft I, Stalag Luft III, Stalag Luft VI, Stalag XXA and Stalag 357.

Once in command he assembled an elected committee to help him run the camp, supported by block leaders who relayed information from Deans to the men and from the men to Deans. 'I found that I was fairly au fait with all that was going on in the camp,' he recalled. 'I had my finger on the pulse. I knew if anything was going wrong, what it was that was causing the upset. And I could do something to put it right.'

Dixie Deans had that rare distinction of being a commander who was genuinely loved by his men. Post-war accounts written by RAF NCOs are universal in their praise for him. Alfred Jenner spoke for many: 'Dixie's great achievement was based on gaining the respect of the Germans by his patent honesty, courage and ability to command the unquestioned loyalty of the young men who came under his leadership and care.' Deans's ability to speak German fluently – gained partly from pre-war holidays in Germany – became not only a means of effective communication but a way of understanding his captors' psychology. 'I was dealing with the Germans day-in day-out,' he recalled. 'I knew I could get over to them what I wanted, and what I wanted was what the camp wanted. I had a fair degree of confidence on what was reasonable to ask them and what I could insist on.'

Deans was the hub of a large and complex organization. Although not directly involved in escape activities, he oversaw the escape organization and provided materials and other assistance to the escapers. Trading with Germans was properly organized, and the bribery of susceptible guards was carefully fostered; vital materials, such as parts for clandestine radios, were brought into the camp for a minimal outlay in cigarettes and other Red Cross-parcel items. Deans had also been instructed by MI9, the branch of British intelligence responsible for POWs, in the use of a secret letter code. He was able to send back useful intelligence gleaned by him and other POWs via his wife, Molly. She was somewhat disconcerted to find strange phrases in his letters, although she was subsequently warned by the War Office not to intimate any puzzlement in her replies.

One of the many who fell under Deans's spell was an Australian airman, Calton Younger, who wrote of his leader:

> The work of camp administration and external relations allowed him little respite, yet any man could take to him a personal problem, and know when he came away at least some of the burden was transferred to the sturdy shoulders of the camp leader. There were men his senior in rank, but they, like everyone else, were loyal beyond belief. In the prison community there was the constant suspicion of men with any kind of privilege; always the scandalmonger was there to whisper accusations, to cry 'Rackets'. The obvious man to decry was the camp leader, but in three years I never heard a murmur against his benevolent despotism.

Deans was an exceptional man, at the opposite end of the spectrum from the corrupt, incompetent or weak leaders to be found in some POW camps. Although it is impossible to quantify, POW accounts suggest that outright bad leadership was a fairly rare phenomenon. Most criticisms made against camp leaders were relatively mild, describing men who had failed to come to terms with camp life, who were out of their depth in new situations.

Sergeant Arthur Evans, a pre-war regular in the Irish Guards, who had himself been a leader in one of the many work camps at Lamsdorf, had misgivings about the overly authoritarian style of one camp leader. Evans was assigned to work at Gleiwitz airfield, which subsequently came under the control of RSM Brody. According to Evans, Brody was, 'officious, fussy and under the impression he was still on the barrack square. He had failed to learn the lesson that POWs refused to be commanded, but for the sake of orderliness and for the benefit of their welfare generally, willingly responded to a request or suggestion when expressed in a fair manner.' David Wild, a chaplain assigned to Stalag XXA at Thorn, saw a range of leadership abilities on his many visits to work camps located around the main Stalag. On only a few occasions did he feel the need to criticize leaders. One such concerned 'CSM R., an elderly Warrant Officer in a Scottish regiment. He had neither the push to challenge and harass the Germans effectively, nor the personality to gain the confidence of so many men.'

Far more serious were the activities of Sergeant Major 'Softie' Shanker, who took control as leader in the transit camp at Corinth and later in Stalag VIIA at Moosburg. Prisoners thought him too friendly in his dealings with the Germans, and his attempts to smarten up the camp were rejected as a result. Worse, however, Shanker apparently presided over a corrupt regime in which he and his associates took their pick of the prisoners' parcels entering the camp. He certainly earned Sergeant James McGee's contempt. 'The least said about him the better,' McGee wrote; 'suffice to say that for his own protection, he, together with his cronies, were moved out of the main camp and into the German administrative area.'

Arguably as bad as poor leadership was an absence of leadership. This was also rare, and typically occurred only in transit camps or in main camps during the confusion that attended the closing months of the war. Corporal Bob Engstrom was captured during the Battle of the Bulge on 17 December 1944 and spent most of his captivity in Stalag XIIID at Nuremberg and Stalag XIIIC at Hammelburg. By this stage in the war, conditions were deteriorating rapidly, as Engstrom explained: 'There was no real organization in the camps I was in. We were just leaves in the wind. We never had anything to use to bribe the guards like the air force guys did. We had no money and almost no Red Cross parcels. There was no leadership that I know of because the officers were off somewhere else. I don't even remember any staff sergeants. There was simply no one to take charge.'

Hammelburg also contained an officers' compound. Conditions there were also poor and morale low. Henry H. 'Mac' McKee, an officer captured during the Battle of the Bulge and sent to Hammelburg, described the state of the camp:

> I saw a lot of despondency and the loss of morale in prison camps. Much more than I was happy about. There was a considerable let down in discipline. And this was in an officers' camp. Although I agree it is difficult to anticipate beforehand just who will break down, once inside the camps, I think you could predict who was likely to do so. They wouldn't keep themselves clean, and they began to look like tramps. Certain guys would try to talk to them and remind them that they were American army officers. Sometimes it helped, but not with most of them.

That the camp was suffering from inadequate leadership was confirmed by Roger Shinn, who arrived at Hammelburg in March 1945 after his long transit from Oflag 64. Once there he met fellow officers from the 9th Armored Division. 'Almost the first look at the Hammelburg camp', he wrote, 'convinced us that we had been lucky. The officers here were weak and depressed. Their skins were pallid, sometimes yellow. We were thin, but healthy, and our spirits were good. At Hammelburg they were a miserable looking lot. They sat listlessly, spirits almost dead.' Improvement came with better weather and the appointment of Paul Goode as SAO:

> Col. Goode took hold with characteristic energy. He scheduled Saturday inspections when everyone had to be neat and dressed in his prison best. The camp became clean and shining. Letters went to the Red Cross and YMCA. Plans were set up for language classes, and the Colonel repeatedly went to talk to the General [the German commandant]. He never got much out of the General, but the fact that he was talking for us made us feel good.

The problems at Hammelburg were those of poor morale and apathy. As a padre in PG 57 at Gruppignano, Bob McDowall was to witness something more extreme: a complete breakdown of order following the surprise announcement of the Italian armistice on 8 September 1943. The commandant, Colonel Calcatera, was taken aback at the news and partially withdrew his men from the camp. Rumours of imminent release spread among the POWs, and with the sudden relaxation of Calcatera's severe rule groups of prisoners went wild. Indian POWs broke out of their compound and, with Australians and New Zealanders, began to ransack much of the camp. McDowall saw them marching on the magazine holding Red Cross parcels:

> As I stood at the gate watching, suddenly the crowd at the magazine was transformed into a seething mass with groups of men fighting over parcels – heaving, sweating, swearing – and hundreds teeming down the road. I was overwhelmed with shame that such scenes should be witnessed by the Italians and that our men should belittle themselves so. Could stand it no longer. I tackled one group of ten and, by shouting and smiting, dispersed them. Then another. By this time, most of the stuff was gone and I was able to order every man out of the

compound. The Indians climbed through a window into another room and I jumped in after them with a lump of board and they went out three at a time at miraculous speed. A New Zealander was nasty and went but slowly. Things came back to normal quietly but the place was indescribable. The grounds were littered with boxes and rubbish and clothes. Our own men had looted their mates' packs, and went to the wire, throwing away or selling their own mates' articles. All round the camp men were throwing clothes to peasants who were swarming about, gathering a harvest richer than they had ever known.

An angry and profoundly disappointed McDowall was relieved when the Italians returned the following day. He recorded in his diary, 'Went to see Col. [Calcatera] who said that he has taken over the camp again and was treating the men as prisoners, since they had proved so unruly. I was glad.' Two days later the Germans surrounded PG 57, and McDowall and the POWs began their journey to a second imprisonment, in Germany.

In smaller, well-run camps, POW leaders considered the incidence of crime to be surprisingly low. It was in the big camps where discipline was more lax and social cohesion lacking that crime gained a foothold. For British and American leaders, policing the camps and administering justice was far from easy. As well as having their authority regularly questioned by recalcitrant POWs, leaders lacked the range of sanctions available to them in a normal military establishment. Punishments handed out by camp leaders were usually light, typically a form of shaming the miscreant in front of his fellows – much less severe than the vigilante judgements of POWs who caught, tried and punished suspected wrongdoers without recourse to the procedures of formal camp justice.

A prevalent misdemeanour in the hard-drinking camps was, inevitably, drunkenness. There was a tendency to regard instances of drunkenness as relatively minor infractions; however, they could have serious consequences. In Stalag 383 at Hohenfels, a habitual drunk had so annoyed his companions that he was thrown out of their hut and forced to live alone in an empty hut used as a music room. There he continued drinking 'prune juice' until 'carted off to hospital'. At the same camp, Sergeant Ray Ryan was pleased to see action being taken against another drunk: 'A chap who became drunk and abusive has been sentenced by the senior MO [medical officer] to 56 days in hospital, scrubbing floors and cutting wood. This is the first disciplinary punishment given in a POW camp – agree with it myself. Many people consider they can go as they please without restraint, merely because they are POWs.'

A particularly serious example of the dangers of drunkenness took place at PG 57 on 20 May 1943. While a cricket match was in progress a *caribinieri* guard shot and fatally wounded an Australian soldier, Corporal W. 'Sock' Symond. Bob McDowall heard the shot and ran over to see what was going on. As he stood by the dying man, he was told that Symond had been drinking beer while watching the match and had begun an argument with a guard, who from a few feet away cocked his rifle and shot the Australian through the heart. Although McDowall described the incident as 'cold-blooded murder', it confirmed his negative views on excessive drinking.

One of the most serious crimes was the theft of food and other personal belongings. POW views on stealing were uncompromising, as expressed by David Westheimer, an American airman at PG 21 at Chieti: 'Theft in a place where everyone had so little ranked just below murder and collaboration with the enemy.' Accordingly, punishments for those caught stealing were severe.

In PG 21 a bread thief was completely ignored by his fellows until he was removed from the camp at the request of the senior officer. In Oflag VIIC at Laufen there was a spate of thefts during the period of severe food shortages in 1940. The main suspects were German troops and the British orderlies who went through the officers' rooms while they were at roll call. Little could be done about the German soldiers, but one orderly who was caught red-handed received five days in solitary as a result. However, other thefts could be attributed only to a British officer. Captain A. N. L. Munby described the officer's arrest: 'The wretched man was caught at 2.30 a.m. outside R[oom] 65 by people who had waited up for several nights in order to trace the loss of food from lockers.' The man had his bread rations and Red Cross parcels stopped, and was made to clean the barrack room for a month. More painful was the announcement made to the camp: 'Captain Lawton Rm 64 was brought before the Bdr [Brigadier Claude Nicholson, the SBO] and convicted of stealing bread from a brother officer's locker. In this camp it is difficult to imagine a meaner act.'

Bertie Harwood, however, considered this a trifling punishment, and added that Lawton 'didn't appear ashamed of what he had done'.

When a thief was caught in the Stalags he often faced tougher direct punishment. Sometimes the thief would be set upon with fists; at other times the punishment was more ritualistic and might comprise being forced to run, or more accurately walk, the gauntlet. Assheton F. Taylor, an Australian airman in the RAF compound at Stalag IVB, described such a punishment. 'The offender', he wrote, 'was required to strip to his birthday suit within the hut following evening curfew, and was then required to walk the full length of the hut at a slow pace between two rows of prisoners, each with a bed board in his hand. Blows below the head were permitted, and the offender had many cuts and bruises by the time he had reached the far end of the hut.'

When a man stole from his own combine, the sense of betrayal was all the greater. In Roger Coward's combine one of their number was caught taking food and dipping 'his unpleasant fingers' into prized tins of Nestlé's condensed milk. 'We didn't beat him up – much,' wrote Coward. 'We just gave him a few "fourpenny ones", made him get down on his knees and lick up the mess he had made, and then, as the most appropriate punishment anyone could think of, hauled him away, shrieking and protesting, and dropped him into one of our deep latrines.'

The actions of individual thieves were an irritating nuisance, but once the thieves were caught their exemplary punishments acted as a deterrent. Far more problematic was the emergence of gangs who through violence and extortion created an atmosphere of intimidation. Although they did not directly take on the camp authorities, they acted as a criminal underworld, preying on the camp's meagre resources.

During February 1945 the US North 3 compound in Stalag Luft I experienced problems of theft and intimidation as a result of the arrival of a large group of non-commissioned officers transferred from camps in the east. Two NCO ringleaders dominated the group, and when caught engaging in theft they refused to accept the authority of the compound officers – one even attacked an officer with a knife. Colonel Hub Zemke, the SAO, recommended that both face courts martial on their release and took the extreme step of bringing in the Germans to have them sent to the cooler. On their release Zemke interviewed them again, and when one threatened to reveal camp secrets to the Germans the SAO explained to him what the 'fate of collaborators would be'. American guards were assigned to monitor their movements, and if they attempted to contact the Germans they were to be eliminated.

As the biggest and the roughest of POW camps, it was hardly surprising that Stalag VIIIB at Lamsdorf should have produced gangs engaged in rackets, theft and extortion. The most infamous of these was a Glasgow razor gang of Scottish soldiers captured in 1940; armed with cut-throat razors, they attempted to establish themselves as 'top dogs' in the camp. They were said to roam through compounds at night, stealing the contents of huts and slashing anyone who resisted them. The gang created an atmosphere of disquiet and fear throughout the camp, although when faced by determined opposition they backed down. Trooper Forbes Morton described one such encounter after a fellow Canadian had been slashed by one of the gang: 'We took it upon ourselves to arm ourselves with whatever we could – bedboards you name it – and we went down to their barracks. And we had a battle royal. The Germans didn't step in either. There was nobody killed or anything [but] that was the end of the gang.' Despite this defeat by the Canadians – and by other groups – various accounts suggest that the gang continued its activities until the camp's closure in 1945.

The exercise of leadership and the imposition of discipline were difficult tasks in a prisoner-of-war camp. With a few exceptions, it would seem that British and American POWs could count themselves fortunate that the men in charge of them maintained high standards of leadership, and in more than a few cases were men of exceptional ability who made decisive contributions to their welfare.

7

Forced Labour

THE 1929 GENEVA Convention gave the Detaining Power the right to use prisoners for work purposes, and the Germans ordered the compulsory employment of British prisoners within months of their victory in the west in 1940. As the war progressed – with increasing numbers of German men conscripted into the armed forces – so the demand for labour increased, and by February 1944 some 80,000 British POWs were working for the Reich.

Although officers were permitted by the Convention to undertake 'suitable work', in practice neither Allied or Axis officers did so. Non-commissioned officers – from the rank of corporal upward – were only to be compelled to perform work of a supervisory nature, although they might join the main workforce if they wished. The right of NCOs not to work would, however, become a contentious issue in Germany.

The type of work performed by prisoners largely depended on the location of their camp. Those in and around the Polish Corridor – in Stalags XXA at Thorn, XXB at Marienburg and IIB at Hammerstein – focused on agriculture and construction. In eastern Germany, POWs in Stalag IVB at Mühlberg worked in factories and construction, and in Stalag VIIIB/344 at Lamsdorf mining and industry were major employers. Further south, in Austria, the men in Stalag XVIIIA at Wolfsberg were engaged primarily in agriculture, forestry and quarrying.

The main camp would have a sizeable population, comprising non-working NCOs and other ranks in transit, the sick, and those occupying permanent positions within the camp administration. The remainder of the prisoners attached to the camp would be dispersed among the many work parties (*Arbeitskommandos*) and their camps. In early 1944 Lamsdorf contained 10,000 British POWs, with a further

9,000 in 235 work camps attached to the main site. Other camps had a higher ratio of men at work, so that, for example, Stalag IIB at Hammerstein contained 7,200 US prisoners in January 1945, 5,315 of whom were assigned to working parties. Work camps ranged in size from a dozen or so men held on a Polish state farm to well over 100 in a large factory or quarry.

In addition to the ordinary work parties, the Germans also organized BABs (*Bau und Arbeitsbattalionen* – construction and work battalions), semi-mobile groups able to move from place to place as needed. In the event, they became fixed institutions, and the best known to British POWs, BAB 21 at Blechhammer, was over 1,000-men strong and acted as a permanent work Stalag.

While under the overall control of the German armed forces, work parties were hired out to private and state concerns. The working prisoner was paid a small daily wage, some of which was sent to the British or American camp administration and the remainder, in the form of the largely useless *Lagergeld*, to the prisoner himself. The employer and his foremen or overseers were expected to get the most out of their labour, while the guards who accompanied prisoners on work details were responsible for security. Prisoners were sometimes able to exploit the different responsibilities of employers and guards to their advantage – sufficiently so for OKW to send a sheaf of directives ordering guards to take more positive measures to increase prisoner productivity.

In Italy during the first two years of war the economy was not prepared for the introduction of foreign labour, and what work there was for POWs tended to be in local, mainly agricultural, concerns close to the camp. Initially, work was not compulsory for any rank of POW, although those who wished to work were given the incentive of double rations. During 1942 Italian policy began to change and ballots were introduced for labour duties, and by the summer some form of work – within the terms of the Geneva Convention – had become, officially at least, compulsory. Separate work camps were established, most situated in the north of Italy, with the prisoners engaged in agriculture or construction.

The Germans were determined to extract as much work as possible from their prisoners. As part of this policy they tried to hoodwink or intimidate NCOs (and medical orderlies, who were protected personnel) into working. Many British NCO prisoners taken in 1940 were unaware of their rights and were sent out to work. Corporal R. P. Evans at Lamsdorf had to wait until the spring of 1942, nearly two years after capture, before being told by a friend that work was not obligatory. But those NCOs who were aware of their rights fought a long and bitter battle to resist compulsory labour. In fairness to the Germans, some privates and lance corporals gave themselves 'Stalag promotions' to avoid work, and as a result men were sent to work camps unless they could categorically prove their rank. Over time, recognition papers were sent from Britain to prove a prisoner's rank, but these were routinely held back by the Germans.

Corporal Bob Prouse had been assigned to Arbeitskommando 1049 – a satellite of Stalag IXC at Bad Sulza – after the Germans had refused to accept him as a legitimate NCO. After several months spent in the camp – effectively a plywood-production factory surrounded by barbed wire – Prouse and the other NCOs pressed the Germans to recognize their non-working status. The ensuing struggle was not dissimilar to many others taking place in Stalags throughout Germany. Prouse recalled how at Arbeitskommando 1049 the NCOs declared en masse that they would not work after New Year's Day 1943:

> The Commandant called a parade, first trying to reason with us and then quickly changing his reasoning to threats. He said that we would lose all privileges such as the Saturday night boxing matches and concerts that had been organized by the prisoners. Then he threatened to cut off our rations and Red Cross parcels. Finally, after each threat had been met with a cheer, he lost his temper and stated that we would all be taken out of camp, one by one, and shot. When this remark was also cheered, he stamped out of the lager in disgust.
>
> On the day of the deadline, all prisoners arose extra early to see what the day would bring. We did not have to wait long. A large number of guards with fixed bayonets stormed in and herded all the prisoners together, jabbing and butting, until we were completely surrounded. Then a high-ranking German officer marched in, followed by a large group of Gestapo. He ordered that those on the shift due at the factory should march out immediately. There were shouts of refusal from the prisoners and then a barked order from the officer. The guards started

to beat those in the front rows with their rifle butts. As blood started to flow and men fell, our leader called a halt and advised the men that they had better move out since it was hopeless for unarmed men to oppose the Germans any further. We obeyed and those in the morning shift left the building with the Germans following closely behind. It wasn't until this shift returned that we learned what had happened. Apparently the men had entered the factory and stood to attention at their machines but refused to operate them. The guards again started to beat them with rifle butts. All finally gave in except for four men, a 'Taffy' (Welshman), two Englishmen and one Scot. Those returning said that every time one of these four was knocked down, he would get back up, stand to attention and shout 'God save the King'. All were finally knocked unconscious and dragged away, and we later learned that for disobeying an order they were sentenced to two years' hard labour in Polish salt mines.

Such direct confrontations were usually best avoided, although it would seem that this show of defiance did encourage the Germans at Stalag IXC to accept the justice of the men's cause and subsequently recognize their NCO status. In most other camps this battle had already been won, although there was a lingering dispute over those NCOs who had originally agreed to work and then changed their minds. By 1943 most non-working NCOs had either been transported to Stalag 383 at Hohenfels (set up for non-working NCOs) or were held within their own main camps. This change of policy was confirmed in this regulation from OKW: 'British non-commissioned officers who signed a pledge to work but are no longer willing to do so are to be returned to the [main] camp. Their unwillingness is not to be considered as a refusal to work. The employment of British non-commissioned officers has resulted in so many difficulties that the latter have by far outweighed the advantages.'

The victory of the NCOs was part of a wider turning of the tide among British working POWs. Until early 1941 they remained in a desperate position, recovering from the shock of catastrophic defeat in France. They were also without a proper supply of Red Cross parcels, and yet were expected to perform heavy manual work. The arrival of food from the Red Cross helped them regain physical strength, and this, with the arrival of new uniforms during 1941, was a great boost to morale. With access to food, cigarettes and other luxuries came the possibility of bribing corruptible guards, who became increasingly pliable as the years went by.

There were, however, certain camps where NCO non-working status continued to be overruled. This occurred in the US compound of Stalag IIB at Hammerstein as late as the autumn of 1943, when the German officer responsible for assembling work parties, Captain Springer, insisted that NCOs and medical corpsmen be included. According to an American report, when the prisoners refused to work Springer stated that 'he did not care about the terms of the Geneva Convention and that he would change the rules to suit himself'. When the Americans again refused to work, Springer ordered his troops to force them to work at bayonet point.

Other NCOs were, however, prepared to work. Some felt a responsibility to their men to act as a protective barrier against German employers and guards: a smartly turned-out sergeant, confident in his authority, invariably impressed his captors. Other NCOs undertook work for less altruistic reasons: to escape the monotony of camp life and engage in a relatively fulfilling activity; to receive better rations; or to find a good jumping-off point for a future escape. At the same time, all working POWs had to deal with the feelings of guilt associated with making contributions to the Axis cause. These feelings could be assuaged by the thought of tying down as many Axis soldiers as possible to guard them and by conducting go-slows and generally acting the fool – various forms of the expression '*Nicht verstehen*' ('I don't understand') were repeatedly uttered by blank-faced POWs to exasperated German overseers. Also common, but more dangerous, were the carrying-out of acts of sabotage and the instigation of strikes.

Of the various forms of labour that might be assigned to a POW, outdoor work was generally preferred, with many men volunteering for agricultural duties. Working on a farm, it was reasoned, gave greater access to the most important thing in a POW's life: food. This was certainly true of the smaller mixed or non-arable farms, where POWs worked and lived alongside the farmer, his family and their animals, with little or no direct supervision from the guards. The hours were long – especially at harvest time – and the work arduous, but a hard-working and well-fed prisoner would enjoy a quality of life far superior to that found in his main camp.

In the vast state farms in Prussia and along the Polish Corridor – typically between 5,000 and 10,000 acres in size – conditions were far from idyllic, however. The work parties, between ten and forty men, were penned in cramped farm buildings with few facilities, and when Red Cross parcels were not available the standard prisoner rations in no way compensated for the work expected by the employer. During the grain and potato harvests in August and September, prisoners could find themselves working fifteen-hour, seven-day weeks. The prisoners did not work for a local farmer but came under the command of an overseer answering to the landowner, who ran his farms on brutally feudal lines.

In August 1943 Private First Class Thearl Mesecher was sent to a farm attached to Stalag IIB, where conditions were uniformly poor. 'On the Sundays that we don't work,' he wrote, 'we are locked in our squirrel cage, and the guard goes home to the nearest village. We are lucky to have enough water to drink, none to wash with. Some things one must endure are perhaps necessary, or in some cases unavoidable. But a lack of even sufficient drinking water looks very much to me that they either do not wish to be bothered with us, or just want us to realize that we are prisoners.' Subsequently Mesecher went to work for an anti-Nazi former clergyman, who looked after him well and provided filling Sunday dinners. Other POWs were less fortunate, relying on the irregular supply of Red Cross and personal parcels for sustenance.

Other types of outdoor work included quarrying, forestry, rail maintenance, and construction. Rifleman Jim Roberts, captured at Calais in 1940, was assigned to work camps around the Danzig area. In more than four years of toil Roberts and his fellow POWs spent the bulk of their time on construction projects, except during the severe Baltic winters, when they were reassigned to snow-clearing or other duties not dependent on frost-free weather. His first job was on a large housing estate, building apartments for German families. Operating alongside Polish workers, they worked hard at doing as little as possible. 'We did get immense satisfaction', wrote Roberts, 'from the knowledge that it must be the slowest building project ever and the thought that we were putting one over the Germans gave us a boost.' Construction was undoubtedly slow: the foundations were dug in the autumn of 1940, and the first families began to move on to the estate only in the summer of 1943. Low-level sabotage had gone on throughout the construction process: tools were dropped into concrete mixes, drainage pipes smashed, and chimney flues concreted over.

Sabotage was one of the best ways for a POW to feel he was fighting back at his captors. In the non-mechanized agriculture that was typical of Germany at that period there were relatively few ways to scupper the German war machine, but in the industrial sphere opportunities were dependent only on the POW's ability to avoid detection. The most common forms of sabotage included making weak concrete mixes, severing power cables, losing tools, breaking machinery, and adding sand or grit to almost any bearing. It was essential that all such acts should not only be unobserved by the guards but be untraceable to the POWs involved. Those caught for even minor crimes faced savage sentences: a man arrested breaking a shovel received three years in a punishment camp.

In his Italian camp, PG 78 at Sulmona, Jim Witte had evaded calls for labour in the local work camp at Aquafredda, but after his transfer to Germany in the autumn of 1943 there was no way of avoiding employment. The Germans at Stalag IVB at Mühlberg followed the standard procedure of asking new prisoners to list their former civilian occupations, to which many replied facetiously as former undertakers, brothel-keepers, airline pilots, food-tasters and so on. But whether their replies were sensible or not, the jobs assigned to them had little or no bearing to the answers given.

On hearing a call for railway workers, Witte decided to volunteer, hoping for a cushy job as a shunter or porter. To his consternation, he was sent to a vast locomotive repair works at Chemnitz: the work was heavy and hard, and the noise deafening. Gangs of foreign workers carried out specific tasks, and a less than enthusiastic Witte was passed around them before ending up in the 'odd-job gang'. 'The gang', he wrote, 'was composed of useless Englanders, Bolshie Frenchmen and undernourished Russians who got jobs like unloading coal wagons and sweeping up. Such a job meant we could rove the factory at will, for as long as we were carrying a broom or shovel the Germans were happy.'

In the spring of 1944 Witte was transferred to the Engeldorf repair works near Leipzig. There he joined a team of Belgians repairing locomotive cabs. The work was not too onerous, and much of the day was spent hiding in the cabs, smoking and chatting. Any difficulties with the factory foreman were squared with a supply of high-quality cigarettes. But accidents and injuries were common in the works – as they were in other industrial concerns – a consequence of inadequately protected machinery and lack of training among the multilingual workforce. Witte was lucky to escape with just a few cuts.

The even tenor of Jim Witte's working life was disturbed by the arrival of a fanatical guard – nicknamed the Weasel – at the beginning of 1945. The Weasel took a dislike to Witte and, immune to bribery, was determined to bring the Englishmen to book. His chance came when he caught Witte fraternizing with his current girlfriend, the Belgian Adrienne, outside the camp boundaries. Although a minor offence, it was sufficient to earn Witte a month's punishment in a coal mine 20 miles from Leipzig.

It was with feelings of trepidation that Witte was escorted through the colliery gates to a 'barrack-room which was filled with Englanders, some of whom were punishment wallahs like me and the others miners from civvy street who were conned into the job on the promise of extra rations'. Witte attached himself to a Northumberland miner, who showed him the ropes. The environment was unpleasant, the work hard, and the conditions dangerous. While the experienced miners worked at the coalface, Witte's job was to shovel coal into a tub that would then be pushed to the junction with the main track. Difficult as the work was, it was made far worse by poor rations and an absence of Red Cross parcels. It was a grim period, as Witte recalled: 'We went to bed exhausted and woke up exhausted. My trouble was that I wasn't used to graft and I had grown soft with fiddling and living off the fat of the land. No one felt sorry for me, especially when they heard what I was in for, but I just gritted my teeth and got on with it. At the end of the month I was let out more dead than alive.' He was escorted back to Engeldorf by a friendly guard. 'He was shocked at my appearance,' Witte wrote, 'and took me off to a *Gasthaus* and bought me a bite to eat and a reviving beer. Next day I went back to work which was a little different from the slavery down the mine.'

Few men volunteered for work in the mines; most had to be either coerced or tricked into going underground. One of the latter was

Sergeant Arthur Evans, initially imprisoned in Stalag VIIIB at Lamsdorf before being sent to the NCOs' camp at Hohenfels. At Lamsdorf, a German officer offered the men good conditions in a work camp where, he told them, they would avoid the fierce cold of the Silesian winter. Evans took up the offer, only to find himself working in a coal mine. Despite this chicanery, Evans did not find the work intolerable; he got on well with his German co-workers, enjoying the advantage of a hot shower at the end of his shift.

Evans's opinion was a minority one, however, and most POW accounts emphasize the negative aspects of underground work. Cyril Rofe, an RAF sergeant at Lamsdorf who had swapped places with a private soldier for a subsequent escape attempt, was sent down a mine at Jawarzo on the German–Polish border. He wrote:

> I rapidly developed an absolute horror of the long dark passages where large noisy monsters [coal tubs] were liable to bear down upon the unsuspecting wayfarer, rattling by and obliging him to flatten himself against the nearest wall – the hospitals were full of men who moved too slowly – and of the side cuttings where we worked, with their gas-laden air, the steady drip of the water, and the menacing lumps of coal that were constantly falling around us.

The sole advantage of this life, according to Rofe, was the ability to trade Red Cross items and cigarettes for fresh eggs from his Polish co-workers. He also found that he could trade cigarettes for work: 'Being already a non-smoker,' he wrote, 'I soon almost became a non-worker too.'

The conditions encountered in mines and other unpleasant workplaces encouraged prisoners to pull 'krankers' (from the German *krank* – 'sick') to escape work. Injuries or illness might be feigned by a variety of measures, including eating carbolic soap to fake heart trouble and an apparently ingenious concoction that could raise body temperatures to feverish levels. Self-inflicted injuries were another means to avoid work. Labouring in a quarry, Corporal Peter Peel deliberately wrenched his ankle, an injury sufficient for him to be returned to Stalag VIIIB at Lamsdorf, where he secured a permanent staff job on the education and entertainments committee. Others adopted more extreme measures that involved self-induced burns, the infection of cuts, and even the breaking of bones.

Allied medical officers were allowed a quota of up to 5 per cent of the total workforce who might be kept back from work. When this quota was exceeded, the Germans would instigate a clear-out of those whom they believed to be malingerers. Unsympathetic German medical staff were greatly feared by sick prisoners, as they did little to distinguish between those trying it on and the genuinely ill. Bob Prouse recalled the rough treatment he received for an injury to his back, aggravated by heavy lifting in his work camp:

> At the work commando I collapsed and was taken to the village doctor. I was held up between two prisoners while the doctor swung his arm to gain momentum and then brought his fist down on the top of my head. I yelled and fell as the pain hit my spine. His verdict was, 'No blood, no swelling, back to work!' Other prisoners in the camp covered for me by taking my work shifts and moving me from bed to bed as the shifts changed, a deed I'll never forget.

The lack of care shown by German medical staff to Prouse and other Allied POWs was as nothing compared to the treatment endured by a group of American prisoners at the Berga work camp. Some 4,000 Americans captured during the Battle of the Bulge had been sent to the dilapidated and already overcrowded Stalag IXB at Bad Orb, which by late December 1944 had degenerated into one of the worst POW camps in Germany. Once there, eighty Jewish POWs were selected to join a work camp at Berga, but as the work quota was for 350 men they were joined by other GIs – men whose name sounded Jewish and 'troublemakers', with the remainder chosen at random. Berga was in fact a satellite concentration camp engaged in the construction of a deep underground munitions factory. As in other slave-labour camps, the prisoners were slowly worked to death on a starvation diet. Failure to work hard enough or any sign of dissent led to savage beatings, and shootings were common. Approximately seventy of the American prisoners died at Berga – a total that would have been far higher had the camp not been evacuated on 4 April 1945 and the men liberated three weeks later.

In Italy, Lance Corporal Doug LeFevre had an easier and more pleasant time than his comrades working in Germany. After his arrival in Italy he spent the winter months of 1942–3 convalescing in hospital before dispatch to the Anzac camp of PG 57 at Gruppignano. His stay was short, and on 25 April he was sent with a batch of other POWs to work in the rice fields around Vercelli in north-west Italy. LeFevre was assigned to a small work camp of between forty and sixty men at Ronseca. He was comforted to note that a relatively large number of Italians were used to guard them – soldiers removed from the war effort elsewhere. Working conditions in the rice fields were generally good, and discipline was lax.

Prisoners who worked had many advantages over their comrades held in main camps. Increased rations and access to a wider range of foodstuffs made them stronger and healthier. They also met ordinary Italian people for the first time, and the more enterprising prisoners, such as LeFevre, began to learn Italian. These experiences would transform their chances of escape after the armistice. The prisoners could also indulge in trade and some highly satisfying sabotage.

The Australian POW workers proved adept at creating obstacles to increased productivity. When they were loading sacks of rice for transport to Germany, they would insist that two men were required for the job, and, recalled LeFevre, 'when nobody was looking we would put excreta in them or bricks or any dirt that we could think of – anything to sabotage food sent to Germany.' On the farm itself, camp leader Popeye Hanson organized a programme of systematic sabotage of mechanical equipment, which included a Fiat tractor driven by LeFevre for ploughing the rice fields. LeFevre conveniently forgot to pump oil into the pistons before starting up the tractor; after three lengths of the field the engine seized. 'I went up to the padroni,' LeFevre recalled, 'and said that the tractor had gone bung. He said, "Explain it, what do you mean by going bung?" I said, "It is like me, it doesn't work." They had to send the tractor to Milan on a four-wheel lorry and it took them six months before they got it back.'

Another PG 57 inmate, Sergeant George Lochhead, was responsible for a group of 100 New Zealanders sent to work on the construction of a hydroelectric plant near Ampezzo in the Dolomite mountains. Acting in a supervisory role, as well as liaising with the Italian guards and employers, Lochhead found the job a stimulating challenge. The Italians ensured that the POWs were properly fed with double rations and had access to Red Cross parcels. On Sundays they were allowed out on parole walks, although with the stark proviso that if anyone escaped Lochhead would be shot. POWs who worked in Italy were paid a few lire a day, which they could use to buy items on the open market (in contrast to the *Lagergeld* system of the German camps). Lochhead was able to pool the money paid to his men and buy provisions from the local market, which included fruit and some wine. Despite these generally good conditions, on one occasion Lochhead fought the authorities to ensure his men had proper footwear:

> The boots started to wear out. When anyone's boots weren't good enough to work in, I kept them at home. It got to be so many that there was real consternation between the civilian bosses and the army. I got the word that every man had to go to work whether his boots were good or not, so I sent them all to work. They'd go along, fill the barrow up. Sit down. Take their boots off. Shake the dirt out. Put the boots back on again. Go and empty the barrow, and by the time they got there they had to take their boots off again. It just drove those foremen mad, and they sent them back. So they sent all the boots [away] and got them repaired.

Lochhead's oblique tactics proved an astute way of taking on the authorities and winning. Direct confrontation often provoked a violent reaction. Strikes were a good case in point. To British and American soldiers a strike for more food or better conditions was merely a device in the overall bargaining process between employee and employer – as was the case in the civilian world. To the German military mind a strike was a form of mutiny to be stamped out immediately.

An example of this difference in attitude can be seen in a protest mounted by the men of Rifleman Jim Roberts's work camp near Danzig. In the spring of 1944 the Germans announced a cut in the bread ration. At the time, the POWs were well supplied with Red Cross parcels and the reduction was of little practical concern, but almost as a matter of principle the men decided to strike. 'More for a laugh than for any other reason,' wrote Roberts, 'we made banners which read, "*Keine Brot – Keine Arbeit*" ("No Bread – No Work") and paraded up and down just inside the wire by the main gate and directly opposite the German quarters. At the same time we were shouting out the same slogan at the top of our voices.'

The men were in high spirits, and German efforts to order the men back into their huts were met with 'rude signs and comments about their ancestry'. Unknown to the British prisoners, the German commandant had summoned reinforcements, which included several lorries of troops, an armoured vehicle, and a thirty-strong detachment from the local Gestapo. After about half an hour the reinforcements arrived and brought the carnival atmosphere to an abrupt halt. The main gun of the armoured vehicle was trained on the POWs, and machine guns were set up around the camp. The prisoners were subjected to strip searches, and the camp was torn apart in a search that revealed much contraband material, including 'a camera, radio, several farmhouse loaves, eggs, a few sheath knives, electrical equipment and a large amount of wood and coal which we used in the stove for heating and cooking'. One of Roberts's comrades sighed, 'All this fuss over a tiny piece of bread and a small demonstration,' but it was clear that the German reaction was intended to teach the British a lesson. The bread ration was cut and the men were sent out to work.

A similar sequence of events – albeit on a smaller scale – occurred in a protest involving Jim Witte at his Chemnitz work camp. One of his initial jobs was just to file down pieces of metal, night after night. Such was the monotony of the job that the prisoners decided to stage a protest, using the poor food as the bargaining issue. 'We downed files and waited,' wrote Witte. 'The foreman, not hearing any sounds of industrious scraping, came out of his office and was horrified to find the Englanders lounging about.' His demand for work was met with a robust 'Fuck off!'. The foreman then called on higher authority, whose demands met with a similar response. The next step saw the arrival of a guard with a savage Dobermann pinscher, 'which looked ready and willing to bite chunks out of our legs. We took up our files and resumed filing.'

Disputes with the Axis authorities called for a deft touch by POWs and their leaders. But Anglo-American POWs enjoyed benefits denied other prisoner groups under Axis subjugation, receiving vital psychological and material support from home. When provided with new uniforms – along with a good supply of food and cigarettes – British and American prisoners were an imposing presence in war-torn Germany, at variance with Nazi propaganda of an enemy of the verge of defeat. Thearl Mesecher described some of the advantages enjoyed by US POWs in November 1944: 'With clothing from the Red Cross, we dress much nicer than any civilian or soldier around here. We are, even during working hours, as clean and neat as possible. Our general good manners and cleanliness are known and respected in every part of Germany where American prisoners are held. When they read or hear their own propaganda, they look at us, and it becomes very deceiving.'

During 1943 the Germans had become sufficiently concerned by what they saw as the 'arrogance' of working British POWs to commission a study by the SS that drew upon reports of British behaviour from across Germany. A respondent from the Austrian city of Klagenfurt summed up the prevailing view of British working POWs within the German community: 'The British are always decently dressed, their uniforms are always in faultless condition, they are shaved, clean and well-fed. Their attitude is extraordinarily self-possessed, one could almost say arrogant and over-bearing. This, combined with the good impression they give of the nation, influences German people in a way that should not be under-estimated.' Another report outlined an instance of this show of superiority:

> A short while ago some forty British prisoners were sent to an industrial town to be split up among six factories. They arrived at the station with masses of luggage, and ostentatiously carrying large packets of food, corned beef and other things which were very short in Germany at that time. They immediately requisitioned two hand carts, loaded on their luggage, and gave two schoolboys some chocolate to push the carts. The German sentry took no action whatever. On arrival at the camp, they again hailed some German boys, who carried their luggage into the camp for them.

The study concluded that the British 'presence in Germany is thoroughly demoralizing'.

While British and American POWs made a contribution to the Axis economy, it was not what their captors had hoped for. The prisoners' work was reluctantly given and poorly performed. The effects of sabotage aside, the Germans and Italians were forced to provide extra guards, build more camps, and divert other economic resources to the maintenance of working prisoners. But work was also a mixed blessing for the POWs themselves. For some it was an opportunity to escape the tedium of camp life; for others it was a painful and wretched experience under the thumb of a hated enemy.

8

'Time on My Hands': Leisure, Entertainment and the Arts

T ERRY FROST WAS born into a working-class family in
Leamington Spa in 1915. Although showing an early aptitude for
art, he left school at the then quite usual age of 14 to work in a local
cycle shop. The nearest he got to pursuing anything of creative interest was subsequently working at the Whitley-Armstrong aircraft
factory in nearby Coventry, painting RAF roundels on to aircraft
wings. But Frost's pre-war life of modest aspiration and achievement would be transformed by his experiences in a prisoner-of-war
camp.

Joining up in 1939, Frost was sent to the military backwaters of
Lebanon and Palestine. Bored by the inactivity of his Middle East
posting, he volunteered for the commandos, only to be captured by
the Germans on Crete in May 1941. He spent the rest of the war in
POW camps, first in Salonica and then in Poland, before ending up
in Stalag 383 at Hohenfels. Stalag 383 was a vibrant centre of POW
activity of all kinds, and it was there that Frost met the young though
established artist Adrian Heath.

Frost sketched portraits of fellow prisoners, and when Heath saw
one of them he realized that here was real artistic promise. Heath
encouraged his protégé while at Hohenfels, and after the war he
persuaded him to attend art school at Camberwell, securing him
an ex-serviceman's grant to finance his studies. Frost moved to
Cornwall as a member of the St Ives School, working alongside artists
such as Ben Nicholson and Barbara Hepworth. His career blossomed
in the 1960s with exhibitions in the United States followed by a series
of academic posts in Britain. The poor boy from Leamington was
elected to the Royal Academy in 1992, and knighted four years later.

Sir Terry Frost considered his four years of captivity as pivotal: 'In
prisoner-of-war camp I got a tremendous spiritual experience, a more

heightened perception, and I honestly do not think that awakening ever left me.' The encouragement of his fellow prisoners was the spur to new and wider horizons. 'Prison camp was my university,' he concluded. Few Allied POWs experienced Frost's life-changing transformation, but many men could say that within the confines of the camps their intellectual, emotional and spiritual lives had expanded in a way they would never have dreamed possible before capture.

If hunger was the great and enduring tormentor of the prisoner in the physical world, then its mental equivalent was boredom. Officers and most NCOs were not engaged in any form of productive work, and for those imprisoned in the early years of the war their captivity seemed to stretch forward into a mind-numbing, indefinite future. 'Prisoner-of-war life is an interminable weekend,' wrote Major Munro Fraser from Oflag XIIB at Hademar, 'an endless Saturday and Sunday that never succeeds in getting round to Monday.' Lionel Renton, a junior officer captured in France in 1940, had a similar outlook: 'If you have never had the experience you can never imagine what it is like to get up in the morning to face a long empty day with nothing to do except what you invent yourself.'

It was this requirement for self-invention that was the challenge. In all camps there were men who withdrew into themselves, but to do nothing was a counsel of despair; their refusal to engage in POW life only compounded their misery. Doing something to sustain body, mind and spirit was an essential tool of survival, and for a lucky few a means to discover a rare and perhaps unlikely fulfilment.

The German and Italian camp authorities allowed prisoners to take up 'wholesome' pursuits, working on the simple premise that a man occupied in leisure was a man not attempting to escape or otherwise cause trouble. It also gave them a useful lever of control: if POWs misbehaved then privileges would be withdrawn. On the Allied side, the SBO and SAO and their staffs saw the provision of such activities as a means of keeping the men healthy in body and mind.

As well making for a generally healthier and happier body of prisoners, sport was a way of reasserting pride in oneself and one's country. Allied POWs could feel a special identity in the many sports they developed, whether football or cricket for the British or baseball or basketball for the North Americans. A group of British and Australian soldiers, captured in Greece and Crete in 1941 and sent to a French POW camp, provided a telling example of the inspirational quality of sport after some of them found a ball and started an impromptu football match. 'Still shut up in our barracks,' recorded a French prisoner, 'we saw them playing around for an hour, showing a liveliness worthy of far different surroundings. They paid no atten-tion to the German officers whom regulations compelled them to salute, broke one of the windows in the *Kommandantur*, and without turning a hair had their ball returned by one of the secretaries!' This insouciant behaviour came as a revelation to the demoralized French POWs: the Commonwealth troops might have lost a battle, but in refusing to be cowed by circumstances they made it clear that they had not lost the war.

Although a few sports could be improvised from objects around the camp, Allied POWs were fortunate in the help given them by the Red Cross and the YMCA, the latter organization being responsible for delivering vast quantities of sporting kit to the prisoners. During 1943, for example, the YMCA shipped to German camps over 10,000 soccer balls, 6,900 pairs of boxing gloves, 8,000 soft balls, 400 base-balls, 650 American footballs and 25,000 table-tennis balls.

Sports were run along national lines. Football was king for the British, played throughout the year in all weather conditions. Professional players were eagerly sought out to strengthen camp or barrack-hut teams. Rugby and cricket were also popular, especially with Commonwealth POWs, although decent playing surfaces for the latter were hard to find. The US prisoners immersed themselves in baseball, softball, basketball and, to a lesser extent, American football. In winter, when the weather was sufficiently cold, skating rinks were constructed and hockey was played by the Americans and, especially, Canadians. In summer, various forms of athletics were contested, with the annual sports day bringing out the whole camp whether as par-ticipant or spectator. The small water reservoirs used for firefighting purposes became improvised swimming pools.

There were numerous other minor sports with enthusiastic de-votees. They ranged from boxing, wrestling, weightlifting and fencing to gentler pastimes such as badminton, deck tennis and ping-pong. In Oflag IVC at Colditz recreational space was usually restricted to the small courtyard within the castle, which led to the development of a new pastime called 'stool ball', played every afternoon with great enthusiasm. Billie Stephens described the game:

> There were eight or ten players on each side and a stool was placed at either end of the courtyard; the object of the game, as the name suggests, being to touch the stool with the ball. These games were fast and furious; one played ten minutes each way and by the end both sides were in a state of complete exhaustion. It is remarkable that no one got seriously hurt, because the courtyard was paved and the people used to get thrown around in the most frightening way.

One of the obviously difficult sports to play in the tight confines of any camp was golf, and yet at Stalag Luft III a course of sorts was constructed. The sandy soil was ideal for bunkers, although in deference to actual playing conditions the greens were renamed 'browns'. As it was not a practical game in a POW camp, no provision was made by the administrators of the Red Cross and YMCA to supply equipment. But they had not reckoned with the ingenuity of the POW and the deep yearning of the golfer deprived of an afternoon on the links. During the early summer of 1943 a small RAF contingent of would-be golfers discovered a single wooden-handled golf club, an item of equipment sufficient for the foundation of the Sagan Golf Club. When Americans began to arrive at the camp they too took an interest.

One of the founder members, an RAF flight lieutenant, remembers the moment of discovering the golf club: 'I shall never forget the thrill of handling a club again after all that time, as I swung at a home-made ball.' The original course – a highly ambitious eighteen holes (1,220 yards, par 55) – was later modified to a more manageable nine. The best hole was considered the blind shot over the kitchen, although the flight lieutenant noted that 'the "abort" [latrine] hole played from the back tee used to thrill us in the playing of it as well as the unfortunates who came out of the door just as someone drove.' During the summer the single club was supplemented by the arrival of ten more from a source in Denmark and by the manufacture of home-made clubs, with hickory shafts carved from hockey sticks and heads cast from melted-down metal water jugs and stove pipes, the moulds being made from soap or sand. In late September 1943, the flight lieutenant wrote, 'We lived and breathed an atmosphere saturated in golf and most of us revelled in it.'

The onset of winter brought the first experiment in POW golf to a close: 'A few mounds covered in snow are the sole evidence that not long ago there was what we like to call the Sagan Golf Club, where for seven months during a strange summer we found entertainment, exercise and something akin to happiness.'

Strenuous activity was not to everyone's liking, however. Bertie Harwood preferred to tread the boards as actor and producer, or put his feet under a card table. In Germany, Jim Witte had little energy left from a hard day in the locomotive repair works, and what strength he had was devoted to entrepreneurial activities and amorous adventures. The escapers, such as Jimmy James and Billie Stephens, were too busy with their own projects to spare time for anything else. For other men the role of onlooker was preferred to that of participant: one of the virtues of sport was its interest to spectators, and major games attracted large crowds. Tony Howard, interned in the Milag merchant-navy camp, wrote how 'many an hour has been spent enjoying playing or watching a game. In the summer one could take a blanket down [to the sports ground], sunbathe, and watch cricket at the same time.'

In the larger camps – where there was more room and better facilities for sporting activity – sport became increasingly well organized. In Center compound a softball league was established with twenty-five teams, including one composed of senior officers, which Spivey ruefully admitted 'was always in the league cellar'. Stalag IIB at Hammerstein had three separate softball leagues, and in a letter from the camp in 1943 one POW announced, 'Practically every state in the Union is represented by at least one player on one of the many teams. Another item of interest is the age-old feud between North and South. Three ball games have been played between the two factions, and the Rebels have beat the Yanks in two of them.' The British organized league and cup competitions in soccer, rugby and cricket; teams took the names of those they supported at home. Throughout the camp system there were many Arsenals playing similarly large numbers of Wolves, Boltons and West Bromwich Albions.

The attempt to re-create the sporting atmosphere of home in an alien camp environment was most apparent at big matches, which in

British camps took the form of internationals between the British home nations and the Commonwealth. Great effort was made in the staging of the games, with programmes, match reports in the camp newspapers, and appropriately attired teams. In football, England–Scotland internationals became a regular fixture. In PG 78 at Sulmona there were four such matches per year, to which senior Italian officers were invited, and in Stalag 383 at Hohenfels the England–Scotland match was similarly important. 'These games were played with all the verve of a Wembley Cup Final,' wrote one prisoner. 'The Camp Commandant and his aides were invited to the top games and seated – the two teams lined up for kick-off and a military band and a Scottish pipe band were in attendance, marching and counter-marching.' Stalag IVB also hosted an informal world cup, in which an extraordinary forty-eight nationalities were represented. The final was between England and Germany (its team drawn from the guards), which England won 1–0.

Vying with sport for popularity was the more sedentary pastime of cards. In every corner of a barrack room a small group would be playing at any time of day, ranging from simple games of crib and whist to five-day bridge marathons and high-stakes poker schools. And with cards came gambling. The armed forces have had a long tradition of gambling, and the enforced idleness of the POW camps encouraged betting of all sorts.

Once packs of cards had arrived at Oflag VIIC at Laufen towards the end of 1940, as part of a consignment from the British Red Cross, card playing began in earnest. And among the keenest players was Bertie Harwood, a gambler since his Cambridge days. As well as bridge – 'the universal recreation' – Harwood and his friends established a chemmy (chemin de fer or baccarat) school. Harwood considered himself a good card player, but losses could be painful – especially when funds were running low – as he recounted:

> Another evening, playing in my room, I got up from the table losing 12 marks – about fifteen shillings. We normally settled up the following day and I went to bed in an agony of mind wondering how and where I was going to find the 12 marks. Lying awake I suddenly remembered that Jack had been sent out some money, via the Red

Cross, to buy a new set of upper dentures; his old set had inadvertently fallen out during our ridiculous battle in France, at a time he thought it prudent not to hang about and look for them. I decided to ask him if he could spare the 12 marks.

After the count parade [*Appell*] the next morning I grabbed hold of him.

'I hardly like to ask you, Jack, but I'm in a bit of a hole.'

'What's the matter now?' he said, sensing danger.

'The truth of the matter is . . . I hardly like to tell you . . . I feel an awful shit.'

'I suppose you want to borrow some money?'

'I'm afraid I do. Can you spare me 12 marks?' I felt I was asking for about ten thousand pounds.

'Good God! Do you think I'm a millionaire? Have you lost *twelve* marks gambling?' he asked incredulously.

'Yes. Isn't it a sod?' I told him I'd pay him back gradually and after quibbling for a while he consented to lend me the money. He wandered off muttering something about not having enough now to pay for his teeth. I knew this to be quite untrue and it didn't worry me. When I settled up that day I felt like Nuffield writing out the cheque for a new wing of a hospital.

Cards were not the only medium allowing gambling to flourish. Various board games were easily adapted for betting purposes. At Mühlhausen (a satellite camp of Stalag IXC at Bad Sulza) Bob Prouse and two fellow Canadians took over a horse-racing board game from some Australian POWs, and this game overshadowed poker and bridge in popularity until it was subsequently closed down by the Germans. (The German authorities showed little interest in gambling or other prisoner pastimes, but would intervene if they believed good order was being compromised.)

Australians were inveterate gamblers, and introduced two-up to the Stalags. A relatively simple game, it involved the throwing up of two coins from a wooden 'spinner', with the result depending on how the coins fell; betting was intense, and large sums of money or quantities of cigarettes were wagered on the outcome. For others, however, coins and pieces of wood were unnecessary. At Fort XV – part of the Stalag XXA complex at Thorn – one British observer noted the ability of Australian POWs to bet on virtually anything: 'I could usually find a group in fine weather sitting for hours on the top of the

Fort at a point overlooking the main railway that ran eastwards to the Russian front and increasingly carried troops and materials frontwards and casualties westwards. They were betting on the direction from which the next train would come.'

Perennial topics of speculation were the dates for the invasion of Europe and the end of the war. New prisoners tended to be highly optimistic, especially after any Allied military success; older prisoners sided with caution. When news of the Battle of Britain reached the RAF prisoners in Stalag Luft I in October 1940 a sweep was held for the correct date of victory in Europe. 'Most people forecast 1941,' wrote Jimmy James; 'only two predicted 1945. It was, perhaps, just as well that we did not suspect the weary years that lay ahead.'

Gambling thrived at the Milag merchant-navy camp. 'Every day the West Hall was opened up as a gambling den,' one seaman wrote. 'On entering, it reminded one at first glance of a low Western gambling saloon. Thick tobacco smoke hung in the air, crowds of men at roulette tables and poker schools, all were going in full swing. It was always difficult to move around between tables owing to the crowd.' In an attempt to re-create the excitement of track meetings, one gambler trapped mice to employ as the racing animals, but the idea was abandoned when the mice started fighting and killing each other before the race. Betting on human runners was more successful, with the annual sports day attracting its share of bookies from the self-styled Milag Jockey Club.

Other camps had their own bookmakers, who took bets on all sporting events. At Eichstätt, Harwood remembered one novelty competition, the 'pony race', in which the contestants were men under 5 foot 5 inches. Harwood wrote that 'colossal sums of money were won and lost on this ridiculous race. (I call it ridiculous because the one I backed came in second.)'

For Harwood and many other men, gambling was a means of injecting a little excitement into the monotony of camp life. But, as in the outside world, gambling claimed its victims, and it had the potential to dislocate the social balance within the camp. Senior British officers in the Oflags generally tolerated gambling – many were gamblers themselves – but they expected their fellow officers to be able to handle their losses with decorum.

In the Stalags, control was limited and gambling had an increased tendency to be disruptive. As a Presbyterian minister, Bob McDowall was naturally ill-disposed towards gambling of any form, although he enjoyed cards and was a keen bridge player. He had seen the damage gambling could do in his native New Zealand, and nothing he witnessed in the camps made him change his mind on the subject. While in PG 57 at Gruppignano, McDowall fulminated against the craze for two-up, and tried to have it stopped. 'Several men are mentally deranged or ill through betting,' he wrote, citing thefts in the camp as a consequence.

Towards the end of the war an attempt was made by the British War Office to ban gambling, and official letters to that effect were sent out to the camps, but they were generally ignored. In US camps, gambling was officially banned but went on nonetheless. Colonel Spivey, another enthusiastic bridge player, certainly disapproved of gambling, and asked his officers to play their games on a friendly basis only. He insisted that there should be no writing of cheques against home accounts, but this demand was quietly ignored by the officers of Center compound. The compunction to gamble was too strong, even for a man of Spivey's persuasive abilities.

Coexisting with gambling were the pastimes that the authorities preferred, the old-fashioned indoor hobbies of civilian and pre-camp life. During 1940, and at newly established camps, improvisation was at a premium. In PG 59 at Sevigliano one sergeant wrote home, 'We still find it a bit difficult to fill in time, but the chaps have made packs of cards, dice, Monopoly, Ludo, draughts and dominoes out of biscuit cartons etc. A case of necessity being the mother of invention.' The shortages were remedied by the Red Cross and the YMCA, which were quick to respond to requests for indoor games; as well as packs of cards, thousands of chess and draughts sets, darts, dominoes and proprietary board games were dispatched to Italy and Germany.

The range of hobbies taken up by the prisoners was limited only by their imagination. Knitting proved popular, in part because of its practical advantages, but rather more surprising was the interest shown in needlework. One convert to the pastime was Lieutenant General Sir Philip Neame, VC, in pre-war life a keen big-game hunter.

'It took a war,' wrote a fellow prisoner, 'to discover his latent talent as a tapestry maker in fine petit-point.'

British and American prisoners demonstrated their skill in mechanical construction, utilizing the most unlikely materials scrounged from within the camp and home-made, stolen or occasionally borrowed tools. In Stalag Luft I American POWs built model aircraft from bits of wood, while old powdered-milk cans were used to construct a working clock. At Stalag 383 the prisoners held an exhibition of their work, described by Vernon Cooper:

> There was quite a selection of embroidery and needlework and things made with a crochet hook fashioned out of a toothbrush handle. There were all kinds of things made in wood – wood carving and trinket boxes and models of ships and aircraft. There was a model of a 'Spitfire' which had an electric motor in it turning the propeller, the motor itself having been made from bits of scrap metal. But even this was a modest achievement compared with the model railway made by two or three men. This featured a scale model of an express locomotive with coaches and track – all made from scrap metal and tin cans. This train was running – powered by a handmade electric motor. This model railway was truly a marvel of ingenuity and skill. When the Red Cross representative saw the exhibition, he arranged for it to be conveyed to England to be exhibited there. The exhibition was staged in London to raise money for the Red Cross.

As enclosed institutions, prisoner-of-war camps were particularly prone to fads and other temporary enthusiasms. One former medical student at Stalag Luft III, who had received training in hypnotic therapy, instigated a brief craze for hypnosis. Ventriloquism also had its moment in several camps, but after a short time enthusiasm diminished and the prisoners moved on to something else. One craze that had a rather longer life than most was spiritualism. Sessions with Ouija boards and the moving tumbler were popular events in many barrack rooms, especially when prisoners were shut up during long winter nights. Although for most POWs this was just a slightly spooky form of entertainment, for others – many grounded in the vogue for spiritualism between the two world wars – it had greater meaning. A constant problem for the seance-holders, however, was the demand to know when the war would end. This was especially difficult to assess in the period before the Normandy invasion, and when dates came and went with no sign of peace or invasion (the mediums were recklessly optimistic) disillusionment and ridicule set in.

One of the stranger pastimes with which POWs amused themselves and onlookers were imaginary games. In PG 57 at Gruppignano, Doug LeFevre witnessed a fairly simple version. He described how POWs 'used to have a wash and do their hair and smarten themselves up, and they had a piece of string which they would drag along, and they would stop and talk to each other as if they had an imaginary dog. Anybody who saw them would think they were crackers but they weren't really.' At Stalag Luft VI at Heydekrug an RAF airman would shepherd a flock of invisible sheep around the compound. Jim Witte recalled how on one occasion four British prisoners at his work camp near Leipzig suddenly stopped work and played a perfectly choreographed imaginary game of snooker – watched in bemusement by the Germans and other foreign workers in the factory. These games could become increasingly elaborate, and one such piece of play in BAB 21 at Blechhammer was described by Roger Coward:

> A whole room of 24 men would agree to pretend that they were going on a day's outing, say, to Bournemouth. One man would be the engine-driver, another the guard and so on. The rest would be trippers. They would make a noise like a train; the guard would whistle and wave his flag; and the lot of them would form a line, each holding on to the one in front of him, and 'Choo-choo-choo!' all round the camp. The guards would stare in astonishment and grunt to each other '*Alles verrückt*' ('All mad!'). But, if we were, it was only that sort of madness that kept us sane.

Flower-growing became an ornament to the utilitarian vegetable plots that were dotted about a camp. Most horticulture parcels sent through the Red Cross included a few packets of flower seeds, and seedlings and bulbs could be bought from the Germans. In the US Oflag 64 at Schubin the grounds around the hospital block were decorated with a fine display of flowers. In Oflag VIIC at Laufen one British officer revealed his enthusiasm for gardening and nature in a letter home: 'We've made a splendid little rock garden and planted heaps of things in it. They have come up very well. We have two herbaceous borders with Borage, Lupins, Tulips etc. Trees heavenly and the swifts play about all day.'

Among the British officers at Laufen and at Oflag VIIB at Eichstätt were a group of birdwatchers who managed to transform their hobby by making a serious contribution to ornithology in post-war studies based on their observations behind the wire. John Buxton, a commando captured in Norway in 1940, wrote how he decided to put the time to good use:

> In the summer of 1940, lying in the sun near a Bavarian river, I saw a family of redstarts, unconcerned in the affairs of our skeletal multitude, going about their ways in cherry and chestnut trees. I made no notes then (for I had no paper), but when the next spring came, and with it, on a day of snow, the first returning redstarts, I determined that these birds should be my study for most of the hours I might spend out of doors. It seemed to me that we prisoners might watch some birds together, and that several of us working on one kind might discover more than if we tried to make notes on all the birds that should visit us.

Buxton's work was interrupted by the closure of Laufen, but he assembled a team at Eichstätt to begin a detailed study of a single pair of redstarts that comprised 850 hours of observation between April and June 1943. 'No pair of birds has ever been watched so continuously,' Buxton wrote, 'with their every movement recorded.' His work bore fruit with the publication of *The Redstart* in 1950.

Buxton was only one of a number keen ornithologists at Eichstätt, observing a variety of birds. Crested larks and goldfinches were studied by Peter Condor (later a director of the RSPB), wrynecks by George Waterston, swallows by Richard Purchon, and chaffinches by John Barrett.

Prisoners were allowed to keep cats, to deal with rats and mice, and these inevitably became pets. Birds and a few smaller animals were also kept, although the Germans forbade dogs or larger animals. A few months after the opening of Oflag VIIB at Eichstätt, Bertie Harwood estimated that there were a least 200 cats in the camp. 'It is true', he wrote, 'they were sometimes killed and eaten by a few of the more hungry prisoners but for the most part they were cared for and fed out of our own rations.'

★

Drawing and painting was another officially encouraged activity, and many prisoners found a formerly undiscovered talent with pencil and paintbrush. Once again the Red Cross and the YMCA provided materials, although these did not get through to all camps, leaving some erstwhile artists to make do with what they could find around them. Terry Frost and Adrian Heath initially salvaged old pillow cases for canvases, made their own brushes from horsehair, and recycled oil from sardine tins as a medium to mix what pigments they could find.

The actor Michael Goodliffe was also a talented artist. Besides a number of competent watercolours, he produced a series of distinctive pen-and-ink Christmas cards of the various prisons he was incarcerated in – a notable feature being the cloud formations in the shape of the British Isles. (The 1943 view of Eichstätt was published after the war in the *Illustrated London News*.)

Bertie Harwood drew his fellow prisoners: 'There was a great demand for pencil portraits which POWs could send home to their families; it was only on rare occasions that the Germans consented to take snapshots of groups. A few of us with a certain aptitude for this sort of thing were deluged with requests. I enjoyed doing the portraits as it passed the time and I felt I was giving pleasure.' While Harwood did his portraits for fun, other POW artists saw commercial possibilities: in the free economy of the camps, a marketable talent could recoup good rewards. In Stalag VIIIB/344 at Lamsdorf the going rate for a portrait sketch was twenty cigarettes.

Prisoners were issued with YMCA logbooks, and as well as recording their day-to-day experiences many men drew pictures and cartoons illustrating life in the camps. Bob Prouse, who would have been the first to admit he was no artist, left a visual commentary of his time in Stalag IXC at Bad Sulza to complement his prison memoirs.

Hobbies and painting were essentially solo pursuits – at times intensely absorbing to the individual, but obviously lacking in the shared nature of creative communal activity. And communal activity of one sort or another was needed for the well-being of a camp. Apart from sport, this was best provided by theatre and music. Such entertainment benefited both performer and audience. For the actor or musician it was a means to channel energy and an outlet for artistic expression that could absorb a man for months on end. For those in the stalls it was a brief return to civilian life, a source of pleasure when enjoyment was often in short supply. Many prisoners spoke of their joy at being transported from the often grim conditions of everyday life. One wrote, 'I almost forgot I was a prisoner yesterday evening when I went to our latest musical comedy', while another said, 'One could really get away from kriegiedom for a few hours, even if one was sitting in a converted Red Cross box.'

Despite seemingly insurmountable obstacles, nothing was allowed to get in the way of an ambitious programme of dramas, revues and music of all kinds. This did not mean that all productions were of a high order: as in life beyond the wire, standards varied widely. But the problems in getting a concert under way at all meant that both public and critics tended to be generous in their applause.

In Oflag VIID at Tittmoning Michael Goodliffe was the only professional actor in the camp, and in the summer of 1940 he was encouraged to put on shows to improve the men's morale:

> We had space for a theatre and unlimited time for rehearsal, but no stage, no lighting, no plays, no musical instruments, no make-up or costumes, very little money, and apart from my fellow pioneers, not many aspirants to stage fame. We had all been shaved completely bald by our captors 'as a precaution against lice', and as a final handicap our diet (mint tea and elderly potatoes) did not leave us with much energy to spare.

At Laufen, Harwood also experienced problems when 'the professional actors refused to be seen on stage with their heads shaved.' As a consequence, he and a few other amateurs instigated theatrical activity: 'We only put on sketches and short musical turns; I trotted out an old standby from my Footlights days and several others had their pet turns. On looking back on those early shows I can only marvel at the enthusiasm of the audience.' Once the professionals had regrown their hair they began to take a greater interest in the stage. Harwood graciously made way for them: 'Their knowledge and previous experience was, of course, invaluable. The first play we did was Galsworthy's *Escape* which Wally [Finlayson] put on. I played the "padre" (my first straight part) and it was a revelation to be produced by someone who knew the job so well.'

In Center compound, Spivey was determined to emulate the high standards of theatrical entertainment he had first encountered in the British-run North compound:

> We made approximately 250 seats out of Canadian Red Cross boxes, which proved to be very comfortable. They were placed on a reconstructed sloping floor so that there was an aisle on each side. We manufactured tickets, had ushers, and offered reserve seats for all regular performances. The stage was elaborate, with all kinds of lighting effects, including complete fade-outs for the whole auditorium and the stage. The spotlight operators had to lie on their stomachs under the ceiling in order to operate their spots. Rheostats [to dim the lights] were improvised, made with buckets of water and bits of cable, metal and wood . . . The stage became so contemporary that it even had a disappearing section and a revolving section. Nothing was too difficult or too trivial in detail to stump a Kriegie who had nothing but time on his hands.

Costumes were either handmade by the prisoners from blankets, uniforms and any material that could be scrounged or stolen, or were hired from the Germans on a parole basis, despite some (well-founded) reservations that they might be used in escape attempts. In the Bavarian camps of Tittmoning, Laufen and Eichstätt costumes and wigs came from the Munich Opera, while camps reasonably close to Berlin were able to draw upon the services of a theatrical costume company, reputedly the largest in the world. Although prepared to co-operate, the Germans charged a high price for costume hire. Scenery, furniture and other props were made by the prisoners, using anything to hand. The YMCA provided make-up and regular lighting equipment to supplement that scrounged by the prisoners themselves.

At the well-run Marlag and Milag Theatre (MMT) − which put on one or two shows a month throughout the life of the camp − improvisation was a way of life. Make-up was mixed by combining talcum powder, margarine and dyes extracted from crêpe paper. The headdresses for the MMT's acclaimed *Mikado* called for a novel approach. In order to simulate the hairstyles of the Japanese girls, mud was collected from the camp reservoir and slapped on to the actor's head, then removed and after further shaping was baked in an oven before the application of thin strips of paper hair.

Other materials came directly from the Germans without their knowledge. One of the MMT producers described the pleasure in hoodwinking their captors, despite other irritations: 'It was one of the banes of show business in captivity that the senior officers from miles around invited themselves to the opening night of each production. It did, however, lend a certain zest to realize that the officer who had that morning conducted an investigation into the loss of 40 light bulbs, some sheets and blankets, and a vacuum cleaner, could now espy the missing property by merely looking at the stage.'

Shows generally had long runs. In Center compound it was estimated that roughly ten performances were required for all the prisoners to see one play or concert. Tickets were usually allocated on a barrack-room/block basis, and the best seats were drawn by lots. First nights had the excitement and formality of their civilian equivalents, with front-row seats reserved for Axis officers, Red Cross and YMCA dignitaries, and senior Allied officers. Programmes were produced by a local printer, under German supervision, and camp newspapers reviewed the performance in their next issue. In some camps the audience even dressed up for the occasion.

Photographs of some performances reveal surprisingly well-made and imaginative sets; those designed by Michael Yates at Eichstätt and Peter Peel in Stalag VIIIB at Teschen were outstanding. Although his background was as a commercial artist, Peel was also a competent actor, and he appeared as Sebastian in *Twelfth Night*, playing opposite Denholm Elliott's Viola. Elliott was to have a successful post-war acting career, as were other British POWs including Peter Butterworth, Rupert Davies, Roy Dotrice, Clive Dunn, Michael Goodliffe and Sam Kydd. The Germans were sufficiently impressed by the Stalag VIIIB production of *Twelfth Night* to allow the theatre group to tour other camps, scenery included.

Michael Goodliffe organized two well-regarded productions of *Hamlet*, while another performance of the same play at Stalag Luft III's North compound in 1943 bowled over the newly captured Delmar Spivey. 'I was given a choice seat to see *Hamlet*,' he wrote:

> The costumes were the best in the world. The actors were trained within an inch of their lives, every man having spent hundreds of hours perfecting his part under highly professional guidance. I was absolutely

carried away both by the performance and by the music, which was played from a real orchestra pit. The stage trappings were beautifully done and the 'women' were so realistic that at first I could scarcely believe any man could impersonate so perfectly.

The playing of female roles by male actors was initially a cause for merriment among the camp audiences, but this attitude swiftly changed, and Goodliffe found that 'unless the presentation of female roles was intelligently tackled any serious productions were impossible.' According to Vernon Cooper at Stalag 383, the solution to the problem of finding the right sort of person to play female parts was not primarily a question of finding men 'good looking enough to pass as girls when suitably made up, but rather men who could act and who braved the challenge of playing a female role'.

Dedicated actors and producers worked hard on the classics and productions from the pre-war repertoire. POWs generally preferred lighter pieces – especially revues and comedies in which music and theatre came together. These were also easier to produce and perform. Gilbert and Sullivan was a favourite with the British, while minstrel shows and reworkings of Hollywood and Broadway musicals worked best with the Americans. Camps also wrote their own entertainments, which, as well as the usual comedies, included some straight dramas. Spivey encouraged each barrack block to write and produce a simple one-act play for performance in the compound theatre.

Almost inevitably, comedy was divided along national lines, with British and Americans separately adapting comic routines of the day to special POW circumstances. Another distinction was the radio show. While the British staged the occasional radio play (with scripts from the BBC), the Americans replicated the radio shows that had become commonplace in the United States during the 1930s. In Stalag Luft III radio shows, complete with spoof advertisements, were actually broadcast over the camp public-address system, with compounds having their own facetious call signs: WPOW for Center and KRGY for South. They proved a good vehicle for satirizing recent camp events while simultaneously acting as a reminder of home.

Films were shown in most camps on occasion. Some were silent (but provided with ribald commentaries from the prisoners), though most were German 'talkies', with a few old British and American releases. In Stalag IIB at Hammerstein, after accepting parole, the prisoners were escorted into the local town to watch a film, but vociferous complaints from local people regarding 'soft treatment' of POWs brought this experiment to an abrupt end. Films never made the impact of theatre: they were too few in number, and lacked the involvement of live performance.

Gramophones – along with heavy, brittle shellac 78-rpm records – found their way into the camps, most being supplied by the YMCA and the Indoor Recreations Fund, with others bought directly from the Germans. Some camps were well equipped – Oflag VIB at Warburg apparently had the use of 250 gramophones with a good stock of records – while others were less fortunate and might have only a few in the entire camp. In the otherwise generally well-equipped Stalag Luft III, gramophones had to circulate around the barracks: each block had its own private record session once a month. The wind-up gramophones were not dependent on an uncertain electricity supply, and so were able to play music outside or after lights out. For music-lovers they were a lifeline to another world, for musical educators they were a valuable illustrative tool, and for others they provided a generally pleasant accompaniment to camp life. In one of the RAF compounds at Stalag Luft III, 'Time on My Hands' became the signature tune of the dance club.

Music performed live was what really mattered, however, and the prisoners threw as much enthusiasm into this as they did into their acting. Until instruments and sheet music could be secured from the YMCA, the Red Cross or the Germans, POW musicians had to rely on the human voice and good memories. A padre captured in 1940 remembered his arrival at Fort XV in the Stalag XXA complex around Thorn: 'The first sound I ever heard in Fort XV was a choir of twenty men singing out a triumphant rendering of "And the Glory of the Lord" from the *Messiah*. None of the singers could read music, and they had learnt every note of the parts by ear from their conductor, Corporal Brown of the Royal West Kent Regiment, who had been a chorister at Westminster Cathedral.'

In 1940 the bulk of British officers captured in France were sent to Laufen, which was a former palace of the Archbishop of Salzburg,

Mozart's sometime patron. Perhaps appropriately, the camp contained an unusually large proportion of musically gifted and energetic officers. Among these was Lieutenant Richard Wood, a rifleman captured at Calais and a professional singer in civilian life. He described the beginnings of music at Laufen:

> We were a dismal lot when we arrived in June, hungry, with a defeatist complex mostly, and found ourselves in overcrowded quarters, with no books, and with nothing to do. The first concerts were sing-song affairs, very popular, and continued to be so when they eventually moved into the theatre . . . In early October some instruments dispatched by the YMCA in Geneva arrived, and from that moment real musical work could start. What an opportunity for music! 1,600 men with nothing to do, nothing to read, little food, little warmth, and getting only intermittent letters. How quiet and how orderly the sound of the concert compared to the continual pandemonium in the rooms! No wonder anyone would come to any show, no matter what it was, either to enjoy, fill up time, or to have a real seat of one's own and a quiet read!

The YMCA provided most musical material, and tried to ensure that each camp would have enough instruments to form a good-sized dance band and a small orchestra. This meant a certain amount of doubling-up of instruments, with saxophones sometimes taking the place of horns in the orchestra. The Red Cross also organized the dispatch of complete 'compact orchestras' to smaller camps; those destined for Italy comprised a large piano accordion, two violins, two banjos, a guitar, a trumpet, four ukuleles, and a set of drums. The sending of sheet music could cause problems with the Axis censors: they were suspicious that the notes might be concealing a code, and the Italians – who were unhelpful in these matters – banned the sending of sheet music altogether. Both Germans and Italians did, however, allow Allied POWs to buy instruments and music and manuscript paper from local sources.

The main musical styles played to listeners were classical, dance band and jazz. All were popular, and many men felt that their musical knowledge had been enriched by their POW experience; prisoner narratives often speak of the uplifting effect of performances of classical music, whether on gramophone or played live. The musicians gained much from being able to perform, although they sometimes bemoaned the conservatism of their audiences. The banned composer Felix Mendelssohn (of Jewish ancestry) was popular with performers, as they could take quiet satisfaction in knowing they were reintroducing his music to Germany, albeit in a limited way.

The American airmen in Center compound were short of experienced musicians, especially when compared to some of the other compounds. A Glen Miller band – under the baton of Major C. R. Diamond – was based in the American South compound and performed a highly successful tour of the other compounds in November 1943, the only fly in the ointment being an overloud rendition of the US and British national anthems which was heard by the commandant and led to a temporary impounding of the band's instruments.

Music in Center compound began to prosper with the arrival of Henry 'Nick' Nagorka, a former student of the Warsaw Conservatory and graduate of the Juilliard School of Music. 'Nick Nagorka', wrote Spivey,

> organized a sixty-piece symphony orchestra which practised hour after hour, while Johnny Ward whipped up one of the loudest and fanciest jazz bands I have ever heard. After we got our loudspeaker system and hundreds of symphonic recordings from the YMCA, we would darken the theater in the early afternoon and Nick would play Mozart, Beethoven, or some other famous composer, explaining the music as it was played. The theater would almost always be filled on such occasions.

Finding suitable places to practise and rehearse was a chronic problem, especially for beginners. In an overcrowded camp, a novice making his first forays on an instrument like the violin could cause much pain to fellow prisoners. At PG 78 Jim Witte noted that a hut was specially set aside for the use of the 'mad musicians'; at Laufen the cells were used as rehearsal rooms; at Eichstätt piano practice took place in a potato store, where the smell of rotting potatoes could be asphyxiating, while the washroom became a trombonist's semi-permanent home.

Despite the lack of space in the main camps, these musicians could be considered fortunate in receiving instruments and music at all. For those in isolated work camps, materials and facilities were few. But where there was sufficient enthusiasm great things were possible. At the small agricultural camp at Koseltiz – one of 190 or so satellite work camps of Stalag XXA – there was a small but thriving musical community: David Wild wrote, 'Among the twelve men perhaps two [were] competent musicians, one of them something of a composer. In the course of time all the other men on the party had taken up and learnt to play some instrument, and so they had formed a band. When any of them heard of an instrument for sale in the neighbourhood, they pooled their available *Lagergeld* to buy it.'

For sheer musical accomplishment the laurels would have go to a group of musicians who came together at Laufen in the summer of 1940, and with the closing of the camp moved to Warburg and then to Eichstätt. While other camps had good orchestras, dance bands and choirs, what singled out this group was its ambition: once a successful performance had been given, something bigger and better was attempted next.

The first project was a re-creation of the King's College Chapel Festival of Nine Lessons and Carols, given at the prisoners' first Christmas, in 1940. Sheet music was in short supply, so that music and words were taken down from memory and the result was scored for male voices and orchestra. Three separate performances were given to accommodate all the POWs. A large Christmas tree was erected, lit by candles. 'The lessons were read just to one side of the tree,' Richard Wood wrote, 'the whole room was beautifully decorated in green and silver, two ugly stoves cast out a warm glow and we all felt very near home. The choir sang really beautifully and the whole service was a revelation.' The Laufen music group grew in size and proficiency, and an abridged version of Bach's *St Matthew Passion* was chosen to celebrate Easter 1941. The project was all-involving, as Wood explained: 'Getting the musical score and four vocal parts; translating, arranging choral and orchestral parts; teaching the singers and players (the Jesus by ear, for the copy put him off), lecturing on it, and fitting in rehearsals, was an adventure in itself.'

The genesis of the next musical project came to Wood while shaving one morning in October 1943. 'I had often had in my mind the thought of a musical festival,' he wrote, 'and now the whole idea unfolded and the rough (though fairly detailed) form of the Festival took shape there and then.' Planning began at the end of October, and the Eichstätt Music Festival opened on 18 February 1944.

Six concerts were organized: symphonic, light orchestral, choral and orchestral, dance band, chamber music, and a show entitled 'Round the World with Song and Dance'. The high point of the festival was a specially commissioned choral piece from Benjamin Britten – *The Ballad of Little Musgrave and Lady Barnard* – which received its world premiere behind barbed wire. The origins of the work went back to the winter of 1942–3 when Wood received records of Britten's *Seven Sonnets of Michelangelo*. Under the auspices of the Red Cross, Wood wrote to Britten to say how much he enjoyed the song cycle, and asked him to write something for the prisoners at Eichstätt. Britten readily agreed, although through the procrastination of British censors the piece arrived only in mid-February 1944, leaving just three weeks of frantic copying and rehearsal before its premiere in the choral and orchestral concert.

Britten dedicated the piece to 'Richard Wood and the musicians of Oflag VIIB'. For music-lovers more attuned to Schubert and Mozart, Britten's extended ballad, lasting eight to nine minutes, was undeniably difficult. Wood described its reception: 'The choir (35 to 40 voices) started by cordially disliking the work but finally they all thoroughly enjoyed it. It grew on us all the time and the audience took to it immediately or were at least brought up short by it.' One suspects the latter, although there was sufficient demand for four separate performances. Altogether, the festival lasted 33 days, during which there were 35 performances and a total attendance of 6,663, from an overall prison population of around 1,800 men. Under any circumstances the Eichstätt Music Festival would have been a noteworthy event; in a prisoner-of-war camp it was nothing less than a triumph.

Those individuals engaged in artistic activity had an advantage over their fellow prisoners. Not only did their endeavours defeat the dreaded enemy boredom – with all its attendant problems – they were also able to transform what might have been wasted years into journeys of self-discovery and artistic enrichment. Terry Frost's experience at Stalag 383 was a springboard to a career as a distinguished artist; young actors such as Denholm Elliott employed their time in captivity as an extension of their drama studies; and Richard Wood was given the opportunity to conduct, arrange and organize music on a scale otherwise impossible for a budding singer in pre-war London.

When Wood summed up his time as a POW musician he could have spoken for the other various artists in the scattered barbed-wire world: 'Those of us who were doing music had the very good fortune to have a daily job. For five years I had the great joy of seeing a community thrive on music, more and more music, better and better music . . . And I am convinced that, through the music we were able to do, many of us have brought back either a deeper, or a new, permanent happiness in our lives.'

9

The Written Word: Internal Escape and
Self-Improvement

'WE COULD NOT have lived without books,' wrote RAF officer Robert Kee. 'They were the only sure support, the one true comfort. When food was short, clothing scarce, blocks overcrowded and underheated, and war news bad, there were always books. In reading one had a pleasure of which, like sleep, one could never be deprived. I remember the books which I read in that time with a great love.'

Many other prisoner narratives echo Kee's praise for the temporary liberation provided by reading. Captain John A. Vietor, in Stalag Luft I at Barth, considered the library to be 'the most important morale factor in [the] camp'. Vietor made a list of his reading – a common practice among POWs – and by the time of his release he had worked his way through 212 books, a rough average of 15 volumes a month, ranging from literary classics – Shakespeare, Thackeray, the Brontës, Dickens, Twain and Conrad – through westerns and detective mysteries to history and biography.

In Kee and Vietor, educated at Oxford and Yale respectively, a passion for books was hardly surprising, but zeal for the printed word extended beyond academic circles to include men with little formal education. Jim Witte, who had left school at 14, found reading a consolation in his North African transit camp:

> The best antidote to boredom that I know of is a book, any book. I bought a Sexton Blake off a chap for five English fags and went away well content. After I had finished reading how the great detective tracked the master criminal I went round the barrack room, calling out, 'Any books to change?' I soon got an offer; this time it was a lurid gangster yarn well laced with amatory adventures in down-town hotels. But what I really wanted was a hardback with some meat in it. There was a studious-looking soldier lying down on his pit with a large

tome propped on his chest, which must have taken some lugging around. I got chatting to him and asked whether he would care to swop it for my well-thumbed James Hadley Chase, plus ten English fags. To my surprise he jumped at the chance and I became the owner of William Prescott's *History of the Conquest of Mexico and Peru.*

Even gambling-mad British Guards and cavalry officers were not immune to the enchantment of reading, and a few turned away from the card tables to the library. In the Italian camp PG 49 at Fontanellato, Eric Newby only half-humorously described an outburst by one such officer to his fellows: 'Since I've been captured I've been locked up alone for a bit and I've been thinkin'. I've decided to take up readin' and I've written to Mummy askin' her to send me the *Tatler* and the *Book of the Month.'*

Among the committed, books were a compulsion. When they were scarce, anything would be read. While Jack Vietor was in solitary in Dulag Luft a guard handed him a book of pro-German propaganda ostensibly disproving German atrocities in Belgium in 1914. 'For lack of other entertainment,' Vietor recalled, 'I read it four times.' The Revd David Read, a chaplain with the 51st Highland Division, captured at Saint-Valéry in 1940, was disconsolate when he discovered that his haversack containing a Bible and Herbert Read's anthology *The Knapsack* had been stolen in the aftermath of the battle. He railed against the prospect of being 'utterly bookless', and was correspondingly delighted when he remembered that tucked away in a pocket was a miniature Greek Testament. During rests on the long march across France towards captivity in Germany, Read was able to console himself by attempting 'to commit to memory the Greek of the Prologue of St John'.

Fortunately for British and American prisoners of war, Allied humanitarian organizations made the supply of books a priority. Under the overall control of the International Committee of the Red Cross, based in Geneva, a number of bodies, led by the various national Red Cross organizations and the YMCA, began to organize a book-supply system from October 1939 onwards.

In Britain, the Red Cross set up the Educational Book Section in February 1940, to supply books of solid worth to assist in the education of POWs, while later in the year the somewhat more frivolous Fiction and Games Section (subsequently renamed the

Indoor Recreations Section) was appointed for the dispatch of light reading along with games of Monopoly, chess, draughts, dominoes and packs of cards. When the United States entered the war in December 1941, the American Red Cross handed over the responsibility of supplying books to the YMCA, which already had a system in place in 1939 complete with book-distribution centres in neutral Sweden and Switzerland. Private individuals were also allowed to send one 5-lb book parcel per month, although it could not come directly from the individual but was to be dispatched from a bookseller or publisher, which forwarded it to the appropriate censorship office, either in Oxford or in New York.

All books were double-censored, first in the Allied country and then in Germany or Italy. On the Allied side, the prohibitions were quite straightforward: nothing was to be sent abroad that might aid the Axis, so that, for example, books containing detailed maps, charts and tide tables of the home country were banned (or the offending articles were removed), as were works on weapons and the military as well as the latest scientific and technical books.

In Germany, and to a lesser extent Italy, the situation was more complex. Beside a standard prohibition on books that might help any potential escaper or saboteur, the sender also had to be careful not to offend the delicate sensibilities of the totalitarian state. Anything that might be seen to disparage modern Germany and Italy – and especially their leaders – was banned, as were works by émigré, Communist and Jewish authors, as well as those who promoted internationalist causes. The strange and often arbitrary nature of Axis censorship was revealed in these comments by Major Elliot Viney, POW librarian in Oflag VIIB at Eichstätt:

> It is interesting to note that [H. A. L.] Fisher's *History of Europe* was forbidden by the Germans not for the chapter on Nazi Germany, but because of the first sentence of the Introduction ['We Europeans are the children of Hellas']. The banned list was extraordinarily thorough, but had some delightful omissions: John Buchan's war novels *Greenmantle*, *Mr Standfast* and so on were forbidden, but the omnibus *Adventures of Richard Hannay* remained untouched; the American novelist Winston Churchill was of course banned in toto, but *My Early Life* by Winston Spencer Churchill was not attributed to the then Prime Minister and was let in. Other gems on the black list were the

Golden Treasury (because Palgrave was a Jew) to *Scouting for Boys* (the Boy Scouts are of course a vital part of the British Secret Service); Spinoza's ethics were banned on racial, *Gil Blas* on patriotic, and *No Orchids for Miss Blandish* on moral, grounds. However, there were usually ways of evading censorship, and the only banned work we never succeeded in obtaining was the most curious of all – the English translation of *Mein Kampf*.

Italian censorship was similarly random. Edward Ward, held at PG 78 at Sulmona, noted how the censor let through an anti-fascist book, *Fontamara* by Ignazio Silone, but confiscated a copy of *Alice's Adventures in Wonderland*.

On one occasion, at least, an unsuitable book slipped through the censorship net, with unfortunate consequences for the prisoners. After his transfer from Oflag VIIC at Laufen to Stalag XXID at Posen in 1941, Lieutenant Harwood and his comrades underwent a routine search. 'We queued up,' wrote Harwood, 'and were furious to find they were confiscating all our treasured "Penguin" books (we had bought little else because "Penguins" were so light and easy to carry).' An advertisement on the back cover of a Penguin book had aroused German anger by including a drawing of a British soldier with fixed bayonet chasing a cartoon Hitler. The result was a mass confiscation of all Penguin books, although the ban was subsequently relaxed.

To guide private book-buyers in making suitable choices, and to avoid censorship gaffes, the Allied Red Cross provided some useful tips. As a weight-saving exercise, paper-bound Pocket Library reprints were recommended over hardbacks (all weights being helpfully appended with prices). Florence Haxton Bullock, a book reviewer for the *New York Herald-Tribune*, put forward a list that included *The Forest and the Fort* by Hervey Allen (an adventure tale of Native Americans and frontiersmen; $2.50, 1 lb), the hefty *The Valley of Decision* (a family epic centred on the Pittsburgh steel industry; $3, 1¾ lb) and *The Robe* by Lloyd C. Douglas (an aristocratic Roman soldier embraces Christianity; $3, 1 lb). For the 'literary-minded' Miss Haxton Bullock recommended the *Penguin Book of Sonnets* and the *Pocket Book of Verse* (both 25 cents and ¼ lb).

Not all reading matter was quite so prim and proper. Canadian airman Flight Lieutenant Dallas Lasky was held in Stalag Luft III. His hut received a copy of D. H. Lawrence's *Lady Chatterley's Lover*, then banned in Britain. He wrote, 'I remember when *Lady Chatterley's Lover* came into our room, it came in units of ten pages, and you'd read ten and pass them along.'

Books poured into Germany and, to a lesser extent, Italy. Exact numbers are hard to quantify. Over a million books from the YMCA were sent to American POWs alone. The US-based *Publishers Weekly* estimated that over half a million books were dispatched to Anglo-American prisoners in Germany in 1943, with double that number in 1944. And when the American and British POWs were liberated, in 1945, approximately a million books were left behind on the camp shelves.

The flow of books into Germany and Italy took time, however. For those captured in the summer of 1940 the painful wait for reading matter lasted several months, and new camps usually had few books with which to start a library. Supply tended to be worse in Italy, mainly because the Italian censors were more suspicious than their German counterparts and took longer to assess a book's suitability for dispatch to a POW camp.

Jim Witte marched into PG 78 at Sulmona with the first large batch of prisoners in the summer of 1941. Facilities were sparse throughout 1941, although a small library had been organized by some of the original, mainly naval, prisoners. Witte described its rough-and-ready nature: 'On issuing day one of the matelots appeared with about fifty books, which he laid on the floor, whilst the queue remained outside. He opened the door and we all surged in, grabbing the nearest book. It didn't matter what it was about as long as you got one. When you had read it, you returned it to the matelot, who dished it out again. Next time you tried for another.'

In the officers' camp of PG 21 at Chieti, a few miles to the east of Sulmona, there was no library at all until early 1943. A few books were in circulation through the camp, but these remained in private hands as a precious bartering resource. David Westheimer, shot down over Italy in December 1942, was among the first of a growing number of Americans in Chieti. Once established in the camp, he began the search for something to read. 'Men who owned books', he wrote, 'tended to trade reads and what books were available to nonowners had long waiting lists, so I became an owner, trading fifty cigarettes to Peter Glenn for *Dombey and Son*. I didn't buy *Dombey* because I was partial to Dickens. I'd only read him when I'd had to in school. I bought *Dombey* because it was the only book on the market.'

Fifty cigarettes seemed a high price to pay – especially set against the five that secured Witte his first Sexton Blake mystery – but it turned out to be currency well spent, as Westheimer became an enthusiastic Dickensian, reading most of the classic novels before liberation in Germany in 1945. *Dombey and Son* also became a useful device for securing further books, as Westheimer described:

> Books trickled into the camp from the Red Cross and the YMCA and from British personal parcels. The prisoner staff started a library in one of the small front rooms across the road from our bungalow. There weren't enough books on the shelves for general circulation so the library had a priority system. Contribute two books, you got an A card and went first. One, a B card and went second. No card got the leavings, and very slim pickings they were. I contributed *Dombey and Son* and got a B card. After that I read a lot.

Libraries grew steadily over time, so that those in long-established camps, especially the Oflags, were substantial entities by 1945. The librarian at Eichstätt recalled that the camp library had started (at Laufen) with 40 books donated by the YMCA in June 1940, and expanded to 15,000 by 1945. By the end of the war the camp also had 60,000 privately owned books, many of these circulating among the prisoner population on an informal basis. This impressive tally reflected both the good work of official organizations like the YMCA and the British Red Cross and the generosity of the officers' friends and relatives.

Other camps tended to have more modest resources. Fairly typical was the US officers' camp Oflag 64 at Schubin. Roger Shinn made good use of the camp library, profiting from a wide array of books that included E. M. Forster's *Passage to India*. The Oflag 64 library grew from a small nucleus of 250 volumes in June 1943 to around 7,000 titles by January 1945. Over 250 books were taken out daily, with fiction dominating the withdrawals. Among the more popular choices were *Arundel* by Kenneth Roberts, *Lee's Lieutenants* by Douglas Freeman and *The Robe* by Lloyd C. Douglas. The library held thirty-five copies of the last of these – a reflection, perhaps, of the strength of Florence Haxton Bullock's recommendation. (After a year's wait, Bob Prouse got hold of a copy of *The Robe* just before his camp was evacuated in April 1945 – 'I managed to read it while marching and found it took my mind off the aches and the pains.')

In the Stalags, book provision varied widely. Although some libraries held a reasonable number of titles – Stalag IIB at Hammerstein had around 5,000 in August 1943, rising to 10,500 in November 1944; Stalag IIIB at Fürstenberg over 6,000 by December 1944 – others were poorly provided for: Stalag XIIA at Limburg (albeit a transit camp) had apparently acquired just fifteen volumes by the autumn of 1944, and in Stalag IIIA at Luckenwalde, in the final months of the war, reading was confined to private books, each with a waiting list of twenty to thirty names written on the flyleaf.

Non-working NCOs had the time to read and access to POW libraries; privates and working NCOs were not so fortunate, and for those men in isolated industrial and agricultural detachments an English-language book could be a rare commodity. One attempt to get books to working POWs was the institution of 'travelling libraries' (*Wanderbüchereien*). Boxes capable of holding up to fifty volumes were sent from the main camp to work detachments, where they would be circulated among the men for a period of three weeks before being returned to be replaced by another box. Unfortunately for those POWs in work detachments, the system was not common in practice.

Writing, a companion activity to reading, provided POWs with an opportunity for self-expression and communication. To write and receive letters was essential to most POWs' well-being, acting as a tangible link with home and an expression of hope for a future beyond the wire. Under the terms of the Geneva Convention, other ranks were allowed to send two letters and four postcards per month. Officers were given a higher monthly letter allocation: junior officers up to four letters; senior officers, padres and medical officers up to six letters. Both incoming and outgoing letters were censored by the Axis and the Allies, which forced writers to be circumspect in what they wrote.

The volume of mail was enormous, and put the postal and censorship services under great strain. In November 1943 Stalag 383 at

Hohenfels had a population of just over 4,500 men, and during a single week in that month 8,052 letters were sent and 5,586 letters received. The average time for a letter to arrive in Hohenfels was 32 days from Britain, 42 days from Canada and 72 days from Australia and New Zealand – but the service was not only slow, it was maddeningly arbitrary. Jack Vietor's description of mail deliveries at Stalag Luft I is fairly typical:

> Mail arrived inconsistently and irregularly, being first sent to Sagan, Stalag Luft III [for censorship], and then forwarded to us. On the average a prisoner did not receive his first letter until eight months after being shot down. The inconsistency was extraordinary. One man received a weekly letter from his family for two years. Another received thirty-six letters all at once, all written on different dates. Smedley [a room-mate] received two letters from his wife on the same day. One had been mailed in March 1943, and the other in March 1945.

Waiting for a letter could be agonizing, as David Westheimer in PG 21 at Chieti remembered. 'During mail call', he wrote, 'I couldn't breathe listening for my name. When it wasn't called I'd almost be physically ill with disappointment. And when it was, let Heaven and Nature sing.' After more than six months in captivity, RAF Sergeant Richard Passmore received his first mail – two letters from his family that had a profoundly beneficial effect. Passmore wrote, 'It would be no empty cliché to say that a new life awoke within me. Those letters were the end of a precious lifeline and I put them down after the umpteenth reading and consciously resolved that I should never again accept the possibility of not returning home, that somehow and however difficult the intervening years might be, I should bear with them.'

Not all letters brought good news. The fear of wives and fiancées deserting them was common among prisoners, and when, in rare instances, it was confirmed by letter the result could be devastating. The break-up of the relationship was made worse by the prisoner's helplessness, confined and isolated far from his loved one. In defiant mood, some prisoners apparently pinned their Dear John letters on camp noticeboards, along with other crassly written missives. Over time they entered camp folklore, becoming increasingly apocryphal as time went on (the half-dozen or so favourites are repeated almost verbatim in rather too many POW memoirs). Flying Officer N. G. Price in Stalag Luft I recorded these chestnuts:

I'm so glad you were shot down, before flying became dangerous.

Our engagement has ended, as I'd rather marry a '44 hero than a '43 coward.

A POW thanked a woman in England for a sweater received via the Red Cross; he received this reply: 'I am sorry to hear that you got my sweater as I knitted it for a fighting man.'

Don't bother to hurry home as I am living with an American and having a lovely time, I'm having his baby soon but forgive me as Mother has done. Ted is sending you cigarette parcels.

Letters could contain other unpleasant surprises. On Christmas Day 1944 Jack Vietor was pleased to receive three letters from home. 'Got my first two from my father,' he wrote, 'filled with news and after reading them, opened the third one. It was from a friend offering condolences for the death of my father. It was a stunning shock and with his letters lying in front of me, even though they were dated in October, it was unbelievable news. I had made so many plans of what we might do together when I returned. For the next two months I continued to receive letters from him.' Bob McDowall had had some inkling that his mother was close to death: 'Got my first letter from [wife] Pat today and two lovely photos. Mum died five months ago. I had so long expected it that it did not so deeply affect me as I thought it would. Writing to her so often and knowing in all prob- ability that she was not there had made me feel quite prepared.'

YMCA logbooks were an invaluable aid to jotting down notes, making drawings, writing verse, or maintaining a diary or journal. Other writing materials were also made available by the YMCA and Red Cross, or could be obtained from the Germans, so that few men were without an opportunity of making a record of their time in captivity. A common reason cited by POWs for keeping a diary or notebook was simply to stave off boredom, but behind this was the desire to preserve an important period of their lives. These essentially private writings were retained by thousands of POWs through their captivity and beyond. Many were forgotten, left in drawers or attic boxes; some were subsequently lodged in museums and libraries, and a few prepared for publication.

The other type of writing was public – writing not for family or self and posterity, but for fellow POWs through contributions to newspapers and magazines. The first camp newspapers were usually handwritten (occasionally typed with a borrowed machine) on to single sides of paper and passed among the POWs or, more usually, pinned up on noticeboards. These simple, single-copy bulletin-board papers were easy to produce, and if a publication failed then others would arise to take its place. One such publication produced daily at PG 53 consisted of six handwritten pages posted on a noticeboard at 8 o'clock each morning.

The great leap forward was to produce a printed multi-copy version, making possible proper camp-wide circulation. Such a move normally involved the co-operation of the captors, which in turn forced the papers to moderate any anti-Axis sentiments. The British *Prisoner's Pie*, produced in Stalag XXA at Thorn, was of a semi-professional standard, with 480 copies printed outside the camp and distributed free of charge. It contained the usual news of activities in the main camp and its satellite work detachments, with crosswords, puzzles, competitions, cartoons, drawings and short stories.

The forging of links between the main and the work camps was one of the reasons behind the publication of *Barbs and Gripes*, the camp paper of the Americans in Stalag IIB at Hammerstein. The predominantly agricultural work detachments contributed their own features to the paper, under such titles as 'Down on the Farm' and 'Out in the Fields', with some fairly heavy-handed humour thrown in for good measure – 'IIB or not IIB' on whether life was better in the main or a work camp. Other elements of the paper included a section on educational matters, reviews of camp plays, classified ads, and a 'Letters from Home' column.

Stalag Luft III proved to be fertile ground for the growth of journalistic talent, with several papers and magazines in each of the five compounds. In Center compound, Spivey oversaw the activities of two papers – the *Gefangenen Gazette* and the *Kriegie Times* – and a short-lived but highly admired magazine, the *New Yorker*, based closely on its famous namesake. Due to paper shortages, they were single-issue bulletin-board publications, but were highly popular with the POWs.

POW WOW, the underground news-sheet of Stalag Luft I, claimed to be 'The Only Truthful Newspaper in Germany'. Making effective use of the BBC news picked up by the camp's clandestine radio, it ran continuously from March 1944 to May 1945, despite German efforts to have it suppressed. Once copies of the paper had been read they were destroyed, to prevent them falling into German hands. *POW WOW*'s finest hour came with the special D-Day edition ('to be read silently, quickly, in groups of three') which scooped news of the landings twenty minutes before New York.

Closely associated with the newspaper was the newsroom, where all information – from German and, where there was a radio, Allied sources – was collated and a digest of the progress of the war issued to the camp. The task of dissemination was performed by individuals acting as 'town criers' relaying information around the barrack blocks, or through a newsboard with a map plotting the progress of the Allied advances.

Not all publications were intended for a general camp readership: some were the private, literary expressions of a small group, others club journals or hobby magazines. One of the simplest was *Our Mag* from Stalag VIIIB at Lamsdorf, a 36-page exercise book passed around twenty-one men who recorded their thoughts and observations of camp life. In the British camps, county and town associations were common and some published magazines. One of the more ambitious was produced by the White Rose Club in Stalag Luft VI at Heydekrug, taking the form of a house journal entitled the *Yorkshire Post: Kriegie Edition* (subsequently reprinted as a souvenir edition by the actual Yorkshire paper).

Of the hobby magazines, particularly outstanding was *The Flywheel*, produced by the MMC (Mühlberg Motoring Club) in Stalag IVB at Mühlberg from May 1944 to March 1945. The MMC began life as a group of six POWs who wanted to fill time and indulge their shared interest in motor vehicles. The club soon grew to be 200 strong, and club president Tom Swallow suggested producing a magazine.

Resources were particularly scarce, even by Stalag standards. Writing some time after the war, Swallow described how Arthur Pill, the 'production manager', managed to get the magazine up and running: 'There was nothing to write on and nothing to write with but by adopting a system of beg, borrow, buy or barter (stealing from

Jerry was taken for granted), he slowly began to get his act together. Arthur begged a pen-holder, borrowed a nib, bought some ink with *Lagergeld* (camp money) and bartered cigarettes for something to write on. Someone liberated some quinine tablets from the German sick bay for colour.' Millet soup – a staple at Stalag IVB – was left for a few days to ferment into a strong glue and used to stick down the artwork.

A particular feature of the magazine was the quality of the illustrations – most by Bill Stobbs and Dudley Mumford – and the hand lettering by Tom Rodger, who took the contributors' articles and painstakingly rewrote them on to the exercise-book paper of *The Flywheel*. Swallow described the difficulties faced by Rodger while working within a barrack-block environment: 'It was not very easy trying to hand script a magazine in a room occupied by about 200 other inmates each doing his own "thing" such as making mugs and plates from empty tins, trying out newly written songs on home-made instruments, rehearsing plays, shouting, singing, cursing and farting (the food was awful!).'

Although there were a number of articles on the car of the future, as well as pieces on motor sport and practical advice on repairs and engineering, much of the magazine's content looked back nostalgically to the world of pre-war motoring. Contributors wrote about their experiences in Britain and abroad, and Bob McDowall took time away from his pastoral duties to write a couple of articles on motoring expeditions through New Zealand.

Some German-published magazines and newspapers were available in the Oflags and, despite their obvious propaganda tone, before being consigned to their inevitable fate as toilet paper they were read by those wishing to improve their German. English-language versions of *Der Adler* (the Luftwaffe magazine) and *Signal* (based significantly on *Time* magazine, using many colour photographs) had a wider readership. Towards the end of 1944, as conditions worsened in Germany, the supply of magazines began to dry up, with just a few titles, such as the Nazi stalwart *Der Völkisher Beobachter*, continuing in circulation.

There were, however, some more focused attempts by the Axis to influence the prisoners, by publishing newspapers exclusively for POWs. The Italian-produced *Prisoner of War News* had limited circulation and an even more limited effect. Somewhat more influential were two German-organized publications: *The Camp*, primarily for British readers, and *O.K.* ('Overseas Kid') for Americans. Both emphasized German triumphs and Allied setbacks, as well as including slanted articles on social problems in the respective home countries. Alongside this fairly overt propaganda were the usual staples of newspapers and magazines: sport, short stories, humour, letters and quizzes. These latter inclusions made the paper quite readable. The editorial staff also made extensive use of contributions from POWs, either unaware or uncaring of the papers' intended role.

Reading allowed the prisoner internal escape from his camp, and writing an opportunity for self-expression. But for some POWs this was not enough. They wanted to take up some form of organized study, so that the time seemingly wasted behind the wire could be redeemed through self-improvement and attainment of qualifications. Learning could then be a way of giving meaning to an otherwise largely pointless existence. Major Cyril Whitcombe, who was to spend nearly five years behind barbed wire, considered it his duty to 'come out of this hole as I went into it, or better; not bitter, still young, still cheerful. I am also trying to keep my brain working and to put something in it.'

In the non-working camps, where time hung most heavily, large numbers of men would sign up for study courses. The enthusiasm for education was remarked on by Captain C. J. Hamson, education officer in Oflag IXA at Rotenburg: 'The most striking phenomenon in officer prisoner-of-war camps in Germany, of which alone I can speak, was the *demand* for education. It was so widespread as to be universal, and it was also both tenacious and urgent. Though by profession a university don, I have not in peacetime encountered its equal.' A letter home from an American POW in Stalag Luft III revealed the exhilaration of learning: 'At present I'm engrossed in two courses – French and the history of English Literature. At the completion of the latter I plan to study journalism with an eye to the future. I've gone rather "high-brow" in my reading and am at present reading Tolstoy's *War and Peace*, a very enlightening and interesting piece of literature.' Not all students kept up their studies, however, and these sudden, intense enthusiasms would often swiftly evaporate.

Education began on an informal basis, and in a few camps remained at the level of impromptu talks by a POW on a subject sufficiently interesting to gain an audience. Many men had knowledge or experiences that they could pass on to their fellows. In Stalag Luft I, Jack Vietor, a former member of the American diplomatic service, gave weekly lectures on international affairs. British POWs were intrigued by tales from the further reaches of the Empire and Commonwealth, so that in PG 57 at Gruppignano Doug LeFevre found himself in demand for talks on his life as a teamster on cattle stations in Western Australia.

During March 1945 Roger Shinn was imprisoned in Stalag XIIIC at Hammelburg, then effectively a transit camp. Library facilities were poor, and when books were in short supply the demand for knowledge was supplied by lectures and talks. He wrote:

> Lectures were scheduled once or twice every day. The subjects were agriculture, economic geography, insurance, psychology – anything some officer could lecture about. We attended by the hundreds. Every lecture or church service had a crowd, not so much because crowds were interested, but because there was nothing else to do. Having got there, we became interested. I remember a vigorous panel on socialized medicine. It almost ended in a fight between a doctor and an economist. I had not thought there was so much energy in Hammelburg.

The learning of languages was popular, especially the language of the captor. A working knowledge of German or Italian was a useful tool for prisoners, especially to bargain for better conditions from guards and civilians. For escapers, some proficiency in the enemy's language was almost essential: Jimmy James and Billie Stephens immersed themselves in German on arriving at their first POW camps, and James, with a natural aptitude for languages, also learned Russian.

Although finding suitable study materials was initially difficult, once books began to pour into the Oflags and non-working Stalags so did the syllabuses, exam papers, textbooks and other educational aids necessary for proper study. In the working camps, however, not only were books and free time in short supply but the Germans often refused to provide assistance for prisoners wishing to study. As men could be called away from the main camp to work in a labour detachment at any time, courses were regularly disrupted. For education officers and students alike it was a frustrating business. In Stalag IVA at Hohnstein, the education officer, G. Tavender, found the Germans especially obstructive, so that when he received details of a proposed manual-trades instruction scheme he was forced to turn it down. Tavender reluctantly concluded, 'If the Germans had thought our "lads" had time for study in the evening (which they hadn't), they would have lengthened the working hours.'

A less tangible factor that affected POWs as they grappled with their studies was a sense of inertia and lack of concentration. Virtually all commentators agreed that this was an enduring problem in POW camps. It was put down to chronic food shortages and the nature of confinement, which, according to one POW, had 'the likeness of eternity. Thus any work attempted resembles walking up a long featureless hill whose summit is out of sight.' Men would sign up for courses and then drop them a few weeks later, only to take up another course and similarly drop that. The seasons and the state of the war also played their part. In warm, sunny weather men preferred to lounge outside, and following major Allied successes – notably the Italian armistice and the Normandy invasion – the levels of excitement within the camps made concentration particularly difficult.

Despite these problems – both physical and psychological – many men did undertake periods of extended study in the POW 'universities'. Essential to the success of these improvised educational institutions was help from outside. From its headquarters in the New Bodleian Library, Oxford, the Educational Books Section of the British Red Cross Prisoner of War Department made a point of persuading educational institutions and professional bodies to provide study facilities and to recognize examinations held in POW camps. It was this far-sighted decision to involve outside organizations that made the work of the section so successful.

The idea of holding exams was accepted by the Germans in 1942, although not by the Italians, which inevitably put a brake on the development of the PG 'universities'. Exam scripts were sent to the camps via Geneva, invigilated by education officers in the camps, and then returned to Britain for marking and grading. It was a formidable logistical challenge, always subject to delay, but with the co-operation of the British and German authorities it worked sur-prisingly well in practice. Exams certainly helped counteract POW inertia. One education officer noted, 'Where there were no exam-inations to cover the course of reading, the reading was generally very desultory and short-lived. Where there were examinations, reading and classes were carried on with great enthusiasm, with higher attend-ances from start to finish.'

The first such examination course was in English (honours-degree standard), compiled in the summer of 1941 at Oxford University by two renowned men of letters, Professor J. R. R. Tolkien and C. S. Lewis. Other courses followed: a total of 136 examining bodies were involved in the scheme, responsible for preparing 6,091 different exam papers, with 88 camps in Germany holding the examinations. By the end of the war, exam papers had been sent out to some 17,000 candidates, with a pass rate of 78.5 per cent. Apart from a small amount of extra time to complete exams, the POW students were given no special concessions. 'It was a point of honour in all prison camps', wrote the historian of the Educational Books Section, 'that a prisoner of war's success should rank equally with a success under home conditions.'

Most Oflags and the larger, better equipped Stalags had their own 'universities', and foremost among them was arguably the NCOs' educational facility in Stalag Luft VI, run by Sergeant Eddie Alderton and dubbed the Barbed-Wire University. The enthusiasm for learn-ing at Stalag Luft VI gained extraordinary momentum, with nearly half the prison population taking part in some form of educational activity. By the spring of 1944 the Barbed-Wire University comprised 10 classrooms with 104 lecturers giving 500 lectures a week to 3,000 registered students. Even when the camp was evacuated in August 1944 – to Stalag 357, first at Thorn and then at Oerbke – teaching and examinations continued. When the camps were liberated in April 1945, Alderton and his fellow lecturers were able to hand over com-pleted exam scripts for dispatch to Oxford.

Although lacking some of the advantages of the well-developed British system, American POWs organized educational pro-grammes on similar lines. The YMCA and affiliated bodies – includ-ing the 'Men of Science – Prisoners of War' service, which utilized the talents and knowledge of American academics, librarians and businessmen – provided the necessary outside assistance, sending textbooks and other study aids to the US camps.

Oflag 64 constituted its own 'Altgebund Academy', and the US compounds in Stalag Luft III had their 'Kriegie Colleges'. In Stalag Luft III's Center compound some twenty-five to thirty-five courses were on offer, ranging from accounting to zoology. The Americans faced the disadvantage of not having an externally recognized exam system. Spivey was aware that this was a contributory factor in the tailing-off of attendances. Accordingly, diplomas were issued by the tutor on the satisfactory completion of the course – and counter-signed by Spivey as the compound's SAO. On the certificate was a request to any potential academic institution in America that this diploma be recognized as a college credit. Assisted by the YMCA, the accreditation scheme was accepted by American colleges 'in almost every case'.

Alongside formal study, prisoners took up other pursuits of a broadly educational nature, including general lectures, discussion groups and debating. One of the more intriguing experiences – demonstrating a fierce commitment to education – took place late in 1944 in Oflag IXA at Rotenburg, and was described by Robert Holland:

> With the aid of a single candle, in a disused bath house, an audience of some thirty officers (of whom two knew Greek, and they not much) listened to a reading by Mr C. J. Hamson, Trinity College, Cambridge, of Sophocles' *Electra*, with such introduction, translation and comment as occurred to the reader. The entire text, including choruses, was read aloud in the original Greek. The course occupied thirteen periods of rather more than an hour each, and it was so successful that it was pro-posed to continue with the first book of the *Iliad*, when food supplies finally broke down rather too seriously to permit the necessary effort.

Not all work was so intellectually rigorous. In Oflag VA at Weinsberg a presentation called 'Bringing up Children' demonstrated a more touching side to the British soldier. A senior officer in the camp described the project: 'Officers lent photographs of their children, and they were used, along with cartoons, to illustrate in about fifty wall sheets the natural development of the child from birth to adolescence, covering physical, intellectual, emotional and social aspects, schools and toys, and emphasizing the way in which parents can assist that development.'

Making profitable use of time was the watchword of the camp educators. Reading was an excellent means of passing time, but through study the POW could expand his intellectual horizons and win a small personal victory over the Germans and the confining circumstances of prison life. Towards the end of the war one idealistic camp education officer wrote to the Educational Books Section about the importance of their work. His prose may have been a little overwrought, but it accurately reflected the sense that through education anything was possible: 'We try to communicate the faith that there are things of the mind unbounded by time and place and that captives may escape beyond the barbed wire into fields of knowledge and delight. Those who know this freedom of the intellect are the happiest people in this camp and they will go out of here the best citizens when the gates are opened.'

10

Other Nationalities

D ESPITE THE USUAL separation of prisoners along national lines, substantial numbers of American servicemen spent time in British camps, and in Italy the relatively few American prisoners captured by the Italians were combined with the British. As a result, there was direct contact between British and Americans throughout the war. British and American POWs functioned well together, successfully putting up a united front to their captors despite attempts by the Axis to drive a wedge between them. This international unity was a reflection of two nations' fighting together and sharing similar political beliefs and a common language.

On a practical level, solidarity entailed the sharing of Red Cross parcels and cigarettes. During 1943, when Americans first began to arrive in POW camps in substantial numbers, they were short of provisions and relied on the British for aid. In the main, help was readily given and gratefully received. Colonel Delmar T. Spivey in Stalag Luft III at Sagan wrote, 'From the very beginning the British Commonwealth, acting through the International Red Cross, took care of us and continued to do so until November 1943, at which time appreciable amounts of American food and clothing began to arrive. The British shared and shared alike with us everything which came from benevolent organizations.'

Americans were also beneficiaries of British assistance on an individual level. A. D. Azios, captured during the Battle of the Bulge, was transported with other American enlisted men to the grim Stalag IIIA at Luckenwalde; once there they were told there would be no food for them. 'The British prisoners, who were next to us, separated by a barbed-wire fence, heard the bad news,' wrote Azios. 'When we were dismissed, the British POWs called us to get next to their fence. They gave each one of us a cup of tea, their tea for the day. Only a prisoner of war can imagine what a sacrifice that is: starving men, giving their cup of tea to strangers. I had a cup of unforgettable hot tea which gave me a new life, as I was literally starving.'

Americans, in their turn, reciprocated British generosity. Alfred Jenner, a British airman, ended his POW odyssey in Stalag 357 at Oerbke, a camp that included Americans and British among its vastly overcrowded POW population. He described an example of American open-handedness that took place at the end of February 1945:

> Somehow a truckload of Chesterfield cigarettes earmarked for the sole use of the Americans arrived at what was left of Fallingbostel station. We all thought, 'the lucky so-and so's' for Virginia cigarettes were as good as currency. To our astonishment – and eternal gratitude – the Americans decided to share their good fortune with the lot of us, amounting, if I remember rightly, to 200 each. Shortly after we were all marched out to live off the land for a month on whatever we could beg, borrow, steal or barter. The value of that great example of unselfishness on the part of the Americans was incalculable.

Mutual generosity apart, British and American POWs tolerated each other's national traits; some even got to like them. David Westheimer, an American airman held in PG 21 at Chieti, found the British – who formed the bulk of the camp's population – an interesting topic for study. He was impressed by British enthusiasm for educational schemes, picked up British slang and styles of swearing, and enjoyed joshing with British prisoners – as one told him, 'the difference between the Americans and the English was that the Americans thought they were best and Englishmen knew they were.' Bertie Harwood, incarcerated in various Oflags since 1940, welcomed the arrival of a group of US officers in 1944: 'A number of American prisoners were sent to Eichstätt [Oflag VIIB] for a short time and we found that this vital and entirely new blood did us the world of good. Being a nation apart we welcomed the novelty of their outlook, but at the same time did not regard them in any way as aliens; we got on very well.'

Needless to say, Anglo-American relations were not all light and harmony. Some old British hands disparaged the poor psychological condition of US Army prisoners, especially those captured in the final stages of the war. Americans resented the often officious or patronizing tones of the British and their tendency to maintain control over the running of shared facilities. At Stalag Luft VI at Heydekrug, the American Man of Confidence, Technical Sergeant Frank Paules, had to tactfully remind Dixie Deans and his RAF prisoners that the camp's theatrical facilities should be equally available to all. The British assumption of seniority was noticed by American journalist Edward Beattie at Luckenwalde following the collapse of German control in April 1945: 'The truth is that Englishmen have a knack of taking over, blandly and as a matter of course and with no prejudice to the others concerned, all the best positions. If the fact is pointed out to them, they will share the jobs. If it is not, the thought never occurs to them.' Beattie – in fact something of an Anglophile – conceded that the British were 'doing a good job'.

Having observed both British and American POWs amicably sharing West/South compound in Stalag Luft I at Barth, Jack Vietor noted how the 'British disliked the Germans intensely. Americans were more tolerant perhaps because of knowing the German character less well and of having seen less German brutality.' American artillery officer Joseph S. Frelinghuysen noticed a similar British antipathy towards the Italians, while Delmar Spivey witnessed a trenchant example of British belligerence shortly after arriving in the then mixed American–British Center compound at Stalag Luft III. At the approach of Christmas, some of the Americans suggested making a collection of chocolate for a colony of German children recently evacuated from Berlin. When asked to contribute, the compound's SBO, Squadron Leader S. G. Pritchard, issued an emphatic no, declaring, 'I'd like to kick the teeth out of each one of the little bastards!'

Spivey had great admiration for the fighting spirit of the RAF, but the heavy-drinking, hard-swearing, goon-baiting, escape-mad mavericks of the North and East compounds seemed a little too close to disorder for his liking. He was undoubtedly relieved when the last British and Commonwealth flyers were transferred from Center compound.

Britain was fortunate in being able to draw upon fighting men from around the world. As well as India and the Dominions of Canada, Australia, New Zealand and South Africa, servicemen came from many other, smaller, nations, so that the British armed forces fielded units from places as disparate as the Caribbean, West Africa, and Palestine. The sheer range of nationalities in British uniform bemused Axis captors, who often quizzed these prisoners on why they had taken up arms on Britain's behalf.

The 'Free' forces of occupied Europe supplied a further category of soldier fighting alongside the British, and these included contingents of French, Poles, Czechs, Greeks and Yugoslavs as well as individuals from all the European nations under German domination. When captured, their status as British combatants became subject to German legal scrutiny, until OKW pronounced that 'the *uniform* is the determining outward factor in establishing the fact of the prisoner's belonging to the respective armed forces.' Czech POWs were, however, considered a possible exception. Czechoslovakia had never been a belligerent power, as the Czech half of the country had either been incorporated into the Reich or become a German protectorate before the outbreak of war. On this basis it was proposed that captured 'Free' Czechs should come under German civil jurisdiction and be tried as traitors. Although this assertion was never tested in court, Czech POWs remained in an uncomfortable limbo for much of the war.

British defeats in North Africa and the Mediterranean fell heavily on South Africans, New Zealanders and Australians, while Dieppe and Normandy pushed up Canadian prisoner totals. Nearly 15,000 South Africans from all three services were captured by the Germans and Italians (10,000 of them in one fell swoop at Tobruk), followed by just over 9,000 New Zealanders, 8,200 Australians and nearly 8,000 Canadians. It was a disproportionately high total.

How much Commonwealth POWs differed from their British counterparts remains a matter of debate. Commonwealth soldiers liked to see themselves as representing something of a unique national fighting spirit, and yet the present-day distinctions between Britain and the British-settled colonies were far less marked in the 1940s, so much so that the Revd Bob McDowall – a New Zealander of Scottish ancestry – could unselfconsciously use the expression 'we English'. In so much as there were differences between the Commonwealth nations, the Afrikaans-speaking soldiers from South Africa found themselves at a remove from their English-speaking comrades.

The journalist Edward Ward became aware of this distinction after being sent to Oflag XIIB at Hademar:

> We had a majority of South Africans there, many of whom very naturally talked to each other in their language, Afrikaans. This, quite unreasonably, irritated many other POWs who, the longer they remain in the bag, become increasingly unreasonable. But it had the effect, broadly speaking, of splitting the camp into two factions, South African and non-South African. The South African members of the camp certainly tended to stick together rather on their own in a way which the Australians and New Zealanders never did.

Flight Lieutenant Dallas Lasky, a Canadian airman held in Stalag Luft III, believed that his countrymen 'had a vitality and an openness, and a kind of exploratory attitude. I think that they did a lot to keep spirits up. And, certainly, Canadians had an identity. Anyone who was there would realize that they were Canadians. It wasn't just a matter of accent or grammar. We weren't burdened with the heavy hand of tradition.' McDowall took a special interest in his New Zealanders: 'Our own fellows are distinctive and have on them a different march from all the others. One gets to know their look after a while and is proud of them.'

Anzac Day was scrupulously observed by Australians and New Zealanders, to commemorate the landings at Gallipoli on 25 April 1915. In Stalag 383 at Hohenfels, the 1944 Anzac Day became a celebration of Commonwealth solidarity: the Australian and New Zealand march past was joined by men from Britain, Canada, South Africa, Palestine and Cyprus. The other central feature of the day was a series of sporting events, in which British and Commonwealth nations competed in their traditional sports.

At various times the Germans tried to loosen the ties between Britain and the Commonwealth. When Bob Prouse was led away from the battlefield at Dieppe, the Germans and the Vichy French authorities attempted to open up a rift between French Canadians and their English-speaking compatriots. The men of the *Fusiliers Mont-Royal* were offered food parcels and cigarettes, which they readily accepted – but only to share them with the other Canadians.

Although Canadians were a prime focus for the shackling order – when POWs were forced to wear handcuffs in retaliation for Canadian orders to bind German prisoners at Dieppe – Canadian prisoners in German camps were offered improved conditions, ostensibly as a reward for the good treatment experienced by German prisoners in Canada. According to Bob Prouse, the Germans 'posted a notice offering all Canadian prisoners a chance to move to a separate and better camp for the use of Canadians only. The offer was turned down flatly by the senior Canadian representative and the Germans were advised that we were all one and the same and, if the whole camp was not included, we didn't want any part of it.'

Many prisoners at Stalag 383 were among those subject to the shackling order, but here the Australians were targeted for a relaxation of the order. 'The Germans are unshackling the Australians,' wrote Australian infantryman Sergeant Raymond Ryan, 'and have issued us with passes stating that we are *"nicht zu fesseln"* [not to be fettered]. By unanimous vote the Australians have decided to hand all the non-chaining passes back to the Germans and tell them we do not wish for preferential treatment as compared with NZ and other Englishmen.'

Although in some cases Commonwealth troops were forced to accept these 'privileges' – and encouraged to do so by British camp leaders – this had no effect on the relations existing among the Dominions. For men who had travelled halfway across the world to fight in support of their 'mother' country, such clumsy efforts to turn their loyalties met with derision.

One other major group of British-uniformed POWs fared rather differently: black servicemen and other non-Europeans from the Empire. The majority of these prisoners came from the Indian Army: approximately 15,000 Indian soldiers entered Axis camps, most captured during the North African campaign. The Italians and Germans attempted to subvert the loyalties of the Indian prisoners and form them into anti-British legions. The German effort took precedence, and during 1942 Indian POWs were transported to Germany, most sent to Stalag IVD/Z at Annaberg as part of a recruitment drive for the Free Indian Legion. Following the surrender of Italy in September 1943 the remaining Indian POWs in Italian camps joined British and Commonwealth troops on their journey north to Germany.

The Indian Army contained several religions, whose complex dietary practices were to cause Indian prisoners many problems in

Europe. Hindus made up 41 per cent of the Army, followed by Muslims (34 per cent), Sikhs (11 per cent) and Gurkhas and other races (14 per cent). Beef was forbidden to Hindus and Sikhs, and Muslims were prohibited from eating pork.

These proscriptions were further complicated by strict laws governing the killing and handling of meat, especially for Muslims. At the merchant seamen's camp, Milag, Asian sailors were held in the *Inderlager*. In order to sort out conflicting views on the acceptability or otherwise of eating meat, the *Inderlager* Man of Confidence, Captain Herbert Jones, wrote to the principal of a madrasa at Lucknow in India for a fatwa on the eating of meat, only to receive the less than helpful ruling that consumption of all kinds of tinned meat was forbidden them, as meat could only be bought from a fellow Muslim.

As a consequence of such restrictions, Indian prisoners depended on the regular supply of special Indian Red Cross parcels, which substituted meat with fish and traditional Indian foods. On many occasions, however, Indians received standard parcels, which obliged them to trade or give away their meat to European POWs. White prisoners were surprised at the actions of the Indians, who could have sold prized meat tins for good prices but seldom pushed home their bargaining advantage. Bob McDowall, in Stalag IVB at Mühlberg, tried to trade raisins for curry powder, but the Indians refused his offer and simply threw a tin of curry powder over the wire dividing their compounds.

The sight of Indian POWs also came as a surprise to many – not least Americans, who had not had contact with Indian soldiers before. One of these Americans was Roger Shinn: 'They wore turbans on their heads and looked not at all like soldiers from this war. They were marvellously clean, for such a home as Limburg, and extremely friendly. We liked to watch them crouch around their tiny fires in the yard and cook. Because of the various dietary rules of the Indian religions, their Red Cross supplies included no meat, but were strong in grains, so the Indians cooked and cooked and cooked.'

Indian POWs, in fact, rarely had sufficient access to cooking stoves, and suffered from chronic fuel shortages; in the *Inderlager* Captain Jones fought a long campaign to get better kitchen facilities for the Indians in his care. In Oflag VIB at Warburg some Indian officers even requested standard parcels, because of the difficulties in preparing and cooking food from Indian parcels.

Confined in separate camps or compounds, Indians had fairly limited contact with British and Commonwealth prisoners. Relations were mixed, with an undercurrent of racism coexisting uneasily with comradeship against a common enemy. Fraudulent trading with Indian POWs was not uncommon, McDowall noting that in PG 57 at Gruppignano 'our NZ chaps passed tins of pudding to Indians as butter, taking off the wrappers'. Another reflective observer, Sergeant Reginald Dexter, was shocked at 'having to see Indian soldiers pushed away from water taps'.

One Indian who did have extensive contact with British and Commonwealth POWs was Captain B. N. Mazumdar, a medical officer captured in 1940 and shuttled through a total of seventeen German camps. Mazumdar refused to have anything to do with the Indian Legion, despite personal entreaties to join from its leader, Subhas Chandra Bose. His belligerent attitude towards the Germans eventually led him to Colditz. But he also had a poor opinion of his fellow British prisoners. Mazumdar thought that those he encountered directly after capture were demoralized and lacking in spirit, and he accused the padres he lived with of hoarding food for themselves and their friends. A somewhat contradictory character, he was proud to hold an officer's commission but was open in condemning British rule in India.

At Colditz, Mazumdar's uncompromising attitude was admired by some British officers, but he irritated others and found himself isolated as the only Indian in the castle. He put forward an escape request which was dismissed out of hand by the escape committee. Angered by this rejection Mazumdar went on hunger strike, demanding to be sent to an Indian camp. After three weeks the Germans relented and sent him to a camp in France, from where he escaped to Switzerland. Mazumdar took great pleasure in sending a postcard to the British SBO at Colditz to inform him of his success.

Of the South Africans who entered captivity in North Africa, 2,270 were men of the Non-European Army Services (NEAS), consisting of black, Indian and coloured troops. Although not intended for front-line service, large numbers of non-Europeans were captured in the desert campaigns, first at Sidi Rezegh in 1941 and then in Tobruk the following year. Treated by their own side as second-class soldiers, they were treated as second-class prisoners by the Axis.

Conditions for all Allied prisoners were poor in North Africa, but the Axis forces – both German and Italian – were especially harsh in their dealings with non-Europeans. During a ration stop for POWs of the South African 5th Infantry Brigade, on their march from Sidi Rezegh to transit camps in the rear, white troops were given biscuits and water first, leaving the non-Europeans until last – by which time the water had run out. Non-European troops were kept in North Africa for extended periods, assigned to labouring duties which included the unloading of munitions in direct contravention of the Geneva Convention. When a British officer complained about this to the Italians he was brusquely informed that the Convention did not apply to those who were not 'regular' soldiers. A South African medical officer, Captain E. D. Hyland, made notes for a report on the conditions of non-European prisoners in North Africa: 'S. A. [South African] natives, Free French, Mauritians and Indians singled out for bad treatment. Rifle butts, whips and sticks by Italian officers and men. Several shot.' Dr L. E. Le Souef, an Australian medical officer in Germany, treated a Senussi tribesmen from Libya, who he noted had 'suffered much at the hands of the Germans on account of his colour'. Many such prisoners did not speak English – let alone German or Italian – and were unable communicate with their captors, another factor militating against good treatment.

The Italians abused black prisoners for propaganda purposes, and in one instance forced them to cavort naked in front of film cameras. Another propaganda stunt backfired, however, when Primo Carnera, the Italian former world heavyweight boxing champion, was lined up against Kay Masaki, a Zulu soldier from the Native Military Corps, whose powerful physique had caught the attention of the Italian film director. A filmed three-minute bout was organized to demonstrate the superiority of the white man; Masaki had no boxing experience, and was deprived of food in the days leading up to the fight. Initially all went to plan as Masaki was dumped on to the canvas within the first minute. But the South African was undeterred, and getting to his feet he carried on boxing before landing a perfect right hook that knocked out Carnera. The cameras were packed away, the film undeveloped.

★

The US armed forces practised strict racial segregation and only reluctantly accepted blacks in a combat role during the Second World War. At the point of capture, black soldiers faced greater dangers than white troops, and there were instances when they were killed by the Waffen SS, who had apparently been given the order that 'Negroes are not to be taken prisoner'. By contrast, Lieutenant Alexander Jefferson – a pilot in the famous black 332nd Fighter Group, the 'Tuskegee Airmen' – received no ill-treatment, from the time he was shot down on a strafing mission over the South of France to his imprisonment in Stalag Luft III. 'Quite naturally having a black prisoner was a little odd for the Germans,' he recalled, 'but I was treated with all the rights and privileges of an American officer; in fact I had no trouble at all with the German authorities because I was black.' Other captured officers from the group received similar good treatment.

Within Stalag Luft III black prisoners were integrated fairly well among the overall white population. For most white POWs this was the first time they had met blacks as equals, and was something of an education. When black airmen began to arrive in the camp in numbers it became a point of honour for a barrack hut to take one in. Roger Shinn observed changes in white attitudes while on his march from Stalag XIIIC at Hammelburg into Bavaria during the closing stages of the war: 'On this march there was one colored lieutenant and several Negroes in the enlisted men's platoon. Racial friction had been marked in England and France. Here there was none. The Negroes were accepted more completely than in any other army group I had ever seen. One Alabama lieutenant, who in the past had often spoken contemptuously of "niggers", became entirely cordial to the Negro lieutenant.' Shinn believed the reason for the change lay in the sense of brotherhood shared by soldiers who had experienced combat, as well as a common solidarity against their captors. 'Strange', he mused, 'that it should take Nazism, with its fanatical racial tyranny, to make Americans democratic.' But the true democratic test would lie in the way the white world treated black soldiers on their return home.

Whatever the disputes among British, Commonwealth and American prisoners, they were always between close allies. The French had, of course, been allies of the British, but after the French surrender in June 1940 relations between the two nations became increasingly fraught. Each side blamed the other for the disaster, with bad feeling compounded on the French side by the British attack on the French fleet at Mers-el-Kébir in July.

In the immediate aftermath of the French surrender the Germans successfully encouraged dissension between British and French prisoners, and the British were certainly enraged at the preferential treatment accorded the French in the grim 1940–41 period. After such a bad start it was perhaps not surprising that Anglo-French prisoner relations were often poor. The British accused the French of operating rackets at their expense, of not being prepared to share Red Cross parcels, and of displaying collaborationist tendencies towards the Germans. On an individual basis British and French prisoners could get on very well, but in the main the relationship was an uneasy one.

For the most part British and French prisoners had only limited dealings with each other, being separated in different camps or compounds. One exception was Colditz, which was shared between Polish, British, French and Dutch prisoners until 1943, when it became predominantly British. At this camp, at least, the French were highly regarded for their anti-German spirit, and on a social level there was co-operation advantageous to both sides. But in February 1945 a large and hungry contingent of French POWs suddenly arrived at the castle, and in this instance, with food in very short supply, relations between the two groups of prisoners could only be described, at best, as mixed.

There were few reservations about the Poles that the British POWs came across in Colditz and elsewhere. Within the castle the Poles were described in glowing terms: a 'wonderful crowd . . . marvellous chaps'; 'absolutely magnificent'; 'old and trusted comrades'. Jimmy James first came across Polish prisoners while in transit to Stalag Luft I at Barth, and was immediately impressed by the way they shared their limited resources with the RAF prisoners. A couple of years later James was transferred to Oflag XXIB near the Polish town of Schubin. 'The Poles', he wrote, 'were extremely co-operative, in spite of the death penalty if they were caught helping prisoners of war. Polish workmen came into the camp nearly every day and regularly lent us their passes and other documents for copying; through them we were in contact with families in the neighbourhood and also with the Polish Underground.' Other prisoners in POW camps in Poland often spoke of the generosity of local people in giving them food or other help.

After the defeat of the 1944 Warsaw Uprising, survivors of the Polish Home Army were scattered across several POW camps in Germany, including Stalag XIB at Fallingbostel. They included men, women and children who, according to British camp leader RSM John Lord, 'behaved in an exemplary fashion'. Lord recalled that 'seeing the Polish women march up from their compound, swinging their arms across their bodies, singing the whole way, collecting their meagre rations and marching back must have made a profound impression on the men of the 1st Airborne Division. It made many men think; it certainly did me.'

In the neighbouring camp – Stalag 357 at Oerbke – RAF prisoners under the command of Warrant Officer James 'Dixie' Deans demonstrated their respect for the Poles, as John Dominy described:

> Our little brush with the Warsaw rising was a poignant one. Some of the women and children prisoners were brought to our bath house to be de-loused after their long journey from Warsaw. The Germans forced the women to strip outside the bath hut before they went in for a shower to cleanse themselves, then made them stand naked outside while their clothes were cooked to kill the lice. An excited German rushed into the camp office to tell us about the 'peep show', which had been put on for our benefit. Jimmy Deans immediately called for his news readers, explained the situation and sent out orders that no one was to approach the perimeter of the camp where the Polish women were exposed to public gaze. Most people stayed in their huts or at the other end of the camp.

One of the ubiquitous themes of Anglo-American POW literature was the plight of Germany's Russian prisoners. During the war on the Eastern Front, the Germans captured approximately 5.7 million men and women of the Soviet armed forces, and through a process of shooting, beating, starvation, disease or overwork killed 3.3 million of them. As the Soviet Union was not a signatory to the Geneva Convention (and had little interest in its own captives), Russian prisoners did not receive assistance from a Protecting Power or from the Red Cross or other humanitarian organizations.

Many British and American camps had an adjoining compound housing ragged and emaciated Russians. The contempt – and fear – the Germans felt towards Russians was abundantly evident to all POWs; even in their weakened state Russians were assigned the hardest and most unpleasant jobs, and were beaten or even shot by German guards on the slightest pretext. The sight of cartloads of Russian dead – stripped of their clothes – being dragged out for burial in mass graves became a common sight.

Prisoners threw cigarettes and tins of food into the Russian compound, although this had to be done surreptitiously as the Germans normally prohibited any such help. In some camps, assistance for the Russians was well developed. At Stalag XVIIIA at Wolfsberg, Howard Greville described how British, Australian and New Zealand POWs decided against individual donations and instead 'agreed that as each man drew his weekly Red Cross parcels he should make a voluntary gift of clothing and one or two tins of food to a central pool, which was then given to Russian camp leaders for distribution. Nobody declined to contribute, and considering our very mixed origins and backgrounds that was rather remarkable.' The Russians gave their benefactors small wood carvings and metalwork in gratitude.

In Stalag IVB at Mühlberg British POWs lobbed tins over to the Russians in a rather disorderly fashion. In return, the Russians offered British POWs dental care. While visiting a female Russian dentist, the Revd Douglas Thompson was politely requested to ask the British prisoners to desist from throwing food over the wire and instead bring it hidden in towels during dental visits, so that it could be distributed in an organized manner. The donations did seem to become more orderly; the camp history explained that 'British P/Ws voluntarily gave up one article from their Red Cross parcels for the relief of P/Ws of other nationalities in hospital. All German food which P/Ws did not consume was also given over.'

The sheer scale of the problem of helping the Russians – and the knowledge that gifts could only be token ones – had its effect on British and American POWs. The Revd David Wild was overwhelmed when sent to the Kopernikus camp, which contained several thousand starving Russians: 'Hundreds were so sick or mutilated, and so ill-clothed, that seen individually they would have caught one's eye and attracted one's sympathy anywhere. At Kopernikus Lager there were so many in such a condition, that after a time we ceased to notice them as anything unusual.'

Although it would seem that Russian prisoners were often suspicious of the 'capitalist' British and Americans, they too were eager to help when possible. Roger Shinn came across a small encampment of Russian prisoners, who, relatively well fed, offered the Americans salt. 'They gave it to us liberally,' wrote Shinn, 'and passed out other little items of food, though they must have been nearly as hungry as we. Though we could not talk, except for a few German words that both they and we might know, their friendliness was exuberant. We automatically pulled out our cigarettes to trade with them, but they wanted nothing in return. Seldom in my life have I seen such generous friendliness.'

The Nazis considered Russians to be subhuman, but their greatest hatred was reserved for Jews. The fate of Jewish prisoners of war depended on the nationality of the army in which they were captured. If they had the misfortune to be members of the Soviet armed forces, a swift death was their best hope. If they were captured as regular soldiers of nations signatory to the Geneva Convention they could expect the basic protections of the Convention, although as the war progressed so the Germans became increasingly hostile to Jewish prisoners, segregating and harassing them. Jewish POWs in the British and American armed forces were undoubtedly the best protected of all Jews in Nazi Germany, although some were better treated than others. Once again the Germans moderated their behaviour for fear of Allied retaliation against their own prisoners.

During the fraught period of capture, some Jews threw away their identity discs (which recorded a man's religion); those who did not were sometimes roughly treated, and during the Battle of the Bulge in December 1944 SS troops were reported to have beaten and even killed Americans they identified as Jewish. Once in enemy hands, some men kept quiet about being Jewish; others could not bring themselves to deny their religion and background and defiantly proclaimed themselves as Jews. Norman Rubenstein was captured at Calais in 1940: 'We had been told to destroy our identity discs and I had already done so. Nevertheless, I decided that I was going to remain Norman Rubenstein and register in whatever camp I was in as being Jewish. To hell with them, I thought. I am British and I am Jewish, and that's how it will always be.'

For one group of Jewish POWs there were no options for anonymity of any kind. The British had raised a number of pioneer companies in Palestine, and, while some of their members were recruited from the Arab population, the majority were Jewish. The Palestinians were captured en masse during the campaign in Greece and Crete, and some 1,500 Jews ended up in Stalag VIIIB at Lamsdorf and its satellite work camps. These men were recent emigrants from central Europe; most spoke German, and some had the uncomfortable experience of returning to areas they had fled in their youth. Relying on the protection of their British Army status, they fought tenaciously for their POW rights against guards, Nazi Party officials and German employers. Their pugnacity – in a dangerous position – earned them admirers at Lamsdorf.

Attempts were made by the Germans to chip away at the 'privileged' position of Anglo-American Jewish prisoners, but the combined efforts of the British and American governments, the Swiss Protecting Power and the Red Cross, along with camp leaders and prisoners, acted as a largely successful barrier to these moves. One early example of the German Army's POW anti-Semitism – directed against Palestinian Jews – was the unsuccessful claim made by legal officers of the Twelfth Army (which had captured the Palestinians) that those of German origin were 'fugitives from justice' and should not be accorded the status of prisoners of war.

Treatment of Jewish prisoners by camp guards and other Germans varied considerably. Wounded after being shot down over Germany, Jewish RAF airman Sergeant Cyril Rofe was sent to a hospital full of German soldiers and was fearful of his reception. 'They soon found out I was a Jew,' he wrote, 'but this made little difference to most of them, who said: "He is a soldier like us, and therefore we must treat him as one of us."' Other Jews, by contrast, were insulted or threatened by guards. In the main, such harassment remained relatively low key, although the Germans refused to work with camp leaders if they knew them to be Jews. Towards the end of the war Jewish POWs began to experience greater levels of intimidation and even violence from guards. These incidents did, however, tend to occur in newer – usually American – camps that lacked the protection provided by firm leadership in the established camps.

One of the more uplifting elements of the prisoner-of-war experience was the efforts made by British and American camp leaders to protect Jewish POWs. At Lamsdorf, RSM Sidney Sherriff thwarted an attempt by the Germans to prevent Palestinian Jews from receiving Red Cross parcels sent from Britain. He immediately told the Germans that if this order were implemented then all British prisoners would forgo parcels. Fearful that such a move would create an international incident, the Germans backed down and the Palestinians received their parcels. Sherriff was also instrumental in ensuring, against German opposition, that a Palestinian prisoner who had died of pneumonia was given a burial with full military honours – as was the practice with other prisoners – and that his grave be marked with a Star of David.

The German policy of segregating Jewish prisoners met with success in a few camps, but an attempt to do so at Stalag Luft VI at Heydekrug was firmly rebuffed by the RAF prisoners and their camp leader, Dixie Deans. John Dominy described the incident:

> Taking parade that morning, Ron Mogg was astonished to get an order that all Jews were to parade separately and be segregated in a single barracks. Naturally he refused to comply and the usual Teutonic hubbub ensued. Mogg was about to tell the Germans to 'get knotted' when a greatly incensed Jimmy Deans arrived. In clipped German, he outshouted them all; the order, he told them forcefully, would not be passed on. He sharply pointed out that the prisoners were members of the King's Service and it was one of the rules of that Service that the faith of all denominations should be respected – 'even bloody tree-worshippers', he added (at the time tree-worshipping and other pagan rites were being actively promoted by Arch Crackpot Goebbels). The Germans gave in.

Also at Stalag Luft VI, the American camp leader Technical Sergeant Frank Paules would have no truck with attempts to alienate Jewish prisoners. 'Up at Luft 6', he recalled, 'the guards distributed anti-Jewish hate literature to all the barracks. They were trying to separate the Jewish fellows. So, I sent out a crew to collect all that stuff. We took it into the middle of the lager and put it in a pile, in plain sight of the guards. I lit a match to it, burned it down and that was the end of that.'

In Stalag Luft III the Germans were half-hearted in their efforts to segregate Jews. Delmar Spivey remembered that 'on two occasions we had been directed to turn in the name of Jews to headquarters, but the official answer I gave was that we had no Jews . . . that the men were Americans and were descended from Jewish, English, Negro, German and many other ancestries. I gave the order that no such lists would be given. The Germans never pushed the matter.' David Westheimer – himself a Jew – recorded an example of defiance by a Jewish POW in South compound, who formed his own YMHA (Young Men's Hebrew Association) teams in basketball, softball and touch football. 'You didn't have to be Jewish to be on one,' wrote Westheimer. 'He'd post game notices on the cookhouse bulletin board. We never knew if our hosts knew what the initials stood for but relished the idea of a Jewish organization flourishing deep in Naziland.'

Of the larger, well-established camps Stalag Luft I had the unfortunate distinction of having its Jews sent to a separate barrack block in February 1945. Apart from a separation in sleeping quarters the Jews were treated as other prisoners, however, but for those involved it was understandably an anxious time.

Relations between Jewish and non-Jewish prisoners were good for the most part, although there were instances of anti-Semitism not untypical of life outside the wire. A few more serious altercations took place between British POWs and Palestinian Jews; how much these incidents were anti-Semitic in origin or were a consequence of traditional British views rubbing up against behaviour from a foreign culture remains hard to discern. In the desperate conditions encountered within the transit camp at Salonica arguments took place over queuing and the allocation of resources. At Lamsdorf, Ike Rosmarin, a South African Jew, reported 'a number of physical skirmishes between Jewish and Gentile prisoners', which he believed were a consequence of German anti-Semitic propaganda. A group of non-working NCOs from the Palestinian contingent had been sent to Stalag 383 at Hohenfels, and had set themselves up as traders. According to R. P. Evans, 'They even started buying bread from the Germans, for cigarettes, and re-selling it for a profit. This didn't please some sections of our community at all, and some of the Scots, reputedly Glasgow "Billy Boys", formed a gang to stop it. I think the senior British Warrant Officer had to step in to prevent a riot. Thereafter, they confined themselves to obtaining bread for others, on commission.' This last incident would seem to have been a case of traders, regardless of religion or race, becoming unpopular through securing what was seen as an 'unfair' monopoly.

British prisoners in BAB 21 at Blechhammer and in the many work camps around Lamsdorf worked alongside slave labourers from all over Europe, and occasionally encountered work companies from the concentration camp at Auschwitz. As the British dental officer Julius Green noted, 'Although we were not too badly off, we were surrounded by misery.' British POWs were shocked at the appearance of these unfortunates, and surreptitiously passed over food and cigarettes when possible. The Palestinian Jews took the lead in helping local Jews, first in the ghettos and then in the concentration camps. They smuggled in food, cigarettes and medicine, and were able, through hints in letters home to Palestine, to say something of what was happening in the death camps. But the suffering was so wide-spread that it dulled moral sensibilities. 'One of the significant and terrible things about being in daily sight and contact with such horrors', Green wrote, 'was that one became inured to it. I had to keep reminding myself that this was *not* normal, and that these poor wretches were fellow human beings, very often fellow Jews.'

From a reverse perspective, the writer and Auschwitz survivor Primo Levi recalled coming across a British prisoner in the latrines at the Monowitz-Buna plant, 'with his face splendidly shaven and rosy and his khaki uniform neat, ironed and clean, except for a large KG (*Kriegsgefangener*) on his back'. Levi also remembered how one Jewish inmate cultivated British POWs: 'In his hands they become real geese with golden eggs – if you remember that in exchange for a single English cigarette you can make enough in the Lager not to starve for a day.' That a few cigarettes could be the difference between life and death was a stark reminder of the distinction between a POW, safe-guarded by the Geneva Convention, and those who languished outside the Convention's protection.

11

Medical and Spiritual Matters

MEDICAL OFFICERS AND padres shared an anomalous position within the POW system. They were not technically prisoners of war, but with a few exceptions they remained in Axis custody throughout the conflict. As 'protected personnel' they were allowed a few extra privileges, the chief among these being permission to travel in the vicinity of the camp, either for visiting hospitals and other camps on official business or for simple parole walks. And, while the vast bulk of non-working prisoners had to think of things to occupy their time, medical officers and padres had a ready-made and enormous challenge thrown down at them: to look after the prisoners' physical, mental and spiritual welfare.

Medical care after capture was part of the lottery of being a prisoner of war. Dieppe veteran Bob Prouse, with shell splinters in both legs, received proper medical attention after being sent to the British prison hospital at Stalag IXC, where his wounds were tidied up and the splinters removed. Doug LeFevre had a tougher time with the arm wound sustained on Ruin Ridge in North Africa. He received no treatment until his arm was inspected by an Italian doctor on the Mediterranean crossing to Italy. By then it was infected, and LeFevre was sent to a hospital in Brindisi, where conditions were primitive, as he recounted:

> The day came when I was to be operated upon and, lo and behold, six rather large Italians came and took me away. They stripped me of my clothes and the doctor laid me on the table and the six Italians sat on me, and I wondered what the devil was going on. The doctor said in English, 'I am very sorry but this is going to hurt as we haven't any anaesthetic.' The doctor sliced my arm open, removed the piece of ironmongery and stitched me up; and the six Italians got off my chest.

Jack Vietor, with bullet wounds to the leg and a cut in the hand, was denied medical attention until his arrival in Stalag Luft I at Barth. Once in the camp, Vietor's injuries received skilful treatment from the compound's British doctor; the wounds were cleaned out, and he was given sulphanilamide powder to counter a dangerous infection. Although soon to be superseded by penicillin, the new antibacterial sulpha drugs were invaluable in healing infected wounds, but remained in very short supply within occupied Europe. While LeFevre spent months slowly convalescing in Italian hospitals, Vietor was up and about in a matter of weeks.

For doctors, life as a medical officer in a POW camp was a combination of frustration – at shortages of medical supplies and Axis bureaucratic restrictions – and professional fulfilment through the range of cases and problems presented to them. Bruce Jeffrey, a young Scottish doctor in the 1st Airborne Division captured at Arnhem in September 1944, wrote to his parents of the variety of work in his prison hospital attached to Stalag IXC at Bad Sulza: 'We do all sorts of exciting operations here. I assist at those and get a chance of seeing the operation all through. In fact I'm getting far more experience than I would have got if I had got back over the Rhine at the end of the Arnhem business.'

Most medical officers were highly regarded by their POW patients. Some, like Dr Leslie Caplan, achieved near legendary status. As the American medical officer in Stalag Luft IV at Gross Tychow he worked tirelessly on his patients' behalf in the face of bitter German hostility, and on the 'death march' to the west in February 1945 he was an inspirational presence, looking after the sick and encouraging those who could stand to keep moving. A few doctors were criticized by POWs for neglecting their duties, but they were usually nameless and little is known of them. But one medical officer who earned infamy among Royal Navy and merchant-navy POWs was Dr Graham MacDiarmid, discovered by the senior doctor at Milag, Major Robert Harvey, to be stealing morphine from the patients to feed his own addiction. MacDiarmid was suspended from all medical work and was eventually repatriated in disgrace, but not before he had been beaten up by prisoners for allegedly making homosexual advances to junior ratings.

All camps would have some sort of medical facility, ranging from a first-aid post to a multi-ward hospital. An Axis doctor was in charge of the hospital, but the work was carried out by British or American medical staff (in both RAF and USAAF camps, doctors came from the British Army).

In Italy medical provision was haphazard, made worse by shortages of basic medicines and other medical supplies, as well as an often obstructive attitude from the Italian authorities. The large camp of PG 70 at Monturano was supplied with just two doctors, from South Africa, who had little more than aspirin to treat their patients. The Revd Douglas Thompson, the camp's padre, noticed how one of the doctors found his posting increasingly stressful, so that eventually he 'became very, very morose and silent; wouldn't speak to any one'. Dr Norman Rogers, the medical officer in PG 8 at Benevento, was particularly concerned with diarrhoea, jaundice and malaria – diseases that accompanied the patients from North Africa. The 120 men suffering from malaria at PG 8 had previously been misdiagnosed by the camp's Italian doctor, who, out of pride, initially refused to accept Rogers's diagnosis. After a long battle, the Italian finally gave way and the men were able to receive quinine and mepacrine as treatment.

In Germany the medical system was better organized, although German medical staff could be difficult and even hostile towards both POW staff and patients. The Germans, like the Italians, suffered from shortages of medicines during the course of the war, and Allied prisoners were a low priority in the allocation of supplies. Fortunately, the Red Cross came to the rescue, providing not only basic medicines but a wider range of items that included spectacles, artificial limbs and surgical instruments. As a consequence, the larger camps were able to provide a wide range of medical services. The hospital in Stalag VIIIB at Lamsdorf had space for 600 beds in six separate blocks, comprising two surgical wards, one medical ward, one psychiatric ward and two infectious-diseases wards isolated from the other blocks. There were four further blocks for laboratories, kitchens and accommodation. Blood plasma was sent out from Britain – essential during complex operations – although the absence of penicillin and a restriction in the use of sulpha drugs to only the most seriously ill meant that infections were slow to heal.

Supplementing the camp hospitals were a small number of specialist hospitals that concentrated on a specific illness or medical condition, to which seriously ill POW patients were sent from camps throughout Germany. They included the hospital at Bad Haina for the treatment of the blind, Rothenburg for skin diseases, and Königswartha and Elsterhorst for men suffering from tuberculosis.

The Germans were fearful of the spread of infectious diseases from prison camps to the civilian population, and took some measures to eradicate them at source. Their greatest fear was the spread of typhus from Russian prisoners, and, although they did little or nothing to help the Russians, they took steps to prevent its spread to British and American prisoners by regular delousing (lice being the carriers of the disease) and by inoculation programmes that involved a painful injection into the chest. These measures, and the good work of Allied medical officers, ensured that cases of typhus were rare among the Anglo-American prison population.

A more serious problem was tuberculosis, which thrived in the confined and poor conditions of POW camps. In 1942, in response to a potentially serious outbreak of TB, the Germans instituted routine mass radiography. As was the case with typhus, the German response was primarily that of self-interest: Dr A. L. Cochrane, a TB specialist in several POW hospitals, explained, 'I was told verbally by a German that their reason for doing this was not humanitarian, but their fear that tuberculosis POWs would infect German civilian workers.' The German follow-up to the screening was erratic, however, so that the programme had limited value. Although TB never became a serious problem overall, it was nonetheless a significant killer of Allied prisoners. Cochrane surveyed the cemetery at Hospital 1251 – a mixed surgical and medical hospital – and found that '80 per cent of the graves were filled with victims of tuberculosis'.

In work camps and smaller camps, access to good medical facilities was more limited, although ill men should have had the opportunity be sent to the main-camp hospitals or to German civilian hospitals if necessary. On many occasions medical staff had to rely on older, simpler forms of medicine. Charcoal became the standard treatment for the gastrointestinal problems that were common throughout the POW system. Graham King, a British medical orderly held in a POW camp in Poland, reverted to the old practice of 'cupping' for the treatment of bronchitis and pneumonia (heated glass jars were placed on the patients' back, and as the air inside cooled it reduced in volume, producing a vacuum effect to hold the cup to the skin). This treatment was essentially psychosomatic, as were others that proved surprisingly effective. King related how 'one patient with "severe arthritis" was cured after an intra-muscular injection of 20cc of sterile water in the buttock. Next day he was enjoying full mobility and was quite embarrassed in his gratitude to the wielder of the syringe – me!' In PG 57 at Gruppignano the doctor was not adverse to giving distilled-water injections to hypochondriacs.

One of the duties of the medical officer was to protect ill men from being sent to work by the Germans, who were generally indifferent to the individual prisoner's welfare. There would be a quota for the number of men allowed off work at any one time – typically a 5 per cent maximum. When the number of genuinely ill cases was below the quota, camp doctors would be prepared to give otherwise well POWs a 'holiday' through some spurious illness or complaint. Desperate men would at times inflict real injuries on themselves to get away from the harder jobs such as mining or quarrying.

A rather unusual but officially sanctioned ruse involved circumcision, medical officers claiming to sceptical Germans that the procedure was required for reasons of hygiene. According to trainee doctor H. C. M. Jarvis, the operations were in fact 'a very useful way of getting some of the lads off work parties for a few weeks'. One prisoner who voluntarily opted for circumcision was R. P. Evans, who described the operation:

> It was not a pleasant experience, under local anaesthetic, to watch a surgeon perform on you. There was only a mild sensation of pain, but mind triumphed over matter and I obligingly passed out. On recovery I found the Australian medical officer had tied a piece of blue ribbon around the bandage, as a sort of accolade. I think the subsequent extreme discomfort was a fairly heavy price to pay for the week's soft living in hospital.

Evans was perhaps fortunate that he had not come under the scalpel of Dr Nichols, a medical officer in Stalag Luft I. According to Jack

Vietor, Nichols 'had been one of the most promising brain surgeons in England' before the war, and had gained a reputation in the camp for being overly 'knife happy'. He had a unique approach to carrying out circumcisions, as Vietor explained: 'During the performance, Doc Nichols, wishing to improve the operation aesthetically, embellished ruffles and frills on the parts concerned, decorations that the hapless recipients viewed with mixed emotions.'

Dental care remained a problem area within the overall medical service for POWs. Not only did prisoners need basic dental treatment, many of them had false teeth – some of them complete sets – which required repair or replacement. When Bob McDowall lost the top half of his false teeth on the crossing from North Africa to Italy, he had to wait months for another set, causing him great anguish in the interim.

The larger camps had the services of a dentist with basic equipment and a small dental laboratory. Anaesthetics remained in short supply, so that even reasonably well-appointed dentists carried out simple extractions without the benefit of analgesia. While at Milag, dental officer Julius Green earned the nickname the 'St Valéry Terror' because 'the lack of equipment and, above all, anaesthetics in the dental room made my ministrations less than pleasant'. A severe toothache forced Jim Witte to visit a German civilian dentist, and the prospect looked grim as he waited his turn, listening to the cries of POW patients being treated ahead of him. But, in his inimitable manner, Witte turned events to his advantage:

> The dentist was huge with a face like Julius Streicher, the eminent Jew-baiter. He motioned me to the chair and asked, 'Englander?' I nodded. He began arranging his implements very slowly and methodically. And then it dawned on me. I drew out twenty Players from my pocket and put them on his tray. 'Ach,' he said. 'Gut.' I watched his thick, hairy wrist fascinatedly as he prepared a shot of cocaine, another commodity in short supply in Germany. He injected my gum very gently and pulled out the infected tooth in one deft movement. I have yet to have a tooth pulled out so efficiently.

The fear of 'going round the bend' made many POWs feel anxious. Stories of men who had slit their wrists or, in a mania of desperation, had thrown themselves at the wire to be shot by the guards were well known in all POW camps. Although such incidents did take place, they were infrequent occurrences: it was their tragically spectacular nature that made them so memorable. For the most part, the mental-health problems faced by POWs comprised a low-grade depression reflecting their miserable circumstances and the simple fact that they were deprived of freedom. For those men captured in the early stages of the war there was no chance of an early release, and the indeterminate nature of the 'sentence' undermined hopeful thoughts of freedom. Over time, POWs became worn down by incarceration – a slow, remorseless erosion that sapped the strongest spirits. For these reasons alone, some form of depression was to be expected.

The trauma of capture had varying degrees of effect on most prisoners. Jack Vietor noted how aircrew relived the terrors of being shot down, one pilot suffering nightmares as a result of baling out and then seeing 'his co-pilot and best friend pass him, falling free without a parachute and screaming'. The guilt of surrender continued to haunt others, especially those Army officers and NCOs who had made the surrender decision. And a post-war study suggested that the relief that men felt at having survived the events leading up to capture was in itself a stimulus to subsequent guilt, which in a few cases became a 'potent factor in precipitating the onset of depression during the POW period and of difficulties on repatriation'.

For those prisoners so severely injured that they could not be considered a military threat in the future there lay the possibility of repatriation. Bilateral exchanges of prisoners had been developed during 1914–18, and the system continued into the Second World War, although efforts were slow and faltering. British and American medical officers would propose those prisoners they believed were suitable for repatriation, who were than examined by a Mixed Medical Commission comprising a doctor from the Detaining Power and two other doctors from neutral countries. Allied doctors would do their best to 'coach' the patients to present their condition in the worst possible light. The decisions made by the commissions often seemed arbitrary to the prisoners themselves, so that on occasion amputees might be rejected in favour of men with seemingly lesser injuries. As well as the sick and wounded, some surplus medical staff – doctors and medical orderlies – could also obtain repatriation by accompanying the patients home.

During 1941 Britain and Germany had opened negotiations for an exchange, with 1,153 British prisoners passed for repatriation. By October the repatriation party had moved to a camp in Rouen preparatory to crossing the English Channel. But at the final hurdle negotiations suddenly broke down, and the despairing patients were returned to their camps – all hopes of a Christmas at home brutally dashed.

British negotiations with Italy proved more successful, and in April 1942 a first exchange took place in the Turkish port of Smyrna, allowing 1,229 British and Commonwealth prisoners to return home. Three smaller exchanges took place in April, May and June 1943 – involving a total of 1,080 repatriables – while a subsequent exchange was eventually thwarted by the collapse of Italy, the patients falling into German hands.

The setback of the aborted Anglo-German exchange was compounded by the continuing dispute over retaliation for the Canadian shackling incident. But in early 1943 negotiations resumed, and four repatriations took place. The first was via Gothenburg in October 1943 (approximately 5,000 British, Commonwealth and American repatriables); the second via Barcelona in May 1944 (over 1,000); the third via Gothenburg in September 1944 (2,560), and the fourth and last via Switzerland and Marseilles in January 1945 (2,500).

For the other prisoners, repatriation invariably evoked bitter-sweet emotions: delight that severely wounded comrades were being spared the rigours of POW life, but a feeling of emptiness in that they themselves would continue to endure captivity without a release date in sight. For those being repatriated the experience was emotionally turbulent. During his period of imprisonment Bertie Harwood had begun to suffer from acute neuritis – a severe inflammation of the nerves – in one of his legs. By early 1944 he was having trouble standing or walking any distance, and had become a regular visitor to the camp hospital. In the autumn he went before a Mixed Medical Commission. 'Within ten minutes,' wrote Harwood, 'I had been interviewed, medically examined and told I would be leaving with the next party to be repatriated.'

Throughout November and December, Harwood and a small group of other repatriables waited for the order to leave Oflag VIIB at Eichstätt, their home for the past two years and more. Harwood had mixed feelings: 'I was congratulated by all my friends and acquaintances on my good fortune and felt extremely uncomfortable at the obvious sincerity of their good wishes. I felt, somehow, that I was letting them down at the end of the journey after we had travelled such a long way together.' On 5 January 1945, after a succession of false rumours, a German guard confirmed that Harwood's group would leave the camp the following day.

The train journey to Switzerland was long and slow. Harwood recorded his feelings of suppressed excitement as he travelled through a snowbound Germany: 'The exquisite pain of knowing that each yard we moved was a yard nearer freedom was almost more than I could stand.' Eventually the train drew into the station in the Swiss half of Constance, to be met by a reception from the British consul's wife and other members of the British community in Switzerland. Harwood found the sound of joyful, feminine voices speaking English overwhelming: 'The whole scene became blurred for I found tears of sheer thankfulness and happiness springing to my eyes.'

The train carried on through Switzerland and liberated France to Marseilles, the now former POWs looked after by some formidable nurses from the American Red Cross. As his ship sailed for Britain, Harwood faced the realization that freedom could be as daunting as it was liberating: 'The contemplation of being let loose and of having to organize my life was quite terrifying.' But in this respect Harwood would be one of many.

Like the medical officer, the padre was a part of the military establishment. But in contrast to the doctor, who had a well-defined role to play before and after capture, the padre's purpose behind barbed wire was somewhat vague. On the positive side this allowed an energetic and dedicated clergyman to carve out a position for himself that would be of great benefit to those under his care, but there were too many chaplains who did not rise to the challenge.

As honorary officers, padres were initially imprisoned in officer camps, leaving the camps containing other ranks without pastoral care. Although the Axis authorities – especially the Germans – preferred to keep clergymen locked away in officer camps, they did permit the transfer of padres to other ranks' camps: the Revd David

Wild's request to leave Oflag VIB at Warburg for a Stalag took just three weeks to be granted. But in Germany the imbalance between padres in Oflags and Stalags was striking: at various times Oflag IXA (Spangenberg) held 35 padres, Oflag IXA (Rotenburg) 21, and Oflag VIIC (Laufen) 18, while otherwise well-organized Stalags – many times the size of the largest Oflag – might only have two or three. In those camps without recognized clergy, lay preachers – usually Nonconformists – and other committed Christians took the position of clergymen, and were sometimes granted a degree of recognition by the Axis camp authorities.

The idea of padres preferring a 'cushy billet' to the hardship of the Stalags was common among prisoners, and even those clergymen who were in Stalags were not immune from criticism. H. C. M. Jarvis, the trainee doctor at Lamsdorf, was unusual in his virulent dislike of the clergy, and his account of POW life lists numerous examples of their failings. On one occasion he wrote, 'Feelings were very resentful against the padres. They were regarded as parasites. Tales of deceit and theft came in from working parties. The padres were allowed to visit these parties, but anything they were asked to bring in was lost on the way.' This intemperate out-burst was clearly based on hearsay, but whatever the truth of the matter it illustrated the intensity of antipathy that some prisoners felt towards men of the cloth.

But those clergymen who went out and engaged with their flocks earned high praise. The dental officer Julius Green worked along-side padres in several camps, and wrote that 'they did not neglect their calling. I remember them with admiration and affection.' As was the case with medical staff, Air Force camps lacked military chaplains of their own and relied heavily on (mainly British) Army padres.

Jack Vietor rejected the idea that capture and imprisonment might open men's hearts to religion: 'The minister who stated early in the war that "there are no atheists in the foxholes" was talking through his clerical hat. It was very rare that even the most harrowing combat altered anyone's religious outlook.' An even more gloomy view was held by Father Cyril Scarborough, a Roman Catholic padre who ministered in several camps, including Oflag IVC at Colditz. 'It's a mistake', he recalled, 'to think that prisoners of war are good at practising their religion. They're not. It doesn't drive people to God or religion, they just feel fed up.' And a report on religious life in Stalag Luft VI at Heydekrug concluded that the majority of prisoners were 'completely indifferent to religion in its organized form'.

Religious motivation was also questioned. An inmate of several Italian camps, Sergeant Reginald Dexter, wrote, 'I'm afraid many of us were hypocritical. In adversity, so easy to turn to the Church for comfort – to attend the services merely as somewhere to get out of the rut of idle camp life.' From his Italian camp, PG 35 at Padula, George Millar considered that only half of POW churchgoers were really religious, although he believed that many prisoners took some comfort from religion; he estimated – with surprising precision – that 'about thirty per cent of officers and four per cent of the batmen' attended religious services. In American camps, however, there was greater interest in religion, with higher attendances at services. Center compound at Stalag Luft III was especially religious, and its Sunday services were packed with worshippers. In short, it would seem that those of a religious disposition gained solace from the provision of religious services, and their beliefs may well have been deepened by their POW experience. The irreligious, however, carried on as before.

Clergymen of different denominations were recruited to reflect the various religious persuasions of the armed forces, but once in the camps the system broke down and padres soon found themselves ministering to men of denominations other than their own. Church of England padre David Wild was careful to hold services that would 'suit men of various denominations'. As the sole minister in the American enlisted men's camp Stalag IIA at Neubrandenburg, the Catholic padre Francis L. Sampson held twice-weekly non-denominational services for Protestants. In Stalag IVB at Mühlberg, Bob McDowall and his group of padres took the ecumenical spirit a stage further. As well as holding Catholic, Church of England and other-denomination services on Sundays and Wednesdays, they took part in interdenominational services, with the ministers taking different parts of the service. It was in these German POW camps that early signs of later ecumenical harmony could be discerned, so that, for example, the Catholic Father Coates was persuaded to join the Protestant pastors in a service in Stalag VIIA at Moosburg to mark the death of President Roosevelt.

Adherents to religions other than Christianity had to make their own ad-hoc provision. Hindus, Muslims and Sikhs of the Indian Army were free to hold their own services, as were Jews, although in their case a measure of circumspection was required. In one of the American compounds at Stalag Luft I a tent was set up for religious services, and was made available to Jewish POWs by the British Catholic chaplain, Father Michael Charlton – this being permitted by the Germans despite the separation of Jews within the camp. Attendance was high, in part, according to one Jewish airman, as a means 'to piss the Nazis off'.

For those without any particular faith, prison-camp life could still possess a spiritual dimension. Bertie Harwood wrote:

> I shall always be grateful for those years as a POW in one respect. The drab monotony of that life and the continual pangs of hunger seemed to open my eyes and make me see the small and commonplace things of this world for the first time. I saw fresh beauty in the most ordinary flowers – flowers one had always taken for granted – and the colouring of the trees in their spring foliage was more vivid that I had ever known it.

That hunger heightens the senses has been well known to religious mystics, who have fasted to gain greater spiritual awareness. The artist Terry Frost, held in Stalag 383, certainly believed that lack of food gave him a heightened perception, both visual and spiritual. And for those prisoners interned in the more scenic parts of Germany and Italy the beauty of the surrounding countryside was a spiritual consolation of sorts.

German attitudes towards padres were ambivalent at best. While individual Germans may have welcomed the work carried out by padres, the Nazi party and OKW did not, especially in the working Stalags. The Nazis were hostile to all manifestations of Christianity, while OKW had an almost paranoid fear that an unchecked clergy would encourage dissent among the prisoner workforce. And yet at the same time they were compelled by the Geneva Convention to allow padres into the Stalags. As a consequence, padres had to tread a fine line when providing secular as well as spiritual support to POWs: if they exceeded '*seelsorgerische Tätigkeit*' (soul-caring activity) too far they could find themselves transferred elsewhere.

German anxiety lay primarily in the content of sermons, which they thought might be used as a platform for incendiary anti-German statements. Standard procedure was to have them vetted, and to ensure that the padre kept to his script an interpreter might attend the service. When the American Presbyterian padre Eugene L. Daniel was transferred from Stalag VIIA at Moosburg to Stalag Luft III at Sagan he was pleased to discover a more relaxed attitude. 'Unlike the Army-run prison camps,' he wrote, 'the Luftwaffe did not require me to submit sermon outlines in advance, nor were they present at our services of worship or Bible classes.'

In the Army-administered Stalag IVB, Bob McDowall was largely left alone by the Germans, although he believed his diary was surreptitiously looked over by some of the English-speaking guards. One of his fellow padres was less fortunate, however. The Methodist minister Douglas Thompson had decided to preach a series of sermons on the Hebrew minor prophets, and, although his plans were initially passed by the German interpreter, when details reached higher authority Thompson was told that anything to do with these prophets was prohibited in the German Reich. The hapless Thompson was disciplined by being sent to Jacobstahl, a former Jewish concentration camp converted into a punishment camp for Stalag IVB.

As well as conducting the main services and overseeing Bible classes and other forms of scriptural or religious study, padres also performed their traditional roles of visiting the sick and officiating at funerals. But arguably as important as their religious duties was the secular work carried out on behalf of the POWs in other ranks' camps. As they held officer rank, padres had a degree of influence over their guards, and were able to use the threat of reporting them to higher authority if they mistreated prisoners. In an Italian camp McDowall discovered that guards were illegally confiscating cigarettes from prisoners entering the hospital, a practice that was stopped after he wrote a strongly worded letter to the commandant. At Stalag IIA, Father Sampson worked closely with the American Man of

Confidence, hiding a radio in the chapel pulpit and acting as one of the men's representatives to the German authorities.

Padres issued with passes to visit work camps were especially effective in protecting the rights of POWs. Prisoners in the more far-flung camps had little contact with NCO leaders in the main camp, and could be subject to the tyranny of employers or guards. The Revd David Wild visited many work camps attached to Stalag XXA at Thorn, and not only liaised with camp leader CQMS Reg Granger but in extreme cases took up matters directly with the German commandant. On one occasion he reported the poor behaviour of a guard in charge of a work camp to the Stalag adjutant, which led to the guard's removal and improved conditions for the British prisoners, while on another he ensured that a man crippled by varicose veins received hospital treatment that had formerly been denied him.

A padre's position could be lonely and difficult, especially when working on his own. 'In the armed forces,' wrote Eugene L. Daniel, 'the chaplain is often without much spiritual support from those around him. Even more so in a POW camp.' In Italy Bob McDowall suffered many conflicting emotions after volunteering to go into captivity. He confided in his diary, 'I came away doing, as I thought, my duty, but it was a sad mistake. I should never have come.' And yet, while he could feel 'inexpressively lonely' at times, he was also uplifted by his work, almost to the point of ecstasy. After one Bible class he wrote, 'These passages of Scripture are so paralysingly beautiful and rich. We read Psalm 116, and I was so moved I could hardly get through it.' And elsewhere he added, 'Am full of happiness at the work. The prison experience has brought me riches beyond dreams.'

McDowall spent nearly two years in Italy. In some ways this period acted as an apprenticeship for his chaplaincy in Germany. Although he never lost his tendency towards awkwardness – both physically and socially – his Italian captivity forced him to open up to the world, to become more understanding of the men around him. The Serb prisoners taught the formerly teetotal Presbyterian that alcohol need not be the 'demon drink'; they also introduced him to new religious experiences. In January 1942, shortly after his arrival in Italy, he was invited to a Greek Orthodox Serb service, which proved something of a revelation. 'Went to the service,' he wrote, 'and was greatly impressed with the sense of wonder and mystery conveyed in it. There is something in these services which proclaims the whole faith, and holds the imagination.' McDowall's growing ecumenicalism subsequently extended to an appreciation of the Church of England: 'I like [their] service far better than our own. Reverence is expressed in its action and worship. Ours is a repetition of the rite.'

McDowall's interest in other denominations did not, however, stop him taking a critical view of some of their practitioners. At the end of January 1944 he was sent to Oflag VIIB at Eichstätt – probably by administrative error – and spent six weeks there before, to his relief, being allowed to return to Stalag IVB. Refused permission to work as a padre in Eichstätt, he had plenty of time to observe the shortcomings of his fellow clergymen. He also remained resolutely self-critical, castigating himself for insufficient faith in God, for poorly delivered sermons, and even for his failings as an actor in the small drama group he attended.

At Stalag IVB McDowall had become the senior member of a small team of British padres. He was now more confident and relaxed, and the success of his German ministry can be gauged in part by the way he was able to draw prisoners to his services. In North Africa, out of a potential congregation of 1,500 soldiers, he was pleased to see 22 men turn up. By contrast, in Stalag IVB McDowall was regularly attracting congregations of between 600 and 900 men. A comparison can also be made of the comments made about him. In North Africa, the New Zealand padre the Revd M. L. Underhill described McDowall as 'a man who didn't have many mates', and during his first year in Italy Ivor Hopkins, a soldier captured in Crete, called him 'a bit of a dour bastard'. But in Germany John Tomlinson considered him a good padre. 'I admired [him],' he wrote, 'because he could have been in the officers' camp with their privileges but chose to stay with us. All of us will remember him with affection.' Derrick Hawthorne, another Stalag IVB prisoner, wrote, 'He had a very pleasant cheerful face and was well liked by all. There was something about him that made me think he was a deeply spiritual man.'

In captivity, Bob McDowall and padres such as David Wild and Eugene L. Daniel flourished. They had followed the Christian way in helping those less fortunate than themselves, and had gained from it as a result. They – and the other great carers, the medical officers and their staffs – had the satisfaction of knowing that by making a significant contribution to the welfare of others their imprisonment had not been wasted time.

12

Resistance, Punishment and Collaboration

AFTER HIS ARRIVAL in Stalag Luft III in the summer of 1942, Canadian airman Kingsley Brown was summoned by the SBO, Group Captain H. M. Massey, who put it to Brown that as a former journalist he might like to get involved in propaganda work. Thrilled at the prospect of being 'some kind of Scarlet Pimpernel', Brown marched off to meet Squadron Leader 'Taffy' Williams, the officer in charge of propaganda. As a block leader, Williams had his own cubicle, which to Brown's eyes had all the clutter of the keen hobbyist. From a table covered with jam jars, glue, paper and scissors, Williams handed Brown a jar filled with an angry buzzing of trapped bees. Brown described how the meeting developed:

> I handed back the jar of bees, and in return he passed me a tiny slip of paper. It was almost tissue paper, not unlike the paper used for airmail letters. It was about four inches in length, and had been cut in the triangular shape of a pennant. On one side of it, it said DEUTSCH-LAND KAPUT. On the reverse side it said HITLER KAPUT. The nature of the propaganda effort suddenly dawned on me. The bumblebees were to carry our devastating message to the German populace.

An enthusiastic Williams then instructed Brown in the delicate art of attaching the pennants to the bees before releasing them around the camp.

Perhaps surprisingly, this almost surreal instance of a propaganda offensive against the Nazi state was not a one-off. The idea had been pioneered at Stalag Luft I, with hornets pestering the people of nearby Barth with messages of despondency. And in Oflag IVC at Colditz an RAF officer built a model glider in the shape of a Spitfire and attached it to a hornet, which buzzed its way around the castle courtyard during a roll call to the consternation of the Germans and amusement of the POWs below.

Much of what became known as 'goon-baiting' was undoubtedly childish, but as the guards had the guns so the prisoners had to look for oblique strategies to counter the enemy's material superiority. Both German and Italian guards made much of their military honour and dignity, and this of course made them vulnerable to the ridicule that manifested itself as schoolboy pranks. And, with many POWs only just out of school and with a great deal of time on their hands, goon-baiting was inevitable.

The twice daily *Appells* became a focus for ill discipline. Attempts to count the prisoners were frustrated by men dodging around at the back, so that a count that should have lasted minutes might go on for two hours or more. Here, at least, there was a serious point to this horseplay, however: when POWs escaped it was vital that their absence be unnoticed for as long as possible; their comrades made sure that some men were counted twice to cover for the escapers. As well as fouling up the count, prisoners would typically attend roll-call parades in a slovenly manner: poorly dressed, smoking, reading, talking loudly to a companion, and jeering the guards. Axis commands were deliberately misunderstood or carried out as badly as possible. To underscore the contempt felt towards the enemy, a British parade for a special occasion, such as the King's birthday, was conducted in an exemplary manner, with a smart turnout and crisply executed drill.

Prisoners in Colditz and the RAF camps were the most enthusiastic goon-baiters. They tended to push things further than anyone else, helped, admittedly, by some generally forbearing guards. In the NCO compound at Stalag Luft III, Richard Passmore recorded how one morning the count was disrupted by the simple expedient of a prisoner called John Edgar wearing a full-blown Mohican haircut. 'The following day,' Passmore continued, 'John had a rival: another man had his head shaven apart from two monstrous horns, carefully shaped and stiff with some kind of grease. Again the interpreter lost his count in the mental confusion. Within a week every variation possible on the theme appeared: monastic tonsures, a five-of-dice pattern, a transverse ridge dressed to resemble a halo.' Aware that this was some form of disobedience, the Germans eventually banned unusual haircuts on pain of three days in solitary, but the POWs believed they had won the moral argument.

The ways in which to infuriate the Germans were almost endless. In Colditz water bombs were dropped on guards; in Oflag VIB at Warburg the honey wagon removing excrement from the camp latrines was found to have the word *Kultur* painted on the side during an inspection by a German general; German marching songs were mercilessly parodied by the POWs, as was the veneration of the Führer – the 'German greeting' ('*Heil Hitler!*') was supplemented by '*Heil Churchill!*' and even '*Heil Stalin!*'. Ironic cheering – a traditional standby of other ranks in the face of authority – was used to good effect to puncture the more bombastic of German announcements. Bob Prouse recalled a typical instance in the Molsdorf camp attached to Stalag IXC at Bad Sulza:

> One day the camp Commandant called a parade to inform us, through an interpreter, how the war was progressing. It was a tale we had heard often, telling us of how the brave German army had repulsed the enemy, leaving large numbers of our comrades dead. The prisoners' spontaneous reply was a loud and ringing cheer. The Commandant threw his hands up in disgust and told us that he would not give us any more news as we must be totally stupid to be cheering the death of our comrades.

The chief goon-baiter at Colditz, Flight Lieutenant Peter Tunstall, considered it his duty to create trouble, although he admitted he paid a high price for his misdemeanours: 'four hundred and fifteen days in solitary, the record in Colditz, and five court-martials, more than any other prisoner during the Second World War'. Others, however, were less enthusiastic. They considered such antics counter-productive, and even demeaning. While Jack Vietor agreed that 'fouling up the goons' could be an enjoyable pastime, 'our pleasure in German mishaps was never really commensurate with the punishments we received.' The RAF leaders Dixie Deans and Wings Day put a brake on some of the more extreme forms of goon-baiting, but tolerated a lot of bad behaviour on the basis that it was a disciplinary problem for the Germans to deal with. Delmar Spivey took a less lenient view, especially in regard to dodging *Appells*: 'It became my policy to discourage such action as it caused an even greater inconvenience to all the POWs who had to stand outdoors, often in frigid weather, while the Germans searched around looking for the missing prisoner.'

Spivey would also have regarded much of this behaviour as being beneath the dignity of an American officer, a view echoed by Calton Younger, an Australian NCO airman. 'The practice of "Jerry baiting"', he wrote, 'was carried on zestfully by many prisoners, but it was the for the most part crude, schoolboy stuff, which, vitiating our own dignity, only encouraged the Germans to a deeper belief in their superiority.' But South African squadron leader T. D. Calnan disagreed: 'To us it was an outlet for our frustration and an antidote to our despair. To infuriate our captors, to make them look ridiculous, was the best morale-builder we had. The satisfaction of winning a small and temporary victory was very sweet and gave renewed courage during the blacker days of the war.'

Apart from goon-baiting and escape – the ultimate act of resistance for a prisoner – there was not a great deal a non-working POW could do to continue fighting the war within a camp. A working POW had the option of sabotage in the workplace; for a non-working POW, sabotaging the camp hurt him more than it hurt the enemy. There were, however, a few possibilities open to the enterprising prisoner. The Germans could be somewhat careless in leaving objects lying around. Any tradesman working in a camp had to guard his tools with his life; the slightest carelessness and they were gone. On one occasion a bicycle was left unattended for a few moments; it was immediately broken down into its constituent parts, which were shot over the wire using the rubber tyre as a catapult. In both Stalags Luft I and Luft VI POW records were stolen from the Germans and destroyed. More controversially, old razor blades were dropped into waste food intended as pigswill. On a more positive note, the NCOs at Stalag 383 at Hohenfels raised money for the purchase of a Spitfire. Staff Sergeant James McGee described the process: 'Through the Protecting Power, it was possible to make allocations from individual pay accounts. The camp adopted the idea with enthusiasm and almost everyone made a contribution thro' an allotment of pay. The plane was purchased, christened "Unfettered Spirit" and flew in combat.'

The frustrations of the prisoners were taken out on the guards where possible; any changes in the balance of power were exploited to the full. In PG 49 at Fontanellato officers were allowed out on parole walks on Sundays, and Stuart Hood, one of the walkers, remembered how 'we took our small revenges as we strode out, marching the short-rumped fourth category guards off their feet.' Bob Prouse described a common tactic, which he admitted was cruel though effective. 'The guards loved Canadian cigarettes,' he wrote, 'and, when they were plentiful (after receiving a carton from home), a favourite trick was to light up in front of a guard, take a couple of puffs, then throw the cigarette at his feet. You could see his eyes widen, waiting for you to move on so that he could retrieve the butt. Instead you would grin at him, step forward and grind it under your heel.' A similar way of getting one over the Germans was the very visible consumption of Red Cross luxuries, especially chocolate. While in transit to Stalag VIIIB at Lamsdorf, Billie Stephens and a group of POWs were forced to wait on a station platform:

> Someone had a very good idea; he got a large slab of chocolate out of one of our Red Cross parcels and unwrapped it very ostentatiously and then offered a small portion of this delicacy to a stray dog. There were probably about 30 to 40 Germans, who were watching us, and who doubtless had not seen chocolate for two or three years. The effect on the crowd was electrifying; after a good deal of talk amongst themselves they came towards us en masse in the most menacing fashion and I believe that, had it not been for the prompt intervention of our guards, they would probably have tried to lynch us. I may say that it hurt us considerably seeing the dog get the chocolate, but it was quite worthwhile.

Gaining a sense of superiority over Germans might be satisfying, but more effective was to subvert their loyalties to the Reich. The development of a 'tame goon' – who was sympathetic to the prisoners, usually through bribery and the threat of blackmail – was an important part of an effective escape organization. Another method of moderating the behaviour of the guards in the prisoners' favour was to issue them with good-conduct references. This became an increasingly useful tool as the war turned against the Axis and guards began to consider their post-war future among the vanquished. As well as handing out good references, RAF prisoners in Oflag XXIB at Schubin made it clear that hostile guards were liable to face post-war retribution. To emphasize this, the names of these guards were publicly listed around the camp, with a small black Maltese cross – cut from the 'In Memoriam' section of German newspapers – appended to each name.

Clandestine radios were simultaneously a means of communication and of resistance. The Axis authorities set up loudspeakers in POW camps, broadcasting popular radio programmes complete with news bulletins of German military triumphs and Allied setbacks. To counter this, the POWs began to construct their own radio receivers to listen to the BBC. Given the extensive electrical knowledge to be found within bomber crews, it is no surprise that the first camp to possess its own radio was Stalag Luft I, where in the NCOs' compound John Bristow built a radio receiver from odds and ends he found in and around the camp. Dixie Deans considered Bristow capable of making 'anything out of nothing'. The only problem for the radio-builders was to locate valves, which could not be home-made, and these were either stolen from German radios or bought from corrupt German guards. In camps where the POWs lacked the necessary electrical knowledge to build their own receivers, entire radios were smuggled into the camp, sold to them by foreign workers.

Each evening a wireless operator would tune into the BBC, while a man with shorthand knowledge would take down the news. This would be edited and transcribed on to news-sheets and given to news-readers, who went from hut to hut to read out the bulletin to the entire camp. The news-sheets were then destroyed, to prevent them falling into enemy hands. Even if the news was bad, the radio was at least a direct link with home, and when the news was good it was a great morale-booster.

The Germans always suspected that the prisoners had access to outside news sources, and devoted much attention to tracking down covert radios. Consequently radios were ingeniously hidden – in beer barrels, medicine balls, accordions – and were rarely discovered. In those camps with several radios, one might be left to be found by the Germans to take the heat off the other radio operators. A few camps had radio transmitters, although they were to be employed only in an extreme emergency, such as to report a possible German order to kill the POWs.

The sending of coded letters – where the code was hidden inside an otherwise innocuous family letter – was a more direct if slower form of communication between British and American prisoners and their governments. A small number of British POWs had set up their own private codes to communicate with their families – known as 'dotty codes', because they often used punctuation marks to indicate the coded sections of the letter. Captain Rupert Barry, one of the original Colditz inmates, was desperate to get British intelligence to provide him with escape materials. Although no coding details had been agreed with his wife beforehand, Barry knew that she was an excellent crossword-puzzler and so wrote her a deliberately odd letter hoping that she would realize there was a hidden code to be unravelled within. At first she thought he had gone mad, but with help she decoded the phrase 'Go to the War Office . . .' The letter was passed to MI9 – the branch of military intelligence responsible for POWs – who replied to Barry in his own code. The letter instructed him to wash out some handkerchiefs (sent to two other prisoners) that revealed the workings of the new HK code, which, in a number of variations, would be used throughout the war.

Although time-consuming, the HK code was reasonably simple to use and proved very secure; despite German suspicions, it was never broken. The code – developed in 1940 – was passed on to responsible members of the armed forces and soon spread to all Oflags and a large number of Stalags. Initially used to alert POWs of the imminent arrival of contraband goods in disguised parcels, it also became a useful intelligence tool, allowing prisoners to send information back to MI9, who in turn could ask for specific information from the camps. The system was inevitably slow: seven weeks for a return of letter was considered very good going in Germany, with seven months for Italy. To supplement and speed up the system, MI9 sent coded messages over the radio. The chosen vehicle for these messages was the regular Wednesday-evening talk to the armed forces given by the 'Radio Padre', the Very Revd Dr R. Selby Wright. If he began with the phrase 'Good evening, forces' a coded message was contained within the talk.

New prisoners were interrogated by the POWs' camp-intelligence officer, not only to establish their bona fides but to see if they had worthwhile intelligence on their capture that could be forwarded to London. Aircrew were particularly useful in describing new enemy weapons and tactics, or defects in their own aircraft and equipment.

British POWs in a work-camp quarry attached to Stalag VIIIB at Lamsdorf

US airmen in Stalag Luft III broadcast a radio show over the camp's PA system

The cast of the 1940 Christmas panto, Oflag VIIC at Laufen – Bertie Harwood is in the back row, centre, with moustache and peaked cap

An accordian–guitar band from a British Stalag. The instruments were supplied by the YMCA and the Red Cross

A Christmas card of Oflag VIIB at Eichstätt by Michael Goodliffe. His distinctive inverted UK cloud formation is apparent

A scene from Michael Goodliffe's 1944 production of *Hamlet*. Richard Wood – the organizer of the Eichstätt Music Festival – is on the left

The forged *Ausweis* of Billie Stephens that managed to fool the rail authorities, the German Army and even the Gestapo

Wearing civilian clothes, a British POW redraws a map of Germany in preparation for escape

A trolley used to move spoil from the 'Harry' tunnel used in the Great Escape

Wing Commander H. M. A. 'Wings' Day, the indomitable escaper and escape leader

The prisoners' courtyard in Oflag IVC, Colditz. Although well guarded, the castle was far from escape-proof

Left: Conspicuously marked to avoid Allied aerial attack, a convoy of Red Cross trucks – nicknamed White Angels – prepares to enter Germany in the final months of the war

Below: British POWs enthusiastically open a consignment of Red Cross parcels, on this occasion from the United States

The contents of a typical American Red Cross parcel

The representative from the Swiss Protecting Power (second from right) discusses conditions at Stalag Luft III with the SBO, Group Captain H. M. Massey (bareheaded)

Above: Allied POWs cheer their liberation from Stalag XIB at Fallingbostel

Left: A group of emaciated POWs from Fallingbostel, immediately after liberation

The scientist Howard Cundall, who had been shot down as a passenger in a bomber over Brittany and sent to Stalag Luft III, was able to provide MI9 with details of new innovations in Luftwaffe airborne radar. Other useful information came from captured crews of the X-craft that had severely damaged the battleship *Tirpitz* at its harbour in Norway.

Additional intelligence supplied by coded letters came from prisoners' observations of what was around them. Even from the limited viewpoint of the camps themselves, intelligence officers were able to glean bits of information from train movements, airfield watches (including the early use of jet aircraft) and the observation of nearby bomb damage, and to suggest other possible targets for Allied bombers. More useful still was information gained from corrupt or anti-Nazi guards. In work camps attached to Stalag XVIIIA, Howard Greville was given information from anti-Nazi Austrians on the whereabouts of a German aircraft plant and the movement of oil from Romania to Germany. He passed this information to an intelligence officer operating within the main camp. In Stalag Luft III the POW intelligence organization was able to worm out information through many different avenues, including details – from two separate sources – of the German rocket programme at Peenemünde. The usefulness of the intelligence sent back to MI9 remains hard to assess. Knowledge of Peenemünde came from many sources, but the information provided by the prisoners from Stalag Luft III would have formed a useful part of the intelligence mosaic that led to the successful RAF raid against the Peenemünde site on 17/18 August 1943.

Acts of resistance tended to be followed by punishment. Escapes could produce violent reactions from the camp guards, as they were often punished themselves if they were found to have been at fault in a prisoner's escape. Escapers – especially from the other ranks – who were recaptured by their own guards could typically expect a severe beating, and in a few extreme cases guards escorting men back to the camp killed them and claimed that they had been 'shot while trying to escape'. Uncooperative prisoners on work parties could also experience rough treatment from their guards. POWs had to walk a fine line when resisting orders or indulging in goon-baiting.

Beyond such ad-hoc reprisals from angry guards, prisoners were subject to set disciplinary punishments for most misdemeanours and to judicial punishments – involving a court martial – for serious crimes such as attacking guards, sabotage, mutiny and sexual relations with German women. Disciplinary punishments came under the jurisdiction of the commandant and usually involved time in solitary confinement, with a maximum sentence of thirty days to be awarded at any one time. Bob Prouse received seven days in the cooler for laughing and smoking during the morning *Appell*. Conditions in solitary varied slightly from camp to camp. Prouse was left in a bare cell lacking direct sunlight, its only furnishings a bed without a mattress or pillows; two blankets were issued, but only at night as he was not allowed to lie on the bed during the day.

POWs convicted by a court martial faced sentences in military prisons, first at Fort Zinna at Torgau and from 1942 at Graudenz in the Polish Corridor. Conditions were uniformly grim. Few, if any, Red Cross parcels or other comforts were permitted, and the food was so poor that men undergoing sentences of more than a few months began to starve. The guards were heavy-handed – if not outright sadistic – and breaches of discipline were punished with severe beatings and shackling. David Hunter, a naval lieutenant held in Colditz and sentenced to three months at Graudenz, described its harsh regime:

> Graudenz was a professional prison, and they made it damned clear to you from day one that you marched double speed everywhere you went, put your hands on top of your head to make sure that you weren't carrying anything, and you stayed in your cell for twenty-three hours out of twenty-four. You had no one to talk to and nothing to read. Every time somebody came and looked through the peephole, you had to spring to attention and say who you were and what your number was.

Conditions at Graudenz did, however, begin to improve when the prison came under the administration of Stalag XXA at Thorn in the summer of 1943. The camp leader at Thorn, CQMS Reg Granger, persuaded the Protecting Power and the YMCA to visit Graudenz and fought an energetic campaign to establish a proper interchange of letters for the prisoners and a regular supply of Red Cross parcels.

By the spring of 1944 the starvation diet had been improved and the prisoners began to lose the dreadfully emaciated appearance that had previously shocked visitors to the prison.

Although strictly against the terms of the Geneva Convention, the Germans instituted various collective punishments for escapes and larger-scale misdemeanours. Sometimes they were disguised as water or power failures, or the inability to distribute Red Cross parcels due to unforeseen circumstances. After an escape at Marlag, Red Cross parcels were stopped by the Germans. The SBO, Captain G. F. W. Wilson, sent a subordinate to ask why this had been done. 'He received the amazing reply', Wilson noted in his diary, 'that this was no punishment, but as the men who supervised the issue of parcels were engaged in the search, none could be given out.' Astounded at the German effrontery, Wilson simply wrote, 'Comment is superfluous.' One undoubtedly sadistic collective punishment that could not be explained away in any form took place in Stalag IIIE at Kirchhain after an escape by nine men in 1941. The prisoners were rounded up, ordered to take off their shoes and socks, and made to wear clogs. Then, at gunpoint, they were forced to run around the compound for three hours, some men collapsing with exhaustion, all with bleeding feet. While this was going on, the prisoners' barracks were torn apart in an ostensible search for escape materials.

The Germans enacted a second type of collective punishment for what they perceived as failings by the Allies in the treatment of their prisoners. German and Italian POWs were better looked after than their Allied counterparts, although there were occasional lapses and these were seized upon by the German authorities to instigate punitive reprisals against Allied POWs. In February 1941 batches of British officers at Oflag VIIC at Laufen and Oflag IXA at Spangenberg were transferred to forts at Thorn and Posen in retaliation for the supposedly poor conditions experienced by German officers at Fort Henry in Canada. Bertie Harwood was one of the officers sent to Posen and quartered in the dank, underground and lice-ridden fortress, with poor drinking and washing facilities and even worse sanitation. Having discovered that conditions in Canada were not as bad as originally thought, the Germans closed down the forts in May and dispersed the prisoners to conventional Oflags, with Harwood being sent to the positively pleasant Oflag VB at Biberach.

This cycle of offence and retaliation continued throughout the war. When German prisoners had their boots confiscated after an escape attempt in Canada, POWs in Stalag XXID at Posen lost theirs for six weeks in reprisal. In September 1942 officers at Spangenberg suffered the confiscation of their personal belongings – including washing and shaving gear – for alleged bad treatment of German officers aboard a prison ship. When the possessions were returned two months later the officers were in the midst of a beard-growing competition.

A more serious and widespread German reprisal came in the aftermath of the Dieppe raid of August 1942. The Germans discovered documents and other evidence that German prisoners had had their hands bound, which the Germans believed went against the terms of the Geneva Convention. The Germans threatened to shackle British and Canadian POWs unless there was a formal apology. The situation escalated in October when, in a commando raid on Sark, more German prisoners were bound, and some of them shot. The Germans then put manacles on some 1,300 British and Canadian prisoners. Encouraged by Winston Churchill, the British responded by shackling a similar number of German prisoners in Canada. The Germans raised the ante so that 4,128 men now had their hands bound. The British then backed down in a battle they could only lose, and with the encouragement of the Swiss Protecting Power and the Canadian government (which had not favoured shackling from the start) the Germans were unbound in December 1942.

The British POW camps targeted for shackling were Stalag 383 (Hohenfels), Stalag VIIIB (Lamsdorf) and Oflag VIIB (Eichstätt). During 1942 the Germans instituted the policy with considerable thoroughness, making life miserable for the men involved. Those who were caught unlocking the manacles (a fairly easy operation) were punished by being forced to stand to attention for eight hours with the manacles on. During 1943, however, German attitudes began to relax, and while the edict remained in force until November 1943 its enforcement declined to the point that in Stalag 383 a guard would come round to the huts in the morning, drop off the manacles, and return in the evening to collect them.

Although irritating, these reprisals were a reminder to the Allies that the Germans were deeply concerned at the fate of their own POWs, and, if only for that reason, would ultimately protect the lives and welfare of British and American prisoners.

Collaboration has always been a topic that arouses fierce emotions, and those POWs who went over to the other side or in some way supported the Axis cause have received much coverage. But their numbers were minuscule, and their overall effect minimal. The only real damage came from those who willingly gave information to their captors under interrogation, or acted as stool pigeons to discover intelligence from other unsuspecting prisoners. Although the Germans did use stool pigeons, the prisoners' fear of them was possibly exaggerated. Bob Prouse certainly believed that he and his comrades were victims of one such informer, who worked his way into their confidence while they were digging an escape tunnel from the work camp at Niederorschel. When the man suddenly disappeared, the tunnel was discovered. A similar occurrence was experienced at Spangenberg, when an unknown officer departed as suddenly as he had arrived, to be followed by an intensive search by the Germans that revealed the presence of a tunnel and much otherwise well-hidden escape material.

One informer with an unusual story was RAF Sergeant Michael Joyce, initially held at the Dulag Luft transit and interrogation camp. The fact that he was a cousin of the infamous collaborator William Joyce – 'Lord Haw Haw' – may not have helped his cause, but he aroused suspicions among other prisoners and did nothing to allay their doubts by his friendliness towards the German camp staff. Joyce eventually asked to be transferred from the camp, and in May 1942 he was taken to Rome and then to North Africa via Crete. There he posed either as a representative of the Red Cross, issuing bogus Red Cross forms, or as a fellow POW shot down in North Africa. He was not particularly successful in gaining information from genuine British and American airmen, and following a bout of dysentery he was returned to Germany.

Joyce's tale then took a bizarre turn when he was ordered to infiltrate one of the civilian escape networks whose lines began on the Luxembourg–Belgium border. Kitted out as a newly downed airman, Joyce managed to contact an escape line, but instead of slipping away to inform his German superiors of the network's existence he simply carried on down the line to Bordeaux, before arriving in Britain in November 1942. Joyce kept quiet about his activities as an informer, and was commended for his bravery and initiative, being awarded the Military Medal and promoted to flight lieutenant. It was only after the war that the truth came out. Joyce escaped prosecution, but lost both his MM and his commission.

Another informer became too well known for his own good. Sub Lieutenant E. W. Purdy, a member of the British Union of Fascists before the war, was recruited by the Germans in the Marlag naval camp. He was taken to Berlin, where he joined a number of other British renegades broadcasting anti-British propaganda. While in Berlin he fell out with his German minders and in March 1944 he was sent to Colditz, where he offered his services to the camp officer, Reinhold Eggers. The prisoners in Colditz were always wary of new arrivals unable to vouch for themselves, but Purdy's misfortune was to be identified as a German sympathizer by Julius Green, then in Colditz but formerly the dental officer at a number of other camps, including Marlag. After interrogation by the security committee and the SBO, Purdy broke down and admitted his past. The SBO, Colonel Willie Todd, then told the commandant that unless Purdy was removed from the camp he would be unable to guarantee his safety. It would seem that this was no idle threat, as, according to one account, some of the Colditz officers had decided that Purdy should be hanged as a traitor there and then. Their intentions were frustrated when Purdy was whisked away after spending just three days in the castle.

The idea of raising a military unit from British POWs to fight on the German side was first raised by the renegade John Amery, a committed fascist who broadcast pro-Nazi propaganda to Britain from Berlin. Although sceptical of the idea, the Germans gave Amery permission to begin recruiting for his grandly titled League of St George in April 1943. He managed to recruit just one member, a 17-year-old ship's boy from the Saint-Denis internment camp outside Paris. Interest from Hitler saved the project, which was then taken over by the SS. In January 1944 the renamed British Free Corps (BFC) came into being, with the initial intention of raising a platoon of thirty men who could be trained and sent into combat.

Two 'holiday camps' had been set up by the Germans, attached to Stalag IIID outside Berlin. Special Detachment 999 was for officers and was establised in a suburban villa at Zehlendorf, but later moved to a country house in Bavaria. Although suspicious of the whole set-up, British officers accepted the offer of short breaks of up to six weeks in pleasant surroundings. To their surprise, no attempt was made to suborn them to the Nazi cause, and it would seem that the 'holiday' was just that. (The Anglophile German Foreign Office official and 1944 July Plot conspirator against Hitler Adam von Trott zu Solz implied that he was the inspiration behind the holiday camp, thereby suggesting a benign motivation.)

The camp for other ranks – Special Detachment 517 at Genshagen – was rather more sinister. The camp staff included a few of the men who were to become the nucleus of the BFC, their role being to persuade incoming POWs to join them in the 'Crusade against Bolshevism'. But little attempt, if any, was made to screen appropriate recruits before arrival, and the vast majority of POWs simply ignored the staff and enjoyed the superior conditions of Genshagen before returning to their parent camps.

Another factor militating against success for the Germans was the presence of camp leader BQMS John Brown, one of the more intriguing and seemingly contradictory figures in the POW system. An Oxford graduate, committed Christian and pre-war member of the British Union of Fascists, Brown was captured in 1940 and sent to the Blechhammer work camp. He used his position as a senior NCO to become a highly successful racketeer, whose blatantly pro-German sympathies were bitterly resented by many of his fellow prisoners. But he was in fact acting as a double agent, having at some point been given access to one of the MI9 letter codes. He was able to get himself sent to Genshagen to run its administration – something beyond the riff-raff who made up the BFC. According to his own account, he managed to sabotage the recruitment efforts of the BFC while sending back reports of the activities of British pro-Nazi sympathizers, including John Amery, to MI9.

During 1944, BFC recruiting leaflets were distributed to POW camps, but were treated with contempt. As Bob Prouse noted, 'They insulted the intelligence of POWs by expecting us to believe this nonsense. The only result in our lager was one of ridicule and laughter.' In a few cases BFC members managed to talk to prisoners directly, but once again with very limited success. Despite the recruitment drive the BFC was never able to reach its very modest target of thirty men (it peaked at twenty-seven in January 1945), and, although it began infantry training, it never saw any front-line action. Its members – an assortment of pre-war fascists, malcontents, opportunists and the mentally confused – drank, womanized and quarrelled among themselves until the end of the war. From a German point of view they were a waste of time and resources.

In 1939 the IRA 'chief of staff', Sean Russell, suggested to the Germans that they raise an anti-British force from Irishmen in the British Army. The Germans were initially doubtful, but in September 1940 they made some tentative moves towards organizing an Irish Brigade with recruits drawn from German POW camps. Although the initiative received some response, none of the volunteers seem to have had any interest in the German cause. Some went along to monitor what was happening and to report back to the British authorities; others were tempted by the idea of greater freedom and improved conditions. Of nine officers who were sent to a camp for possible recruitment, three were code-writers in contact with MI9. The officers were soon returned to their camps, with the exception of one man who was not even Irish but a journalist looking for a story. Realizing that the Irish were a lost cause, the Germans effectively abandoned the project in 1943.

From a German perspective, a more promising source of recruits was provided by POWs from the Indian Army. The genesis of the Free Indian Legion resulted from the arrival of Subhas Chandra Bose in Germany in January 1941. Bose, an Indian nationalist leader under virtual house arrest in Calcutta, had slipped out of India and, after travelling through Afghanistan and the Soviet Union, had reached Germany in the hope of lobbying Hitler for military support against the British in India. While Hitler and the German Foreign Office debated the issue, the sudden capture of over 1,000 Indian troops in North Africa in May 1941 transformed Bose's plan to that of raising a German-equipped Free Indian Legion. The number of Indian POWs steadily increased to around 15,000 by the end of 1942, providing a well-stocked pool of potential recruits.

Batches of Indian POWs were sent from Italy and North Africa to the German camp at Annaberg, where they were subjected to an intensive recruitment campaign by civilians from the German-sponsored Free India Centre. Those POWs thought suitable were sent to another camp at Frankenberg for further attempts at persuasion and, if successful, military training. There was certainly an anti-British undercurrent within the Indian POW population that the Free India propagandists were able to exploit with some success: roughly a quarter of those captured went over to the German side – approximately 4,000 men. The figures would have been higher if Bose had not insisted that all recruits start on the bottom rung, thereby alienating NCOs and Viceroy's Commissioned Officers (VCOs – ranks roughly between a senior NCO and an officer), who, in addition, had dependants back in India relying on their British pay and subsequent pensions.

Bose's modernizing zeal extended to abolishing the traditional distinctions of religion, region and caste. Although in many ways commendable, these changes tended to unsettle many of the Indian Legion soldiers. Another unsatisfactory reform was Bose's choice of Hindustani as the language of command, replacing the Urdu of the British Indian Army. As a consequence, German, English, Urdu and Hindustani were all spoken at various times.

Despite these problems, recruitment and training continued, the intention being to raise a force comparable to a German infantry regiment of three 1,000-strong battalions. A small German staff of senior NCOs and officers would provide overall leadership. By February 1943 the Indian element of the Legion stood at 2,270, and by the summer of 1944 it had reached a maximum strength of 3,115 Indian troops, which with the German staff made a total figure of around 3,500 men. The deployment of the Legion remained a problem. Initial hopes that victory on the Eastern Front would enable it to be used as a spearhead to invade British-occupied India were irrevocably dashed by the spring of 1943. Designated *Infanterie Regiment 950*, the Legion was initially deployed in the Netherlands in May 1943, performing construction duties, before being transferred to France as part of the German occupation force.

Morale steadily declined. There were outbreaks of violence between different religious groups, and at least one mutiny. The men of the Legion began to feel increasingly isolated from all that was familiar to them. Discipline began to waver, and there were accusations of drunkenness, looting and rape while in France. The historian Milan Hauner wrote of the Legion in France, 'Without spiritual guidance many Indians saw "Europeanization" as a process of throwing away their own religion and habits. The imitation of Europe sometimes took rather grotesque forms when some of the Indians preferred to speak broken German among themselves rather than Urdu, for instance.' After the Allied breakout from Normandy the Legion was withdrawn from France – a transfer that included skirmishes with the French Resistance, the Legion's only form of military action. Stationed first in Alsace and then near the Swiss border in Germany, it took no part in the final battles of 1945 and tamely surrendered to the Americans in April 1945. While the ring-leaders of the Legion were court-martialled in India after the war, it was felt by the British that too many men had been either tricked or coerced into joining the Legion to merit any further disciplinary action.

For the Germans, the Free Indian Legion had seemed to show genuine promise, but as it ultimately failed in both the military and propaganda spheres it turned into the largest of their collaborationist white elephants. Perhaps anticipating failure, the Germans seemed half-hearted in their attempts to bring over Allied POWs to their cause. They had some undoubted successes with camp informers, but even there results were limited. The history of Allied POWs in Germany and Italy is one not of collaboration but of sustained and spirited resistance.

13

Escape from Germany

SHORTLY AFTER HIS arrival at Colditz in September 1942, Lieutenant Commander Billie Stephens teamed up with Major Ronnie Littledale to consider possibilities of escape from the castle. Within days they had worked out a rough plan that involved climbing out of a window in the prisoners' kitchen, a dash through the courtyard of the guarded *Kommandantur* and then, somehow, a breakout through the walls of the *Kommandantur* and across the dry moat and the park to scale a final row of barbed wire. Once over the wire they would take trains to Switzerland, some 400 miles away. Despite some misgivings, the Colditz escape committee approved the plan and brought in Captain Pat Reid, a former Colditz escape officer and locksmith, and Canadian flight lieutenant Hank Wardle.

Although Reid introduced some refinements, the plan remained decidedly risky, but preparations for the escape were remarkably thorough. Civilian clothes were made up from military uniforms and German wool blankets. The escape committee supplied 100 Reichsmarks to each man as well as the necessary papers and maps. Stephens and Littledale were to assume the identity of two Frenchmen working in Germany but travelling back to France on leave. Their papers – an identity card and a leave pass giving them permission to return to France – were prepared by a team of forgers and propmakers under Major W. F. 'Andy' Anderson. Stephens's papers had impressions from six different stamps, each cut out from India rubber with a penknife, as well as a passport-style photograph he had acquired from home. 'These were the most brilliant forgeries I have ever seen,' Stephens recalled; 'Ronnie's and mine actually passed two Gestapo check-ups without question.' The maps were based on knowledge that past escapers had provided of the surest routes and details of the frontier itself, including the positions of pillboxes and sentry posts.

MI9 sent useful intelligence through coded letters; Airey Neave, who had successfully reached Switzerland the previous January, suggested a suitable approach march to the border.

At 6.30 p.m. on 14 October the escapers broke into the kitchen and removed the window bars. As Reid would need time to pick the door lock on the far side of the courtyard, he was the first man out, carefully dropping from the window down on to a flat roof and then to the ground. Not only was the whole courtyard floodlit and overlooked by dozens of windows from the *Kommandantur*, there were as many as three guards patrolling the area.

Within the courtyard were a few buildings and areas of shadow, and the escapers had to flit between these to the far side without being observed. This would have been all but impossible without the presence of POW watchers who could observe the courtyard and the guards. A group of musicians – under the baton of legless air ace Douglas Bader – were used as a signalling device. Looking out of a window, Bader would signal the musicians to stop whenever the guard had turned away on his beat and the coast was clear. Although the musicians were forced to quit playing early, the four escapers made it across to the relative safety of a pit on the far side of the yard.

Reid began to work on the lock, but after an hour he was forced to admit defeat; it could not be picked. The situation seemed hopeless: the four men were stuck in the German part of the camp. But luck was with them. Reid had noticed a hole with some steps leading down to a cellar. Walking into the cellar, stinking with the smell of escaped sewage, they saw a flue leading up to the ground on the far side of the *Kommandantur*, and, although it was barred, a simple tug pulled the bars away. Stephens and his comrades could hardly believe their good fortune. Although the flue was very narrow – and necessitated the larger Stephens stripping off to his underwear – the escapers squeezed out on to a terrace above the dry moat.

They lowered themselves with bed sheets to the bottom of the moat and clambered up the other side. A guard then walked past them only 10 yards away, but they remained unseen. The breakout was completed when they hauled themselves over the single-strand perimeter fence. Stephens remembered being amazed when he looked down at his watch to see that it was 3 a.m.; they had taken over eight hours to escape from Colditz.

The two parties separated, with Stephens and Littledale walking to the nearby station at Rocklitz to catch the morning train to Chemnitz. So confident were they of their forged papers that they did not take the usual escaper's choice of local trains (where papers were rarely checked) but instead boarded the express (*Schnellzug*) to Stuttgart; although they were questioned by railway police, their story and papers were deemed satisfactory. They had previously been advised by a Polish officer in Colditz that it would be unwise to book a train from Stuttgart directly towards Switzerland, and instead took a local train to a suburb before buying tickets for Tuttlingen, 20 or so miles north of the Swiss border.

They boarded a compartment that they soon discovered contained two decidedly pro-Nazi French youths. 'This was very unfortunate,' recalled Stephens, 'and we prayed that they would not start to try and talk to us and discover that we spoke very little German and extremely bad French.' Luckily the two escapers were ignored, and they moved to another compartment at the next stop. The strain was beginning to tell on the usually unflappable Stephens: 'I then began to have the most dreadful fit of nerves; we were so near our goal and our luck had been so wonderful that I was sure it couldn't hold.'

Stephens and Littledale decided against taking a train from Tuttlingen to Singen, a few miles from the border, correctly reasoning that the frontier zone would be closely guarded, and their presence as French workers ostensibly on their way to France would be highly suspicious to anyone checking their papers. After walking out of Tuttlingen station they took a wrong turning and spent the night in a wood before working out their true position in daylight. The next evening they cautiously began walking towards Singen. Even with reasonably good maps it was easy to get lost, especially now that they were hungry, thirsty and tired after three days on the run. Walking in the wrong direction near Singen they ran into a guard, who inspected their papers and, to Stephens's surprise, accepted the story that they were working in the area and politely redirected them on the right road to Singen.

Rather than push their luck further, they holed up for the night in a wood to prepare for the final crawl to the border the following evening. It rained steadily the next day, leaving the escapers cold, exhausted and extremely bad tempered before darkness finally allowed them to creep from their hiding place towards the frontier just a few hundred yards away. Despite moving as quietly as possible they were spotted and challenged by a border guard who demanded to see their papers. When the guard ordered them to follow him, the escapers ignored him and made a dash to the border line. Incredibly the guard did nothing to stop them, and the two men carried on running, crossing the frontier a few moments later.

Fearful that they might walk back into German territory, given the meandering nature of the border, Stephens and Littledale waited until daylight, when, in Stephens's words, 'we saw a bullock cart approaching with a very old man driving it. He soon put our minds at rest, welcoming us with open arms. We were in Switzerland at last but were almost too tired to appreciate it. Forty-eight hours later we had arrived at the British legation in Berne where we were royally welcomed and life began to seem brighter.' Told the news that Reid and Wardle had also arrived safely in Switzerland, an overjoyed Stephens could reflect that they had taken on the Nazi police state and won. No other victory would ever taste so sweet.

Although Stephens and Littledale were experienced escapers, supported by an excellent committee in Colditz, the most distinguishing feature of the whole escape had been the officers' amazing good fortune. In the breakout from the castle, the plan was overly dependent on the guards in the *Kommandantur* being exceptionally unobservant; and Reid's inability to pick the door lock would have stopped the escape in its tracks had they not fortuitously discovered a passage that took them right outside the castle walls. While the professionalism of Stephens and Littledale in travelling through Germany could not be faulted, their mishaps in the dark near the frontier led to two encounters with border guards, who should have arrested them on the spot or shot them while trying to get away. While so many other escape attempts ended in disaster at the Swiss frontier, luck had been with them to the end.

Escapers were universally agreed that the best time to escape was as soon after surrender as possible. The newly captured were not registered by the enemy, and there were many more opportunities for escape during transit from the battlefield than there were in a permanent camp. And soldiers escaping in friendly territory could call upon help from the

254

civilian population. Many British soldiers captured in 1940 upbraided themselves for not being more escape-minded during their march through France. But it was at this moment that the potential escaper most lacked the initiative to make a run for it. He was a defeated man, often in a poor physical state, and with even lower morale. For those in such a demoralized condition the thought of escape was typically deferred until a time when strength could be rebuilt in a permanent camp. But by then the potential escaper would be held in a well-guarded prison within a hostile country.

But even for POWs who had been registered in a permanent camp, transit between camps offered new escape possibilities. Most of these journeys were conducted by train, and unguarded cattle trucks were vulnerable to resolute escapers, who would cut holes in the wooden floors or force the locks on the sliding doors. It took a great deal of nerve for an escaper to throw himself out of a moving train, especially at night, when he could not see what he might be jumping into. But sufficient numbers of men were prepared to take the chance that the Germans began to deploy guards within the wagons if they thought the POWs were at all escape-minded.

The types of escape from a permanent POW camp could be broadly classified as over (the wire), through (the gate) or under (the wire). Going over the wire was the riskiest form of escape, as guards would often shoot on sight any prisoner they saw clambering up the perimeter fence. To attempt to cut through the double-wired perimeter fence seemed all but suicidal, although a few men did get through when new buildings or other obstacles obscured the view from German watchtowers. A particularly bold attempt of this type was made from Stalag Luft III at Sagan by flight lieutenants 'Nick' Nicholas, an American in the RAF's Eagle Squadron, and Ken Toft. With remarkable coolness they cut and wriggled their way through the wire in broad daylight, relying on the distraction of the guards in the two adjacent watchtowers by other POWs.

The most ambitious of the over-the-wire schemes was Operation Olympia, better known as the 'Warburg Wire Job'. The escape was based on the discovery by a POW in Oflag VIB at Warburg that the searchlights and perimeter lights could be controlled from within the camp by the prisoners. Four specially hinged ladders were secretly constructed to span the double perimeter fences. On the night of 30 August 1942 the lights were fused and four teams rushed the wire. The surprised guards opened fire at the noise made by the escapers, but in the darkness they managed only to wound one man in the foot. Of the forty-one prisoners involved, twenty-nine got clean away from the camp and three succeeded in reaching home.

Attempts to escape through the gate were generally less dangerous. They involved either hiding within a container or vehicle being taken out of the camp or somehow bluffing the sentries at the gate, usually by impersonating another guard or a 'neutral' such as a tradesman or even an inspector from the Protecting Power. Hiding in rubbish to be evacuated from the camp was a common if unpleasant method of escape. On one occasion a POW was covered by a sack – with hundreds of Red Cross tin cans attached – and deftly dropped into a cart taking out a pile of cans to a rubbish tip, only to be discovered by an attentive guard checking the pile with his rifle and fixed bayonet. Similar ruses included hiding under a departing truck and even clambering into one of the honey wagons carrying excrement from the camp, although in this instance the Polish driver was in on the act and had emptied and rinsed out the container.

When impersonating a German NCO or officer, the prisoner would require a first-rate copy of a military uniform, appropriate documentation, and the natural authority to persuade the guard at the gate to let him through. While at Colditz, Airey Neave teamed up with Tony Luteyn, a Dutch soldier who spoke fluent German. Both of them dressed up as German officers, and on the night of 4/5 January 1942 they calmly walked out of the castle. It was a bravura performance: at one point Luteyn even upbraided a guard for not saluting him. Both men reached Switzerland.

Impersonation attempts normally worked on the principle that the man being portrayed would be a 'generic' German, and therefore unknown to the guard. But the process was turned on its head in another escape attempt from Colditz, so that the lead escaper – Lieutenant Mike Sinclair – assumed the role of one of the better-known guards in the camp, the veteran Staff Sergeant Rothenberger – nicknamed Franz Josef because of his bushy white moustache resembling that of the former Austro-Hungarian emperor.

The plan was for Sinclair, with two other bogus guards, to dismiss the actual guards from one sector of the castle to allow a mass escape of thirty other British POWs. A good German-speaker, Sinclair devoted himself to catching Rothenberger's accent and mannerisms, and during the attempt, on 4 September 1943, he managed to convince several guards with his impersonation. At the last moment, however, Sinclair was unmasked by one suspicious and obstinate soldier who demanded his pass, which turned out to be a day too old. The escape was foiled, and in the turmoil of recapture Sinclair was wounded in the chest by a pistol shot from an enraged guard.

An ingenious scheme at Warburg involved the impersonation of a visiting team of Swiss inspectors. While the Swiss were in the camp, two POWs dressed as the inspectors and an escort of three 'German' guards marched up to the gate and demanded to be let through. The escapers' preparations had been thorough: their uniforms and clothes were well-tailored, their German sufficiently good, and their manner convincing. The guards hurriedly obeyed the order to open the gates, and the escapers were free of the camp in minutes, although all were subsequently recaptured before reaching Switzerland.

A rather different form of impersonation was tried at the naval Marlag (O). The camp showers were situated beyond the main perimeter wire, and groups of officers were escorted to the shower block by a less than attentive guard. Lieutenant David James and his accomplices built a lifelike dummy – nicknamed Albert – which was covertly taken to the shower block and assembled. While the prisoners were in the showers, James climbed out of a back window and walked out of the camp. After their shower, the other officers returned to their compound with Albert marching along in the middle of the group, and at the gate a simple head count arrived at the correct tally. To cover James's escape, another prisoner – also named James – took his place at roll calls.

Working on the principle that the multitude of uniforms prevalent throughout Germany would confuse most security personnel, James wore his own naval uniform but assumed the persona of a Bulgarian naval officer, whom he facetiously named Lieutenant I. Bagerov. James did well initially, but was recaptured at Stettin and returned to Marlag. The Germans, however, had not worked out how he had escaped, and so he was able to use Albert again. On this occasion James sensibly adopted the disguise of Swedish sailor (he spoke some Swedish) and reached Stockholm after boarding a Finnish ship sailing from Danzig. Once in Britain, James and MI9 sent back information to Marlag that helped in the subsequent escapes of lieutenants S. W. L. Campbell and D. Kelleher − both of whom successfully reached Sweden via Baltic crossings.

The most extreme form of impersonation involved faking an illness serious enough for repatriation. This was a far from easy ploy, and only the dedicated and the lucky succeeded. Paddy Byrne, an RAF officer in Stalag Luft III, managed to convince a Mixed Medical Commission that he had gone mad; it took a long struggle over many months, and his antics had driven his friends and room-mates almost to the point of insanity. When Byrne was told he was due for repatriation he opened up a 'Lunacy School' to teach others the best methods to convince the Commission of their mental instability − four passed the test with tickets out of Stalag Luft III.

For those choosing the medical route, their physical symptoms had to perfectly replicate those of a serious − generally life-threatening − condition. Richard Pape, a prisoner in Stalag Luft VI at Heydekrug, had attempted a number of more conventional escapes before deciding, in April 1944, to be nominated for repatriation. He carefully studied the symptoms of a patient suffering from acute nephritis, a kidney disease whose external symptoms included dizziness, swollen ankles, and a pronounced yellowing of the skin. With the help of a sympathetic medical orderly, blood and urine samples were supplied using liquids from the genuine nephritis sufferer. Pape recalled that before examination a British physiotherapist spent several hours carefully flicking 'my ankles with wet towels until they ballooned out without the slightest trace of bruising'. To achieve the jaundiced look, Pape swallowed four pieces of soap and rubbed his skin with dye from some yellow crêpe paper to complete the fabrication. This was sufficient to convince the German doctor that he was very ill, although as an insurance policy Pape also replicated the symptoms of TB. He easily passed the repatriation board in May 1944, reaching Sweden on 7 September.

In contrast to the theatrical nature of impersonation, tunnelling under the wire was slow and arduous. It also drained the camp's resources, whether in bed boards to shore up the tunnel or in large gangs of prisoners for digging and dispersal of soil. But tunnels had their advantages. Aidan Crawley – an RAF officer who broke out of the Asselin tunnel in Oflag XXIB at Schubin and subsequently prepared a 'manual' on escapes from Germany – described their positive aspects:

> This was one of the safest methods of getting outside the wire because when the tunnel was being built no one was in danger of being shot, and when finally completed there was a good chance of crawling away unobserved. Tunnelling also demanded less from an individual than most methods of escape. With the exception of the experts who designed the entrance and did the skilled work, those who built the tunnels worked in teams and did as they were told. Most of the oper-ations became a drill which needed perseverance and stamina but little more, and by working in teams men built up an *esprit de corps* which was otherwise so difficult to achieve in prison life.

Tunnels could be divided into two types: the long tunnel that led from one of barrack huts to a point well outside the wire, and the shorter – sometimes improvised – tunnel that was started as close to the wire as possible. The long tunnel was an elaborate business that might take months to dig, but had the advantage of allowing a mass breakout. Some seventy-six men got away from Stalag Luft III in March 1944. Other notable mass escapes by tunnel included those from Stalag IIIE at Kirchhain in May 1942 (fifty-two escapers) and from Oflag VIIB at Eichstätt in June 1943 (sixty-three) – despite the success of the breakouts, however, in both instances all the prisoners were eventually rounded up by the Germans.

Of the smaller tunnels, a good example was a 'Blitz' tunnel dug by Jimmy James and John Shore from Stalag Luft I at Barth. A small brick building that held camp rubbish – known as the incinerator – was situated close to the perimeter wire, beyond which was the football field, surrounded by a single wire fence that would be fairly easy to climb. Although the incinerator was in clear view of the guards, it was also used as a viewing point by spectators during football matches. Accordingly, the escape committee organized a series of football matches during mornings and evenings, with attendant crowds of spectators, to allow James and Shore to go in and out of the inciner-ator unobserved. After four days' work the tunnel was ready. The next night-bombing raid – when the camp lights were turned off – was chosen for the escape.

An air raid on the evening of 19 October 1941 doused the lights, and Shore crept to the incinerator followed by James. Unfortunately for James, just at that moment several guards walked by. He was forced back into the shadows, but as he again attempted to crawl to the incinerator he was caught in the flashlight of the camp security officer. Shore, meanwhile, wriggled out of the narrow tunnel and under the barbed wire around the football field and was soon clear of the camp. Walking by night he reached the port of Sassnitz, and after some hair-raising encounters at the dockside he successfully climbed onboard a ship bound for Sweden. Ten days after the escape Shore was back in Britain, where he was awarded the Military Cross. James, meanwhile, was awarded two weeks in solitary, although he was congratulated for the audacity of the escape by the commandant (a POW in the First World War), who gallantly wished him better luck next time.

The distinctions between the shorter tunnels with only a few escapers and the long-tunnel mass escape highlighted differing attitudes to escape. Two or three well-prepared men had a greater chance of reaching home: they were better equipped with clothes and papers; their absence from the camp could be covered for an extended period; and their escape did not automatically lead to a nationwide manhunt as would be the case with a mass escape. But the proponents of mass escape argued that, while only a few prisoners had any real chance of getting away, the other escapers tied down large numbers of the enemy in the ensuing search. The tunnel breakout from Eichstätt apparently tied down 50,000 Germans – police, army, home guards and Hitler Youth – and some 300,000 troops and police were said to be involved in the search for the RAF escapers who had tunnelled out from Oflag XXIB at Schubin in March 1943.

The different escape techniques used by POWs were in part a consequence of the escapers' previous experience and their individual temperaments. Some men, like Jimmy James, were out-and-out tunnellers, while others, such as the RAF warrant officer George Grimson, preferred to fool the Germans. Pat Reid, with an engineering background, considered schemes to tunnel or physically break out of Colditz, while the barrister Airey Neave preferred to talk his way through the front gate.

Some prison camps were harder to escape from than others. Stalag Luft III at Sagan was one of the more secure camps, not particularly because of its physical constraints but because of the quality of the German staff and guards. The camps holding the more enthusiastic escapers tended to be allocated the more observant and escape-conscious guards, and in Staff Sergeant Glemnitz and his team of ferrets Stalag Luft III had guards who were almost a match for their prisoners. Oflag IXA at Spangenberg was also one of the most escape-proof of camps, mainly because of its position – it was built on solid rock and surrounded by a deep moat with a single, well-observed and well-guarded entrance and exit.

Although Colditz was exceptionally well guarded – with more guards than prisoners – and possessed a forbidding appearance, it was not as secure as its reputation suggested, being honeycombed with false ceilings, bricked-up rooms and secret passages. The escape of Billie Stephens was only one of several utilizing tunnels and shafts that should have been known to the Germans and blocked off. A governor of a modern high-security jail would have been horrified at the lack of observation and containment of prisoners. At Colditz, POWs roamed through much of the castle at will, and with their superior knowledge of its complex layout (through MI9 the prisoners had been sent a detailed plan of the building, discovered in the archives of the British Museum) they had an advantage over their captors.

Escapes from permanent POW camps were always difficult; considerably easier were those made from work parties and their associated camps. For prisoners working outside – in agriculture, transport or quarries – it was relatively easy to slip away unnoticed, and most work camps were poorly guarded when compared with the main Stalags and Oflags.

Even in the better-guarded work camps – such as at Niederorschel 1049, where Bob Prouse was held – breakouts were not unduly difficult. Prouse and two other prisoners worked hard on an escape plan, acquiring money, civilian clothes and forged papers stating they were Czech workers. Although the camp was behind wire and well guarded, on 27 April 1943 Prouse's team slipped into civilian clothes and managed to mingle with some Germans who worked in the plywood factory within the camp grounds and were on their way home. Although the alarm was raised as the escapers were going through the gate, they were able to run clear of the camp and hide in a forest. From there they jumped a freight train at the nearby marshalling yard to Kassel, and then took a series of country trains towards München-Gladbach and the Dutch border. As their progress had been so good to this point, they decided against walking to the frontier town of Dalheim, as originally planned, and instead board-ed the train. This turned out to be a fateful mistake. Conditions of travel were far stricter in border regions than anywhere else in Germany, and as they got off the train at Dalheim they were arrested by two policemen.

They were informed by their jubilant captors that the swastika on their papers faced the wrong way, and that they had no special papers to allow Czechs to be so close to a border. And to Prouse's displeasure he was laughingly told that 'with a nose like mine I had to be an Englishman'. The recaptured POWs passed through several military prisons – which involved interrogations and strip searches – before being returned to Stalag IXC at Bad Sulza and, after a long delay, a sentence of twenty-one days in solitary.

Escape-minded officers and RAF NCOs were aware of the advan-tages of running off from work parties. Stalag VIIIB at Lamsdorf had a great tradition of escaping, and from its RAF compound – well within the main camp – airmen regularly traded places with soldiers; half of RAF home runs came from Lamsdorf.

What made a prisoner want to escape? All POWs had a duty to escape if a reasonable chance presented itself. But escapers were a small minority of the overall camp population. As Wings Day observed, many prisoners would have considered escaping if it had 'been handed to them on a plate', but they lacked the necessary initiative and appli-cation to plan and carry through an escape themselves; they were unable to overcome the powerful inertia that prevailed in all POW camps.

While duty provided the official reason for escape, other factors probably played a more important part in a prisoner's bid for freedom. At a basic level, escape was an antidote to the boredom of everyday camp life. Pilot Officer William Ash, an American serving in the Canadian Air Force, explained that 'for one thing, it made the time pass a lot more quickly.' Some enjoyed the sense of adventure and risk that escaping provided. There was also the furtiveness and sense of conspiracy that appealed to the schoolboy in every prisoner. It was no surprise that Pat Reid – the most exuberantly old-fashioned of escape chroniclers – agreed with the sentiment that 'escaping is the greatest sport in the world'.

Flight Sergeant Cyril Rofe had been sent to the RAF compound at Lamsdorf, and there encountered the impromptu escaping that was such a feature of the camp; according to one member of the escape committee, once spring came 100 men were escaping from work camps every month. Rofe described how these escapers considered it as a risky form of sport: 'It broke the monotony. They did not expect to succeed; they merely wanted something to do. The planning passed the time, the escape was a great adventure. When they were recaptured they would do a few days in the cooler, then return to start planning once more. A dangerous sport, certainly, but it was not everyone who could settle down to a life of nothing but intellectual or cultural pursuits.'

For a small group of men, the very fact of imprisonment was unbearable. Sergeant Ernest de los Santos – a B-17 gunner shot down in 1943 and held in Stalag VIIA at Moosburg – was a self-confessed loner who 'never could stand being locked up'. He made three escape attempts from Moosburg; on the first he was caught scaling the wire and was extremely lucky not be shot; on the other two occasions he got away safely but was recaptured while on the run. Sergeant de los Santos described the feeling behind his determination to escape:

> I just had to try and break out. The other prisoners wouldn't even try. I don't know why. If you don't try, you'll never do it. I just wasn't going to sit in the barracks. I didn't really have any friends, so I'd go out for a walk and start looking around to see how I could get out – and I'd find a way. Each day I'd think about it a little more, and then I'd decide to take a chance. You knew you were going to get caught, but you just chose to go anyway.

British officer George Millar held a similar revulsion towards confinement: 'To live inside a perimeter of barbed wire was a constant agony for me . . . It is the monotony of a steady existence, of fixed and secure prospects, that wears me down. I was unfitted to be a happy prisoner.'

Wings Day estimated that of escapers there was a small hard core of prisoners – about 5 per cent of the whole camp – who were totally devoted to escaping: men prepared to put up with any discomfort and prepared to take potentially fatal risks. De los Santos was one such, and so too was Jimmy James. When James wrote, 'for some of us escaping became a way of life,' this was no idle expression. In his five years of captivity James was involved – at various levels – in twelve escape attempts, including the Great Escape, the mass break-out from Stalag Luft III. One of the few to be spared execution after this, he was sent to Sonderlager A in Sachsenhausen concentration camp, where he joined a nucleus of hardened escapers from Stalag Luft III including Day, Sydney Dowse and Johnny Dodge. After the trauma of recapture – and in the hands of the ruthless SS – it would have been reasonable to have given up any ideas of escape, but shortly after their arrival in Sachsenhausen in April 1944 a tunnel was begun. Planned by Dowse and James, the most experienced tunnellers, it was to be over 100 feet in length, but without lighting or extra air intakes the work was dark, airless and lonely. James was also concerned that 'we might strike an electrified wire below ground.'

In June, Day discovered news of the murders of the Great Escape prisoners. James was called to a meeting with the other tunnellers to discuss the changed situation, where recapture would almost certainly mean death. But Day and his comrades had always believed that escaping was analogous to an operational mission; and in the same way that airmen did not shirk a dangerous bombing raid over Germany, so it was with escapes. James, with typical understatement, described the meeting's conclusion: 'After a short discussion we decided unanimously that we would carry on with our escape plans. We had made good progress with our dispersal trenches, there had been no searches to date, and we felt we had a good chance of digging the first tunnel from a concentration camp which the Germans considered escape proof.' James and Dowse were the diggers – assisted by new arrival from the commandos, Colonel Jack Churchill – and on 23 September the tunnel was broken with all five escapers getting safely free of Sachsenhausen.

Lacking the forged papers that could be provided only in a large POW camp, the escapers travelled on foot or by freight wagons. James had paired up with Jack Churchill, and they lasted for two weeks before being picked up only a short distance from the Baltic ports. The others were recaptured earlier. A national alert had been ordered immediately after the escape, and a furious Himmler demanded the deaths of the escapers following *Verschärfte Vernehmung* (interrogation under torture). Two Gestapo agents had been sent to Sachsenhausen to carry out the executions, but because the men had been arrested by the ordinary criminal police their presence was known to a wider world, and the SS, under pressure from the police, backed down. After a period in the camp's punishment block, the five men were returned to the relatively good conditions of Sonderlager A.

Captain Terence Prittie was another seasoned escaper, and made five breakouts during 1941–3. After escaping from Eichstätt he was sent to the more secure castle at Spangenberg. He described how the idea of escape dominated his very being:

> I thought and talked about it most of the day. Most nights I dreamt of it. As a result of continuous study from the map of a small section of the Swiss frontier I was able to visualize that piece of country almost exactly as it must, in fact, exist. I knew by heart its roads and railways, its woods and villages, the swelling slopes and the curves of its hillsides. My waking day was spent discussing and planning how I could reach that frontier area once more. In my sleep I stalked boundary posts and the stretches of barbed-wire fence that ran in-between, watched ghostly German patrols steal by in the gloaming, and after they had passed, ran stumbling and panting towards that legendary land of safety and freedom beyond.

But such intensity of thought and action had its negative side – so much so that by the summer of 1943 Prittie was burnt out as an escaper. While escape 'afforded tremendous scope for physical endeavour', he acknowledged that it also made him 'short-tempered, absurdly secretive, and muddle-headed about the details of ordinary life'. He noticed what he called 'escape psychosis' in others: 'They became moody, vaguely and meaninglessly mysterious, almost morbidly self-interested. Often they seemed to be only "half-there", for their thoughts were nearly always periscoped round the corner of the castle battlements or down through the flagstones of its courtyard into the bowels of the earth.' In July 1943 the Germans – probably assisted by a British informer – made a series of searches that discovered not only a half-dug tunnel but the radio and several caches of escape and other contraband material. After this setback Prittie retired as an active escaper and devoted himself to education and writing.

Alongside the men who planned and worked to get out beyond the wire – and sometimes succeeded – were those who liked the idea of escape, but lacked the determination to see it through. Robert Kee witnessed this type in Oflag XXIB at Schubin and in Stalag Luft III. He wrote:

> All schemes involved weeks and sometimes months of furtive planning, decisions on route and disguise, invention of a suitable story for travelling purposes and sometimes even the learning of a new language . . . [The would-be escaper] would live in a world by himself conscious as he watched the humdrum routine of his fellow prisoners that he was destined for higher things and happy in the knowledge that he was not as other men.
>
> For weeks it would go on like this and then suddenly one day you would notice him just lying in the sun instead of studying his map, or reading a novel instead of his German grammar . . . And you would know at last he had called his own bluff.

Escapers were a small minority who made great demands on the camp's resources and brought hardship to all POWs through the inevitable German retaliation that followed an escape attempt. Not surprisingly, there was always a degree of ambivalence towards escaping. Many accepted that it was a part of their duty to resist the Germans, and even if not active escapers themselves they were prepared to accept its consequences and assist in the more mundane tasks. A few, however, actively discouraged escapes.

Sergeant Richard Passmore, an RAF NCO in Stalag Lufts I, III and VI, held that ambivalent attitude towards escape. While he helped out in tunnelling duties – and suffered the nightmare of a cave-in – he thought the whole enterprise was a 'form of escapism', because the chances of a home run were so small. 'The official line', he wrote, 'was that it was our duty to escape, or to try continually to do so, with the purpose of distracting the enemy and tying down numbers of his men. Against this, many of us felt that we had already taken enough risks for our country and that it was a miracle that so many of us had survived. There were men at home, both in and out of uniform, who were doing quite nicely out of the war.'

The RAF NCO escapers had developed an effective escape organization, called Tally Ho, but they believed it lacked authority to compel the ordinary prisoner to provide support for escaping. The NCOs' section of the Stalag Luft III camp history filed this complaint: 'The Escape Committee had no official standing and had no means at its disposal for issuing orders, or enforcing their wishes. The inability to direct other POWs was the greatest difficulty with which the Committee had to contend. Comparatively few NCOs were deeply interested in escape. The majority did not consider that they were duty bound to make an attempt to get away.' Such a complaint would have been common among many escape committees across Germany, but there can be little doubt that the NCOs were comparing their position with the officers' compound at Stalag Luft III, which was run by escapers. Wings Day and his escape officers, first Lieutenant Commander Jimmy Buckley and then Squadron Leader Roger Bushell, expected other camp activities to be subordinated to escape.

Not all camps were as escape-conscious as Stalag Luft III or Colditz. POW camp administrations that opposed escaping – or were even lukewarm towards it – made life much harder for escapers. In some camps there were rumours that tunnels had been betrayed to the Germans in order to prevent the status quo being disturbed. To the escapers such actions were treason, but to those less escape-inclined they were a way of protecting the majority from what they saw as the enthusiasms of a selfish minority.

Stalag IVB at Mühlberg was not an escapers' camp, and according to its camp history this was very much a consequence of the anti-escape attitudes of the Man of Confidence, Warrant Officer Jack Meyers, supported by Major White, the senior medical officer. The camp history noted that the two men 'agreed to take the view that if there were attempts to escape it would bring reprisals on the heads of the P/Ws remaining and many privileges would be stopped and so make the lives of the ones remaining even less comfortable'.

Meyers's refusal to recognize the camp's escape committee rankled, as did, it was claimed, his decision not to hand on escape materials received from MI9. Some idea of the animosity directed at Meyers by the escapers can be seen in a report submitted to MI9 by Warrant Officer R. L. Davies, who bluntly asserted, 'I consider that W/O Meyers acted as a collaborator.' Although there were many attempted escapes from the camp, the lack of an effective escape committee hampered these operations. Escapers did, however, receive help from the large number of French POWs also held in Mühlberg. The experiences of Pilot Officer James Branford – who made the camp's only British home run – seemed to bear out these criticisms. He found that 'our own escape committee was of a negative quality,' and instead he relied on the French for assistance. He swapped places with a French worker, sneaked out of the camp with a coffee fatigue in May 1944, and then travelled by freight trains to the Netherlands, where he was put on an escape line to Britain by the Dutch underground.

MI9 had increasing influence in the escape process as the war went on; it sent general information to camps on how to operate as an escaper and specific intelligence from previously successful escapers, as well as escape materials smuggled in special parcels. These parcels were sent by thirty-two fictitious philanthropic organizations that included the Authors' Society, the Welsh Provident Society and the Women's United Services Association. The Historical Record of MI9 described the activities of one of its more unusual funds: 'An impudent scheme, by which money and maps, hidden in Christmas crackers and sent by an imaginary "Lancashire Penny Fund" direct to the German Camp Commandant, was successful in a large number of camps. A letter with the crackers requested the Camp Commandant in each case to pass them to the SBO or Camp Leader to help brighten their Christmas Party.' It was thought that half of them got through to the POWs.

Brigadier Norman Crockatt, head of MI9, made a point that Red Cross parcels were never to be tampered with, in case discovery should lead to the severing of this lifeline. Of the parcels sent from MI9, 5,173 were innocently packed with tobacco to provide cover for the 1,642 parcels containing escape aids; the POWs were tipped off which parcels contained contraband materials and were usually able to spirit them away from the Germans as they were unpacked. The volume of material arriving was far from negligible. As well as a large supply of Reichsmarks (and lire for Italy), MI9 dispatched 9,247 maps, 3,138 compasses, 1,119 hacksaws, 1,942 passes, 297 blankets (to be used for tailoring) and 427 sets of dyes. Maps were hidden in records; tools in the handles of baseball bats; hacksaws in combs and toothbrushes; compasses and money in bars of soap. Apart from their obvious material value, MI9's interventions were a boost to morale: escape was a slow, often frustrating business, and for the escaper to know that his efforts were being supported by an official organization from home was a source of strength and encouragement.

MI9's help was only part of a developing escape system that in some camps was organized on an almost industrial scale. This was especially true in the North compound of Stalag Luft III, where in April 1943 preparations were begun for a mass breakout that would become known as the Great Escape. Instead of the profusion of ad-hoc tunnels that sprouted from most camps, there would be just three – code-named Tom, Dick and Harry – of great length and depth to avoid the German listening devices dotted around the camp perimeter. The driving force behind the plan was Roger Bushell, a South African-born former barrister, whose Spitfire had been shot down in 1940 over France. On his first escape he was caught within sight of the Swiss border, and in a subsequent escape through Czechoslovakia he was sheltered by the Czech Resistance only to be recaptured in the aftermath of Heydrich's assassination in Prague – the Luftwaffe rescued him from the clutches of the Gestapo, who had informed him that if they captured him again he would be shot. Jimmy James described Bushell as 'a man of forceful personality, his penetrating gaze was given an almost sinister twist by the permanent droop on his left eye caused by a skiing accident.'

In a compound of approximately 1,500 men, some 600 POWs were directly engaged in the operation. The escape committee was divided into self-contained sections covering the various requirements for escape: tunnelling, dispersal of soil, intelligence, security, forgery, mapping, clothing, food. Though the camp contained some of the most experienced and dedicated escapers, the German ferrets were a particular nuisance – not only because they discovered tunnels and escape plans, but because their presence inhibited many escape activities such as tailoring and forgery. In order to contain the activities of the ferrets, the prisoners instituted the Duty Pilot scheme: a man sat by the gate carefully logging all German arrivals and departures, so that knowledge of an influx of ferrets could be relayed throughout the camp. Staff Sergeant Glemnitz – a man with a sense of humour – used to check with the Duty Pilot on the movements of his own men, on one occasion sentencing a ferret to four days in the cooler for evading duty.

The three tunnels produced a total of over 230 tons of spoil that had to be dispersed throughout the camp, a task made more difficult by the tunnel sand being of a different colour from that of the darker camp topsoil. Over half was dispersed by 'penguins', men equipped with trouser sacks – one to each leg – which carried 8 lb each and had an opening at the bottom operated by a pin attached to a string leading to the trouser pockets. The 'penguins' would release their sacks and tread the sand into the topsoil, the attendant waddling motion giving them their nickname. The rest of the spoil was hidden in or under blocks and other buildings.

In September 1943 the main tunnel, Tom, was discovered shortly before completion. Tunnelling work was stopped while the Germans ransacked the camp, and when it resumed in January Harry was selected as the escape tunnel, with Dick relegated as a storage area for escape equipment. By early March Harry was nearing completion: the tunnel was 365 feet in length and reached a maximum depth of 28 feet. It was one of the most advanced tunnels built in Germany, complete with wooden trolleys on rails for ease of movement, a ventilation system driven by bellows with an air line made from klim tins, and electric lighting powered from the German mains.

Bushell's ambitious plan envisaged an escape by at least 200 men, its prime aim being to cause maximum disruption throughout Germany. It was accepted that only a few men had any real chance of getting home: these were mainly those with good language skills, who would be first out of the tunnel and be supplied with excellent forged passes and appropriate travel documents. The first 100 were selected from those who had worked most closely on the tunnel; the remainder were chosen from a ballot of 500 names. Jimmy James was number 39, and teamed up with Sortiras Skanziklas, a Greek fighter pilot in the RAF. They would take a train towards the nearby Czech border and then hope to pass through Czechoslovakia and down through the Balkans to Greece and Turkey. Those travelling on foot – the 'hardarsers' – had more limited documentation and would have to do the best they could.

While the tunnel was in progress the German POW administration began to take an increasingly severe view towards escaping. Escapes were not, of course, the preserve of British and American prisoners. Germany was plagued with roving bands of escapers of all nationalities, the Russians – with little to lose – being particularly troublesome. Attempts were made by the Germans to remove the legal protection granted escapers by the Geneva Convention. Although escape itself remained as a basic disciplinary offence (with a maximum of thirty days' solitary confinement), penalties for such related activities as damage to property were increased, and in April 1943 an order threatened prisoners caught in civilian clothing or German uniform with a court martial and a possible death sentence.

The Gestapo were also taking an interest in POW affairs, and issued an order that recaptured prisoners were not to be handed back to the military authorities but were to be kept by them. In March 1944 a secret decree – *Aktion Kugel* ('Operation Bullet') – demanded that all recaptured POWs, with the exception of British and Americans, were to be executed in a concentration camp. With these developments in mind, the commandant of Stalag Luft III, Colonel von Lindeiner, called a meeting of the senior Allied officers to warn them of the changed political atmosphere in Germany and the increased dangers of escape. His warning was politely acknowledged by the escapers and ignored.

Fearful that the operation would be discovered by Glemnitz's ferrets, Bushell decided to break the tunnel on the night of 24/25 March, earlier than originally planned. As the escape got under way, a series of delays forestalled any possibility that the full complement of 200 men would get away, and at around 5 a.m. the decision was made to shut down the operation. While the last men were crawling out of the tunnel, a patrolling guard almost fell into the tunnel mouth and raised the alarm. By then some seventy-six men had got away and were fanning out across a snowbound Germany.

James and Skanziklas boarded a local train and headed towards Boberöhrsdorf and the Czech frontier. They tried to walk across the mountains into Czechoslovakia, but heavy snowstorms forced them down on to lower ground, where they decided to take another train. But the alarm had been raised, and they were arrested at a station by an alert policeman and taken to a local prison. James was interrogated by the Gestapo, bullied and threatened, but not tortured. Over the next few days all but three of the escapers were recaptured.

Hitler raged at the news of the escape: he demanded that all those recaptured be shot. In a conference with Himmler and Göring and OKW chief Field Marshal Wilhelm Keitel, he then slightly moderated his demands and decided that fifty should die – in complete contravention of the Geneva Convention. The selection – apparently made by SS General Arthur Nebe – was largely arbitrary: of the leading troublemakers, Bushell was shot but Day was spared; Skanziklas was killed but not James, who, to his surprise, found himself in a group of four *Prominente* prisoners sent to Sonderlager A at Sachsenhausen. The murder of the fifty officers was kept secret: they were shot in small groups, and their bodies were cremated to prevent any subsequent post-mortem examinations. The official reason for their deaths was that they were killed 'while trying to escape', but this fooled no one, least of all the prisoners.

The realization that the Nazis were prepared to carry out such a barbaric act came as a profound shock to POWs throughout Germany. A new tunnel was started by a defiant escape committee in North compound in May 1944, but the killings had a salutary effect on all potential escapers – although more important to a lessening interest in escape was the news of the Normandy invasion in June. At the same time, the Allied governments released the prisoners from their duty to escape, without forbidding escape attempts altogether. Captain John A. Vietor, in Stalag Luft I at Barth, summed up the prevailing view on escaping after D-Day: 'Attempts to escape varied with the war news. If the news was good, escape attempts lessened. If the news was bad, efforts were stepped up. During the Russian offensives [in early 1945] the end of the war seemed in sight and although there were still sporadic attempts, the energy and enthusiasm to escape largely diminished. Liberation seemed a certainty and the rewards of escape were not equal to the risks.'

But for those who did make it over the wire there was the possibility of freedom in the near and not the distant future. The exhilaration of successfully breaking out of a POW camp was never forgotten. Of his escape from the prison hospital at Obermassfeld in June 1943, Bill Edwards wrote, 'The great moment for which I had thought, dreamed, talked and planned for three weary long years had arrived. I was free! I took several deep breaths of night air – to me it seemed sweeter than any I had breathed since 1940.' After breaking out from a Lamsdorf work camp, Cyril Rofe and his escape companion rested for a moment: 'As we lay there watching the sun rise, our cocoa tasted like nectar. We might have been the gods on Olympus, only we felt happier . . . No other day was ever like it.' Looking back at his escape from Stalag Luft III, Kingsley Brown recalled that he had 'never known the pure, sweet joy of living, tempered so deliciously with the sense of danger, as I knew it during the four days that elapsed between our escape and recapture'.

Once out of the camp, the escaper had to put as much distance as possible between himself and the camp before the alarm was raised. The destinations chosen by escapers were remarkably varied, a spread of countries surrounding Germany. According to MI9, the chosen destinations of home run escapers were, in percentage terms, Sweden 29.79, western Europe 24.49, Switzerland 18.50, Russia 14.29, Balkans 12.93.

Regardless of destination, the prime obstacle facing escapers was the transit of a hostile and very alert Germany. As subjects of a police state, the German people were constantly harangued to be on the lookout for undesirables, and a culture of observation and informing – on both neighbours and strangers – was well established by 1939. The escaper faced not only a capable police force, well supported by the Wehrmacht where necessary, but all the other organizations of the Nazi system, in particular a rejuvenated home guard – whose members, according to one escaper, were 'far more agile and vigorous than men of fifty to sixty-five have any right to be' – and the Hitler Youth, whose enthusiasm for tracking down enemies of the state was a constant danger to any man on the run.

Britons and Americans tended to make poor escapers when on the run. Playing the part of a German was exceptionally difficult and usually best avoided in favour of impersonating another Continental European who possessed some knowledge of the German language and had a reason for being in the country. The presence of several million foreign workers in Germany provided the escaper with good social camouflage, without which there would have been few home runs. But Britons and Americans also had difficulty in acting the part of a Czech, Danish or French worker – not least because they had

had little or no experience of seeing one, let alone pretending to be one. This weakness was highlighted by Terence Prittie and his four companions, who in their escape from Warburg disguised themselves as Hungarians. He subsequently wrote, 'Too many Germans have travelled extensively in Central Europe ever to permit us the choice of so unlikely a nationality. Englishmen will seldom realize how much better informed the average German is regarding the manners, appearance and speech of his Continental neighbours.' It was perhaps no coincidence that of three POWs making home runs from the Great Escape, one was Dutch and the other two Norwegian.

As well as deciding what disguise to adopt, an escaper had to choose his method of travel. Trains were generally considered to be the most effective method of reaching the border: they were fast, and did not draw upon the escaper's reserves of physical energy. But they required some knowledge of German and the railway system, money, and identity papers and other travel documents, as well as a disguise that had to be scrupulously maintained at all times and a good deal of confidence to deal with any awkward situation.

For those without these resources and talents, the choice was between jumping a freight train and walking. Escapers generally had little difficulty in getting aboard freight wagons, but destinations were often hard to discern, and even those escapers on a wagon with an appropriate destination marked could find themselves literally sidelined for days without hope of movement. For those on foot the question was whether to walk only at night or to risk daylight travel. Whatever the choice, finding a safe place to lay up to sleep was always difficult, and after a few days food supplies would be exhausted. Walking also proved more physically and psychologically exhausting than most escapers ever envisaged, especially in bad weather. After a few days the hungry, tired and dispirited escaper began to take the risks that tended to get him caught. As a result, long-distance travel on foot was considered over-ambitious, although the three successful escapers from the Warburg Wire Job managed to trek cross-country for more than 120 miles, over a period of 15 days, and walk across the frontier into the Netherlands unobserved – a great feat of endurance and self-discipline.

If escapers were the military elite of the POW world in Germany, then arguably the finest of these warriors was a quiet, normally unassuming sergeant in the RAF called George Grimson. Not only did he carry out several particularly audacious escapes, he took the whole concept of escaping to a higher level by setting up his own escape line in German territory.

Grimson was shot down in 1940, and after a spell in the RAF compound at Lamsdorf was sent to Stalag Luft I and then followed the NCOs' route to Stalag Lufts III and VI. Once captured he set about learning German, and by thorough application he was able to speak the language at a colloquial level. Grimson was not a tunneller but preferred to bluff his way out of prison camps. His greatly admired breakout from Stalag Luft III typified this carefully thought-out yet seemingly nerveless approach to escaping. In May 1943 the NCOs were told they were to be moved to a new camp, Stalag Luft VI at Heydekrug. This was a perfect opportunity for Grimson to slip out of the camp. His escape was witnessed by POWs, both in the camp and at the local station in Sagan, where the first batch of prisoners was preparing to leave for Heydekrug. This is Calton Younger's version of Grimson's escape over the wire:

> Dressed as a ferret, wearing earphones made from boot-polish tins, and using a home-made ladder, he was pretending to repair the seismograph wire immediately beneath a *posten* [sentry]-box. Suddenly he dropped his pliers, making sure that they fell into the German compound on the other side of the German fence.
>
> He swore with feeling. It was too far to go round by the gate to retrieve the pliers, he declared; instead he would climb the wire. He bridged the gap between the fences with a short plank, and a moment later he was picking up his pliers.
>
> Warning the guard to see that none of the prisoners used the ladder while he was away, he murmured that he was going for a cup of coffee. Under his ferret's dungarees he wore civilian clothes, and it was as a civilian that he walked out of the German compound.
>
> At the station we were waiting for the train to start. Our carriage was drawn up immediately opposite the station canteen, and, enviously, we watched one man drink a pot of beer almost in a single swallow, and order again. He drank like a man who had not tasted beer for a long time, like one of us for instance.
>
> 'Bloody Grimson,' said someone in an awed voice.

Grimson travelled north to the Baltic coast, but was recaptured five days later trying board a Swedish ship.

At Stalag Luft VI Grimson and the escape committee discovered that two of the German staff – the camp interpreter, Adolph Munkert, and a Pole of German origin called Sommers, who was actually working for the Polish Resistance – were favourably disposed towards the Allied cause. Grimson was keen to exploit this opportunity in order to set up an escape line along the Baltic ports to get men away from Heydekrug to Sweden on a regular basis. Although German territory, the area contained many Poles as well as French workers and seamen from the Baltic states who, Grimson hoped, would work with him to establish the escape line.

On 21 January 1944 Grimson bluffed his way out of the camp in a German uniform, supplied by Munkert, and took a series of trains to a friendly Polish forester's cottage suggested by Sommers. He kept in contact with the camp through letters delivered via Munkert. Although forced to leave the forester's cottage for security reasons, Grimson managed to contact a few Poles in the port city of Danzig who were prepared to help him.

A couple of weeks later Warrant Officer Paddy Flockhart escaped from the camp and contacted Grimson in Danzig. The dock area was fenced off from the rest of the port and well protected. Flockhart and Grimson spent a frustrating couple of days trying to find a Swedish vessel that was not too closely guarded. Finally Flockhart, supplied by Grimson with a workman's cap and overalls, was able to edge his way alongside a Swedish vessel and convince the guard he was one of the crew by careful examination of the mooring warps. He then walked up the gangway unchallenged, hid himself in a hold sufficiently well to avoid the German pre-sailing search, and arrived in Sweden a few days later. The escape committee's plan had been for the first escaper to Sweden to remain in place and encourage Swedish sailors to help escapers, but, fearful of compromising relations with a neutral country, the British Embassy put Flockhart on a flight to Britain.

Grimson continued to develop the escape line. After trying several ports, he decided to concentrate on Danzig, which seemed to have the most Swedish shipping. He secured fairly safe lodgings, and rented two rooms in different parts of the port for use by escapers. Regular trips were made from Danzig to Heydekrug to meet Munkert, who gave him supplies and messages from the escape committee. Grimson was leading a lonely and psychologically draining life, but, although suffering from ill health, he refused to escape or give up on his mission; indeed, he apologized to his comrades in camp for not having had more success.

German security grew tighter – partly as a result of the Great Escape – and on one train journey Grimson was made to show his forged identity papers on twenty-seven separate occasions. While he was on one of these trips two more men escaped from Stalag Luft VI, Warrant Officer R. B. H. Townsend-Coles and Sergeant Jack Gilbert. They broke out on 3 April and had originally intended to head east via Lithuania, but turned west and eventually rendezvoused with Grimson in Danzig, where they were taken to a safe house. Knowing a Swedish vessel was in harbour, Grimson took the escapers through a hole in the dock fence to the ship, which was guarded by a German sentry. Grimson went forward to distract the guard's attention and allow the others to slip up the gangway and board the ship. Unfortunately the sentry saw Townsend-Coles and grabbed him by the arm and dragged him off the gangway. The ensuing scuffle provided the perfect cover for Gilbert, who was able to get onboard (and reach Sweden). The guard dragged Townsend-Coles away, but, rather than join Gilbert, Grimson shadowed Townsend-Coles in the hope of effecting some sort of rescue. Townsend-Coles apparently saw Grimson on the train taking him to the prison at Insterburg, but there was no rescue.

Further setbacks would spell disaster for the escape line. At Heydekrug another escape attempt went wrong, and the escaper was captured with his documents (they were the same forgeries being used by Grimson, making him vulnerable to subsequent searches). This arrest and that of Townsend-Coles suggested to the Germans that the RAF escapers were receiving German help. This was confirmed by the seizure of papers from the Polish Resistance that linked Sommers with the escape committee.

The whole escape line began to unravel. Sommers bravely took his own life, fearing that he might give away information under torture. Munkert was interrogated and shot, as was Townsend-Coles, who, according to the German account, had subsequently 'offered resistance' after his arrest. Six POWs, whom the Germans believed to be the chief ringleaders, were arrested, roughly treated, and sent to other camps. As for Grimson, he disappeared. For months afterwards the

RAF prisoners hoped that he might have escaped or still be in hiding, but it seems most likely he was caught and killed by the Gestapo. It was a tragic end to a great escaper. Grimson could have got away across the Baltic on a number of occasions, but he heroically stayed out in the cold to help his comrades.

On a simple cost–benefit analysis, escapes were arguably not worth the enormous investment of human effort and the lives lost. Although few could have foreseen the murderous German reaction to the Great Escape, the work put into escaping – not only by the escapers but also by the far larger backroom staff – yielded only modest returns in the ledger of home runs. In terms of the disruption caused within Germany, escapers had greater success, and, if the mass breakouts did not quite achieve the amount of disorganization claimed for them, they were nonetheless a thorn in flesh of the Nazi state. But, more than anything, escaping was a demonstration that the war was still being fought by Allied POWs; that, even if bloodied, they remained resolutely unbowed. When judged by these more intangible criteria, escapes can be seen as something of triumph in the story of Allied prisoners of war in Germany.

14

An Italian Adventure

Prisoner-of-war camps in Italy were of similar construction to those in Germany and were guarded in similar manner, but Allied escapers there had a much lower success rate than their counterparts in Germany, not only in breaking out of camps but also in getting back home. The Italian War Ministry reported 602 escape attempts up to July 1943, of which just 6 were converted into home runs. This was certainly a disappointing total, especially given prisoner numbers in Italy that by August 1943 had reached a total of 42,194 British, 26,126 Commonwealth and Empire, and 1,310 Americans behind the wire.

But, as MI9 pointed out, prisoners in Italy were 'guarded with much greater care than in Germany'. German guards tended to be stolid men of little imagination; the Italians, by contrast, were more curious and were encouraged to follow up their curiosity with action. Brigadier James Hargest – one of the few escapers to make a pre-armistice home run from Italy – explained that the Italian guard was 'as sharp as a needle, and many attempts at escape were frustrated because our fellows failed to recognize this fact'. Parcels were also more thoroughly searched in Italy, which made the passage of contraband escape materials difficult (and MI9 recorded that it been unable to establish good letter communications with Italian camps, through the inefficiency of the local mail system).

Yet, even though Italian camps were harder to break out of than those in Germany, the problems only really began once escapers were beyond the wire. In Germany, millions of workers from all over Europe provided cover for men on the run; in Italy foreigners were a rare and strange sight. Eric Newby, held in PG 49 at Fontanellato, wrote that the Italians were 'fascinated by minutiae of dress and behaviour of their fellow men', and that the disguises and forgeries which might work in Germany would seldom 'fool even the most myopic Italian ticket collector and get the owner past the barrier, let alone survive the scrutiny of the occupants of a compartment on an Italian train'.

Newby's comments were borne out by other POWs, including the escaper George Millar, who was eventually sent to the 'bad boys" camp of PG 5 at Gavi. He described a failed escape by two fellow officers who slipped out of PG 35 at Padula dressed as workmen. They were well prepared and suitably attired for the escape, except that the 'Italian foreman had noticed that their boots were peculiar.' Norman Rogers, a medical officer who walked out of PG 49 after the armistice, was intrigued that Italians always recognized him as British despite his best efforts to pass himself off as a local. But, like their counterparts in Germany, the British officer class did not make good social chameleons. The Italian peasants that Rogers encountered explained to him that his hair was parted the wrong way, that he walked and sat in the wrong way, and that 'anyone as scruffy as you wouldn't have glasses in Italy.'

The most memorable of the pre-armistice escapes was made from PG 12 at Vincigliata, a nineteenth-century mock castle that housed senior British officers – those of brigadier rank and above – captured by the Axis in North Africa. The six-man escape team, led by Lieutenant General Sir Richard O'Connor, also included Air Marshal Boyd, Major-General Carton de Wiart, VC, and brigadiers Combe, Hargest and Miles. The high value of the prisoners made certain that the camp was well guarded, and the Italians congratulated themselves on having foiled a number of escape attempts. But the weakness of PG 12 – as of other castle prisons – lay in the prisoners' ability to avoid observation by their captors in the passageways and small rooms that made up the jail. A hole (partially hidden in a lift well) was knocked through a wall into a disused and blocked-up chapel. This provided a perfect staging post for digging a tunnel – no elaborate trapdoor was required, and the spoil was simply stored in the chapel.

Work began on 1 September 1942. The ground was hard, and the generals' digging tools were limited to 'some broken kitchen knives and a small crow bar'. Noise was also a problem, and tunnelling was confined to the mornings and the afternoon siesta period, when the guards were less vigilant. Progress was slow and irregular. According to Hargest, 'Some weeks we made only a very few inches; some we made as much as three feet.' By Christmas Day they had only pushed forward a little under 20 feet. But the generals were not downhearted, and they continued chipping and scraping away at the rocky soil until the end of March, when the tunnel was ready to break.

The escapers received the full support of the others in PG 12. Lieutenant General Sir Philip Neame, VC, the camp's SBO, used his engineering knowledge to plan the route of the tunnel, while the forging of identity cards became the responsibility of Major General M. D. Gambier-Parry, a talented artist, who also organized the camp's musical life. Hargest recalled how Gambier-Parry was sent catalogues to select records for his weekly gramophone recitals:

> By a queer chance he discovered that the artists' photographs in the catalogues were the exact size of, and printed on similar paper to, those on identity cards. He sent for further catalogues and set up a small committee to choose likenesses. The results could not have been better – all six of us seemed to have more or less a counterpart in German or Italian opera. They found me a celebrated German tenor, and G.-P. gave him my moustache more painlessly than I cultivated his right-hand hair-parting.

On the night of 30 March 1943 the tunnel was successfully broken. Hargest expressed his feelings on emerging from the tunnel: 'It was a tremendous experience. Not even the need for action could suppress the wave of exaltation that swept over me. Here was the successful achievement of a year of planning and seven months of toil. I remember thinking, with a new kind of awareness, that whatever the immediate future held, at this moment I was alive and free. I have never been able to recapture in retrospect the fullness of that moment.'

The escapers split into three pairs: O'Connor and de Wiart decided to walk the 150 or so miles to the Swiss frontier; the others took the train north from nearby Florence. The decision taken by O'Connor and de Wiart was a mistake: although they were resolute and fit, their ages – 53 and 63 respectively – told against them, and, more significantly, as walkers they were more likely to be challenged than rail travellers. After eight days on the run they were arrested by suspicious *carabinieri*, delighted on finding they had recaptured such illustrious prisoners.

Combe and Boyd successfully reached Milan, but there became separated. Combe was picked up the following day in Milan while gazing into a shop window, but Boyd managed to jump a freight train to Como – close to the border – before a moment of impatience led him to climb down from the waiting train and be recaptured. Hargest and Miles also reached Milan, but they immediately took a north-bound train to Como before knowledge of their escape had been broadcast throughout the country. From Como they walked to the border town of Chiasso and then took to the mountains, crossing the frontier wire at 10.30 p.m. on the night of 31 March – just twenty-five hours after leaving PG 12. Later in the year they travelled through occupied France to Spain. Unfortunately their story did not end happily: Miles died in Spain, and, although Hargest reached Britain safely, he was killed in action in Normandy on 12 August 1944.

During 1943 the situation of Allied POWs in Italy was transformed by the overthrow of Mussolini on 25 July and the formation of a government, under Marshall Pietro Badoglio, which, while still at war, began secret peace talks with the Allies. Even before these negotiations were initiated, the British and US governments – and their respective escape organizations, MI9 and MIS-X – had begun to consider the fate of their prisoners within Italy. While concerned that the Germans might insist on the prisoners' removal to Germany, the Allies were even more fearful that mass breakouts by POWs would lead to reprisals by the Germans.

It is believed that the commander of the British Eighth Army, General B. L. Montgomery, was behind what became the controversial 'Stay Put' order following a visit to London in May–June 1943. From the start there was confusion over what the escaped prisoners would do on their release. The view expressed by MI9's chief, Brigadier Norman Crockatt, seemed to suggest that they might engage in forms of guerrilla warfare, but given their lack of weapons, knowledge and interest in such matters this was an unlikely option – a POW's overriding aim was to get back home as quickly as possible. As early as 7 June, Crockatt had signalled to MI9 Cairo that orders were to be dispatched forbidding mass breakouts. By radio transmissions and coded letters the following order was sent to POW camps in Italy: 'In the event of an Allied invasion of Italy, Officers Commanding prison camps will ensure that prisoners-of-war remain within camp. Authority is granted to all Officers Commanding to take necessary disciplinary action to prevent individual prisoners-of-war attempting to rejoin their own units.'

Churchill was unaware of the order, and had insisted in the negotiations with Italy that Allied prisoners should be safeguarded by the Italians from any German interference, or be released and helped on their way to Switzerland or along the Adriatic coast to southern Italy. An order to this effect was sent by the Italian War Ministry to POW camp commandants on 6 September, a couple of days before the announcement of the armistice. How many of these orders reached the camps is unknown, but if they did they were largely ignored.

While Crockatt insisted on the prisoners being kept in place, contrary efforts were made by MI9's senior officer in the Middle East, Lieutenant Colonel A. C. Simonds, to aid prisoner escapes. His early efforts to set up an escape organization were rebuffed, however, and it was only on 8 September that a newly deployed 'A' Force was given responsibility for assisting the passage of POWs to Allied lines. But by then a golden opportunity had been missed, and 'A' Forces' lack of resources prevented it from making a significant contribution during September 1943 – the vital month before the Germans and Italian fascist forces gained control of the country, and when escaping was at its easiest.

Reports of Allied victories in Tunisia and the fall of Mussolini had raised hopes among Allied prisoners, and during the summer of 1943 rumours of impending release were a feature of camp life. But the actual news of the armistice on the evening of 8 September came as a complete shock to the prisoners – and most of their captors. Some Italian guards threw away their rifles and returned home; others, however, stuck to their posts and awaited orders from their superiors. The reaction of the camp commandants was crucial. A few followed the new orders to actively help the POWs; others carried on guarding their prisoners, albeit without much enthusiasm, although a substantial number did all in their power to hand them over to the Germans. The reason for such obstructiveness is hard to discern. Some camps certainly contained a fascist hard core who threw in their lot with the Germans, but it is also possible that a few commandants deluded themselves that they would be able to defend their camps against German intervention, while others, after years of holding men in captivity, simply could not bring themselves to let their prisoners go.

The Germans' reaction to the armistice was swift and uncompromising. Betrayed by their former ally, they crushed any sign of resistance. They took over administrative positions within Italy while reinforcements poured over the Alps to contain the Allied invasion in the south. They also began to look for Allied POW camps, to transport prisoners to Germany. This took time, and it was in the days immediately after the armistice that prisoners had their best chance to get away.

Accounts of the period repeatedly refer to the inertia of the unguarded prisoners: they tended to hang around the camp and do little to organize a getaway. But of course these men were not escapers; they were ordinary prisoners who had had the possibility of escape thrust upon them. Unlike the true escaper – who was mentally and physically prepared for ordeal ahead – these men found the idea of marching hundreds of miles in a foreign and potentially hostile country daunting, if not overwhelming. The Stay Put order also encouraged them to do little, and there were circulating rumours that Allied seaborne landings and parachute drops would make escape unnecessary.

As PG 5 at Gavi contained persistent escapers, it was not surprising that the armistice encouraged a wave of escape bids there and a desperate attempt by the SBO to persuade the Italian commandant to release them. Unfortunately for the POWs, the commandant maintained an iron grip on the camp until the very swift arrival of the Germans on 9 September. Many prisoners attempted to hide within the camp, but almost all were flushed out by the Germans, so that, according to one report, 'only a captain and a few soldiers had succeeded in escape.'

At PG 57 at Gruppignano, Bob McDowall recorded the confusion that reigned among both guards and captors. The commandant, the usually oppressive Colonel Calcatera, briefly withdrew his troops from the camp, but the prisoners failed to act with purpose. Rumours of Allied landings on the northern Adriatic ran through the camp, and a brisk trade with the local people was begun, fuelled by the ransacking of the Red Cross-parcel store by some of the POWs. The camp was easily isolated by Germans advancing over the Brenner Pass, and within a couple of days the Germans had taken over without resistance from Italians or British.

When news of the armistice reached the other ranks' camp of PG 78 at Sulmona (the officers had already been sent to PG 19 at Bologna) the Italian guards simply walked away. Although the prisoners were subject to the Stay Put order, most simply ignored it and scores of them began to breakout of the camp. The high and barren Abruzzi mountains were a formidable barrier to men poorly equipped and out of condition; a large group made an early attempt to march over the nearest ridge, but were forced back. Prisoners returned to the relative safety of the camp – with its store of Red Cross parcels – or the surrounding neighbourhood, where, to their surprise, they found the people of the area exceptionally friendly.

The inactivity of the Sulmona prisoners came as a shock to Captain Jock McKee, an 'A' Force officer who with considerable initiative had pushed northward to try to scoop up as many ex-prisoners as possible before the front line stabilized. Reaching Sulmona, he found a mass of at least 1,000 men doing nothing. Despite his best efforts to get them to move – including at one point threatening them with his revolver – only twenty-three soldiers accompanied him back to Allied lines. Shortly after McKee left, the Germans arrived in force and rounded up the former Sulmona prisoners. Jim Witte had slipped away from the camp, but his fair hair and height (6 foot 2 inches) made him easy to identify, and he was picked up á by a passing German patrol and soon in a cattle truck to Germany.

The Anglo-American officers' camp PG 21, at Chieti, became the focus for bitter recriminations over the interpretation of the Stay Put order. The SBO, Lieutenant Colonel Marshall, upheld the order despite repeated entreaties from prisoners to be allowed to leave the camp, which, post-armistice, had only a few guards in place, some of whom actually encouraged prisoners to escape. Not only did the SBO repeatedly threaten potential escapers with court martial, he even appointed his own guards to see that the men remained in camp. He was supported by the SAO, Colonel Gooler, who issued similar warnings to the American prisoners. Approximately 40 POWs ignored the order and climbed over the wall to freedom – most safely crossing Allied lines – but nearly 1,300 officers and orderlies remained in the camp. Many officers could not bring themselves to disobey a direct order from a superior and reluctantly stayed put, but at the same time the force of inertia also seemed to hold them as firmly in place as the barbed wire and the Italian guards. A week after the armistice the POWs awoke to find the watchtowers filled with friendly but battle-hardened German paratroopers.

With the Germans in control, Colonel Marshall limply released the prisoners from the escape prohibition, but by then his authority was in tatters. And the otherwise good relations between Americans and British had become strained. The Germans transported the prisoners to nearby PG 78 at Sulmona, which had become a holding camp after the transfer of its original POWs to Germany. Once at Sulmona, under German guard, the prisoners were paradoxically galvanized into action, as John Verney observed: 'At Vasco [PG 21] we had been as passive as sheep, at Sulmona we became as busy as beavers, and the whole camp echoed to the sounds of excavation.' The wire at Sulmona had been cut and damaged in places, and, with the German front-line troops less knowledgeable about looking after prisoners than regular guards, there were several escape attempts – on one night sixty or so Americans broke through the wire, a number getting clean away. The new-found enthusiasm for escape continued as the prisoners were sent north in cattle trucks, many jumping from the moving trains.

In the officers' camp of PG 47 at Modena, the Italians told the prisoners that they would defend them from any German intervention. The SBO, Lieutenant Colonel Shuttleworth, went along with the Italians, but on 9 September the arrival of German troops in the immediate vicinity and the decamping of the Italian guards made some of the prisoners increasingly uneasy. At a meeting convened by the SBO, permission was given for men to quit the camp, but less than 200 men took this opportunity, leaving approximately 1,000 officers to be tamely arrested by the Germans. While the Stay Put order played its part in encouraging such displays of timidity, it would have taken a rigorous shake-up of the entire camp system in the weeks, perhaps months, leading up to the armistice to have retrained the sedentary prisoners in the attitudes of an escaper.

In one camp, British and Italian leaders co-operated so that all the prisoners walked free. Colonel Eugenio Vicedomini, the commandant of PG 49 at Fontanellato, may have received the order of 6 September, but he had already been working with the British SBO, Lieutenant Colonel Hugo de Burgh, on a response to a German take-over of the camp. Vicedomini's example was unique in a main camp, although a few Italian leaders in work camps in northern Italy were equally helpful to the British. At PG 120/1 the Italian commander advised his prisoners of the best routes to Switzerland and gave them maps, money and a Red Cross parcel each. At PG 148/7 the commander went a stage further and led the forty inmates of the camp to Switzerland himself.

At PG 49 it was agreed that if there were signs of German activity the British would leave to a previously reconnoitred hiding area. Since his arrival in August 1943 de Burgh had instituted a new military regime intended to toughen up the prisoners. At noon on 9 September, Vicedomini's scouts reported the approach of German troops and the escape plan was immediately put into effect: the wire was cut, and over 600 officers and orderlies marched out of PG 49 in good order. When the Germans arrived a short while later they found an empty camp. Vicedomini bravely stayed at his post, and was roughly handled by the now angry Germans. They proceeded to ransack the Red Cross-parcel store before leaving with the former commandant now under arrest. (Vicedomini spent the rest of the war in German camps, and, his health broken, died shortly after his release in 1945.) Over the following two days the former prisoners dispersed, hiding out in the Apennines, or travelling north to Switzerland or south towards Allied lines in the foot of Italy. The leadership displayed by the British and Italians in PG 49 stood in marked contrast to that of PG 21.

Whatever the consequences of prisoner inertia and the Stay Put order, nearly 50,000 of the 79,000 Allied POWs of all nationalities in Italy did move beyond the confines of their camps. Some of these were subsequently rounded up by the Germans. By mid-November 1943 roughly 24,000 POWs had been transferred to Germany, a figure that rose to 50,000 by the end of the year. This meant that there were still something in the region of 30,000 ex-prisoners at large in Italy. More would continue to be arrested by the Germans and fascist forces, but by October 1944, 4,000 former prisoners had crossed the Swiss border, and a further 6,500 reached Allied lines in the south. An unknown figure remained in hiding in Italy, either to escape or to be overrun and rescued by the Allied drive northward, although it is estimated that as many as 2,000 former POWs were never accounted for (a substantial number of them were thought to have settled in Italy).

To the confusion of tens of thousands of former Allied prisoners roaming across Italy were added a million or so Italian soldiers returning home in the autumn of 1943. The POW fugitives would subsequently be joined in hiding by young Italian men on the run from the fascist authorities as well as deserters from the German forced-labour Todt Organisation. That so many former prisoners were able to avoid recapture was a direct consequence of the extraordinary help given them by the Italian people. Numerous accounts by Allied fugitives speak of the kindness and generosity shown by all sections of Italian society. Most striking of all was the help offered by the impoverished peasantry. It became a rule of thumb among escapers that the poor were the best people to approach for assistance. Captain Ian English, released from PG 49, looked for the number of haystacks in a farmyard: 'Five meant the family was too well to do and might be fascist in outlook. Only one haystack indicated the family was too poor, though probably friendly. Two haystacks were about right.'

Although some Allied fugitives exploited the hospitality shown them, the majority were genuinely grateful. As a consequence, Allied escapers were forced to rethink their typically hostile and contemptuous view of the Italian people. While imprisoned, Norman Rogers considered Italians to be 'comic-opera types', but he admitted that his time spent on the run 'changed my view about them entirely; they were very brave, generous people.'

Not only were Allied escapers a drain on the peasants' scarce resources, they were a potentially fatal liability. As early as 19 September 1943 the Germans had issued a 'final warning' to all Italians that anyone helping Allied fugitives faced the death penalty. A number of helpers were executed by the Germans and fascists; others were sent to concentration camps and had their property destroyed. Despite the draconian nature of the German decree, it had limited effect: Allied fugitives continued to receive help, even though it might be provided a little more circumspectly than in the early days of September, when in a fiesta-like atmosphere escapers had had food and drink forced upon them.

After leaving their camp, POWs had to decide what to do next: whether to escape to Switzerland or head south, or to go into hiding helped by friendly Italians and let the war catch up with them. It was a difficult decision to make, especially as many men had only a hazy idea of where they were and how to find the best route to safety.

While the help given to fugitives in central Italy was generally unorganized – spontaneously provided by peasant families scattered over wide areas – those former POWs in northern Italy attempting to escape to Switzerland had the good fortune to be supported by the *Ufficio Assistenza Prigionieri di Guerra Alleati* ('Allied Prisoner of War Assistance Service'). Based in Milan, this branch of the Committee for National Liberation was organized by Giuseppe Bacciagaluppi, the manager of an electronics company, who had an English wife and spoke good English himself. POWs were located by sympathizers and then sorted into small groups led by guides to the border with Switzerland. Trains were used as much as possible, and although fascist militiamen remained a danger – especially when checking passengers' papers – the experienced and wily guides were usually able to avoid them. Once near the border, the escaping POWs were taken over the mountains by smugglers or other locals with detailed knowledge of the terrain. Bacciagaluppi's organization was responsible for the transfer of nearly 1,000 Allied servicemen before his arrest on 3 April 1944. (He subsequently escaped from his imprisonment.)

A few highly enterprising former POWs also took an active role in helping their comrades to safety. Sergeant Edgar Triffett had been sent with many other Australians – including Doug LeFevre – to the rice fields around Vercelli in the spring of 1943. Triffett escaped in June and headed for the Alps, and although close to the border he remained in hiding helped by a friendly priest. On hearing news of the armistice Triffett did not take the obvious and easy step of crossing over the border, but instead returned to the Vercelli region to help his comrades. He picked up 139 former prisoners and led them up to a partisan area in the mountains, where they were given a choice of joining the partisans or crossing the frontier. Most chose the latter option, but Triffett stayed on the Italian side, leading a partisan band and continuing to help escaping POWs. Captured by enemy forces, he managed to escape, eventually leading another group of prisoners into Switzerland. From Switzerland he had hoped to continue his activities, but was forbidden from returning by the British.

The most formidable of the former POWs who helped Allied escapers was another Australian, Private John Peck. Having worked as a drover from the age of 14, Peck joined up (under age) on the outbreak of war and saw action in the Western Desert in 1940 and in Greece and Crete the following year. He was captured twice by Germans on Crete, and escaped twice, spending the winter of 1941–2 in hiding. He helped other evaders and escapers rendezvous with Royal Navy rescue parties, although a bout of malaria prevented him from getting off the island. He was eventually arrested by the Italians in May 1942 and sent to Rhodes, where he escaped but was recaptured and sent to a prison camp in the centre of the island. Almost inevitably he escaped from this camp, and with four companions he stole a boat and began to sail for Turkey. But the boat fell apart in a storm, leaving just Peck and another man to be rescued by an Italian destroyer.

Peck was then sent to Italy and via the transit camp at Bari to PG 57 at Gruppignano, where he learned to speak Italian fluently. He was transferred to a work camp around Vercelli, where he escaped in June 1943. Peck and another escaper actually managed to cross the frontier, but, short of food and daunted by the mountain ranges ahead, they retreated to a shepherd's hut, only to be arrested by the *carabinieri*. While serving time in solitary confinement in a civilian jail in Vercelli Peck was freed by looters breaking into the jail following the armistice. He gathered up a small group of wandering POWs and led them to the crossing point that he had found on his previous escape attempt. Originally he had planned to lead them into Switzerland – a home run on the sixth attempt – but, as he recalled:

I had pangs of conscience and decided that for me to go in to Switzerland and freedom meant now abandoning all my friends, who had no way of knowing which way to go and how to get there. So I decided to get back and get these people and take them into Switzerland. I started off an organization with the Italians and made arrangements on the route for people to pick up and guide the prisoners after I'd started organizing back on the plains.

Peck disguised himself as an Italian businessman, an occupation that provided good cover while travelling around northern Italy supervising his helpers. The work of guiding Allied prisoners was extremely stressful. 'The risks were enormous,' he recalled:

> I was always in fear, because even if I did everything correctly, I could have been picked up just casually like everybody else. But with prisoners who were normally much taller than local men, [and who] normally had fair hair, spoke only English, and had no knowledge of how and where they were going, they were [potentially] sheep led to slaughter, and in many cases this happened with inexperienced couriers and inexperienced guides.

Peck worked closely with Giuseppe Bacciagaluppi and others in the *Ufficio Assistenza Prigionieri di Guerra Alleati*, and had a part in taking approximately 1,500 Allied escapers over the border. It was an incredible feat for a private soldier who was just 21 when the armistice was declared. (He was given a temporary promotion to captain by the British SOE in Switzerland, a commission subsequently confirmed by the Australian Army, although at the lower rank of lieutenant.)

Peck established a base at Luino, near the border, and operated with local partisans against the Germans. The risks began to mount. In January 1944 a mission to blow up a railway line was betrayed to the Germans, and on the night before the attack Peck and others in his group were arrested by the Gestapo. Peck was in a desperate position, not least because he had been captured wearing a German officer's uniform. He endured several tough interrogations by the Gestapo, and was sentenced to death by a military tribunal in Turin before being sent to the prison of San Vittore in Milan pending execution.

Bacciagaluppi was also held in San Vittore, and managed to have Peck selected as part of a bomb-disposal squad. This was an exceptionally dangerous job – digging out unexploded bombs with picks and shovels – and was typically reserved for condemned men, but for someone with Peck's spirit there remained the possibility of escape. The squad was assigned work at a railway marshalling yard, and when it came under an Allied air attack the guards and prisoners scrambled for safety, as Peck recalled: 'The guards ran and so did I – in the opposite direction.' With shots flying over his head Peck dashed across the bomb-pocked marshalling yard and out into the streets of Milan. After taking a train to Novarra he headed north into the Alps and finally crossed into Switzerland.

After a couple of months' rest Peck returned to Italy, acting as a liaison officer with several partisan formations. An attempt by the partisans to set up a liberated area – the 'Republic of Domodossola' – inevitably ended in failure when it was overrun by a well-armed German force in October 1944. Peck and the partisans were forced to retreat into Switzerland, which marked the end of Peck's extraordinary career as escaper and partisan. (After returning to Australia, he moved to Britain, where he married and lived until his death in 2002.)

Lance Corporal Doug LeFevre was one of the many POWs in northern Italy helped by Peck and the Italian escape organizations. LeFevre's experiences were fairly typical of many thousands of British and Commonwealth ex-POWs in that he stayed in the locality of his camp for some months before thinking about escape. In the work camps around Vercelli there were no Stay Put restrictions: the prisoners merely walked away from the camp, as did most of the guards. LeFevre teamed up with fellow Australian Norm Terrell and, having left the camp, they exchanged their British battledress uniform for civilian clothes. LeFevre remembered how 'Norm had a shooting jacket and a grey pair of pants. I had quite a dapper blue outfit.'

Because of his small stature and dark appearance, LeFevre could more or less pass as an Italian, but Terrell – tall and fair – was something of a problem. And because he spoke little Italian – unlike LeFevre – he was forced to adopt the part of a mute. Indeed, during the months after the armistice Italy was full of large, fair-headed 'Italians' with speech difficulties. One such was South African Graham Shepherd of the Natal Field Artillery:

I was 6 foot 4 inches tall, and so conspicuous that on my way south to meet the Allies even my three fellow escapees, with whom I was travelling in company, could not bear it. They asked me if I would mind leaving their group as I was attracting far too much attention. As luck would have it, they all ended in Germany, while after nine months of wandering on my own in the Italian countryside, being fed by the Italian people, I finally met up with the Allies.

LeFevre and Terrell remained as a team through thick and thin. LeFevre described how they survived through the autumn of 1943: 'We were dependent on the kindness of these Italians for our food. We went from farm to farm working where we could, because we soon realized that as generous as these people were we couldn't bludge on them, so we helped on the farms for about a couple of months gradually working our way north.'

By lying low among the peasant communities they were fairly safe from detection – certainly by the Germans, who, LeFevre discovered, had little knowledge of Italian or the Italian people. On one occasion LeFevre and Terrell encountered a German soldier riding towards them on a bicycle while they were drinking at a village water pump. The soldier drew up and asked them in halting Italian to help him put up a poster. After a certain amount of bother the poster was put into place. They stepped back to admire their handiwork, only to find that it read, 'Attention! Citizens of Piedmonte. 5,000 lire will be paid for information leading to the apprehension of escaped prisoners of war.' LeFevre and Terrell looked at each other in alarm, but managed to contain their surprise. The German soldier, his work done, sat down and shared his lunch of bread, baloney sausage and wine with the two Australians. When they were finished, the now tipsy German wobbled away on his bicycle, waving goodbye to a relieved LeFevre and Terrell.

During the winter of 1943–4 conditions worsened: food was scarce, and the Germans and the fascist authorities began clamping down on ordinary Italians, exacting brutal revenge on any harbouring Allied fugitives. Concern over the danger they posed to their Italian benefactors was the prime reason behind LeFevre's decision to head towards Switzerland. A German patrol had been sent to LeFevre's village, but by mistake they went to another in the locality, and there discovered four other Australians, who were taken into custody. LeFevre described how they then 'burnt the village down and took the menfolk away. Well we thought this wasn't good enough. It was bad enough us getting it in the neck, but for civilians all they were doing was being good to people. And if you knew the poverty of these people! This was what really struck home!'

LeFevre and Terrell and two other Australians contacted a POW escape organization in January 1944. They were directed to travel to Vercelli, and there joined a group of fifteen other Allied escapers. From Vercelli they took a train north that ran alongside Lake Maggiore. Rather than risk a security check at a border station, the escape party were instructed to leap from the train when it slowed to cross a trestle bridge over a mountain stream. To the escapers the train seemed to be travelling far too fast, but at the last moment they jumped and all landed safely, their falls cushioned by 12 feet of snow. From there they trudged up a mountainside towards the frontier, even coming across some friendly Italian frontier guards, who gave them food and hot tea. Once over the border they were met by an officious Swiss border-guard officer, who escorted them to an internment camp where they stayed before repatriation to Australia via Marseilles in the autumn of 1944. With the war still on, there were no bands and flags to welcome home the Australian former prisoners. LeFevre was unconcerned: he only wanted to get back to the settlement of Cotteslow, where his wife lived. With typical understatement he wrote, 'No one had bothered to notify her that I was coming back. So I guess she was surprised.'

Another successful escape organization was set up in Rome, using the neutrality of the Vatican state as partial cover for its activities. The guiding light behind what was called the Rome Escape Line was a charismatic Irish priest, Monsignor Hugh O'Flaherty, who had previously worked for the welfare of Allied prisoners in regular POW camps. After the armistice, Rome became a magnet for escaping prisoners, some of whom attempted to find sanctuary within the Vatican itself. Despite O'Flaherty's best efforts to help, the numbers of fugitives entering Rome threatened to overwhelm him. Fortunately he received aid from a number of people, including Sir D'Arcy Osborne, the British minister to the Vatican, and Major Sam Derry, who had jumped from a train taking him to Germany from Sulmona and made his way to Rome. While O'Flaherty acted as a bridge between the relative security of the Vatican and his many contacts within Rome, Osborne discreetly provided funds and other material help, while the energetic Derry – supported by a small hand-picked staff – acted as the billeting officer and overall leader of the organization.

Derry kept as many fugitives out of the city as possible, setting up a network of safe houses in the surrounding region. As always, help from the Italian people was the foundation of success. While the Italian peasantry provided the bedrock of support in rural districts, in Rome the helpers came from a wider social spectrum, not least from the patrician elements of Italian society that made the capital their home. Among these was the aristocratic left-wing film director Luciano Visconti, who looked after five British and American officers for several months during 1943–4. In all, nearly 4,000 ex-prisoners from over 20 nationalities – including 2,776 Anglo-Americans – passed through the hands of the Rome Escape Line before the city's liberation on 5 June 1944.

Former POWs who did not make the push to reach Switzerland or Allied lines had to reconcile themselves to a hard existence of living off the land, working alongside peasant farmers scratching a livelihood in the more remote – invariably mountainous – regions of Italy. Many were asked to join the partisan bands that emerged as a reaction to the establishment of the German-backed fascist republic. The ex-prisoners had military training and technical knowledge that many of the partisans lacked. The partisans also hoped that the inclusion of British and American servicemen would give them a legitimacy with the Allies that might lead to the provision of arms and equipment. But most former prisoners were reluctant to be involved with partisans' activities. Apart from a natural hesitation in joining an uncertain, foreign fighting organization, there was an underlying fear of being caught carrying arms while in civilian clothes, which would deny them any protection from the Geneva Convention. For those who did join there was also a problem of differing objectives. While these former prisoners were prepared to take on the enemy before returning home, the partisans had a complex political agenda that owed as much to securing a good position within any post-war settlement as to simply fighting the Germans.

Some men joined the partisans for relatively short periods, often dropping out to continue their journey towards Switzerland or the Allied lines. Others, however, prospered as partisan fighters, a few becoming leaders of some renown. In addition to his work supervising escape lines, John Peck engaged in sabotage activities. So too did Australian sapper Frank Jocumsen, who served as a courier and then a liaison officer for a partisan group in northern Italy and, like Peck, was considered sufficiently important to receive a temporary British commission as a captain. Armed with a Thompson sub-machine gun, 'Frank the Australian' became something of a legend in the Valesia region, and he was awarded the Medaglia d'Oro, Italy's highest award for bravery, after the war.

The fighting between partisans and German and fascist forces was vicious, and recaptured POWs were invariably executed if thought to be involved in military activity. One Australian taken by fascist forces sent this last letter home, made all the more poignant by its matter-of-fact expression:

> Just a line to tell you that I will not see you again as I am going to be shot by the Fascists in Varallo this morning . . . I hope you are all well just at present so give my love to all the Beggs also Gwen and my girl friend Phyllis and hoping she will be happy without me being there with her. I am with two English boys and they are going with me. I hope you got that letter I wrote a fair while ago. How is Melbourne? I suppose it is just as bad as ever. Lots of love to you all from your loving Brother, Mick. Goodbye.

Although the partisan war was a sideshow in the wider scheme of the Italian campaign, it was still a means by which Allied POWs could fight back at the Germans. More significant, perhaps, was the return to uniform of several thousand former prisoners, some of whom were able to play a part in the final stages of the war. For these men, at least, their adventure in Italy had been a resounding personal success – very different from the experiences of those prisoners who had been transported over the Alps and were to endure a further nineteen months of imprisonment in Nazi Germany.

15

Migration and Liberation

'THE FIRST NEWS of the D-Day landings in June 1944 set the camp dancing,' wrote one American prisoner. 'But when weeks passed and not much seemed to happen, there was letdown and despair.' His comments would have been seconded by almost every POW in Germany: the heady optimism occasioned by Allied success in France during the summer of 1944 was dashed by the slowdown in the autumn and the prospect of another winter behind the wire. Ominously, the supply of Red Cross parcels began to falter, and this was made worse by the German decision to further reduce food and fuel rations.

Their own fate was a continuing anxiety for many prisoners as the war entered its final phase: would they simply be released as the Allied armies drew near, or would they be used as bargaining counters in a futile attempt to stave off unconditional surrender? Or, worse still, would the Nazis kill them all in some final act of vengeance? These anxieties were, in fact, well founded. On 19 February 1945 Hitler suggested to his top military aides that Germany should disown the Geneva Convention with regard to British and American prisoners. At OKW, Admiral Karl Dönitz and General Alfred Jodl were asked to submit their opinions on the matter. The Allies, however, now held twice as many prisoners as did the Germans, and solely for fear of Allied countermeasures both men recommended no public repudiation of the Convention, although Jodl cynically suggested to Hitler that a formal agreement to uphold its terms need not necessarily be carried out in practice. Fortunately for the POWs, no such retrograde steps were taken against them, although the conditions they were to endure in 1945 were severe enough.

POW camps in central Germany became increasingly overcrowded following the evacuation of camps in the east from December 1944 onward. By the end of the war they had doubled or even tripled in size: sports areas and parade grounds were taken over by vast canvas encampments, while the barrack huts were filled to overflowing, with several men sharing a bunk and others sleeping on concrete floors. The lack of food and fuel added to the misery; old hands began to make comparisons with the terrible first winter of 1940–41. Some thought things were getting worse. Even in the best-run camps conditions were becoming intolerable. At one such camp – Stalag 383 at Hohenfels – Australian POW Ray Ryan described the worsening situation:

> It is noticeable how the strain of cold, food, smokes, boredom and worry is beginning to tell on a number of chaps to a large degree and on everyone to a lesser degree. It is especially hard on those who have had bad news recently. One chap I know whom I haven't seen for several weeks was standing on the corner today when I passed him. It gave me a shock to see how he had altered. He had always been one of the more cheery types. Now his face is lined and his eyes vacant, mouth open, hat on the back of his head, hair untidy, boots unlaced. Other chaps have given up the struggle and stay in bed for days at a time, without washing or having the slightest interest in anything.

Aware of deteriorating conditions, the Red Cross persuaded the Germans to let them set up a holding centre in the Baltic port of Lübeck, and to supplement rail transport (now on its knees as a result of Allied bombing) with a fleet of trucks. Painted white, with the distinctive Red Cross emblem, these 'White Angels' began to operate out of Lübeck on 12 February 1945, taking supplies to camps in northern Germany and to the columns of marching POWs. Finding sufficient drivers was a problem, although this was solved when the Germans let paroled prisoners drive the vehicles. A similar system had been put into operation for camps in southern Germany, with soldiers from the Swiss Army and paroled prisoners driving relief trucks from Switzerland.

Prisoners also had to contend with the increasing intensity of the Allied strategic bombing campaign. The great fleets of US B-17 and B-24 heavy bombers flying over Germany were an awesome sight to the prisoners looking up from below, as were the vivid illuminations of the RAF night attacks. When flying to targets further afield the bombers were a welcome reminder of Allied military might. For those closer to the targets, the stress of the raids wore down the strongest nerves. Bob Prouse – whose work camp near Stalag IXC at Bad Sulza lay on a main flight path – found the growing frequency and intensity of the bombing an uncomfortable and potentially dangerous disruption to camp life. In every raid he and the other prisoners were forced down into the lice-ridden castle dungeons that acted as an air-raid shelter. At the end of March 1945, when the bombing campaign was still at its height, he jotted in his notebook that in that month there had been 179 alarms lasting 235 hours, the longest alarm being 16½ hours long. 'No wonder we were getting "bomb-happy"!' he recalled.

Working at a locomotive repair works on the outskirts of Leipzig, Jim Witte not only saw the devastation wrought by the bombers but found himself at the centre of a major attack. He witnessed the great RAF and USAAF bomber streams that destroyed Dresden on 13 and 14 February 1945. On the morning afterwards, Witte and the other POWs

> went to work to find a thoroughly demoralized ashen-faced lot of German workers. My foreman, who was quite a decent bloke, was literally shaking: 'Dresden,' he said, 'alles Kaput.' Apparently, thousands of its citizens had been killed in a ferocious fire-storm like the one that had destroyed Hamburg. What could we say? We worked with the Germans and ran the same risks from the bombers. They did not take it out on us. And I was not filled with any sort of jubilation.

With the Allied planners running out of major targets, it was inevitable that the locomotive repair works would be on the list. On one early-spring afternoon the air-raid siren wailed and Witte and his fellow workers raced from the factory towards nearby fields to take shelter in whatever ditches and hollows they could find. He described the attack:

> Half way to the fields we heard a mighty roar getting nearer. I glanced up and saw two Pathfinders. They dived to mark the target, our works. We started to run as hundreds of Flying Fortresses blackened the sky, and I dived into a fold in the ground. The noise was hellish; I thought my head was going to split open. I felt the blast travel all over me and I tried to burrow deeper into the ground. And then suddenly there was

silence. We rose or staggered to our feet like zombies and carried out a kind of roll call. To our horror six of our mates were killed, and what made it worse was the fact that the war was nearly over. We survivors helped the Germans to collect their own casualties, which were huge. This was a terrible job carrying badly mutilated corpses of men, women and children to a makeshift mortuary. My last body was that of a Russian whom I found by a large crater; his intestines lay beside him and his right leg rested by his head. He died with a smile on his face. This was one of my most abiding memories as a POW.

Many POW camps were sited in the eastern and central areas of Greater Germany, and it was here that prisoners wondered whether they might be liberated by the Red Army. The Wehrmacht was, however, determined to hold on to its prisoners, and during January and February 1945 the camps in the east were evacuated.

The prisoners began their marches in a poor condition: many were suffering from malnutrition, and almost all were out of condition for the strenuous journey ahead. The winter of 1944–5 was particularly harsh, and throughout January and into February the men had to contend with heavy snowfalls and sub-zero temperatures by day and night. Although they were issued with Red Cross parcels as they left their camps, these soon ran out, leaving them largely dependent on inadequate German rations. Contaminated drinking water caused gastrointestinal problems. The worst of these was dysentery, a potential killer for men having to contend with such desperate conditions. Piles of bloody faeces were a common sight along the route. Adding to the prisoners' problems, Allied fighter-bombers roamed over Germany, and the long columns of prisoners presented inviting targets. There were numerous incidents of POWs being strafed by Allied aircraft, sometimes within a few days of the war's end.

Those prisoners who were ill or incapable of marching were left behind to be overrun by the Red Army. The Soviet forces provided some limited help for the wounded, although able-bodied prisoners had to look after themselves. They were told to make their way to the Black Sea port of Odessa, and many former prisoners were reduced to hitching rides on trucks or trains returning eastward from the front line. The Revd David Wild remained with the sick at the Kopernikus hospital and was liberated by Soviet troops at the end of

January. He and his men were held for two months in the Polish spa town of Ciechocinek, before the cumbersome Soviet bureaucracy permitted them to undertake a ten-day rail journey to Odessa. From there they boarded the SS *Duchess of Richmond* to begin their voyage home.

Roger Shinn and the US Army officers from Oflag 64 at Schubin left camp on 21 January on a 350-mile trek that would take them from Poland along the Baltic to a railhead at Parchim near the river Elbe. The men from this camp were relatively fortunate: they were well equipped and organized, and the commandant and his guards demonstrated a basic regard for prisoner welfare. Despite these advantages, the prisoners found it tough going, as Shinn recalled after the opening day of the march:

> We walked on hour after hour, growing dreary and weary. Our column began to stretch out. Muscles unused to exercise grew sore, and the freezing weather helped to make them ache. Stragglers fell far behind. There were no longer any recognizable platoons, any military order. Now there was just a mass of men, moving slowly and painfully forward, strung out for miles . . . After the first hour there were no organized halts; if the head of the column stopped, the tail was too far away to know it. As each group of men got too tired to walk, they stopped awhile and then trudged on. The guards grumbled and protested, but were too tired themselves to really care.

The march took its toll: by 14 February just 500 men out of an original force of nearly 1,500 were still on their feet – and they still had another two weeks to go before reaching the railhead. To the Germans' credit, those men who had fallen out were reasonably treated; taken to collecting centres, they were sent on by train when rolling stock became available.

The march gave the fitter and more enterprising prisoners opportunities for escape. Lieutenant Frank J. Diggs, from Oflag 64, escaped with a comrade on the second day of the march. Disguised as Polish civilians, they climbed over a barbed-wire fence penning the Americans within a large barn for the nightly stop. There were no Germans in the area, and the two men were looked after by a Polish family until the arrival of Soviet troops a couple of days later. They met up with some other American former prisoners, and by truck and train reached Odessa on 1 March. Private Jim Roberts was evacuated from his work camp at Stolzenberg on the Baltic on 18 February, and, like Diggs, escaped while on the march westward and then slowly made his way to Odessa with a small group of British soldiers, arriving at the port on 3 April. Altogether, approximately 2,500 Allied servicemen were repatriated through the Black Sea port.

In Stalag Luft III at Sagan, preparations for a possible march to the west had been anticipated for some time. In Center compound, Colonel Delmar T. Spivey had been storing food for such an eventuality since December, and had instituted a programme of circuit-bashing so that by the end of January every man was supposed to be walking 4 miles a day. On the evening of 27 January, with Soviet artillery rumbling in the background, they were given orders to leave the camp immediately, and in the early hours of the 28th approximately 10,000 American and British airmen marched out of Stalag Luft III into a light snowstorm.

The early high spirits that characterized the move evaporated after the first day, as cold and exhaustion and then hunger bit into the men's resolve. After four days Spivey found that he 'was very tired and irritable, and many times caught myself snapping at the men when I should have been encouraging them'. But he was pushing himself to the limit, walking up and down the column urging his men to press on to the schools, churches, factories, barns and outhouses that became their resting places at the end of the day's march. Exhausted POWs now began to drop out.

Although the German officers in charge threatened to shoot stragglers, the guards were generally helpful, and those POWs genuinely unable to march were allowed to catch up with the main party. The Germans also allowed several extended halts of a day or more, enabling the prisoners to regroup and regain their strength. On 5 February the march came to a halt at Spremberg, where the prisoners were put into cattle wagons and taken to other camps – most of the Americans to Stalag VIIA at Moosburg, and the British to the naval camp at Marlag. There, in desperately overcrowded conditions, they would await liberation.

It was at Spremberg that Spivey was ordered to attend a secret meeting in Berlin – along with Brigadier General Vanaman and other officers, all of whom were told this would lead to their swift repatriation. Spivey was devastated to be separated from his men, and bitterly resented the order. After arriving at a small camp outside Berlin, the Americans were left to wait, and it was only in mid-March that they met a representative from SS General Gottlob Berger – then the head of POW affairs in Germany – to discuss the plight of Allied POWs. Although Spivey and Vanaman gave their support to negotiations between the International Red Cross and Berger's office to allow Red Cross vehicles to enter Germany and provide relief to the POWs, the real reason for their summons became apparent on 3 April when they were taken to meet Berger.

In an attempt to save his skin, Berger proposed that the Americans take a message to General Eisenhower to open negotiations with the SS to end the war. Whatever their thoughts on this ludicrous proposal, Spivey and Vanaman judged it wise to take the offer of an escort to Switzerland, especially now that Soviet tank armies were pressing towards the German capital. On 5 April they left Berlin; taking a tortuous route, they finally crossed the Swiss border on the 23rd. The two men were flown to Paris and then to the Allied HQ in Reims, where they were able to relay their message. But by then the war was virtually over, apart from which a bargaining offer from a relatively minor SS leader would have had no influence on the Allied imperative of unconditional surrender. After two weeks' waiting in Reims, Spivey was able to grab a flight to the United States. He arrived on home soil on 7 May, to a joyful reunion with his wife and young son.

The forced marches from other ranks' camps were generally less well organized than those of the officer camps, and the guards tended to be rougher in their treatment of the POWs. Also, the other ranks often had further to walk. Roger Coward, along with others in Silesia, marched over the mountains into Czechoslovakia in mid-winter. The weather conditions were terrible, and unsympathetic guards made it a march from hell. The only redeeming feature was the kindness of the Czech people, who threw food to the POWs whenever possible. Coward was on the road for twelve weeks, walking from Czechoslovakia into Bavaria, where he collapsed suffering from dysentery, pleurisy and diphtheria. Only the intervention of a German doctor saved him from death.

By April 1945 the Third Reich was in its death throes, but the Wehrmacht and especially the SS continued to fight on. The great columns of men marching from camps in the east found themselves mixed up with prisoners who had been evacuated from camps threatened by Americans and British in the west. In some instances prisoners would see another column of POWs marching past them in the opposite direction. No matter how pointless the exercise, the Germans were determined to hold on to their captives until the end.

The British and American NCO airmen from Stalag Luft VI (Heydekrug) and Stalag Luft IV (Gross Tychow) experienced some of the worst conditions on the long march westward. Staff Sergeant Joseph P. O'Donnell left one of the US compounds of Stalag Luft IV on 6 February to begin an odyssey that only ended eighty-six days later on 2 May with his liberation by the British Army. After five weeks of trudging through snow, ice and slush O'Donnell was at an all-time low. At one of the rest halts he happened to be sitting by a puddle. 'I sat in silent solitude,' he wrote, 'and stared at my reflection in a dirty, ice-encrusted pool of water, filled by melting snow. From my roadside resting place, I saw my face for the first time in 35 days. I saw a harried, starved, unshaven and unbathed skeleton, that once walked with pride and dignity as my companions. I now walked with animals as my companions.'

When men were close to the edge they needed all the help they could find – firstly from their comrades, and then from their leaders. The RAF NCOs who had left Stalag Luft VI were inspired by Warrant Officer James 'Dixie' Deans. In the latter part of their ordeal he rode up and down the long columns of men on an old bicycle, helping and encouraging them and persuading the Germans to look after the sick and wounded. While in Stalag 357 at Oerbke he arranged for a consignment of Red Cross parcels to be sent from the supply dump in Lübeck to the now starving POWs. And on the final march in the last days of the war Deans again secured more life-saving Red Cross parcels, before finally convincing the German commandant to disobey his orders and give up the hopeless quest of taking the prisoners to an imaginary 'northern redoubt'.

The *Prominente* – considered by the Nazis to have some possible use in the future – faced an anxious time, especially when the Germans began to move them from their regular camps to unknown destinations. Those at Colditz were escorted from the castle by the SS in April 1945, but after taking a roundabout route through southern Germany they were liberated by the Americans without harm. Pilot Officer Jimmy James – held in Sachsenhausen concentration camp – was one of the many *Prominente* under direct SS control. Their prospects seemed bleak, especially as Himmler had issued an order that such individuals were to be executed rather than fall into Allied hands.

On 3 April James and the other Sachsenhausen *Prominente* were hurriedly assembled and driven south, past the ruins of Berlin, to begin a macabre Cook's tour of Germany's remaining concentration camps. They were taken to Flossenburg and then Dachau. After a short halt they travelled to a punishment camp outside Innsbruck, having picked up more *Prominente* on the way. These included members of the German aristocracy and officers implicated in the July bomb plot (along with forty family hostages), French and German clergy (including Pastor Martin Niemöller), and senior officers and politicians from all over Europe who Œhad fallen foul of the Nazis. Among the latter were the former French premier Léon Blum and the Austrian chancellor Kurt von Schuschnigg. The 150 or so *Prominente* were guarded by 50 SS troopers, who as they prepared to leave Innsbruck on the evening of 27 April were reinforced by another SS squad under the command of a particularly vicious killer called Bader.

With virtually nowhere else to go, the SS led the seven buses containing the hostages slowly up the hairpin bends of the Alps to the Brenner Pass and into Italy, where, short of petrol, the party stopped at a village called Niederdorf. By now the SS leaders, having lost contact with their headquarters, were increasingly unsure of their next step: should they kill the prisoners now or await further orders? But, unknown to the SS, an Italian *Prominent* had made contact with a local partisan group. They surrounded the village, and a plan was hatched to overpower the guards. But as this would have undoubtedly caused heavy casualties it was decided to postpone this idea in favour of a hopefully more peaceful solution proposed by Colonel von Bonin, a German *Prominent* officer. He phoned through to the German Army headquarters in Italy, and managed to get a military unit sent to disarm the guards.

On 28 April a German Army patrol of just fifteen men entered Niederdorf and, with help of von Bonin, managed to persuade the much larger SS group to surrender. A furious Bader commandeered a lorry and with a few of his soldiers drove down the pass to join other SS units in Italy. The Italian partisans made sure they did not get far: Bader and his comrades were later found hanging from telegraph poles. With the SS gone, James recalled how the 'whole village relaxed and took on a festive air'. A few days later an advance unit of the US 339th Infantry Regiment arrived, and the British contingent began the journey home. They were driven to Naples and then flown to Britain in a transport version of a Wellington bomber – the aircraft in which James had been shot down nearly five years earlier.

Odette Churchill would also be liberated from the SS in decidedly unusual circumstances. Incarcerated in the Bunker – the prison cells at Ravensbrück concentration camp – she had few illusions that she would be spared in the final frenzy of killing. But, for the camp's commandant, Fritz Sühren, Odette's talismanic assumed surname held the possibility of protection from the retribution that would surely follow Germany's defeat. Disobeying Himmler's order of 16 April 1945 to kill all inmates in the Bunker, Sühren decided to flee the camp, taking with him incriminating documents and Odette. On the morning of 28 April – her thirty-third birthday – Sühren marched into her cell and told her to gather up her things. Odette and a few others were packed into the back of a police wagon and driven away from Ravensbrück. While she had been there she had seen almost nothing of the camp – 'all my experiences were sounds' – but as she prepared to leave she witnessed the terrible sight of cannibalism among the prisoners: 'I saw a girl of about 18 – her head was shaved but she was still fresh-looking – shot down [by a guard], and the women around her attacked her like dogs. They were starving, they were demented, they were crazy.'

Odette was taken to a camp at Neustadt, but this was only a temporary stop. On 3 May she was summoned by a guard and put into a large Mercedes car with Sühren at the wheel. They were escorted by two other cars, occupied by SS soldiers. Her mind numbed by torture, ill-treatment and months in solitary confinement, Odette had little interest in their destination, assuming only the worst. But after two hours Sühren halted the convoy, gathered up the documents, and took them and Odette a short distance from the car. After carefully burning the papers, Sühren invited Odette to join him in a picnic of sandwiches, crystallized cherries and a bottle of red Burgundy. While the SS escorts waited patiently, they finished their surreal lunch, returned to the car, and drove off. It was now that he told Odette that he was taking her to the Americans.

She thought that this might be a typically cruel Nazi trick to raise her hopes, but in the evening the convoy was challenged by a US patrol. Sühren gravely announced that his passenger was a relation of the British prime minister. To his discomfort this cut little ice with the GIs manning the roadblock. More to the point was Odette's rejoinder: 'And this is Fritz Sühren, Commandant of Ravensbrück Concentration Camp. Please make him your prisoner.' While her former captor was led away to face justice (and an eventual death sentence), Odette spent the remainder of the night in the Mercedes, mentally preparing herself to rejoin a world outside the horror of the camps.

After their winter march across northern Germany, Roger Shinn and the officers from Oflag 64 were packed into boxcars at the railhead at Parchim and transported south into Bavaria, reaching Stalag XIIIC at Hammelburg on 10 March. At Hammelburg Shinn witnessed one of the more bizarre episodes in the final stages of the prisoner-of-war experience: an attempt, ordered by General George Patton, to release the American prisoners held in the camp. Despite the objections of his divisional and corps commanders, Patton decided to send an armoured column of 50 vehicles and around 300 troops to Hammelburg, up to 60 miles behind enemy lines. It would seem that Patton had wanted to release his son-in-law, Lieutenant Colonel John Waters, in some type of grand gesture, possibly to expiate guilt over Waters' capture in North Africa.

During the afternoon of 27 March, the Hammelburg POWs heard machine-gun fire and saw German soldiers in retreat. Shinn observed the fighting swirling around the camp: 'A tank started rolling down the hill. Lt. Col. Waters walked out to meet it with the American flag. I, who had always hated parades and the dramatics of patriotism, thrilled when I saw that flag.' The moment of liberation seemed at hand. A vast crowd of cheering prisoners milled around the American vehicles, and Shinn clambered onboard a half-track. Within minutes, however, it was soon clear that there were far too many prisoners for the available transport. Shinn climbed down to look for food and maps, essential provisions for an attempt to reach American lines on foot. Finding nothing, he – and most of the other POWs – trudged back to the camp, just before German forces launched their counter-attack.

The audacity of the American advance had caught the Germans by surprise, but even in their weakened state they were capable of mounting a devastating response. None of the task-force vehicles made it back to American lines, and only a handful of men avoided death or recapture. As if to underline the pointless nature of the mission, Waters was severely wounded in the early stages of the fighting.

The following day Shinn and a group of POWs left Hammelburg and resumed their march southward. Their dejection at the rescue mission's failure did not last long. Conditions on the march were good: there was sufficient food, German discipline was relaxed, and the warm spring weather and scenic Bavarian countryside lifted the men's spirits. Apart from the terrifying ordeal of an Allied bombing attack, the march passed without incident. On 2 May the column halted for the last time: two American jeeps rolled up as the prisoners were eating their evening meal. Shinn described their liberation:

> We gave greetings to the American soldiers. They showered us with K-rations, candy, pencils and paper, cigarette papers, and all the odds and ends that the American army carries. The certainty of freedom overwhelmed us. So smoothly had the operation gone that it seemed almost unreal. There had been none of the tremendous excitement of the tank battle of Hammelburg with its noise and fire and wild elation. But this time we *knew* we were free. That knowledge was a wonderful thing. Behind the barn was a tiny Catholic shrine, a place where one or two could kneel. I walked back to it, entered, knelt, and prayed. Then I went into the barn and slept.

Another prisoner liberated while on the move was Jim Witte. As the US Army closed in on his work camp near Leipzig, he had hoped to sneak away and join his Belgian friends, Louis and Adrienne, but he was gathered up in a column of prisoners from many nationalities and marched away from the front line. They were strafed by Allied fighters and given no food, although they were able to forage for potatoes in the fields adjoining the barns where they were held at night. On the third day – with the Red Army squeezing Nazi-occupied territory into a narrow strip – the marchers turned westward towards Torgau. With the Americans so close, Witte and another British POW gave their demoralized guards the slip during a halt in a village:

> We hurried off and we were stopped by two men in strange uni-forms who got out of what looked to us like a staff car. None of us had ever seen Yanks in combat dress before, but that was what they were. They were both officers, splendidly accoutred with holstered pistols, grenades in lapels and carrying rifles. We told them about the lads we left behind and the Germans in the village. They roared away supremely self-confident and captured 600 Jerries single-handed. Meanwhile we carried on and reached the American armour, an entire division camped on the bank of a tributary of the Elbe. We were free at last, and so overjoyed that we couldn't speak.

Bob Prouse had hoped that he would be liberated in his work camp, but at 2 a.m. on 2 April the POWs were abruptly woken and told they were to prepare to leave camp. Six hours later they walked through the gates of Mühlhausen to join the chaos of thousands of prisoners and German troops and civilians on the move. 'It was a mad beehive of activity,' Prouse recalled, 'and I felt certain that our guards had orders to march us in circles to avoid having us freed by the advancing British, Canadians and Americans on one side and the Russian army on the other.' After several days of desultory marching, the prisoners ended up in Stalag IXC's main camp at Bad Sulza, and waited as battle raged around them. On 11 April the guards entered the British enclosure and ordered the prisoners to move out. With freedom so close, the prisoners refused. The Germans threatened to shoot them. Prouse described the stand-off:

> The prisoners held their ground and glared in defiance. For a moment there was an ominous silence, suddenly broken by the unmistakable sound of approaching tanks. We knew this was our salvation and let out a thunderous cheer. The Jerrys took to their heels, rushing out of

the main gate and disappearing in full flight. At 5:05 p.m. on April 11, the tanks of the American Third Army arrived at the gates of the camp. We rushed out to greet them and they showered us with cigarettes and field rations. One trooper even stripped off his battle jacket and handed it to me, no doubt feeling sorry for my ragged appearance. The officer in charge laid out a map, asking directions and locations of other POW camps. We pointed these out and also gave them the general map location of our still marching comrades. Before they left, we told them the direction that the fleeing guards had taken and asked them to give them hell.

Liberation by the Americans and British was a joyous experience, but in those camps overrun by the Red Army there was justifiable unease. The friendly but unpredictable and often drink-fuelled behaviour of the Soviet soldier was a cause of concern, as was the Red Army's slowness in getting the Anglo-Americans back to the west. For the 8,000 or so American and British airmen at Stalag Luft I at Barth, freedom seemed a long time in coming. Towards the end of April they could hear the rumble of Soviet artillery growing in intensity. The German commandant had ordered Colonel Hubert Zemke to prepare his men to evacuate the camp, but the SAO refused to move. The balance of power had swung from captors to captives, and the commandant shrugged his shoulders and on the night of 29 April the Germans quietly moved out, allowing the prisoners to take over the camp. But, to the chagrin of many old POWs, the Anglo-American camp authorities insisted that the men stay in the camp.

A couple of days later the Russians arrived; the barbed-wire fences were ripped down, and the former prisoners spilled out into the surrounding countryside. Although Zemke and his staff attempted to maintain basic military discipline, some men had had enough, and gathering up as much food as they could carry they set off westward towards the advancing British. The remainder stayed in and around the camp as talks were started with the Russians to allow American aircraft to land at a nearby airfield and ferry the officers home. As a German-speaker with some knowledge of Russian, Jack Vietor was not confined to camp but acted as an interpreter for the American negotiators. Much of his time was spent attending drunken banquets hosted by the Russians. He described the conclusion to one typical

Even the plight of the guards elicited sympathy from former prisoners. Soldiers from the liberating armies were surprised to find guards being protected by their former captives. Bob Prouse's response to his guards' new situation was perhaps not atypical:

> We began rounding up Jerry prisoners in the immediate vicinity. For years I had dreamed of this moment of revenge but when I came face to face with the first Jerry to surrender to me, all I could feel was compassion as I saw the fear in his eyes and noticed his trembling lips and hands. I escorted him to our camp, where we had set up a temporary prisoner compound, and even handed him a cigarette and let him show me snaps of his wife and children.

But these sympathies coexisted alongside eruptions of ridicule and violence directed towards the ex-POWs' former tormentors. Private Adrian Vincent – who had been behind the wire since 1940 – provided this thoughtful comment on the turning of the tables as he observed his comrades mocking their former guards: 'As I watched them it suddenly struck me that the expressions on their faces were very much the same as those I had seen on the faces of some of the Germans who had taunted us as we walked through the French villages on our way into Germany.'

Those guards who were known to have mistreated prisoners could expect rough justice. Some might receive a beating or be humiliated; others were killed. John White, a POW who had endured the march from Stalag VIIIB at Teschen, recalled the fate of one guard, nicknamed the Farmer's Boy because of his red cheeks. This guard had shot dead a British soldier who, sitting by the roadside, had not moved after the command to march had been given. When freed by an American patrol, the POWs were asked if anyone had ill-treated them. 'We told them that one of our companions had been murdered,' remembered White, 'and that was the end for the Farmer's Boy, who was taken away and shot.'

In another instance the POWs themselves administered the punishment. Lance Bombardier Edward Stirling had escaped in Czechoslovakia during the march from BAB 21. On his recapture he was beaten by his guards and briefly sent to Theresienstadt concentration camp, where he endured terrible conditions. He was then marched with prisoners of various nationalities towards an unknown camp, and was again poorly treated. When the column was overrun by the US Army, Stirling was determined to exact revenge: 'The Hauptmann [Captain] and 11 swines of postens [sentries] were picked out by us and the Yank prisoners and we riddled them with bullets and left them where they dropped. We had told them before when they starved us and hit the boys that we'd get them and we did in the end.'

While a few liberated prisoners enjoyed their new-found freedom by letting off steam in Germany – acquiring supplies of petrol from the Allies and joyriding in cars was a popular pastime – most were keen only to get home. But at the same time there was a lurking anxiety about what 'home' would be like, especially for those who had been captured early in the war. Would wives still love them – or even be there? And would children recognize or remember them? Some men had undoubtedly become institutionalized, and found the prospect of leaving their old camps – with their fixed routines and certainties – a frightening one. But, whatever their worries, the former British and American POWs were fed into the system that would take them home and deliver them back into civil society.

16

Homecoming

A S EARLY AS July 1942, the British War Office began to make plans for the evacuation of prisoners from Germany and Italy at the war's end. This demonstrated considerable foresight and, with the parlous state of British military fortunes at the time, even greater optimism. Following the invasion of Europe in 1944 the whole concept of POW repatriation took on a more realistic aspect, and British plans were combined with those of the United States. An Ex-Prisoner-of War section (PWX) was formed to enable specialist units to follow the attacking forces and organize the orderly evacuation of former prisoners from their camps and their safe and swift repatriation.

The vast majority of Allied POWs were liberated in the space of just a few weeks in April 1945, in often highly chaotic conditions. PWX wisely accepted that a speedy evacuation must be a priority over an orderly one. Once a camp was liberated, PWX officers organized fleets of trucks to ferry the former POWs back to a series of transit centres, of which the largest were in Brussels (British) and Reims (American). There, men were assembled for air transport: for the British, to reception centres in south-east England; for Americans, to Camp Lucky Strike outside the port of Le Havre, in preparation for embarkation to the United States.

The former prisoners were certainly in no mood to wait patiently in their old camps. Many had already decided to make their own way home, hitching lifts with westward-bound vehicles or commandeering German cars and driving towards the Channel. The work of PWX was made even more difficult by other groups of former prisoners deciding to stay on in Germany and enjoy their new freedom in as wild a way as possible. Despite these problems the transfer of ex-prisoners from Germany was remarkably swift and efficient. Fleets of bomber and transport aircraft were requisitioned for the use of former POWs, so that by the end of May the vast majority were either home or, in the case of the Americans, well on their way home. Although former prisoners were expected to return to the world of military discipline, it was realized that this transition needed to be gradual; minor misdemeanours were overlooked, and the staff at the transit centres treated their charges with considerable tact and kindness.

For most British soldiers and sailors the flight home was their first time in an aircraft, and the sense of occasion was heightened as they saw below them the white cliffs of southern England – a deeply emotional moment. The reception centres scattered throughout south-east England provided a warm welcome. After being deloused and given new uniforms – complete with appropriate rank insignia and medal ribbons sewn on to the tunic – the men were fed, often with a traditional cream tea to underline that they were back home. They were also prepared for the world outside: relatives were contacted, and ration cards and travel warrants issued, as well as a limited amount of pay. Many encountered women for the first time in years; for some the sound of female voices speaking English was spellbinding, although Sergeant Ray Ryan was less sure. 'The women's voices', he wrote, 'sound queer and high pitched.'

Although grateful at what had been done for them, the returning POWs were also bewildered at the sudden change from prisoner to free man. A general feeling of anxiety was commonplace. Bertie Harwood – who had arrived at Liverpool in the repatriation of January 1945 – felt this acutely. Having enjoyed the dockside welcome of a brass band and flag-waving crowds, he was ambivalent about going ashore: 'I was definitely not as balanced as I had imagined. I longed to disembark and get going, but at the same time I was petrified at the thought of meeting people again. The idea of entering a room full of strangers was quite terrifying.'

As Harwood travelled south to a military hospital at Aldershot he experienced the strangeness of Britain in 1945: 'It was not the same England I had left in early 1940. There was a tense, workmanlike atmosphere. Everyone was going about his or her business with utterly weary faces but with grim purpose.' Another common emotion experienced by former prisoners was a dislike of bureaucracy in any form. Harwood was aggrieved when told he was to stay in the hospital for a couple of days, although he managed to persuade one of the doctors to allow an early release. He caught a train to London to meet a girlfriend, and from there he returned to his home in the village of Wye, near Ashford in Kent.

Jim Witte was one of the few ex-prisoners who was in less of a rush to get home. While still in the American-occupied part of Germany he had engineered a brief affair with a German single mother whose husband had been killed on the Eastern Front. Although somewhat reluctant at first, she had succumbed to the food and chocolates supplied by Witte and a rather vague promise of marriage. Witte had got used to the free and easy atmosphere under the Americans, and when he was eventually transferred to Brussels he was disconcerted to find it 'staffed by the British with all the old attendant bullshit'. He moderated his view somewhat when, after getting blind drunk one night, he was helped back to his temporary barracks by the military police with a solicitousness that was as surprising as it was welcome.

Witte was impressed by the good reception he received on arriving in Britain and the efficiency of the whole processing system. He was given a rail warrant home, and arrived at Liverpool Street station for the short journey to Rayleigh in Essex. Once again the strangeness of everyday life in England hit home as he caught an afternoon commuter train: 'No one said anything to me, merely contenting themselves with the midday editions. It was all very unreal and I began to get a feeling of anti-climax. Although I had written home to say that I had arrived safely in England, there was no one at the station to meet me. So much for the "hero's return", I thought. I found myself queuing for a bus amongst a lot of women chattering about the availability of bananas.'

Commonwealth POWs liberated in Germany were evacuated to Britain before returning to their home countries. Bob McDowall was delighted to be arriving in England in springtime, although he too found his new life unnerving. He wrote to his wife, Pat, to say that he needed to 'get readjusted to life in normal conditions. We are all in a rather strange state, and need some time to be able to move easily among people.' But a short while later he was able to write, 'It is beginning to dawn upon me at last that I am free again and I am slowly returning to a normal human being. The interval of prison life is beginning to feel like a strange interlude and I am, as it were, making contact on the other side of it once more.'

While waiting for shipping for their homeward journey, Commonwealth former prisoners were given the freedom to travel around Britain, and with free rail passes many made the most of the opportunity to visit relatives and get to know the 'home country' better. Bob Prouse decided to delay his rail excursions 'until I could regain some of the fifty pounds I had lost in weight. I wasn't too proud of my appearance and wanted to lose that gaunt look and fill out some of the hollow spots before visiting friends and sightseeing.' The visiting Commonwealth ex-POWs were well received: the New Zealand official historian recorded that 'the British people were lavish in extending the freedom of their homes to our men.'

As well as travelling to see relatives in Birmingham and to Glasgow to say goodbye to his old escape pal Tommy Glassey, Prouse made a special trip to London on 8 May:

> It was VE Day and I'll never forget the wild celebration in Piccadilly Circus. The pandemonium was a fitting end to almost six years of war. I personally had a feeling of thankfulness that I had come through OK and, apart from some injuries, was relatively healthy. The main feeling I had was of being free, free to come and go as I wanted. The other important part of freedom was being able to buy food and drink; the glorious feeling of waking up to a meal of bacon and eggs, toast and hot coffee; the absolute thrill of a dish of vanilla ice cream; the wonder of white bread.

On 30 May Prouse set sail from Liverpool; he landed in Halifax, Nova Scotia, on 7 June. His military life was drawing to a close: 'On July 14, approximately five years and three months after my enlistment, I received my discharge and commenced the task of putting my life back together. It was a relief to be home again and great to be alive.'

Most American former POWs ended up at Camp Lucky Strike. Jack Vietor had arrived there at night after escorting a group of wounded men from Reims. He described the scene:

> The following morning I had the opportunity to look over the milling maelstrom of Camp Lucky Strike. The camp was an embarkation point

and processing center. Returning prisoners and combat troops swamped the already overtaxed facilities. There were now 25,000 men at the camp and more were arriving every hour. Shipping space Stateside was scarce. Desperate efforts were made to repatriate men on a first come first served basis but it was an almost impossible job. Efforts were made to keep the restless men satisfied with movies, P-X, volley ball, etc., but they made poor makeshifts for home. Many men waited at Lucky Strike for as long as six weeks before getting on a boat.

Most men did not in fact have to wait that long; Victor and Roger Shinn were away in a matter of days. Shinn discovered that his time at Lucky Strike gave him a chance to recuperate and to enjoy good and plentiful food:

> We got new clothes, learned again the feel of money, read old issues of *Time* and *Life* and *Newsweek*, rested, and ate. Eating was a strange experience. Each new old American food tasted inexpressibly good. Gradually we controlled our appetites. Gradually we achieved the psychology of free men – of men who can eat a meal and remember that there will be more meals tomorrow and the next day, who can walk into a place without their eyes roving about for something to eat or burn in a fire.

The transatlantic crossing was uneventful for the two returning POWs. Both Shinn and Vietor sailed into Boston harbour. 'There was a brass band,' wrote Vietor, Red Cross girls with coffee to meet us and a few casual onlookers. We weren't worried about what kind of reception we had. We were home at last.'

In the US armed forces ex-POWs received ninety days' leave and, in most cases, were discharged without further military obligation. In Britain they were allowed a more parsimonious six weeks away and were then – if fit and young – returned to military duties. There had been some expectation that they might be deployed in the Far East, but the Japanese surrender on 2 September 1945 rendered this irrelevant. Most former POWs did not make enthusiastic soldiers: they believed that they had served their country well enough, and that it was time for others to do their duty. With the war over they waited for demobilization – a desultory countdown to a return to civilian life.

For regular officers and NCOs, captivity was generally considered to be disastrous for their careers. For ambitious junior officers captured in the early years of the war there was no denying that they had lost out in the best years for promotion. Long-term prisoners released in 1945 felt very aware that the world and the military profession had moved on since their capture in 1940–41. And yet some former prisoners seemed to be able to advance up the ladder. Jimmy James converted his temporary commission into a permanent one, and reached the respectable rank of squadron leader. Corran Purdon – a 20-year-old commando officer captured on the Saint-Nazaire raid – survived captivity and eventually retired from the Army as a major general. Delmar T. Spivey also rose to the rank of major general, and might have advanced further had he not been forced to retire from the Air Force for health reasons.

Once out of uniform, men had to resume their lives and pick up their pre-war careers or, failing that, at least find work. They also had to reintegrate themselves with their families. This proved more difficult than imagined. Feelings of disappointment, anxiety and restlessness and a sense of isolation were experienced by many returning prisoners, and these were not emotions that helped a man find his way in the working world or at home. RAF Sergeant W. P. Wood wrote perceptively of the 'condition':

> I suppose the most common sensation of a returning prisoner was one of anti-climax. It had been a long time coming and the imagination had created a sort of mirage. Life in England fell far short of this illusion of course . . . For some time, life in a house caused me a discomfort amounting almost to claustrophobia. I recall too a triviality and lack of purpose in civilian conversation which produced at times a need to escape as strong as any experienced in Germany. Yet where could you go? Escape to the past was clearly impossible. Strangely enough, one felt most comfortable in the company of other 'kriegies', a company so long and often irksome. Only their reaction and behaviour seemed completely logical, predictable and understandable.

While it would seem that there was little official provision to offer psychological help in the United States, in Britain attempts were made to support those who found it hard to adjust. In fact, on the basis of pre-war psychiatric studies of Great War prisoners and studies of those recently repatriated, there was a tendency by the medical authorities to be overly anxious about the mental condition of all returning prisoners. Not everyone suffered psychological problems as a result of imprisonment, and for most of those that did the symptoms faded in time. Some men resented the patronizing tones adopted by the medical authorities, especially when they discovered that wives and families had been given advice on how to 'deal' with them.

In order to help men make the passage into civilian life as smoothly as possible, the British government set up twenty Civil Resettlement Units (CRUs) across the country. Nearly 20,000 men attended voluntarily, and, while there was suspicion of the psychological testing conducted at the centres, the teaching of vocational and social skills was welcomed. But CRUs were intended only as a temporary measure, and after their closure in 1946 the former POWs were on their own.

In the succeeding decades it slowly became obvious that a substantial number of former POWs were in fact suffering from mental-health problems. Typically, their symptoms did not manifest themselves in a manner to alert public attention, but the sleep disorders and nightmares, relationship difficulties and intrusive recollections from captivity were acutely painful for those involved. Many POWs simply lived with these problems as best they could, suffering in silence. A psychiatric study conducted in the early 1990s of former American prisoners living in the Midwest suggested that a high incidence of post-traumatic stress disorder (PTSD) was common among former POWs. Of the 191 men who had undergone captivity in Europe, 19 per cent were diagnosed as currently suffering from PTSD and 44 per cent from lifetime PTSD. By contrast, soldiers who had experienced heavy combat had a significantly lower lifetime PTSD level of 30 per cent.

As well as psychological problems, veteran POWs reaching old age began to suffer from a multitude of general medical problems – such as arthritis and respiratory, skin and stomach disorders – that they believed stemmed from their POW experiences. A major difficulty lay in convincing the authorities that this was indeed the case, especially as this would be the first stage in securing an appropriate disability pension. It took Jim Witte many years to persuade his medical board that the tinnitus he suffered was a consequence of the intense noise he endured in the locomotive repair works in Chemnitz and Leipzig.

Leslie Caplan, the doctor who had valiantly accompanied American POWs on the long march from Stalag Luft IV, had no doubts regarding the special needs of ex-POWs. As a professor of psychiatry at the University of Minnesota he wrote, 'Every POW should automatically be service-connected for these ailments or any ailments related to them. All he should have to do is prove he was a prisoner of war.' This has not, however, been a majority view within those governmental departments responsible for POW welfare, and for a number of former prisoners the battle for their rights continues.

The consequences of imprisonment were not always psychological or physical impairment. Former prisoners could look back at their captivity and discern positive aspects amid the predominantly negative. How they viewed their time in German and Italian POW camps depended on their experiences and their temperament. But all were agreed that the war and imprisonment were events of central importance that continued to have a profound influence on their post-war lives. The distinguished broadcaster and writer Robert Kee spent his years of captivity in Stalag Luft III and Oflag XXIB. Despite a varied and successful career and a life that, in his own words, could be 'regarded as reasonably full', he conceded that 'everything that has happened to me since seems somehow secondary to what happened then.'

A few years after the war had ended, Roger Shinn reflected on what being an infantry officer and POW had meant to him:

> My adventure in war was over. It had been harsh in fact, but was rich in memory. I had asked for it and had taken it. I recalled E. M. Forster's *Passage to India*, which I had read in the cold, dim-lit barracks of Oflag 64. Of his heroine, he said, she had left Britain to question India and life. Before she returned, 'she was no longer examining life, but being examined by it.' If I had gone into the army with perhaps too conscious a desire to question war, I could now say war had questioned me.

Many former POWs believed their captivity had made them more tolerant of others, and had taught them how to endure privation. 'It made me realize what hardships really were,' recalled RAF airman Wilfred Davies, 'and being able to get along on a small diet, and [it] generally gave me an insight to human nature.' And while Jim Witte still had nightmares of his time in Germany, he felt that his prison experience did him no lasting psychological damage. 'Captivity', he said, 'made me appreciate the value of everyday things, the value of water and of three square meals a day. And, above all, of being free to come and go.' Rifleman Jim Roberts wrote how imprisonment in work camps in Poland had 'moulded me into a better, more mature person [with a] willingness to help others whenever possible'. American infantryman Clifford Fox had always tried to make the best of things. His optimistic and outgoing view on life had stood him in good stead in captivity, and continued to do so:

> I think this experience changed me as a human being. Since then it's been easier for me to accept setbacks because I've seen so many people who could not handle adversity. It also changed my attitude about people. We Americans tend to think we're the greatest, but there are great people all over the world. So being a POW made me more appreciative of what I do have. The old saying 'Life is what you make of it' is pretty much true. You can be sad and depressed, or you can decide to just go on when things don't go the way you want them to. I wouldn't take anything for my POW experiences, but I sure would not want to go through them again.

Something all POWs were agreed upon was the value of comradeship. For many this was the cord that bound them together in their darkest hour. To have a few close friends who would look out for each other could, in the worst circumstances, be the difference between life and death.

There was also an inspirational aspect to friendship that left its mark. The dental officer Julius Green had wide knowledge of conditions in Stalags and Oflags throughout Germany, and his simple summary of his time as a prisoner was testament to the enduring power of comradeship. 'Any regrets?' he wrote. 'I am sorry I was taken prisoner, but I am glad I found myself among the men with whom I spent five years behind barbed wire. The patience, coolness, courage, perseverance and integrity of my fellow prisoners has been a constant example which I have striven to follow. I have not always succeeded but at least I try.'

Postscript

A FEW DAYS before leaving for France in April 1940 Bertie Harwood had met a girl called Betty, the daughter of a local doctor in his Kent village of Wye. They corresponded regularly during his imprisonment. 'Curiously enough' he wrote after the war, 'we had got to know each other quite well. At least we thought we had and that was why we got married within three weeks of my arrival in England.' Unfortunately the marriage was not a success, and to make matters worse Harwood's health began to decline. By the late 1950s he was a very sick man, living with his mother and suffering from an incurable neurological disease, from which he died in 1963.

After a difficult start in the post-war world, Jim Witte was to prosper. He received £287 in back pay – 'a tidy old sum for 1945 with beer 4d or 5d a pint and fags ten for sixpence' – and waited for his 'demob', which came in January 1946. He returned to his old firm, Unilever, but, although they were happy to take him on, his copy-writing post in the advertising department had gone. He spent the next few years in the doldrums, bored in a series of poorly paid clerical jobs. His home life also took a downturn. Witte's Dutch-born father had died while his son was in PG 78, and his mother subsequently remarried. Witte did not take to his stepfather, and for a while he seriously thought about rejoining the Army. But, in his own words, 'all was not gloom.' In 1947 he met Elizabeth, and two years later, on 4 September 1949, they were married. Two children quickly followed, along with a mortgage on a two-bedroom bungalow in Rayleigh. In the mid-1950s Witte's career took a turn for the better: he was offered a post as assistant editor on the Unilever staff magazine, and subsequently became editor of the company newspaper. He left Unilever in 1978, and in his retirement wrote a vivid account of his time as a soldier and prisoner of war in Italy and Germany.

The Very Revd Bob McDowall returned to New Zealand in August 1945, and after three months' leave resumed his former life as minister at St Luke's church in Auckland. Always a hard worker, he was active in parish affairs and in the wider role of the Presbyterian Church in New Zealand and in the missions to the Pacific islands and Hong Kong. His daughter Mary believed that his involvement in the interdenominational Church Union was a direct consequence of his experiences at Stalag IVB; while at St Luke's he developed close relationships with the local Anglican and Catholic churches. His progressive outlook extended to pioneering the involvement of women in the Church, and after his induction as moderator of the Presbyterian Church of New Zealand in 1957, three women elders attended the General Assembly for the first time as voting members. Always a very private man, he talked little of his POW experiences except during the sermons and addresses of his moderatorial year. But by then he was suffering from Parkinson's disease, and after a formal diagnosis in 1958 he retired from St Luke's the following year. He died at the age of 64 on 21 August 1963.

Doug LeFevre returned home to Australia in the autumn of 1944 to be reunited with his wife, Eileen, after an absence of over four years. Together they would bring up four daughters. LeFevre briefly worked in a flour mill before setting up a poultry business with Eileen in 1947. They moved on to buy a haulage firm supplying the construction business. The work was hard and the overheads high, and after several years they decided to move into real estate, selling houses to the growing population of Western Australia. He considered his war service and time as a POW to be the making of him. He recalled how he 'went away a very insecure young man. I had a speech impediment, I was against everybody, I was against authority. I went away, as the saying is, a snotty nosed kid and I came back a man.'

Like Doug LeFevre, Bob Prouse had only just married when he was called away to war. His wife, Vera, had to wait five years for his return, but the foundations had been laid for a successful and fruitful marriage. Setting up home in Toronto, Prouse began a new career as a sales manager in a department store. He was a natural salesman, and went on to become the general sales manager at a glassware company. On retiring he developed his many interests and hobbies: skiing, swimming, fishing, metal-detecting, playing cards, reading, and all things military. He died at the age of 88 on 4 January 1999, the much-loved patriarch of a large family that included four children, nine grandchildren and five great-grandchildren.

Roger Shinn went back to the United States not only to be reunited with his wife, Katherine, but to see his daughter Carol, who had been born while he was in captivity – the first of two daughters. Although promoted to major – he was also awarded the Silver Star – Shinn entered the Church, being ordained into the Evangelical and Reformed Church in 1946. A distinguished career as a theologian followed. Among many academic posts he held was that of Reinhold Niebuhr Professor of Social Ethics. The author of at least sixteen books and a contributor to a further forty, he was also actively engaged in the civil-rights movement. Over the years he received numerous awards for his work as a theologian, although also noteworthy was his induction into the Infantry School Hall of Fame at Fort Benning, Georgia.

After her terrible ordeals Odette's homecoming was one of slow and painful recuperation: for her first year she had to walk on her heels and was unable to wear shoes until a series of operations to her feet allowed her more normal mobility. In spite of what she had endured, she harboured no bitterness towards her former captors. In a post-war interview she said: 'You've got to dismiss all that [bitterness] and say I'm healthy, they're sick. I don't have to be bitter because bitterness creates such terrible misery that you live with it inside yourself like some kind of cancer.' Odette was awarded the MBE on her return in 1945, the George Cross the following year, and the Légion d'honneur in 1950. After the death of her first husband she married Peter Churchill, although the marriage was not to last and after its dissolution in 1956 she married Geoffrey Hallowes, who had also served in SOE. Numerous articles and a book and film of her exploits brought her fame – most of it unwanted, however. In her entry in *Who's Who* she called herself a 'housewife', but she was actively involved in many charitable organizations, which she continued to support until her death at the age of 82 on 13 March 1995.

In recognition of his escape activities Jimmy James was awarded the Military Cross and a Mention in Dispatches. His time spent learning Russian in Stalag Luft III was put to good use when – after leaving the RAF in 1958 and spending time in Canada – he was appointed general secretary of the Foreign Office-sponsored Great Britain–USSR Association. This led to a move to the diplomatic service in 1964, and he held consular posts in eastern and western Europe, Africa and finally London. James was married in 1946, and after his retirement in 1975 he lived with his wife Madge in Shropshire, where he continued his active involvement in POW associations, as well as acting as the British representative on the International Sachsenhausen Committee.

A career officer, Colonel Delmar T. Spivey enrolled in the newly formed US War College and after graduating served in a number of command posts as a brigadier general. Following the outbreak of war in Korea in 1950 he was promoted to major general and appointed vice-commander of the Fifth Air Force, based in Japan. Returning to the United States he became commandant of the Air War College at Maxwell Air Force Base, but in 1956 he was forced to retire from the service as a result of problems with his knee, damaged during his crash landing at Gelsenkirchen in 1943. As a prominent US Army Air Force officer Spivey received many awards, including the Distinguished Service Medal and the Legion of Merit, and he was appointed an Honorary Commander of the British Empire. He died on 18 January 1982, aged 76, and was survived by his wife Virginia and a son, two grandsons and one great-grandson.

John A. Vietor returned to the United States to live in San Diego, California. With his considerable private income, Hollywood good looks (he was sometimes mistaken for Douglas Fairbanks Jr) and an enthusiasm for the good things in life, he became a well-known West Coast socialite. His son Marc recalled that he 'was very aware of how lucky he had been to survive, and pursued his pleasures and pastimes unrepentantly. He was an epicurean and loved nothing more than a long night of eating, drinking and lively conversation.' A pre-war friend of Jack Kennedy, he was an active Democrat supporter and worked on the presidential campaign that led to the election of Kennedy in 1960. At various times Vietor was a newspaper columnist, television executive, restaurant owner and philanthropist, and after his second marriage he moved to San Francisco and there founded and published *San Francisco* magazine. He enjoyed swimming, golf, tennis and deep-sea fishing, and was a world-class backgammon player. While on a sea cruise off China in 1982 he died unexpectedly of a heart attack, aged 68.

After his return to Britain in 1943, Billie Stephens served out the war in shore appointments before leaving the Navy in 1945. He went back to live in Northern Ireland, and took over the family shipping firm in Belfast. He subsequently assumed a number of positions in the province, including that of chairman of the Northern Bank and the Northern Ireland Tourist Authority. While in Switzerland, after his escape from Colditz, he met his future wife 'Chou-Chou', who was then running a safe house where he was lodging. They were married after the war, and when Stephens retired they went to live in the South of France. As the last surviving escaper from Colditz he was much in demand by the media, and was present at a number of post-war escape reunions. He died at his home in France on 3 August 1997, aged 85.

Notes

Only those works not listed in the bibliography have been provided with full publishing details.

ABBREVIATIONS

AWM = Australian War Memorial
IWM = Imperial War Museum (Dept of Documents)
IWMSA = Imperial War Museum Sound Archive
PRO = Public Records Office (now National Archives), Kew
SWWEC = Second World War Experience Centre, Leeds

Preface

p. ix A precise number. Numerical data for British, Commonwealth and Empire POWs are contradictory and unclear, especially as to whether figures given for British POWs include Commonwealth and Empire forces, and whether those POWs who were repatriated or who escaped after the Italian armistice are included in overall totals. *Fighting with Figures: A Statistical Digest of the Second World War*, ed. Peter Howlett (London: Central Statistical Office, 1995), registers a POW total of 135,009 men (p. 43, table 3.8) for United Kingdom forces (if Commonwealth and Empire figures are added, the total is approximately 190,000). *The History of the Second World War, United Kingdom Medical Services: Casualties and Medical Statistics*, ed. W. Franklin Mellor (London: HMSO, 1972), has a higher figure of 142,319 (p. 837, table 9) for UK POW losses. Detailed figures are provided in the three-volume list of POWs in Germany in early 1945: British Army, 107,000-plus (*Prisoners of War: British Army 1939–1945*); combined Air Force and Navy, 21,000-plus (*Prisoners of*

War: Naval and Air Forces of Great Britain and the Empire 1939–1945); Commonwealth and Empire armies, 41,000 (*Prisoners of War: Armies and Other Land Forces of the British Empire 1939–1945*). Unfortunately the lists are not complete, and the combined total of just under 170,000 British, Commonwealth and Empire POWs must consequently be too low. On 20 Mar. 1945 a Foreign Office note on POW locations and strengths stated that the 'estimated number of Imperial Prisoners of War in German hands was about 180,000' (PRO FO 1038/34). A figure of 180,000 POWs in Germany was also quoted by the Secretary of State for War in the House of Commons (15 May 1945). Taking this figure and adding to it the numbers of POWs who were repatriated and who escaped captivity in Italy, a very rough total of around 200,000 British, Commonwealth and Empire POWs seems reasonable. See also John Nichol and Tony Rennell, *The Last Escape*, pp. 416–20.

p. ix Figures for the United States. On 1 Nov. 1945 the US War Department issued a figure of 92,965 American POWs in German captivity. In the 1980s the Veterans Administration raised the numbers to 95,532. See Lewis H. Carlson, *We Were Each Other's Prisoners*, p. xvii.

1: Battlefield Surrender

p. 1 Lieutenant H. C. F. 'Bertie' Harwood. H.C. F. Harwood, typescript memoir, IWM Papers. See also PRO WO 1167/718 and WO 217/28; C. R. B. Knight, *Historical Record of the Buffs 1919–48* (London: Medici Society, 1951); L. F. Ellis, *The War in Flanders 1939–40* (London: HMSO, 1953). For a detailed analysis of British surrenders in 1940, see Mark Connelly and Walter Miller, 'The BEF and the Issue of Surrender on the Western Front in 1940'.

p. 1 'No troops'. Knight, p. 72.

p. 2 'Those few weeks'. Harwood, p. 10.

p. 2 'a few light tanks'. Ibid., p. 44.

p. 3 'A voice shouted'. Ibid., p. 67.

p. 4 'He led his men'. *History of the Irish Guards in the Second World War*, noted in John Keegan, *The Face of Battle* (London: Jonathan Cape, 1976), p. 50.

p. 4 'No soldier'. Charles Carrington, in Richard Holmes, *Firing Line* (London: Jonathan Cape, 1985), p. 381.

p. 4 'the defending force'. Ernst Junger, in Holmes, p. 381.

p. 5 Such killings were. See Theodore Draper, 'The Psychology of Surrender'.

p. 5 'because I couldn't'. In Andrew Wilson, 'The War in Vietnam', *The Observer*, 30 Nov. 1969, in Joanna Bourke, *An Intimate History of Killing* (London: Granta Books, 1999), p. 184.

p. 5 The ambivalent attitude. For a full discussion of incentives and disincentives to surrender and accept surrenders see Niall Ferguson, 'Prisoner Taking and Prisoner Killing in the Age of Total War', and Gerald H. Davis, 'Prisoners of War in Twentieth-Century War Economies'.

p. 5 Prisoners could be used. For the importance of reciprocity in the good treatment of prisoners see see S. P. Mackenzie, 'The Treatment of Prisoners of War in World War II', and Bob Moore, 'Unruly Allies'.

p. 6 On 27 May 1940. See Cyril Jolly, *The Vengeance of Private Pooley* (London: William Heinemann, 1958), and Gerald Reitlinger, *The SS Alibi of a Nation 1922–1945* (London: William Heinemann, 1956), pp. 148–9.

p. 6 The massacre at Wormhoudt. See Leslie Aitken, *Massacre on the Road to Dunkirk* (Wellingborough: Patrick Stephens, 1977), and Alfred Tombs, 'Wormhoudt Survivor', IWMSA.

p. 7 During the Normandy campaign. Figures from Syzmon Datner, *Crimes Against POWs*, pp. 43–4.

p. 7 'that it was understood'. In George H. Stein, *The Waffen SS Hitler's Elite Guard at War 1939–1945* (Ithaca and London: Cornell University Press, 1966), p. 277 . See also Datner, pp. 43–4.

p. 7 One particularly infamous SS atrocity. See Charles B. MacDonald, *The Battle of the Bulge* (London: BCA/Weidenfeld & Nicolson, 1984), pp. 216–33, and Stein, pp. 278–80.

p. 7 the worst such war crime. Dear and Foot, *The Oxford Companion to the Second World War*, p. 132.

p. 8 One such incident. See W. Wynne Mason, *Prisoners of War*, pp. 192–3.

p. 8 One of the first. J. H. Witte, IWM Papers. See also *A History of the Essex Yeomanry* (Colchester: Behman, 1950).

p. 9 'Even an orderly'. *Essex Yeomanry*, p. 31.

p. 10 'Next morning'. Witte, pp. 104–5.

p. 10 'When I signed'. Ibid., p. 3.

p. 11 'I was launched'. Ibid., p. 107.

p. 11 A Presbyterian minister. R. G. McDowall, IWM Papers; also held in the Auckland War Memorial Museum Archives, Files 874 (2). See also M. A. Tagg, *The Prisoner Padre*; J. B. McKinney, *Medical Units of 2 NZEF in Middle East and Italy* (Wellington, NZ: War History Branch, Dept of Internal Affairs, 1952), and W. E. Murphy, *The Relief of Tobruk* (Wellington, NZ: War History Branch, Dept of Internal Affairs, 1961).

p. 11 'drink, moral turpitude'. Tagg, p. 4. (Dr Tagg is McDowall's daughter.)

p. 12 'I was always afraid'. McDowall, p. 8.

p. 12 'Took all food'. Ibid., p. 9.

p. 13 'Green and the others'. Ibid., p. 13. Tagg suggests that McDowall had a poor opinion of those padres who remained with the MDS (Tagg, p. 49).

p. 14 Lance Corporal Douglas LeFevre. Transcribed audio interview, AWM. See also Philip Masel, *The Second 28th: The Story of a Famous Battalion of the Ninth Australian Division* (Perth: 2/28th and 24th Anti-Tank Company Association, n.d.); Mark Johnston and Peter Stanley, *Alamein: The Australian Story* (Melbourne: Oxford University Press, 2002).

p. 14 'Our officer lost'. LeFevre.

p. 14 'First light'. Ibid.

p. 15 'We may as well have'. Ibid.

p. 15 'Many of the men'. Masel, p. 89.

p. 16 Bob Prouse. A. Robert Prouse, *Ticket to Hell*. See also Ronald Atkin, *Dieppe 1942: The Jubilee Disaster* (London: Macmillan, 1980).

p. 16 'dim view'. Prouse, p. 7.

p. 16 'I was up to my thighs'. Ibid., p. 12.

p. 17 'I felt no fear'. Ibid., p. 17.

p. 17 One Canadian reported. Atkin, pp. 239–40.

p. 18 This hostility was subsequently. For Hitler's Commando Order see Datner, pp. 139–206, and Jonathan F. Vance (ed.), *Encyclopedia of Prisoners of War and Internment*, p. 62.

p. 19 Captain Roger L. Shinn. Roger L. Shinn, *Wars and Rumors of Wars*. See also MacDonald.

p. 19 'was like no other'. Shinn, p. 17.

p. 19 'This fight was exciting'. Ibid., p. 31.

p. 19 'While daylight remained'. Ibid., p. 41.

p. 20 'So we moved'. Ibid., p. 44.

p. 20 But a group that remained. For SOE see M. R. D. Foot, *SOE in France* (London: HMSO, 2004).

p. 21 Among these was Odette Sansom. For Odette Sansom see Odette Hallowes, IWMSA transcript; Jerrard Tickell, *Odette*; and Peter

Churchill, *The Spirit in the Cage*, pp. 9–21. Born Odette Brailly, she became, through marriage, successively Mrs Sansom, Mrs Churchill and Mrs Hallowes. To avoid confusion the author has used her customary name, Odette.

p. 21 'Am I going'. Hallowes, IWMSA, p. 2.

p. 23 Considering prisoners and missing. Figures from John Ellis, *The Sharp End of War: The Fighting Man in World War II* (Newton Abbot: David & Charles, 1980), pp. 159–60.

p. 24 These British disasters. See Connelly and Miller, pp. 438–9.

p. 24 'We talk a lot'. Lord Slim, quoted in A. J. Barker, *Behind Barbed Wire*, p. 28.

p. 24 'fired off'. Harwood, p. 67.

2: Capture from Air and Sea

p. 26 With this in mind. For B. A. 'Jimmy' James see IWM Papers (also published as *Moonless Night* [London: William Kimber, 1983; Barnsley: Leo Cooper/Pen & Sword Books, 2001]; page references refer to *Moonless Night*) and IWMSA transcript.

p. 26 'I pulled the rip cord'. James, IWMSA, p. 7.

p. 27 'Reassured'. James, IWM/*Moonless Night*, p. 14.

p. 27 'The evader was on his own'. Ibid., p. 15.

p. 28 'polite noises'. Ibid., p. 17.

p. 28 'For you the war'. Ibid

p. 28 Airey Neave. Figures from Airey Neave, *Saturday at MI9*, pp. 20–1.

p. 29 After the first great raid. See Martin Middlebrook, *The Schweinfurt-Regensburg Mission* (London: Allen Lane, 1983), p. 305.

p. 29 Captain Roland L. Sargent. See Arthur A. Durand, *Stalag Luft III*, pp. 26–32, 45–50. For a similar British example see S. C. Masters, IWM, pp. 50–91.

p. 30 Warrant Officer Stan Hope. Stan Hope, SWWEC.

p. 30 Three airmen. Clutton-Brock, *Footprints in the Sands of Time*, p. 202.

p. 31 Two Canadian crewmen. Ibid., p. 203.

p. 31 One source estimates. Figure from M. R. D. Foot, in Dear and Foot, *The Oxford Companion to the Second World War*, p. 747.

p. 31 One of the B-17 bombers. Delmar T. Spivey, *POW Odyssey*. See also Durand, pp. 19–22, and Roger A. Freeman, *Mighty Eighth War Diary* (London: Jane's Publishing, 1981), p. 86.

p. 32 'As I watched'. Spivey, p. 5.

p. 32 'The door opened'. Ibid., p. 6.

p. 32 They would become. Figures from the US Veterans Administration in Lewis H. Carlson, *We Were Each Other's Prisoners*, pp. xvii–xviii.

p. 33 B-24 pilot Captain John A. Vietor Jr. John A. Vietor, *Time Out*.

p. 33 'As soon as'. Ibid., p. 13.

p. 34 'When the leader'. Ibid., p. 10.

p. 34 'were absorbed in'. Ibid., p. 15.

p. 35 'War is a crazy game'. *Prisoner of War Bulletin*, vol. 2, no. 9 (Sept. 1944), p. 9.

p. 35 'heard muttering'. Vietor, pp. 20–21.

p. 35 'Only with the aid of arms'. Goebbels, in Durand, p. 50.

p. 35 'Fighter-bomber plots'. Albert Hoffman, in David A. Foy, *For You the War is Over*, p. 40.

p. 37 The numbers of POWs. *Fighting With Figures: A Statistical Digest of the Second World War*, ed. Peter Howlett (London: Central Statistical Office, 1995), p. 43, estimates 5,518 RN POWs; *The History of the Second World War, United Kingdom Medical Services: Casualties and Medical Statistics*, ed. W. Franklin Mellor (London: HMSO, 1972) estimates 5,629 RN POWs (p. 837, table 9) and 5,720 merchant seaman of all nationalities serving on British registered ships (p. 829). Very few American mariners became prisoners of the Germans and Italians.

p. 37 In charge of the motor launches. W. L. Stephens, IWM Papers. See also the the *Times* obituary of Stephens (15 Aug. 1997), James G. Dorrian, *Storming St Nazaire* (London: Leo Cooper, 1998), and C. E. Lucas Phillips, *The Greatest Raid of All* (London: Heinemann, 1958).

p. 38 'We opened fire'. Stephens, p. 1.

p. 38 'There was practically no firing'. Ibid., p. 2.

p. 39 'It was just'. Ibid., p. 3.

p. 39 'were herded down below'. Ibid., p. 4.

3: The Road to the Camps

p. 40 'I sat'. H. C. F. Harwood, IWM Papers, p. 84.

p. 40 'I felt angry'. John A. Vietor, *Time Out*, p. 24.

p. 40 'terrible feeling'. Douglas Le Fevre, AWM.

p. 40 'deeply disappointed'. A. Robert Prouse, *Ticket to Hell*, p. 23.

p. 41 'Now I was depressed'. Roger L. Shinn, *Wars and Rumors of Wars*, p. 47.

p. 41 'The general attitude'. Willis C. Rowe, 'Ethics of Surrender'.

p. 42 'He made a bee-line'. J. H. Witte, IWM Papers, p. 110. 'Snurdge' was Lieutenant (later Major) N. E. Strutt.

p. 42 'You suddenly realize'. In Allan Kent Powell, *Splinters of a Nation* (Salt Lake City, Utah: University of Utah Press, 1990), p. 41, quoted in Lewis H. Carlson, *We Were Each Other's Prisoners*, p. 28.

p. 42 'In this lonely cell'. Shinn, p. 61.

p. 43 'My throat closed'. Delmar T. Spivey, *POW Odyssey*, p. 11.

p. 43 'I thought of England'. Harwood, p. 96.

p. 44 'This wasn't'. W. L. Stephens, IWM Papers, p. 4.

p. 45 Attempts by French civilians. See J. Roberts, *A Terrier Goes to War*, p. 33; T. C. F. Prittie and W. Earle Edwards, *Escape to Freedom*, pp. 14–15; John Brown, *In Durance Vile*, p. 23; and David Rolf, *Prisoners of the Reich*, p. 28.

p. 45 'to our helpless disgust'. Private Davis, in Rolf, p. 28.

p. 45 'The Germans'. Harwood, p. 76. See also Prittie and Edwards, p. 14.

p. 46 'Whilst on the march'. James Goulden, WO 208/3311, SPG 903.

p. 46 'Leaving the railway yards'. Roberts, p. 37.

p. 46 'The train stopped'. G. E. Lyons, in A. J. Barker, *Behind Barbed Wire*, p. 49.

p. 47 The next great influx. See W. Wynne Mason, *Prisoners of War*, pp. 63–90.

p. 48 'seemingly known'. Howard Greville, *Prison Camp Spies*, p. 14.

p. 49 'weak macaroni stew'. Witte, p. 109.

p. 49 'We had to guard'. Ibid.

p. 49 'were well imbued'. Ibid., p. 111.

p. 49 A mile or so off. See Spence Edge and Jim Henderson, *No Honour, No Glory* for accounts of the sinkings of the *Jason* (*Jantzen* in Mason) and the *Nino Bixio*. Figures for the deaths on *Jason* from Mason, p. 111.

p. 50 'a severe loss'. R. G. McDowall, IWM Papers, p. 17.

p. 50 'Had fair meals'. Ibid.

p. 50 'I felt lonely'. Ibid., p. 18.

p. 50 'to let you know'. LeFevre.

p. 51 'We were taken'. Bertram Martin, in Adrian Gilbert, *The Imperial War Museum Book of the Desert War 1940–42* (London: Sidgwick & Jackson, 1992), p. 124.

p. 51 'I was standing'. LeFevre.

p. 52 'I remember well'. Stephens, p. 12.

p. 52 'I shan't attempt'. Ibid., p. 11.

p. 52 'Rations for the journey'. Ibid., p. 12.

p. 53 'We winced'. Shinn, p. 52.

p. 54 'I was shown'. Harwood, p. 73.

p. 54 'a prolonged process'. Stephens, p. 16.

p. 54 'a mixture of "sweet and sour"'. B. A. James, note to author.

p. 55 The *Durchgangslager*. See WO 208/3269, Oliver Clutton-Brock, *Footprints in the Sands of Time*, pp. 13–27; Arthur A Durand, *Stalag Luft III*, pp. 55–73.

p. 56 Many RAF men passing. See Clutton-Brock, pp. 14–16, and Rolf, pp. 45–7.

p. 56 The first senior British officer. See Sydney Smith, *'Wings' Day*, pp. 35–72.

p. 57 According to one witness. R. M. Clive, RE, in Clutton-Brock, p. 19.

p. 57 Colonel Spivey experienced. Spivey, pp. 22–4.

p. 58 'He told me'. Ibid., p. 23.

p. 58 'served the most heavenly tea'. Ibid., p. 25.

p. 58 Jack Vietor had a more testing time'. Vietor, pp. 23–37.

p. 59 And the best. See Charles Rollings, 'Scharff the interrogator', *Daily Telegraph*, 28 Feb. 1998, p. 15, and Raymond F. Toliver, *The Interrogator*.

p. 59 'that every word'. Toliver, p. 137.

p. 59 'I suspected'. Hubert Zemke, *Zemke's Stalag*, p. 6.

p. 60 'Declining'. Ibid., p. 11–12.

p. 60 Operating behind the lines. See M. R. D. Foot, *SOE in France* (London: HMSO, 2004).

p. 60 But when Odette Sansom. See Odette Hallowes, IMWSA transcript; Jerrard Tickell, *Odette*; and Peter Churchill, *The Spirit in the Cage*, pp. 22–7.

p. 61 'Where's Arnaud?'. Tickell, p. 222.

p. 61 'I know'. Hallowes, p. 11.

p. 61 'I had been blind'. Ibid., p. 7.

p. 62 'He used to'. Ibid., pp. 17–18.

p. 62 'I wasn't going to accept'. Ibid., p. 18.

p. 63 'We were shaved'. Prouse, p. 28.

p. 63 'I was told'. Harwood, pp. 93–4.

p. 63 'One event'. Witte, pp. 120–1.

4: Camps and Captors

p. 66 In October 1939. Figures from Vasilis Vourkoutiotis, *Prisoners of War and the German High Command*, p. 31.

p. 66 In North Africa the Germans. Figures from Roger Absalom, *A Strange Alliance*, p. 23.

p. 68 *'Schiesse am Schweitz'*. William Kalway, in Lewis H. Carlson, *We Were Each Other's Prisoners*, p. 91.

p. 68 'the Germans'. H. C. F. Harwood, IWM Papers, p. 98.

p. 68 'very few of the guards'. A. Robert Prouse, *Ticket to Hell*, pp. 105–6.

p. 68 'the older Germans'. A. N. L. Munby, IWM Papers, note.

p. 68 'Tisch was'. John A Vietor, *Time Out*, p. 91.

p. 68 'Complaints have'. OKW, Sept. 1941, in 'German Regulations Concerning Prisoners of War'.

p. 70 'truly beautiful place'. J. H. Witte, note to author.

p. 70 'Day after day'. Harwood, p. 141.

p. 70 'Good God'. In T. C. F. Prittie and W. Earle Edwards, *Escape to Freedom*, p. 78.

p. 71 The 230 Allied prisoners. Figures from W. Wynne Mason, *Prisoners of War*, p. 212.

p. 72 'Sulmona offered'. Adrian Carton de Wiart, *Happy Odyssey*, p. 186.

p. 72 The main camp at Sulmona. For PG 78 (Sulmona) see PRO WO 224/134; J. H. Witte, IWM Papers, pp. 118–42; Edward Ward, *Give Me Air*, pp. 31–95; Dawyck Haig, *My Father's Son*, pp. 111–18; Mason, pp. 39–40, 119, 207–209.

p. 73 The visibly better conditions. See PRO WO 224/134, visit by US military attaché, 28 May 1941.

p. 73 'lounging around'. J. H. Witte, conversation with author.

p. 73 PG 49 at Fontanellato. For PG 49 (Fontanellato) see WO PRO 224/117; Ian English (ed.), *Home by Christmas?*; Eric Newby, *Love and War in the Apennines*, pp. 30–55; Malcom Tudor, *British Prisoners of War in Italy*, pp. 27–44.

p. 73 'They were of the kind'. Newby, p. 37.

p. 73 'I was still'. Lieutenant Jack Comyn, in English, p. 31.

p. 74 The commandant. For PG 57 (Gruppignano) see PRO WO 224/122; R. G. McDowall, IWM papers, pp. 59–171; Douglas LeFevre, AWM; Mason, pp. 122–4, 214–18, 282–3.

p. 74 According to camp folklore. See Phil Loffman, AWM S557.

p. 74 'You could be punished'. LeFevre.

p. 74 In PG 21 at Chieti. For PG 21 (Chieti) see PRO WO 224/111; David Westheimer, *Sitting it Out*, pp. 40–116; John Verney, *A Dinner of Herbs*, pp. 34–88; Joseph S. Frelinghuysen, *Passages to Freedom*, pp. 60–100.

p. 74 'every bit the perfect villain'. Westheimer, p. 65.

p. 75 The camp was. For Stalag Luft I (Barth) see PRO WO 224/62; B. A.

James, IWM/*Moonless Night*, pp. 24–57; John A. Vietor, *Time Out*; Hubert Zemke, *Zemke's Stalag*; Sydney Smith, *'Wings' Day*, pp. 80–106; Oliver Clutton-Brock, *Footprints in the Sands of Time*, pp. 42–5; Mason, pp. 31–5, 142–3; www.merkki.com – accesssed Mar. 2004.

p. 75 'Cold damp fogs'. Vietor, p. 62.

p. 75 Increasing numbers. For Stalag Luft III (Sagan) see PRO WO 208/3283; James, pp. 58–65, 76–106; Delmar T. Spivey, *POW Odyssey*, pp. 31–117; Westheimer, pp. 163–259; Kingsley Brown, *Bonds of Wire*; Nathaniel Flekser, IWM Papers, pp. 22–85; Arthur A. Durand, *Stalag Luft III*; Clutton-Brock, p. 70–83; Mason, pp. 143–4, 401–3.

p. 76 'All in all'. John Dominy, *The Sergeant Escapers*, p. 57.

p. 76 The new camp. For Stalag Luft VI (Heydekrug) see PRO WO 224/65; Calton Younger, *No Flight from the Cage*, pp. 71–140; Dominy, pp. 89–117; Clutton-Brock, pp. 98–107; Mason, pp. 404–405; www.b24.net/pow/stalag6.htm – accessed Dec. 2003.

p. 76 'Russian-type'. Dominy, p. 89.

p. 77 'He did everything'. Francis S. Paules, quoted in www.b224.net/pow/stalag6.htm – accessed Nov. 2003.

p. 77 Many were sent. For Stalag Luft IV (Gross Tychow) see PRO WO 2224/64; Clutton-Brock, pp. 108–15; www.b24.net/pow/stalag4.htm – accessed Dec. 2003.

p. 77 'treated harshly'. Bill Krebs, deposition to the Judge Advocate War Crimes Investigation, quoted in www.b24.net/pow/stalag4.htm – accessed Dec. 2003.

p. 78 'The Germans'. Ibid.

p. 78 The last Luftwaffe camp. For Stalag Luft VII (Bankau) see PRO WO 224/66; V. V. Cooper, IWM Papers, pp. 116–22; Douglas Smithson, www.pegasus-one.org/pow/douglas_smithson.htm – accessed Feb. 2004; Clutton-Brock, pp. 126–8.

p. 78 'a bastard'. Peter Thomson, in Clutton-Brock, p. 126.

p. 78 The naval camp. For Marlag and Milag see PRO WO 208/3270; W. L. Stephens, IWM Papers; A. C. Howard, IWM Papers and type-script memoir, *'Mein Gefangenschaft'*; G. F. W. Wilson, IWM Papers; Gabe Thomas, *Milag*; Mason, pp. 255, 406–7; Jonathan F. Vance, 'The Politics of Camp Life'.

p. 79 The first POW camp. For Oflag IXA (Spangenberg) see PRO WO 224/78; Prittie and Edwards, pp. 250–3; Mason, pp. 29–30, 234–6.

p. 79 Most officer prisoners. For Oflag VIIC (Laufen) see PRO WO

224/75; Harwood, pp. 92–122; Prittie and Edwards, pp. 54–73; A. C. Whitcombe, IWM Papers; A. N. L. Munby, IWM Papers, 1940–41.

p. 79 Conditions improved. For Oflag VB (Biberach) see PRO WO 224/72; Harwood pp. 137–48; Prittie and Edwards, pp. 78–110; Mason, pp. 83–4.

p. 80 'very old and doddery'. Harwood, p. 139.

p. 80 'He was blind drunk'. Ibid., pp. 140–41.

p. 80 Harwood's stay. For Oflag VIB (Warburg) see PRO WO 224/73; Harwood, pp. 149–60; Prittie and Edwards, pp. 111–53; Mason, pp. 126–9, 236.

p. 80 'much the worst'. See PRO WO 224/73.

p. 81 A former cavalry barracks. For Oflag VIIB (Eichstätt) see PRO 208/3291 and WO 224/74; Harwood, pp. 161–216; Prittie and Edwards, pp. 180–6; Mason, pp. 237–9, 365.

p. 81 'in a beautiful Bavarian countryside'. Mason, p. 237.

p. 81 'A keen soldier'. Prittie and Edwards, p. 183.

p. 81 The most famous. For Oflag IVC (Colditz) see Stephens, pp. 49–60; P. R. Reid, *The Colditz Story*; pp. 62–194; Airey Neave, *They Have Their Exits*, pp. 61–91; S. P. Mackenzie, *The Colditz Myth*; Henry Chancellor, *Colditz*.

p. 82 'We walked'. Stephens, p. 49.

p. 82 'most with one purpose'. Ibid., p. 51.

p. 82 Oflag 64. For Oflag 64 (Schubin) see PRO WO 224/83: Roger L. Shinn, *Wars and Rumors of Wars*, pp. 86–93; J. Frank Diggs, *Americans Behind Barbed Wire*, pp. 21–108; 'The Saga of John Kriegie', *Prisoner of War Bulletin*, vol. 3, no. 3 (Mar. 1945), p. 7.

p. 83 Stalag IVB. For Stalag IVB (Mühlberg) see PRO WO 208/3274 and WO 224/12; McDowall; M. A. Tagg, *The Prisoner Padre*, pp. 99–128; Assheton F. Taylor, *One Way Flight to Munich*, pp. 121–229.

p. 83 The largest camp. For Stalag VIIIB/344 (Lamsdorf) see PRO FO 916/22; Arthur Evans, *Sojourn in Silesia*; Ike Rosmarin, *Inside Story*; H. C. M Jarvis, IWM Papers; Imelda Ryan, *POWs Fraternal*, pp. 64–73, 80–91; Vance; Mason, pp. 30–31, 88–9, 129–32, 239–41, 297–8, 369–70.

p. 85 'where a profusion'. Mason, p. 370.

p. 85 'To have belonged'. Dominy, p. 19.

p. 85 Of the other ranks' camps. For Stalag 383 (Hohenfels) see PRO FO 916/835; M. N. McKibbin (ed.), *Barbed Wire: Memories of Stalag 383*; Ryan, pp. 91–138; Cooper, pp. 81–116; R. P. Evans, IWM Papers, pp. 41–51; Les Foskett, www.pegasus-one.org/pow/les_foskett.htm – accessed Oct. 2003; Mason, pp. 248–9, 388–9.

p. 86 'first class'. J. E. McGee, IWM Papers, p. 11.

p. 86 'was noticeable'. Ibid., p. 16.

p. 86 'After the best part of two years'. Foskett.

p. 86 After his recapture. James, pp. 115–35, 147–63; see also Smith, pp. 192–234.

p. 87 After capture. E. C. Stirling, Diary, 27 February–4 April 1945, IWM Papers. See also Norman Rubenstein, 'Good God, A Jew!', in Tony Strachan (ed.), *In the Clutch of Circumstances*, pp. 135–150.

p. 87 In August 1944. See PRO FO 916/834; Colin Burgess, *Destination Buchenwald*.

p. 88 'This constant shattering'. Ed Carter-Edwards, 'Man's Inhumanity', in Strachan, p. 235.

p. 88 'We respected each other'. Ibid., pp. 236–7.

p. 89 Edgar Hargreaves. E. C. S. Hargreaves, IWMSA transcript.

p. 89 The idea of holding. Odette Hallowes, IWMSA transcript, and Jerrard Tickell, *Odette*.

p. 90 'I give you that'. In Tickell, p. 261.

5: The Fabric of Daily Life

p. 91 'Being shot down'. John A. Vietor, *Time Out*, p. 43.

p. 92 'We had always'. Philip B. Miller, in Lewis B. Carlson, *We Were Each Other's Prisoners*, p. 84.

p. 92 'Layed awake'. Mike Harkovich, in Donald Vining (ed.), *American Diaries of World War II*, p. 393.

p. 92 'The Italians'. Edward Ward, *Give Me Air*, pp. 40–1.

p. 93 'I reached'. Milt Felsen, *The Anti-Warrior*, p. 199.

p. 93 'When the gas explodes'. Joseph P. O'Donnell, *The Shoe Leather Express*, vol. 1, p. 80.

p. 94 'You were compelled'. Vietor, pp. 83–4.

p. 94 'I had seen'. H. C. F. Harwood, IWM Papers, p. 150.

p. 94 'Hell is other people'. Jean-Paul Sartre, *Huis clos* (1944), scene 5.

p. 94 'Rarely in life'. Vietor, p. 71.

p. 94 'we had a roster'. E. C. S. Hargreaves, IWMSA transcript. p. 31. See also B. A. James, IWM/*Moonless Night*, p. 53.

p. 95 'drained each other'. Vietor, p. 130.

p. 95 'Men with'. R. G. McDowall, IWM Papers, p. 20.

p. 95 'I had thought'. Ibid.

p. 95 'I felt'. Ibid., p. 111.

p. 96 'officers from one camp'. Harwood, p. 150.

p. 96 'upper-class officers'. Eric Newby, *Love and War in the Apennines*, p. 38.

p. 96 'Everyone else'. Ibid., p. 39.

p. 96 'They ate together'. J. Ellison Platt, in Margaret Duggan (ed.), *Padre in Colditz*, p. 70.

p. 96 'They spoke'. Harwood, p. 206.

p. 97 'debts and mortgages'. Felsen, p. 211.

p. 97 'there were men'. Calton Younger, *No Flight from the Cage*, p. 89.

p. 98 'A cup of Ersatz coffee'. James, pp. 28–9.

p. 98 'The sour taste'. Ibid., p. 29n.

p. 98 'It was always lukewarm'. Vietor, p. 118.

p. 98 'Dinner: cabbage'. McDowall, p. 34.

p. 99 'Had urgent call'. Ibid., p. 41. See also J. M. Green, *From Colditz in Code*, p. 55; Reginald Dexter, IWM, Rolf Collection, pp. 1–2.

p. 99 'Nothing could rival'. Roger L. Shinn, *Wars and Rumors of Wars*, p. 91.

p. 99 'Hour after hour'. Ibid., p. 120.

p. 100 'When the parcels'. A. Robert Prouse, *Ticket to Hell*, p. 44.

p. 100 'I received'. Edward W. Beattie Jr, *Diary of a Kriegie*, p. 90.

p. 100 A British Red Cross Parcel. The details given are of a Number 1 British Red Cross food parcel sent towards the end of the war, described in P. G. Cambray and G. G. B. Briggs (comps.), *Red Cross and St. John War Organisation 1939–47*, pp. 142–3.

p. 101 'canned creamery butter'. David Westheimer, *Sitting it Out*, p. 56.

p. 102 'usually contained'. Vietor, p. 120.

p. 102 'I hustled excitedly'. Ibid., pp. 120–21.

p. 102 'In my own garden'. Delmar T. Spivey, *POW Odyssey*, p. 66.

p. 103 But J. Frank Diggs. See J. Frank Diggs, *Americans Behind the Barbed Wire*, pp. 57–8.

p. 103 'Fattening the kittens'. Vietor, p. 127.

p. 104 'included one lieutenant'. Shinn, p. 90.

p. 104 'intricate system'. Beattie, p. 249. See also Shinn, p. 90, and W. Wynne Mason, *Prisoners of War*, p. 214.

p. 104 according to one source. Beattie, p. 249.

p. 105 'He eats about'. McDowall, p. 361.

p. 105 'People began to arrive'. Robert Kee, *A Crowd is Not Company*, p. 74.

p. 105 Second only to shortages. For details of POW clothing see Cambray and Briggs, pp. 169–77; Mason, pp. 47, 130, 156, 242; Arthur A Durand, *Stalag Luft III*. pp. 171–3.

p. 105 One of the more outlandish. J. E. Pryce, *Heels in Line*, p. 76. For similar outfits see also Howard Greville, *Prison Camp Spies*, p. 17, and J. Roberts, *A Terrier Goes to War*, p. 52.

p. 106 'We have all'. in Cambray and Briggs, p. 178.

p. 106 'By the summer'. Spivey, p. 55.

p. 106 The vast majority of servicemen smoked. According to the Royal College of Physicians, London, 81% of all British males regularly smoked tobacco during the late 1940s (US figures were similar) – www.rcplondon.ac.uk, accessed Feb. 2005.

p. 107 'dried mint leaves'. Pryce, p. 60.

p. 107 'I realized that'. Ibid.

p. 107 when Center compound. Spivey, p. 119.

p. 108 'They were homogeneous'. R. A. Radford, 'The Economic Organisation of a P.O.W. Camp', p. 37.

p. 108 'they could be clipped'. Ibid.

p. 109 'There was a coffee-stall owner'. Ibid., p. 36.

p. 109 'Partly because'. Shinn, p. 55.

p. 109 'a pair of gloves'. Vietor, p. 106.

p. 110 'You never knew'. V. V. Cooper, IWM Papers, p. 88.

p. 110 'The stall owners'. Raymond Ryan, in Imelda Ryan, *POWs Fraternal*, p. 126.

p. 110 'little of the workings'. Radford, p. 37.

p. 111 'I built up'. J. H. Witte, IWM Papers; conversation with author.

p. 112 'The prices asked'. McDowall, p. 245.

p. 112 'It was immoral'. Shinn, p. 55.

p. 112 'The Germans'. McDowall, p. 388.

p. 112 'In the permanent camp'. Radford, p. 35.

p. 114 'very cloudy'. Anon. seaman.

p. 114 'wine had gone'. Ibid.

p. 114 'Everybody sat around'. Ibid.

p. 115 'Three drinks'. Vietor, p. 125. See also Kee, pp. 117–19, on 'laying down a brew' for some brilliant comic writing.

p. 115 'In the past few weeks'. Major R. C. L. Harvey, in Gabe Thomas, *Milag*, p. 201.

p. 115 'In a meeting'. Anon. Seaman. See also Thomas, p. 201.

p. 116 'These chaps'. McDowall, p. 72.

p. 116 'The determination'. Spivey, p. 80.

p. 116 'There was much conviviality'. Ibid.

p. 116 'This was a mistake'. Ibid.

p. 116 'My reaction'. Ibid.

p. 117 'The sex organ'. George J. Davis, *The Hitler Diet*, p. 3.

p. 117 'A few soldiers'. Prouse, p. 113.

p. 117 'homosexual tendencies'. Spivey, p. 74.

p. 117 'It is to the everlasting credit'. Ibid.

p. 117 'Homosexualism'. J. E. Platt, IWM Diary, in S. P. Mackenzie, *The Colditz Myth*, p. 221.

p. 117 'Jocular references'. Ibid.

p. 118 'whatever loves'. Newby, p. 38.

p. 118 It was in PG 49. See Dan Billany and David Dowie, *The Cage*.

p. 118 'This is where'. Geoffrey Ellwood, in Daniel G. Dancocks (ed.), *In Enemy Hands*, p. 107.

p. 118 'Practitioners could'. Ike Rosmarin, *Inside Story*, p. 79. See also George Moreton, 'Barbed Wire Medico', in H. C. M. Jarvis, IWM Papers, p. 496.

p. 118 'homosexuality was rife'. J. H. Witte, conversation with author.

p. 118 'In winter'. Witte, p. 134.

p. 119 'Dutiful swains'. Ibid., p. 133.

p. 119 'To perform'. Newby, p. 37.

p. 119 'they earned'. Witte, p. 134.

p. 119 'staged an elaborate'. Kingsley Brown, *Bonds of Wire*, p. 123.

p. 119 'would bring women'. Felsen, pp. 208–9.

p. 120 'come to a window'. Harwood, p. 205.

p. 120 'To POWs who'. J. H. Witte, note to author.

p. 121 'I was not'. Ibid.

p. 121 'I was twenty-five'. Ibid.

6: Leadership and Discipline

p. 123 At a punishment camp. J. E. Pryce, *Heels in Line*, pp. 102–3.

p. 124 In Stalag IIB at Hammerstein. 'Stalag IIB: The Final Report', from *American Prisoners of War in Germany* (1 Nov. 1945), reproduced in www.DarbyRangers.com – accessed Apr. 2004.

p. 124 'He was a man'. Kingsley Brown, *Bonds of Wire*, p. 93.

p. 124 'a superb natural leader'. Eugene L. Daniel Jr, *In the Presence of Mine Enemies*, p. 82.

p. 124 'one of the finest'. Delmar T. Spivey, *POW Odyssey*, p. 38.

p. 125 'I had been accustomed'. Ibid.

p. 125 'Windows [were] broken'. Ibid., p. 42.

p. 126 'giving orders'. Ibid., p. 44.

p. 126 'a general clean-up'. Ibid., p. 44.

p. 126 'Some believed'. Ibid., p. 45.

p. 126 'drive each other'. B. A. James, IWM/*Moonless Night*, p. 83.

p. 127 'There was a tendency'. Edward Ward, *Give Me Air*, p. 127.

p. 127 'Under the regime'. Ibid., pp. 145–6. See also Dawyck Haig, *My Father's Son*, p. 128.

p. 127 'Fortune had made'. T. C. F. Prittie and W. Earle Edwards, *Escape to Freedom*, pp. 69–70. For other favourable assessments see H. C. F. Harwood, IWM Papers, pp. 128–9, and J. M. Green, *From Colditz in Code*, p. 53; for one less so, see A. N. L. Munby, IWM Papers: 'He was very affable . . . His division however were not very enthusiastic about him' (diary, 31 Aug. 1940).

p. 128 'We admired Col. Goode'. Roger L. Shinn, *Wars and Rumors of Wars*, pp. 108–9.

p. 128 'The camp reminded me'. Spivey, p. 56.

p. 128 'It was a constant battle'. Ibid., p. 41.

p. 129 'Colonel Spicer was'. Captain Mozart Kaufman, in George Lesko, 'Colonel Spicer's Defiant Speech', in www.merkki.com/speeches – accessed Nov. 2003. See also John A. Vietor, *Time Out*, p. 102.

p. 129 'They are a bunch'. Colonel Spicer, in Lesko.

p. 130 'a pretty tough lot'. Munby, 21 June 1940. See also E. G. C. Beckwith (ed.), *The Mansell Diaries*, p. 35, for a similar view.

p. 130 'Hauptman [Captain] Püpcke'. Alec Ross, in Henry Chancellor, *Colditz*, p. 252. See also, S. P. Mackenzie, *The Colditz Myth*, pp. 145–6.

p. 131 'British orderlies'. Spivey, p. 47 . See also Vietor, p. 152.

p. 131 'We soon became accustomed'. Raymond Ryan in Imelda Ryan, *POWs Fraternal*, p. 73.

p. 132 'His strong character'. Ike Rosmarin, *Inside Story*, p. 44.

p. 132 'a remarkable man'. Green, p. 92.

p. 132 Meyers had the support. Figures from Oliver Clutton-Brock, *Footprints in the Sands of Time*, p. 91

p. 132 'The trouble in the camp'. R. G. McDowall, IWM Papers, p. 358.

p. 133 In the ensuing referendum. Figures from Ryan, p. 108.

p. 133 'Two Sergeant cooks'. Sam Kydd, *For you the war is over*, p. 105. See also CSM Soane, in David Rolf, *Prisoners of the Reich*, p. 85, and Roger V. Coward, *Sailors in Cages*, p. 88.

p. 133 'NZ chaps'. McDowall, p. 111.

p. 134 'there were on many occasions'. Spivey, p. 62.

p. 134 'some individuals'. Ibid.

p. 134 'My name is Lord'. Bombardier Stonard, in Rolf, p. 68.

p. 134 'would be seen'. John Lord, IWMSA.

p. 134 'degrade the British soldier'. Ibid.

p. 135 'ensure that the Germans'. Ibid.

p. 135 'I made sure'. Ibid.

p. 135 'The stench'. Ibid.

p. 135 'to show the POWs'. Ibid.

p. 136 'I found that'. J. A. G. Deans, IWMSA.

p. 136 'Dixie's great achievement'. Alfred Jenner, 'Tribute to Dixie Deans of Stalag Luft', in www.merkki.com/speeches – accessed Jan. 2004.

p. 136 'I was dealing'. Deans.

p. 137 'The work'. Calton Younger, *No Flight from the Cage*, p. 24–5.

p. 137 'officious, fussy'. Arthur Evans, *Sojourn in Silesia*, p. 54.

p. 137 'CSM R.'. David Wild, *Prisoners of Hope*, p. 121. See also pp. 108–109, 110.

p. 138 'The least said'. James E. McGee, IWM, Rolf Collection, p. 10e. See also Ian Ramsay, *P.O.W.*, pp. 17, 36, 40, 56.

p. 138 'There was no organization'. Bob Engstrom, in Lewis H. Carlson, *We Were Each Other's Prisoners*, p. 12.

p. 138 'I saw a lot'. Henry H. McKee, in ibid., p. 108.

p. 139 'Almost the first look'. Shinn, p. 130.

p. 139 'Col. Goode'. Ibid., pp. 130–31.

p. 139 'As I stood'. McDowall, pp. 167–8.

p. 140 'Went to see'. Ibid., p. 169.

p. 140 There he continued. See Ryan, p. 119.

p. 140 'A chap'. Ibid., p. 108.

p. 141 'cold-blooded murder'. McDowall, p. 135. See also Wesley Jack in Megan Hutching (ed.), *Inside Stories*, pp. 134–5, and Richard Lamb, *War In Italy*, p. 173.

p. 141 'Theft in a place'. David Westheimer, *Sitting it Out*, p. 85.

p. 141 'The wretched man'. Munby, 30 Sept. 1940.

p. 141 'Captain Lawton'. Ibid.

p. 142 'didn't appear ashamed'. Harwood, p. 103.

p. 142 'The offender'. Assheton F. Taylor, *One Way Flight to Munich*, p. 128.

p. 142 'We didn't beat him up'. Coward, p. 104.

p. 143 'fate of collaborators'. Hubert Zemke, *Zemke's Stalag*, p. 54.

p. 143 'We took it upon ourselves'. Morton in Daniel G. Dancocks (ed.) *In Enemy Hands*, pp. 99–100. See also, Rosmarin, p. 79, and John Borrie, *Despite Captivity*, p. 214.

7: Forced Labour

p. 144 As the war progressed. Figures from Vasilis Vourkoutiotis, *Prisoners of War and the German High Command*, p. 199.

p. 144 The type of work performed. On an overall percentage basis, 24% of British POWs worked in construction, 23.5% in mines and metallurgy, 18% in other industrial concerns, 17.5% in agriculture and forestry, 10.5% in energy and transportation, and 3% in administrative occupations – from Vourkoutiotis, p. 199.

p. 146 'The Commandant'. A. Robert Prouse, *Ticket to Hell*, pp. 41–2.

p. 147 'British non-commissioned officers'. OKW Directive, 11 March 1942, article 59.

p. 148 'he did not care'. 'Stalag IIB: the Final Report', from *American Prisoners of War in Germany* (1 Nov. 1945), reproduced in www.DarbyRangers.com – accessed Apr. 2004.

p. 149 'On the Sundays'. Thearl Mesecher, in Donald Vining (ed.), *American Diaries of World War II*, p. 350.

p. 149 'We did get'. J. Roberts, *A Terrier Goes to War*, p. 64.

p. 150 'The gang'. J. H. Witte, IWM Papers, p. 160.

p. 151 'barrack-room which was filled'. Ibid., p. 195.

p. 151 'We went to bed exhausted'. Ibid., p. 196.

p. 151 'He was shocked'. Ibid., p. 195.

p. 152 'I rapidly developed'. Cyril Rofe, *Against the Wind*, p. 98. See also Arthur Evans, *Sojourn in Silesia*, p. 22, and Eric Gallagher in Megan Hutching (ed.), *Inside Stories*, pp. 180–81.

p. 152 'Being already'. Rofe, p. 96.

p. 153 'At the work commando'. Prouse, p. 86.

p. 153 Some 4,000 Americans. For the Berga camp see Mitchell G. Bard, *Forgotten Victims*, pp. 72–97, and Lewis H. Carlson, *We Were Each Other's Prisoners*, pp. 194–9.

p. 154 'when nobody was looking'. Douglas LeFevre, AWM.

p. 154 'I went up'. Ibid.

p. 155 'The boots'. George Lochhead, in Hutching, p. 210.

p. 155 'More for a laugh'. Roberts, p. 111.

p. 156 'rude signs'. Ibid.

p. 156 'a camera'. Ibid., p. 112.

p. 156 'All this fuss'. Ibid.

p. 156 'We downed files'. Witte, p. 156.

p. 156 'which looked'. Ibid.

p. 157 'With clothing'. Mesecher, in Vining, pp. 359–60.

p. 157 'The British are'. 'SS Report on Questions of Internal Security', in PRO WO 208/3242, Historical Record of MI9, attachment 'A', appx 'B', p. 16.

p. 157 'A short while ago'. Ibid., p. 17.

p. 157 'presence in Germany'. Ibid., p. 20.

8: 'Time On My Hands'. Leisure, Entertainment and the Arts

p. 159 Terry Frost was born: Terry Frost, IWMSA transcript. See also obituaries in *The Times* and *Guardian*, 3 Sept. 2003.

p. 159 'In prisoner-of-war camp'. Frost, *The Times*, 3 Sept. 2003.

p. 160 'Prisoner-of-war life'. Munro Fraser, in David Rolf, *Prisoners of the Reich*, p. 88.

p. 160 'If you have never'. Lionel Renton, in A. J. Barker, *Behind Barbed Wire*, p. 88.

p. 161 'Still shut up'. Robert Guerlain, in *Prisoner of War*, Oct. 1944, p. 2.

p. 161 During 1943, for example. Figures from *Prisoner of War Bulletin*, vol. 1, no. 5 (Oct. 1943), p. 2.

p. 162 'There were eight or ten'. W. L. Stephens, IWM Papers, p. 53.

p. 162 'I shall never forget'. 'Golf in Captivity', *Prisoner of War*, Oct. 1944, p. 3.

p. 162 'the "abort" [latrine]'. Ibid.

p. 163 'We lived and breathed'. Ibid., p. 4.

p. 163 'A few mounds'. Ibid.

p. 163 'many an hour'. A. C. Howard, IWM Papers p. 157.

p. 163 'was always in'. Delmar T. Spivey, *POW Odyssey*, p. 71.

p. 163 'Practically every state'. *Prisoner of War Bulletin*, vol. 3, no.3 (Mar. 1945), p. 2.

p. 164 'These games'. V. V. Cooper, IWM Papers, p. 88. For details of the Stalag IVB 'World Cup' see Colin Wingrave, www.wartimememories.co.uk/stalag4b.html – accessed Aug. 2004.

p. 164 'Another evening'. H. C. F. Harwood, IWM Papers, pp. 112–13.

p. 165 At Mühlhausen. A. Robert Prouse, *Ticket to Hell*, p. 99.

p. 165 'I could usually find'. David Wild, *Prisoner of Hope*, p. 33.

p. 166 'Most people'. B. A. James, IWM/*Moonless Night*, p. 32.

p. 166 'Every day the West Hall'. Anon. seaman.

p. 166 'colossal sums'. Harwood, p. 185.

p. 167 'Several men'. R.G. McDowall, IWM Papers, p. 113. Although two-up was illegal in Australia, it was played throughout the Australian Army, subsequently becoming an Anzac Day institution.

p. 167 'We still find'. *Prisoner of War*, July 1942, p. 10.

p. 168 'It took a war'. James Hargest, *Farewell Campo 12*, p. 77.

p. 168 'There was quite a selection'. Cooper, p. 104.

p. 169 'used to have'. Doug LeFevre, AWM. See also John Dominy, *The Sergeant Escapers*, p. 107, and J. H. Witte, IWM Papers, p. 169.

p. 169 'A whole room'. Roger V. Coward, *Sailors in Cages*, p. 152.

p. 169 'We've made a'. Richard Wood, IWM Papers, letter to Beryl from Oflag VIIC/H.

p. 170 'In the summer'. John Buxton, *The Redstart* (London: Collins, 1950), p. 1. See also Stephen Moss, *A Bird in the Bush: A Social History of Birdwatching* (London: Aurum Press, 2004), pp. 156–9, and Peter Marren, *The New Naturalists* (London: HarperCollins, 1995), pp. 193–4.

p. 170 'No pair of birds'. Buxton, p. 3.

p. 170 'It is true'. Harwood, pp. 202–3.

p. 171 The actor Michael Goodliffe. For biographical details, and illustrations and photographs of POW theatrical productions, see Goodliffe, www.mgoodliffe.co.uk – accessed Dec. 2003.

p. 171 'There was a great demand'. Harwood, p. 209.

p. 172 'I almost forgot'. *Prisoner of War*, June 1942, p. 8.

p. 172 'One could really'. Flying Officer Bolton, in Rolf, p. 145.

p. 172 'We had space'. Goodliffe.

p. 172 'the professional actors'. Harwood, p. 116.

p. 172 'We only put on'. Ibid.

p. 172 'Their knowledge'. Ibid.

p. 173 'We made'. Spivey, p. 67.

p. 173 In order to simulate. P.O. Herbert Macey, IWM Papers, Rolf Collection.

p. 174 'It was one'. In Rolf, p. 180.

p. 174 Photographs of some of performances. See Goodliffe, and Peter Peel in SWWEC.

p. 174 'I was given'. Spivey, p. 67.

p. 175 'unless the presentation'. Goodliffe.

p. 175 'good looking enough'. Cooper, p. 86.

p. 176 'The first sound'. Wild, p. 50.

p. 177 'We were a dismal lot'. Wood, 'Music in P.O.W. Camps in Germany, 1940–45', pt 1, p. 5.

p. 177 The Red Cross also organized. See *Prisoner of War*, July 1942, p. 10.

p. 178 A Glen Miller band. See Arthur A. Durand, *Stalag Luft III*, p. 242.

p. 178 'Nick Nagorka'. Spivey, p. 69.

p. 179 'Among the twelve'. Wild, p. 221.

p. 179 'The lessons were read'. Wood, 'Music in P.O.W Camps', pt 1, p. 6.

p. 179 'Getting the musical score'. Ibid., p. 6. See also Emily Daymond, 'Music in Prisoners of War Camps', pp. 42–4.

p. 179 'I had often had'. Wood, IWM Papers, 'The Music Festival'.

p. 180 The high point. See Wood, IWM Papers, letter to Mr Grigg 're: The Ballad'.

p. 180 'The choir'. Wood, IWM Papers, *The Times*, February 1945.

p. 181 'Those of us'. Wood, 'Music in P.O.W Camps', pt 2, pp. 15–16.

9: The Written Word: Internal Escape and Self-Improvement

p. 182 'We could not'. Robert Kee, *A Crowd is Not Company*, p. 115.

p. 182 'the most important'. John A. Vietor, *Time Out*, p. 69.

p. 182 'The best antidote'. J. H. Witte, IWM Papers, p. 113.

p. 183 'Since I've been captured'. In Eric Newby, *Love and War in the Apennines*, pp. 42–3.

p. 183 'For lack of'. Vietor, p. 30.

p. 183 'utterly bookless'. David Read, 'Books in Prison', pt 1, p. 595.

p. 183 'to commit to memory'. Ibid.

p. 183 Under the overall control. The various book-supply organizations were the World Alliance of YMCAs, the International Bureau of Education, the Ecumenical Commission for Assistance to Prisoners of War, the European Student Relief Fund, the International Federation of Library Associations and the Swiss Catholic Mission for Prisoners of War.

p. 183 In Britain, the Red Cross. For a full description of the activities of the Educational Books Section see Robert W. Holland (comp./ed.), *Adversis Major*.

p. 184 'It is interesting'. Elliot Viney, in Holland, p. 47.

p. 185 'We queued up'. H. C. F. Harwood, IWM Papers, p. 125.

p. 185 Florence Haxton Bullock. 'Book Suggestions', *Prisoner of War Bulletin*, vol. 1, no. 6 (Nov. 1943), p. 4.

p. 186 'I remember'. Dallas Lasky, in Daniel G. Dancocks (ed.), *In Enemy Hands*, p. 105.

p. 186 Books poured into Germany. Figures from David Shavit, 'The Greatest Morale Factor Next to the Red Army', p. 116.

p. 186 'On issuing day'. Witte, p. 120.

p. 186 'Men who owned books'. David Westheimer, *Sitting it Out*, p. 58.

p. 187 'Books trickled into the camp'. Ibid., p. 71.

p. 187 The librarian at Eichstätt. See Holland, p. 47.

p. 187 The Oflag 64 library. See 'The Saga of John Kriegie' in *Prisoner of War Bulletin*, vol. 3, no. 3 (Mar. 1945), p. 7.

p. 188 'I managed to'. A. Robert Prouse, *Ticket to Hell*, p. 139.

p. 188 Although some libraries. Shavit, pp. 120–1.

p. 188 One attempt. Ibid., p. 125.

p. 188 In November 1943. Stalag 383 figures in PRO FO 916/835, 2/12/43, pp. 1, 4.

p. 189 'Mail arrived'. Vietor, p. 142.

p. 189 'During mail call'. Westheimer, p. 103.

p. 189 'It would be'. Richard Passmore, *Moving Tent*, p. 99.

p. 190 'I'm so glad'. N. G. Price, in David Rolf, *Prisoners of the Reich*, p. 125.

p. 190 'Got my first two'. Vietor, p. 154.

p. 190 'Got my first letter'. R. G. McDowall, IWM Papers, p. 227 .

p. 191 The British *Prisoner's Pie*. 'Their Own Journals', *Prisoner of War*, Nov. 1943, p. 3.

p. 191 The forging of links. ' "Barbs and Gripes" at Stalag II B', *Prisoner of War Bulletin*, vol. 2, no. 10 (Oct. 1944), p. 10.

p. 191 *Gefangenen Gazette*. 'Gazette Celebrates Birthday', *Prisoner of War Bulletin*, vol. 3, no. 4 (Apr. 1945).

p. 192 *POW WOW*. For *POW WOW*, see Hubert Zemke, *Zemke's Stalag*, pp. 31–3; Rolf, p. 129–30; David A. Foy, *For You the War is Over*, p. 88.

p. 192 One of the more ambitious. *Prisoner of War*, Oct. 1944, p. 2. See also Rolf, p. 130.

p. 192 Of the hobby magazines. See Tom Swallow, Arthur H. Pill et al., *Flywheel: Memories of the Open Road*, a 1987 facsimile bound edition of the original magazines.

p. 192 'There was nothing'. Ibid., p. 6.

p. 193 'It was not very easy'. Ibid.

p. 193 Some German-published magazines. See Vietor, p. 139; Delmar T. Spivey, *POW Odyssey*, p. 92, and Edward W. Beattie, *Diary of a Kriegie*, pp. 192–3.

p. 194 'come out of this hole'. Major Cyril Whitcombe, in Rolf, p. 113.

p. 194 'The most striking phenomenon'. Captain C. J. Hamson, in Holland, p. 16.

p. 194 'At present'. *Prisoner of War Bulletin*, vol. 1, no. 5 (Oct. 1943), p. 8.

p. 195 Many men had knowledge. Vietor, p. 69; Nathaniel Flekser, IWM Papers, p. 44; Douglas LeFevre, AWM.

p. 195 'Lectures were scheduled'. Roger L. Shinn, *Wars and Rumors of Wars*, p. 131.

p. 196 'If the Germans'. G. Tavender, in Holland, p. 103.

p. 196 'the likeness of eternity'. In Holland, p. 53.

p. 197 'Where there were no examinations'. Ibid., p. 114.

p. 197 The first such examination course. Ibid., p. 52.

p. 197 'It was a point of honour'. Ibid., p. 59.

p. 197 Most Oflags. For Stalag Luft VI, see Holland, pp. 90–2, and E. Alderton, 'Superior to Adversity'.

p. 198 In Stalag Luft III's Center compound. See Spivey, p. 87.

p. 198 'With the aid'. Holland, p. 102.

p. 198 'Officers lent photographs'. Ibid., p. 116.

p. 199 'We try to communicate'. 'Where There is no Vision the People Perish', in Educational Books Section pamphlet, January 1945.

10: Other Nationalities

p. 200 'From the very beginning'. Delmar T. Spivey, *POW Odyssey*, p. 54.

p. 200 'The British prisoners'. A. D. Azios, letter to the author.

p. 201 'Somehow a truckload'. Alfred Jenner, 'Tribute to Dixie Deans of Stalag Luft', in www.merkki.com/speeches – accessed Jan. 2004.

p. 201 'the difference'. David Westheimer, *Sitting it Out*, p. 75.

p. 201 'A number of American prisoners'. H. C. F. Harwood, IWM Papers, p. 207.

p. 202 'The truth is'. Edward W. Beattie, *Diary of a Kriegie*, p. 297. See also Joseph S. Frelinghuysen, *Passages to Freedom*, pp. 48–9, 53.

p. 202 'British disliked'. John A. Vietor, *Time Out*, p. 98.

p. 202 American artillery officer. See Frelinghuysen, p. 53.

p. 202 'I'd like to kick'. S. G. Pritchard, in Spivey, p. 43.

p. 203 'the *uniform*'. 'Prisoners of war of alien nationalities in enemy armies', OKW, 16 June 1941, translated and published by the American Prisoners of War Information Bureau.

p. 203 Czech POWs. For the concerns of Czech prisoners see Vietor, pp. 50–51, and J. E. R. Wood (ed.), *Detour*, p. 4.

p. 203 Nearly 15,000. POW figures from *Official Year Book of the Union of South Africa, 1946*, in Ian Gleason, *The Unknown Force*, p. 195 (South Africa); W. Wynne Mason, *Prisoners of War*, p. v (New Zealand – includes small numbers captured in Pacific); Hugh Clarke, Colin Burgess and Russell Braddon, *Prisoners of War*, p. 53 (Australia); Jonathan F. Vance, *Objects of Concern* (Canada).

p. 203 'we English'. R. G. McDowall, IWM Papers, p. 72.

p. 204 'We had a majority'. Edward Ward, *Give Me Air*, p. 127.

p. 204 'had a vitality'. Dallas Lasky, in Daniel G. Dancocks (ed.), *In Enemy Hands*, p. 99.

p. 204 'Our own fellows'. McDowall, p. 202.

p. 205 'posted a notice'. A. Robert Prouse, *Ticket to Hell*, p. 131. See also Vance, pp. 133–4.

p. 205 'The Germans'. Raymond Ryan, in Imelda Ryan (ed.), *POWs Fraternal*, p. 86.

p. 205 The majority. Figures from Dear and Foot, *The Oxford Companion to the Second World War*, p. 565.

p. 205 The Indian Army. Figures from Rudolf Hartog, *The Sign of the Tiger*, p. 66.

p. 206 In order to sort out. Captain H. W. Jones, IWM Papers (File 2).

p. 206 Bob McDowall. McDowall, p. 200.

p. 206 'They wore turbans'. Roger L. Shinn, *Wars and Rumors of Wars*, pp. 55–6.

p. 207 'our NZ chaps'. McDowall, p. 128.

p. 207 'having to see'. Reginald Dexter, IWM, Rolf Collection, p. 21.

p. 207 One Indian who. For Mazumdar see Dr B. N. Mazumdar, IWMSA, and Henry Chancellor, *Colditz*, pp. 207–10.

p. 207 Of the South Africans. Figures from Gleason, p. 195. For the experiences of South African non-European POWs see Gleason and David Killingray, 'Africans and African Americans in Enemy Hands'.

p. 208 'S. A. [South African]'. E. D. Hyland, in Gleason, p. 196.

p. 208 'suffered much'. Dr L. E. Le Souef, IWM Papers, pp. 226–7.

p. 208 Many such prisoners. At the end of the war, D. H. Barber encountered a group of East African prisoners who said they had received reasonable treatment in German camps but had encountered difficulties in communicating with their captors (D. H. Barber, *Africans in Khaki* [London: Edinburgh House Press, 1948], p. 96).

p. 208 The Italians abused. See Killingray, p. 196.

p. 208 Another propaganda. See Gleason, pp. 202–3.

p. 209 'Negroes are not'. Killingray, p. 197.

p. 209 'Quite naturally'. Alexander Jefferson, in Lewis H. Carlson, *We Were Each Other's Prisoners*, p. 57.

p. 209 For most white POWs. For white reactions to black POWs at Stalag Luft III see Westheimer, pp. 253–5, and Kenneth W. Simmons, *Kriegie*, pp. 112–13.

p. 209 'On this march'. Shinn, p. 167.

p. 209 'Strange', he mused. Ibid.

p. 210 'wonderful crowd'. Kenneth Lockwood, Peter Allan, Pat Reid, respectively – all in S. P. Mackenzie, *The Colditz Myth*, p. 281.

p. 210 'The Poles'. B. A. James, IWM Papers/*Moonless Night*, p. 70.

p. 211 Other prisoners. See, for example, Sam Kydd, *For you the war is over*, p. 126, and David Wild, *Prisoner of Hope*, p. 178.

p. 211 'behaved in an exemplary fashion'. John Lord, IWMSA.

p. 211 'seeing the Polish women'. Ibid.

p. 211 'Our little brush'. John Dominy, *The Sergeant Escapers*, pp. 150–51.

p. 211 During the war. Figures from Jonathan F. Vance (ed.), *Encyclopedia of Prisoners of War and Internment*, p. 329.

p. 212 'agreed that'. Howard Greville, *Prison Camp Spies*, p. 23.

p. 212 While visiting. Douglas Thompson, IWMSA transcript, p. 14.

p. 212 'British P/Ws'. PRO WO 208/3274, appx C.

p. 212 'Hundreds were'. Wild, p. 233.

p. 213 'They gave it'. Shinn, p. 119.

p. 213 If they were captured. For German attitudes and behaviour towards Jewish POWs of various nationalities see Szymon Datner, *Crimes Against POWs*, pp. 98–108, and 'The "Special Treatment" of Jewish Prisoners of War'.

p. 213 'We had been told'. Norman Rubenstein, *The Invisibly Wounded*, p. 26.

p. 214 For one group. For the Palestinian Jews see Yoav Gelber, 'Palestinian POWs in German Captivity'.

p. 214 Their pugnacity. See Cyril Rofe, *Against the Wind*, p. 31, and J. M. Green, *From Colditz in Code*, pp. 103–4.

p. 214 One early example. See Gelber, p. 101.

p. 214 'They soon found out'. Rofe, p. 14.

p. 215 'Taking parade'. Dominy, p. 126.

p. 215 'Up at Luft 6'. Frank Paules, in www.b24.net/pow/stalag6 – accessed July 2004.

p. 216 'on two occasions'. Spivey, pp. 77–8.

p. 216 'You didn't have'. Westheimer, p. 200.

p. 216 In the desperate conditions. See Gelber, p. 95.

p. 216 'a number of'. Ike Rosmarin, *Inside Story*, pp. 63, 76.

p. 216 'They even started'. R. P. Evans, IWM Papers, p. 42.

p. 217 'Although we were not'. Green, p. 99.

p. 217 The Palestinian Jews. For help to other Jews, see Gelber, pp. 114, 116–17, 119, 120, 134.

p. 217 'One of the significant'. Green, p. 112.

p. 217 'with his face'. Primo Levi, *If This is a Man and The Truce* (London: Sphere, 1987), p. 75.

p. 217 'In his hands'. Ibid., p. 105.

11: Medical and Spiritual Matters

p. 218 'The day came'. Doug LeFevre, AWM.

p. 219 'We do all'. Bruce Jeffrey, in www.pegasus-one.org/pow/bruce_jeffrey.htm – accessed Sept. 2004.

p. 219 But one medical officer. See Gabe Thomas, *Milag*, pp. 131–2.

p. 220 'became very, very morose'. Douglas Thompson, IWMSA transcript, p. 9.

p. 220 The 120 men. See N. C. Rogers, IWMSA transcript, p. 35.

p. 221 'I was told'. A. L. Cochrane, 'Tuberculosis among Prisoners of War in Germany'.

p. 221 '80 per cent'. Ibid., p. 657.

p. 222 'one patient'. Graham King, letter to *Daily Mail*, n.d.

p. 222 In PG 57. See R. G. McDowall, IWM Papers, p. 137.

p. 222 'a very useful way'. George Moreton, *Doctor in Chains*, p. 138 (Moreton was Jarvis's pen name). See also John Brown, *In Durance Vile*, p. 89 .

p. 222 'It was not'. R. P. Evans, IWM Papers, pp. 48–9.

p. 223 'had been one'. John A. Vietor, *Time Out*, p. 55.

p. 223 'During the performance'. Ibid.

p. 223 'the lack of equipment'. J. M. Green, *From Colditz in Code*, p. 66.

p. 223 'The dentist'. J. H. Witte, IWM Papers, p. 171.

p. 224 'his co-pilot'. Vietor, p. 59.

p. 224 'potent factor'. W. H. Whiles, 'A Study of Neurosis among Repatriated Prisoners of War'.

p. 224 Bilateral exchanges. See Jonathan F. Vance (ed.), *Encyclopedia of Prisoners of War and Internment*, pp. 249–50, and David Rolf, *Prisoners of the Reich*, pp. 191–203.

p. 225 'Within ten minutes'. H. C. F. Harwood, IWM Papers, p. 214.

p. 226 'I was congratulated'. Ibid.

p. 226 'The exquisite pain'. Ibid., p. 238.

p. 226 'The whole scene'. Ibid., p. 254.

p. 226 'The contemplation'. Ibid., p. 268.

p. 227 But in Germany. Figures for padre numbers from, respectively, W. Wynne Mason, *Prisoners of War*, p. 235, Eugene L. Daniel, Jr, *In the Presence of Mine Enemies*, p. 42, and S. P. Mackenzie, *The Colditz Myth*, p. 159.

p. 227 'Feelings were'. H. C. M. Jarvis, 'The Barbed Wire Medico', IWM Papers, p. 492.

p. 227 'they did not neglect'. Green, p. 54.

p. 227 'The minister who stated'. Vietor, p. 146.

p. 227 'It's a mistake'. Cyril Scarborough, IWMSA.

p. 228 'completely indifferent'. PRO WO 224/65, Religious Life at Stalag Luft 6, p. 3.

p. 228 'I'm afraid'. Reginald Dexter, IWM, Rolf Collection.

p. 228 'about thirty per cent'. George Millar, *Horned Pigeon*, pp. 90–1.

p. 228 Center compound. For religious life in Center compound, see Delmar T. Spivey, *POW Odyssey*, pp. 76–8; Daniel, pp. 70–3; and Kenneth W. Simmons, *Kriegie*, pp. 116–18. Simmons claimed 98% of the compound attended Sunday services; this seems far too high, however.

p. 228 'suit men'. David Wild, *Prisoner of Hope*, p. 28.

p. 228 In Stalag IVB. See McDowall, editorial note to p. 266.

p. 229 'to piss the Nazis off'. Quoted in Mitchell G. Bard, *Forgotten Victims*, p. 40.

p. 229 'I shall always'. Harwood, p. 202.

p. 230 'Unlike the Army-run'. Daniel, p. 69; see also V. V. Cooper, IWM Papers, p. 82.

p. 230 In an Italian camp. McDowall, p. 84.

p. 231 'In the armed forces'. Daniel, p. 84.

p. 231 'I came away'. McDowall, p. 57.

p. 231 'These passages'. Ibid., p. 95.

p. 231 'Am full of happiness'. Ibid., p. 79.

p. 232 'Went to the service'. Ibid., p. 83.

p. 232 'I like [their] service'. Ibid., p. 286.

p. 232 'a man who didn't'. M. L. Underhill, in M. A. Tagg, *The Prisoner Padre*, p. 111.

p. 232 'a bit of a dour bastard'. Ivor Hopkins, in ibid.

p. 232 'I admired'. John Tomlinson, in ibid.

p. 232 'He had'. Derrick Hawthorne, in ibid., p. 13.

12: Resistance, Punishment and Collaboration

p. 234 'I handed back'. Kingsley Brown, *Bonds of Wire*, pp. 57–8.

p. 235 'The following day'. Richard Passmore, *Moving Tent*, p. 167.

p. 236 'One day'. A. Robert Prouse, *Ticket to Hell*, p. 81. See also Passmore, pp. 170–1.

p. 236 'four hundred and fifteen'. Peter Tunstall, in Henry Chancellor, *Colditz*, p. 119.

p. 236 'our pleasure'. John A. Vietor, *Time Out*, p. 93.

p. 236 'It became my policy'. Delmar T. Spivey, *POW Odyssey*, p. 36.

p. 237 'The practice'. Calton Younger, *No Flight from the Cage*, p. 50.

p. 237 'To us it was an outlet'. T. D. Calnan, *Free as a Running Fox* (London: Macdonald, 1970), in David Rolf, *Prisoners of the Reich*, p. 159.

p. 237 'Through the Protecting Power'. James E. McGee, IWM, Rolf Collection, p. 17.

p. 238 'we took our small revenges'. Stuart Hood, *Carlino*, p. 8.

p. 238 'The guards loved'. Prouse, p. 105.

p. 238 'Someone had'. W. L. Stephens, IWM Papers, p. 35a.

p. 239 'anything out of nothing'. J. A. G. Deans, IWMSA.

p. 240 Captain Rupert Barry. See Rupert Barry, 'Cooking up a Code', in Reinhold Eggers (comp.), *Colditz Regained*, p. 39. For details of the code, see J. M. Green, *From Colditz in Code*, pp. 161–71, and M. R. D. Foot and J. M. Langley, *MI9*, pp. 110–13, 332–4.

p. 241 The scientist Howard Cundall. See Foot and Langley, p. 176.

p. 241 In work camps. See Howard Greville, *Prison Camp Spies*, pp. 64, 67, 70, 82, 87.

p. 242 Bob Prouse received. Prouse, pp. 95–8.

p. 242 'Graudenz was'. David Hunter, in Chancellor, pp. 253–4. See also PRO FO 916/834.

p. 242 Conditions at Graudenz. See David Wild, *Prisoner of Hope*, pp. 120–25, 184–6, and W. Wynne Mason, *Prisoners of War*, pp. 395–6.

p. 243 'He received'. G. F. W. Wilson, IWM Papers, diary, 8 Aug. 1941.

p. 244 The Germans raised the ante. Figures from Jonathan F. Vance (ed.), *Encyclopedia of Prisoners of War and Internment*, p. 270. See also S. P. Mackenzie, 'The Shackling Crisis'.

p. 245 One informer. For Joyce's story see Oliver Clutton-Brock, *Footprints in the Sands of Time*, pp. 183–5.

p. 246 It would seem. For the threats against Purdy see Chancellor, pp. 284–5. (Purdy was sentenced to hang after the war, but his sentence was commuted to life imprisonment.) See also Green, p. 143.

p. 246 The idea of raising. For the British Free Corps see Adrian Weale, *Renegades*, and Sean Murphy, *Letting the Side Down*, pp. 115–42.

p. 247 Two 'holiday camps'. For the camps and Trott's involvement, see PRO WO 224/93.

p. 247 Another factor. See John Brown, *In Durance Vile*. After the war Brown was awarded a DCM for his secret work. See also Green, p. 106, and Weale, pp. 103–13.

p. 247 'They insulted'. Prouse, p. 125.

p. 248 In 1939 the IRA. For the 'Irish Brigade' see Carolle J. Carter, *The Shamrock and the Swastika*. For attempts to suborn officers see T. C. F. Prittie and W. Earle Edwards, *Escape to Freedom*, pp. 73–6, and for other ranks Roger V. Coward, *Sailors in Cages*, p. 132, and Sam Kydd, *For you the war is over*, p. 139.

p. 248 The genesis of. For Indian collaboration see Milan Hauner, *India in Axis Strategy*, Rudolf Hartog, *The Sign of the Tiger*, and Hugh Toye, *The Springing Tiger*.

p. 249 By February 1943. Figures from Hartog, pp. 65, 66, and Hauner, p. 587.

p. 250 'Without spiritual guidance'. Hauner, p. 589.

13: Escape from Germany

p. 251 Shortly after his arrival. For Stephens's escape see PRO WO 208/3311, SPG 997; W. L. Stephens, IWM Papers, pp. 55–78; and Pat Reid, *The Colditz Story*, pp. 185–220.

p. 251 'These were'. Stephens, p. 57.

p. 253 'This was very unfortunate'. Ibid., p. 73.

p. 253 'I then began'. Ibid.

p. 254 'we saw a bullock cart'. Ibid., p. 78.

p. 255 Many British soldiers. See, for example, Terence Prittie, in T. C. F. Prittie and W. Earle Edwards, *Escape to Freedom*, p. 10.

p. 255 The most ambitious. For the Warburg Wire Job, see PRO WO 208/331, SPGs 974, 975, 976, and Aidan Crawley, *Escape from Germany*, p. 134–5.

p. 256 But the process. For the Franz Josef escape attempt, see Henry Chancellor, *Colditz*, pp. 221–36.

p. 257 A rather different form. For James's escape, see PRO WO 2208/3270 and PRO WO 208/3242, SPG 1834, and David James, *A Prisoner's Progress*.

p. 258 Paddy Byrne. See Sydney Smith, *'Wings' Day*, p. 163.

p. 258 Richard Pape. Richard Pape, *Boldness Be My Friend*, pp. 304–8.

p. 259 'This was one of the safest'. Crawley, p. 12.

p. 259 Of the smaller tunnels. See B. A. James, IWM/*Moonless Night*, pp. 45–52, and Crawley, pp. 112–13.

p. 260 The tunnel breakout. Figures for Eichstätt from M. R. D. Foot and J. M. Langley, *MI9*, p. 246; Schubin figures from Crawley, p. 208. It should be remembered that those involved were not elite troops diverted from the front but reserves already in place.

p. 261 Even in the better-guarded. See A. Robert Prouse, *Ticket to Hell*, pp. 51–65.

p. 262 'with a nose'. Ibid., p. 65.

p. 262 'for one thing'. William Ash, IWMSA.

p. 263 'It broke the monotony'. Cyril Rofe, *Against the Wind*, p. 33.

p. 263 'never could stand'. Ernest de los Santos, in Lewis H. Carlson, *We Were Each Other's Prisoners*, p. 134.

p. 263 'I just had to'. Ibid., p. 135.

p. 263 'To live inside'. George Millar, *Horned Pigeon*, p. 55.

p. 264 Wings Day estimated. See Smith, p. 90.

p. 264 'for some of us'. B. A. James, p. 40.

p. 264 'we might strike'. B. A. James, note to author.

p. 264 'After a short discussion'. B. A. James, IWM/*Moonless Night*, p. 128. See also ibid., pp. 203–4.

p. 265 'I thought and talked'. Terence Prittie, in Prittie and Edwards, p. 218.

p. 265 'afforded tremendous scope'. Ibid., p. 220.

p. 265 'short-tempered'. Ibid.

p. 265 'They became'. Ibid.

p. 266 'All schemes'. Robert Kee, *A Crowd is not Company*, p. 77.

p. 266 'The official line'. Richard Passmore, *Moving Tent*, p. 139.

p. 267 'The Escape'. PRO WO 208/3283, pt 2, p. 17.

p. 267 'agreed to take'. PRO WO 208/3274, p. 3.

p. 268 'I consider'. R. L. Davies, PRO WO 208/3274, appx. A/C, p. 2.

p. 268 'our own escape committee'. James Branford, PRO WO 208/3274, appx D, p. 7.

p. 268 'An impudent scheme'. PRO WO 208/3242, p. 77.

p. 268 Of the parcels sent. Figures from Foot and Langley, p. 110.

p. 268 As well as. Figures from PRO WO 208/3242, p. 90.

p. 269 'a man of forceful personality'. B. A. James, IWM/*Moonless Night*, p. 43. For the Great Escape, see Paul Brickhill, *The Great Escape*, Jonathan F. Vance, *A Gallant Company*, and James, pp. 98–106.

p. 272 'Attempts to escape'. John A. Vietor, *Time Out*, pp. 114–15.

p. 272 'The great moment'. Bill Edwards, in Prittie and Edwards, p. 267.

p. 273 'As we lay there'. Cyril Rofe, in Foot and Langley, p. 26.

p. 273 'never known'. Kingsley Brown, *Bonds of Wire*, p. 65.

p. 273 According to MI9. Figures from PRO WO 208/3242, p. 79.

p. 273 'far more agile'. Terence Prittie, in Prittie and Edwards, p. 8.

p. 274 'Too many Germans'. Ibid., p. 164.

p. 274 If escapers were. For Grimson's story, see John Dominy, *The Sergeant Escapers*, and Crawley, pp. 281–97. See also PRO WO 208/3242, SPG 1833.

p. 275 'Dressed as a ferret'. Calton Younger, *No Flight from the Cage*, pp. 65–6.

14: An Italian Adventure

p. 279 The Italian War Ministry. Figures from Roger Absalom, *A Strange Alliance*, p. 23. Absalom's detailed study of Allied POWs on the run considers both Italian and Allied viewpoints.

p. 279 This was certainly. Figures from Absalom, p. 28.

p. 279 'guarded with much greater care'. PRO WO 208/342, p. 80. See also Adrian Carton de Wiart, *Happy Odyssey*, pp. 198, 205.

p. 279 'as sharp as a needle'. James Hargest, *Farewell Campo 12*, p. 69.

p. 279 'fascinated by minutiae'. Eric Newby, *Love and War in the Apennines*, p. 31.

p. 280 'fool even the most myopic'. Ibid.

p. 280 'Italian foreman'. George Millar, *Horned Pigeon*, p. 103.

p. 280 'anyone as scruffy'. N. C. Rogers, IWMSA transcript, p. 48.

p. 280 The most memorable. For the escape, see PRO WO 208/3242, appx J (SPG 1587); Hargest, pp. 102–30; Carton de Wiart, pp. 207–24.

p. 280 'some broken'. Carton de Wiart, p. 208.

p. 281 'Some weeks'. Hargest, p. 101.

p. 281 'By a queer chance'. Ibid., p. 114.

p. 281 'It was a tremendous experience'. Ibid., p. 118.

p. 282 It is believed that the commander. See M. R. D. Foot and J. M. Langley, *MI9*, pp. 156–7. No documentary evidence is given, however, that Montgomery initiated the 'Stay Put' order.

p. 282 The view expressed. Ibid., p. 158.

p. 282 As early as 7 June. See Richard Lamb, *War in Italy*, p. 160.

p. 283 'In the event of'. Quoted in Absalom, p. 27.

p. 283 While Crockatt insisted. See Foot and Langley, pp. 158–65, and Lamb, pp. 161–3.

p. 284 'only a captain'. PRO WO 224/106. See also Millar, pp. 141–52.

p. 285 The inactivity of the Sulmona prisoners. See Foot and Langley, p. 162.

p. 285 The Anglo-American officers' camp. See PRO WO 208/3343; David Westheimer, *Sitting it Out*, pp. 112–18; Joseph S. Frelinghuysen, *Passages to Freedom*, pp. 92–119; and John Verney, *A Dinner of Herbs*, pp. 61–112. So fierce were the accusations directed against Marshall that he faced a post-war court of inquiry. Although exonerated – he had, after all, only been following orders – the bitterness remained. Marshall's failure was to blindly follow an order when circumstances had radically changed.

p. 286 'At Vasco'. Verney, p. 103.

p. 286 In the officers' camp of PG 47. See Absalom, pp. 28–30.

p. 287 In one camp. For the walkout from PG 49, see Newby, pp. 47–55; Stuart Hood, *Carlino*, pp. 7–16; Ian English (ed.), *Home by Christmas?*; Absalom, pp. 127–9; Malcolm Tudor, *British Prisoners of War In Italy*, pp. 33–43.

p. 287 At PG 120/1. Absalom, p. 100.

p. 287 Whatever the consequences. All figures from Absalom, pp. 11–36. (The overall Allied total of just under 80,000 POWs in Italy included Yugoslavs, Free French and Greeks as well as Anglo-Americans.)

p. 288 'Five meant'. Ian English, *Home by Christmas?*, p. 45.

p. 288 'comic-opera types'. Rogers, p. 52.

p. 288 'changed my view'. Ibid.

p. 289 Bacciagaluppi's organization. See Absalom, p. 40.

p. 289 Sergeant Edgar Triffett. See PRO WO 208/4273, and Absalom, pp. 56–8.

p. 290 The most formidable. For John Peck, see PRO WO 208/4265; J. D. Peck, IWMSA; Bill Bunbury, *Rabbits and Spaghetti*; Absalom, pp. 49–56.

p. 290 'I had pangs'. J. D. Peck, in Bunbury, p. 127.

p. 291 'The risks were enormous'. Ibid., p. 155.

p. 292 'The guards ran'. J. D. Peck, PRO WO 208/4265.

p. 292 Lance Corporal Doug LeFevre. For LeFevre's escape see Douglas LeFevre, AWM, and Bunbury, pp. 135–43.

p. 292 'Norm had a shooting jacket'. LeFevre.

p. 293 'I was 6 foot 4 inches'. Graham Shepherd, in D. D. Brown, 'Hope Deferred'.

p. 293 'We were dependent'. LeFevre.

p. 293 'Attention! Citizens'. Ibid.

p. 294 'burnt the village down'. Douglas LeFevre, in Bunbury, p. 136.

p. 294 'No one had bothered'. LeFevre.

p. 294 Another successful escape organization. See Sam Derry, *The Rome Escape Line*; Absalom, pp. 277–303; and Foot and Langley, pp. 165–70.

p. 295 In all, nearly 4,000. Figures from Derry, p. 228.

p. 296 So too did Australian sapper. For Jocumsen, see Absalom, p. 61.

p. 296 'Just a line'. Quoted in Roger Absalom, ' "Another crack at Jerry"?'.

15 : Migration and Liberation

p. 297 'The first news'. Milt Felsen, *The Anti-Warrior*, p. 213.

p. 297 On 19 February 1945. See Szymon Datner, *Crimes Against POWs*, pp. 365–7.

p. 298 'It is noticeable'. Raymond Ryan, in Imelda Ryan, *POWs Fraternal*, p. 132.

p. 299 'No wonder'. A. Robert Prouse, *Ticket to Hell*, p. 133.

p. 299 'went to work'. J. H. Witte, note to author. For an account of the Dresden raid from a POW perspective see Louis G. Grivetti, in Lewis H. Carlson, *We Were Each Other's Prisoners*, pp. 116–19, and Kurt Vonnegut's novel *Slaughterhouse-Five* (London: Jonathan Cape, 1970).

p. 299 'Half way to the fields'. Witte.

p. 301 'We walked on'. Roger L. Shinn, *Wars and Rumors of Wars*, pp. 96–7.

p. 302 'was very tired'. Delmar T. Spivey, *POW Odyssey*, p. 126.

p. 302 It was at Spremberg. See ibid., pp. 131–74.

p. 304 'I sat in silent solitude'. Joseph P. O'Donnell, *The Shoe Leather Express,* vol. 1, p. 35.

p. 305 On 3 April. B. A. James, IWM Papers/*Moonless Night*, pp. 163–97.

p. 306 'whole village relaxed'. Ibid., p. 191.

p. 306 'all my experiences'. Odette Hallowes, IWMSA transcript, p. 23.

p. 306 'I saw a girl'. Ibid.

p. 307 'And this is Fritz Sühren'. Odette Churchill, in Jerrard Tickell, *Odette*, p. 284.

p. 307 'A tank started rolling'. Shinn, p. 138.

p. 308 'We gave greetings'. Ibid., p. 176.

p. 309 'We hurried off'. J. H. Witte, IWM Papers, p. 208.

p. 309 'It was a mad beehive'. Prouse, p. 141.

p. 309 'The prisoners held their ground'. Ibid., p. 148.

p. 310 'The rest of the evening'. John A. Vietor, *Time Out*, p. 179–80.

p. 311 'Four Cossacks'. R. D. McDowall, IWM Papers, p. 493.

p. 311 'We said goodbye'. Ibid., p. 495.

p. 312 'organized parties'. A. J. East, IWM Papers, p. 87.

p. 312 'There is no real hatred'. McDowall, p. 495.

p. 313 'We began rounding up'. Prouse, p. 148.

p. 313 'As I watched them'. Adrian Vincent, *The Long Road Home*, quoted in David Rolf, *Prisoners of the Reich*, p. 251.

p. 313 'We told them'. John D. White, in Robin Neillands, *The Conquest of the Reich: D-Day to VE-Day – A Soldier's History* (London: Weidenfeld & Nicolson, 1995), p. 249.

p. 313 'The Hauptmann'. E. C. Stirling, IWM Papers, pp. 86–7.

16: Homecoming

p. 316 'The women's voices'. Raymond Ryan, in Imelda Ryan, *POWs Fraternal*, p. 141.

p. 316 'I was definitely not'. H. C. F. Harwood, IWM Papers, p. 300.

p. 316 'It was not the same'. Ibid., p. 302.

p. 317 'staffed by the British'. J. H. Witte, IWM Papers, p. 217.

p. 317 'No one said anything'. Ibid., p. 221.

p. 317 'get readjusted'. R. G. McDowall, letter home, in M. A. Tagg, *The Prisoner Padre*, p. 129.

p. 317 'It is beginning'. Ibid.

p. 318 'until I could regain'. A Robert Prouse, *Ticket to Hell*, p. 159.

p. 318 'the British people'. W. Wynne Mason, *Prisoners of War*, p. 502.

p. 318 'It was VE Day'. Prouse, pp. 160–61.

p. 318 'On July 14'. Ibid., p. 161.

p. 318 'The following morning'. John A. Vietor, *Time Out*, p. 190.

p. 319 'We got new clothes'. Roger L. Shinn, *Wars and Rumors of Wars*, pp. 180–81.

p. 319 'There was a brass band'. Vietor, p. 192.

p. 320 'I suppose'. W. P. Wood, in David Rolf, *Prisoners of the Reich*, pp. 279–80.

p. 321 Some men resented. For POW irritation at official views on their supposedly fragile mental condition, see Harwood, p. 207, and René Cutforth, *The Listener*, 19 Dec. 1968, p. 810, in S. P. Mackenzie, *The Colditz Myth*, pp. 395–6.

p. 321 A psychiatric study. See Brian Engdahl, Thomas N. Dikel, Raina Eberly and Arthur Blank Jr, 'Posttraumatic Stress Disorder in a Community Sample of Former Prisoners of War'.

p. 322 'Every POW'. Leslie Caplan, in Stan Sommers, *American Ex-Prisoners of war, Inc., National Medical Research Committee, The European Story, Packet No. 8*, p. 33, quoted in Lewis H. Carlson, *We Were Each Other's Prisoners*, p. 235.

p. 322 'everything that has happened'. Robert Kee, *A Crowd is Not Company*, p. 9 (introduction to second edition).

p. 322 'My adventure'. Shinn, p. 181.

p. 322 'It made me realize'. W. Davies, IWMSA transcript, p. 27.

p. 323 'Captivity', he said. J. H. Witte, conversation with author.

p. 323 'moulded me'. J. Roberts, *A Terrier Goes to War*, p. 171.

p. 323 'I think this experience'. Clifford Fox, in Carlson, p. 249.

p. 323 'Any regrets?'. J. M. Green, *From Colditz in Code*, p. 159.

Postscript

p. 324 'Curiously enough'. H. C. F. Harwood, IWM Papers, p. 299.

p. 324 'a tidy old sum'. J. H. Witte, note to author.

p. 324 'all was not gloom'. Ibid.

p. 325 'went away'. Doug LeFevre, AWM.

p. 326 'You've got to'. Odette Hallowes, IWMSA transcript, p. 26.

p. 327 'was very aware'. Marc Vietor, note to author.

Bibliography

ABBREVIATIONS

AWM = Australian War Memorial
IWM = Imperial War Museum (Dept of Documents)
IWMSA = Imperial War Museum Sound Archive
SWWEC = Second World War Experience Centre (Leeds)

OFFICIAL DOCUMENTS

National Archives (Public Record Office)
AIR 40
FO 3711, 916, 1038
WO 32, 208, 224

UNPUBLISHED ACCOUNTS

Written Material

Arct, B. (IWM, 88/58/1); Ayling, E. (IWM, 78/35/1); Azios, A. D. (letter to author); Barfield, B. O. (IWM, 97/6/1); Carstens, A. A. (IWM, 03/10/1); Carter, G. H. F. (IWM, 96/41/1); Cooper, V. V. (IWM, 02/51/1); Dexter, R. (IWM, Rolf Collection); Dexter, W. (SWWEC); Dunford, R. C. (IWM, 86/25/1); East, A. J. (IWM, 87/35/1); Evans, R. P. (IWM, 90/18/1); Flekser, N. (IWM, 98/82/1); Foskett, L. (www.pegasus-one.org/pow/les_foskett .htm); Glass, J. (IWM, 95/30/1); Goodliffe, M. (www.mgoodliffe.co.uk); Hall, G. (IWM, PP/MCR/340); Hall, R. (SWWEC); Harwood, H. C. F. (IWM, 84/33/1); Hewitt J. D. (IWM, 86/35/1); Howard, A. C. (IWM, 88/5/1); James, B. A. (IWM, PP/MCR/255); Jarvis, H. C. M. (IWM, 89/34/2); Jeffrey, B. (www.pegasus-one.org/pow/bruce_jeffrey.htm); Jones,

H. W. (IWM, 67/325/1–2); Krebs, B. (www.b24.net/pow/stalag4.htm); Le Souef, L. E. (IWM, PP/MCR/10); McDowall, R. G. (IWM, 98/29/1); McGee, J. E. (IWM, Rolf Collection); Macey, H. (IWM, Rolf Collection); Martin, H. L. (IWM, 97/4/1); Masters, S. C. (IWM, PP/MCR/305); Munby, A. N. L. (IWM, 87/25/1); Oflag 64 Prisoner of War Camp (www.rlc.dccd.edu/enrich/cordstud/oflag_64.htm); Paules, F. (www.b24 .net/pow/stalag6.htm); Platt, J. E. (IWM, 84/23/1); Reeves, R. D. ('Peoria to Munich' – www.1p-net.com/pow/html); Smithson, D. (www.pegasus-one.org/pow/douglas_smithson.htm); Stephens, W. L. (IWM, 86/7/1); Stirling, E. C. (IWM, 99/22/1); Sugarman, M. ('Jewish POWs at Colditz' – www.jewishvirtuallibrary.org/jsource/ww2/ sugar6.html); Swinney, D. (SWWEC); Tagg, M. A., *The Prisoner Padre: The Impact of War on a New Zealand Cleric* (MA thesis, University of Waikato, 1997); Wadley, P. L.('Even One is Too Many' – www.aiipowmia.com/research/wadley.html); Weiner, H. P. (IWM, 97/15/1); Whitcombe, A. C. (IWM, 67/37/1); White, R. (www.pegasus-one.org/pow/rishel_white.htm); Wilson, G. F. W. (IWM, 81/6/1); Witte, J. H. (IWM, 87/12/1, and letters to author); Wood, R. (IWM, 90/33/1A).

Interviews, Oral Histories

Abbot, G. (IWMSA, 4843); Ash, W. (IWMSA, 10202); Beeson, W. (IWMSA, 4802); Buckley, P. (IWMSA, 4759); Burton, H. (IWMSA, 4668); Cadden, G. (IWMSA, 4643); Davies, W. (IWMSA, 6128); Deans, J. (IWMSA, 6142); Falconer, E. (IWMSA, 4667); Fennell, S. (IWMSA, 4895); Franklin, I. (IWMSA, 7052); Frost, T. (IWMSA, 961); Goodson, J. (IWMSA, 11623); Hall, E. (IWMSA, 6075); Harding, W. (IWMSA, 6323); Hargreaves, E. C. S. (IWMSA, 5378); Hope, S. (SWWEC); Howard, A. C. (author interview); James, B. (IWMSA, 4987); Jenner, A. (www.merkki.com/speeches.htm); Kitchen, H. (IWMSA, 4628); LeFevre, D. (AWM, S00517); Loffman, P (AWM, S557); Lord, J. (IWMSA, 765); Mazumdar, B. (IWMSA, 16800); Norris, E. (IWMSA, 4639); O'Neill, W (author interview); Pals, L. (IWMSA, 4642); Peck, J. D. (IWMSA, 16667); Peel, P. (SWWEC); Ramelson, B. (IWMSA, 6705); Rogers, N. C. (IWMSA, 4755); Sansom, O. (IWMSA, 9478); Scarborough, C. (IWMSA, 4820); Stovroff, I. (www. merkki.com/speeches.htm); Thompson, D. (IWMSA, 4650); Toombs, A. (IWMSA, 10725); Witte, J. H. (author interview); Worsely, J. (IWMSA, 3173).

PUBLISHED MEMOIRS, DIARIES AND OTHER FIRST-HAND ACCOUNTS

Arct, B., *Prisoner of War – My Secret Journal* (Exeter: Webb & Bower, 1988)

Beattie, Edward W., Jr, *Diary of a Kriegie* (New York: Thomas Y. Cromwell, 1946)

Billany, Dan, and Dowie, David, *The Cage* (London: Longmans, 1949)

Bird, Tom (ed.), *American POWs of World War II: Forgotten Men Tell Their Stories* (Westport, Conn.: Praeger, 1992)

Blythe, Ronald (ed.), *Private Words: Letters and Diaries from the Second World War* (London: Viking, 1991)

Borrie, John, *Despite Captivity: A Doctor's Life as a Prisoner of War* (London: William Kimber, 1975)

Brickhill, Paul, *The Great Escape* (London: Cassell, 2000)

Brown, John, *In Durance Vile* (London: Robert Hale, 1981)

Brown, Kingsley, *Bonds of Wire: A Memoir* (Toronto: Collins, 1989)

Carton de Wiart, Adrian, *Happy Odyssey* (London: Jonathan Cape, 1950)

Churchill, Peter, *The Spirit in the Cage* (London: Hodder & Stoughton, 1954)

Coward, Roger V., *Sailors in Cages* (London: Macdonald, 1967)

Dalton Hight, Rae (ed.), *Voices of World War II Veterans* (Port Orchard, Washington: Mox-Sun-Ray Publishing, 2004)

Dancocks, Daniel G. (ed.), *In Enemy Hands: Canadian Prisoners of War, 1939–45* (Edmonton, Alberta: Hurtig Publishers, 1983)

Davis, George J., *The Hitler Diet, as Inflicted on American POWs in World War II* (Los Angeles: Military Literary Guild, 1990)

Derry, Sam, *The Rome Escape Line: The Story of the British Organisation in Rome for Assisting Escaped Prisoners of War* (London: Harrap, 1960)

Diggs, J. Frank, *Americans behind Barbed Wire* (New York: ibooks, 2003)

Dominy, John, *The Sergeant Escapers* (London: Coronet, 1976)

Duggan, Margaret (ed.), *Padre in Colditz* (London: Hodder & Stoughton, 1978)

Duke, Florimund, and Swaart, Charles M., *Name, Rank, and Serial Number* (New York: Meredith, 1969)

Eggers, Reinhold, *Colditz: The German Side of the Story* (New York: W. W. Norton, 1961)

—— (comp.), *Colditz Regained* (London: Robert Hale, 1973)

Evans, Arthur, *Sojourn in Silesia* (Ashford, Kent: Ashford Writers, 1995)

Examinations in Prisoner of War Camps (booklet)

Felsen, Milt, *The Anti-Warrior: A Memoir* (Iowa City: University of Iowa Press, 1989)

Frelinghuysen, Joseph S., *Passages to Freedom: A Story of Capture and Escape* (Manhattan, Kan.: Sunflower University Press, 1990)

Green, J. M., *From Colditz in Code* (London: Robert Hale, 1971)

Greville, Howard, *Prison Camp Spies: Espionage behind the Wire* (Loftus, NSW: AMHP, 1998)

Haig, Dawyck, *My Father's Son* (Barnsley: Leo Cooper, 2000)

Hargest, James, *Farewell Campo 12* (London: Michael Joseph, 1945)

Hood, Stuart, *Carlino* (Manchester: Carcanet Press, 1985; first published as *Pebbles from My Skull*, London Hutchinson, 1963)

Hutching, Megan (ed.), *Inside Stories: New Zealand Prisoners of War Remember* (Auckland: HarperCollins, 2002)

James, B. A., *Moonless Night* (Barnsley: Leo Cooper/Pen and Sword, 2001)

James, David, *A Prisoner's Progress* (Edinburgh: William Blackwood, 1947)

Junod, Marcel, *Warrior Without Weapons* (London: Jonathan Cape, 1951)

Kee, Robert, *A Crowd is Not Company* (London: Sphere, 1989)

Kydd, Sam, *For you the war is over . . .* (London: Bachman & Turner, 1973)

McKibbin, M. N. (ed.), *Barbed Wire: Memories of Stalag 383* (London: Staples Press, 1947)

Mander, d'A, *Mander's March on Rome* (Gloucester: Alan Sutton, 1987)

Millar, George, *Horned Pigeon* (London: Heinemann, 1946)

Moreton, George, *Doctor in Chains*, (London: Howard Barker, 1970)

Neave, Airey, *Saturday at MI9* (London: Coronet, 1971)

—— *They Have their Exits* (London: Coronet, 1970)

Newby, Eric, *Love and War in the Apennines* (London: Picador, 1983)

Oates, Lynette, with Ian Sproule, *Australian Partisan: A True Story of Love and Conflict* (Loftus, NSW: AMHP, 1997)

Pape, Richard, *Boldness Be My Friend* (London: Elek, 1953)

Passmore, Richard, *Moving Tent* (London: Thomas Harmsworth, 1982)

Prittie, T. C. F., and Edwards, W. Earle, *Escape to Freedom* (London: Hutchinson, 1953; first published as *South to Freedom*, London: Hutchinson, 1946)

Prouse, A. Robert, *Ticket to Hell via Dieppe: From a Prisoner's Wartime Log 1942–1945* (Exeter: Webb & Bower, 1982)

Pryce, J. E., *Heels in Line* (London: Arthur Barker, 1958)

Ramsay, Ian, *P.O.W.: A Digger in Hitler's Prison Camps 1941–45* (Melbourne: Macmillan, 1985)

Reid, P. R., *The Colditz Story* (London: Coronet, 1962)

Roberts, J., *A Terrier Goes to War* (London: Minerva 1998)

Rofe, Cyril, *Against the Wind* (London: Hodder & Stoughton, 1956)

Romilly, Giles, and Alexander, Michael, *The Privileged Nightmare* (London: Weidenfeld & Nicolson, 1954)

Rosmarin, Ike, *Inside Story* (Cape Town: Flesch, 1990)

Royal Air Force School for POWs, Stalag Luft VI, Germany, prospectuses, 1944, 1945 (Red Cross and St John War Organisation, 1944, 1945)

Rubenstein, Norman, *The Invisibly Wounded* (Hull: The Glenvil Group, 1989)

Ryan, Imelda (ed.), *POWs Fraternal: Diaries of S/Sgt Raymond Ryan* (Perth, WA: Hawthorn Press, 1990)

Salvi, R. G., *Whom Enemies Sheltered: A Saga of Human Love in the Midst of World War II* (Bombay: Bharatiya Vidya Bhavan, 1983)

Sampson, Francis L., *Paratrooper Padre* (Washington, DC: Catholic University of America Press, 1948)

Shinn, Roger L., *Wars and Rumors of Wars* (Nashville, Tenn: Abingdon Press, 1972)

Simmons, Kenneth W., *Kriegie* (New York: Thomas Nelson, 1960)

Spiller, Harry (ed.), *Prisoners of the Nazis* (Jefferson, NC: McFarland, 1997)

Stone, James F., *A Holiday in Hitlerland* (New York: Carlton Press, 1970)

Strachan, Tony (ed.), *In the Clutch of Circumstance: Reminiscences of Members of the Canadian National Prisoners of War Association* (Victoria, BC: Cappis Press, 1985)

Swallow, Tom; Pill, Arthur H.; et al, *Flywheel: Memories of the Open Road* (Waltham Abbey, Essex: Fraser Stewart Books, 1987)

Taylor, Assheton F., *One Way Flight to Munich* (Loftus, NSW: AMHP, 1998)

Tudor, Malcolm, *British Prisoners of War in Italy: Paths to Freedom* (Newtown, Powys: Emilia Publishing, 2000)

—— *Escape From Italy, 1943–45* (Newtown, Powys: Emilia Publishing, 2003)

Verney, John, *A Dinner of Herbs* (London: Collins, 1966)

Vietor, John A., *Time Out: American Airmen at Stalag Luft I* (Fallbrook, Cal.: Aero Publishers, n.d.; first published New York: R. R. Smith, 1951)

Vining, Donald (ed.), *American Diaries of World War II* (New York: Pepys Press, 1982)

Ward, Edward, *Give Me Air* (London: Bodley Head, 1946)

Westheimer, David, *Sitting it Out: A World War II POW Memoir* (Houston, Tex: Rice University Press, 1992)

Wild, David, *Prisoner of Hope* (Lewes, Sussex: The Book Guild, 1992)

Wood, J. E. R., *Detour: The Story of Oflag IVC* (London: Falconer Press, 1946)

Younger, Calton, *No Flight from the Cage* (London: Star Books, 1981)

Zemke, Hubert, as told to Roger A. Freeman, *Zemke's Stalag: The Final Days of World War II* (Shrewsbury: Airlife, 1991)

SELF-PUBLISHED WORKS

Beckwith, E. G. C. (ed.), *The Mansell Diaries* (1977)

English, Ian, *Assisted Passage: Walking to Freedom Italy 1943* (1994)

—— (ed.), *Home by Christmas?* (1997)

Daniel, Eugene L., Jr, *In the Presence of Mine Enemies: An American Chaplain in World War II German Prison Camps* (Attleboro, Mass.: 1985)

Howard, Anthony, *'Mein Gefangenschaft'* (n.d.)

Lett, Gordon, *Rossano (An Adventure of the Italian Resistance)* (Hugh Brian Gordon Lett, 2001; first published London: Hodder & Stoughton, 1955)

O'Donnell, Joseph, *The Shoe Leather Express* (3 vols.: n.d., 1986, 1989)

Spivey, Delmar T., *POW Odyssey: Recollections of Center Compound Stalag Luft III and the Secret German Peace Mission in World War II* (Attleboro, Mass.: 1984)

SECONDARY SOURCES

Absalom, Roger, *A Strange Alliance: Aspects of Escape and Survival in Italy 1943–45* (Firenze: Leo S. Olschki Editore, 1991)

Bard, Mitchell G., *Forgotten Victims: The Abandonment of Americans in Hitler's Camps* (Boulder, Colo.: Westview Press, 1994)

Barker, A. J., *Behind Barbed Wire* (London: B. T. Batsford, 1974)

Bunbury, Bill, *Rabbits and Spaghetti: Captives and Comrades: Australians, Italians and the War* (Freemantle, WA: Freemantle Arts Press, 1995)

Burgess, Colin, *Destination Buchenwald* (Kenthurst, NSW: Kangaroo Press, 1995)

Cambray, P. G., and Briggs, G. G. B. (comps.), *Red Cross and St. John War Organisation 1939–1947* (London: Red Cross, 1949)

Carlson, Lewis H., *We Were Each Other's Prisoners: An Oral History of World War II American and German Prisoners of War* (New York: Basic Books, 1997)

Carter, Carolle J., *The Shamrock and the Swastika: German Espionage in Ireland in World War II* (Palo Alto, Cal.: Pacific Books, 1977)

Chancellor, Henry, *Colditz: The Definitive History* (London: Hodder & Stoughton, 2001)

Clarke, Hugh, Burgess, Colin, and Russell, Braddon, *Prisoners of War* (North Sydney, NSW: John Ferguson/Time-Life, 1988)

Clutton-Brock, Oliver, *Footprints in the Sands of Time: RAF Bomber Command POWs:* (London: Grubb Street, 2003)

Crawley, Aidan, *Escape From Germany* (London: HMSO, 1985)

Datner, Szymon, *Crimes Against POWs: Responsibility of the Wehrmacht* (Warsaw: Zachodnia Agencja Prasowa, 1964)

Dear, Ian, *Escape and Evasion: POW Breakouts in World War Two* (London: Cassell, 2000)

—— and Foot, M. R. D. (eds.), *The Oxford Companion to the Second World War* (Oxford: Oxford University Press, 1995)

Doyle, Robert C., *A Prisoner's Duty: Great Escapes in US Military History* (New York: Bantam Books, 1999)

—— *Voices from Captivity: Interpreting the American POW Narrative* (Lawrence, Kan.: Kansas University Press, 1994)

Durand, Arthur A., *Stalag Luft III: The Secret Story* (Wellingborough: Patrick Stephens, 1989)

Edge, Spence, and Henderson, Jim, *No Honour, No Glory* (Auckland: Collins, 1983)

Foot, M. R. D., and Langley, J. M., *MI9: The British Secret Service That Fostered Escape and Evasion 1939–1945 and its American Counterpart* (London: Bodley Head, 1979)

Foy, David A., *For You the War is Over: American Prisoners of War in Nazi Germany* (New York: Stein & Day, 1984)

Garrett, Richard, *P.O.W.: The Uncivil Face of War* (Newton Abbot: David & Charles, 1988)

Gleason, Ian, *The Unknown Force: Black, Indian and Colored Soldiers through the Two World Wars* (Rivonia, Johannesburg: Ashanti Publishing, 1994)

Hartog, Rudolf, *The Sign of the Tiger: Subhas Chandra Bose and his Indian Legion in Germany 1941–45* (New Delhi: Rupa & Co., 2001)

Hauner, Milan, *India in Axis Strategy* (Stuttgart: Klett-Cotta, 1981)

Holland, Robert W. (comp./ed.), *Adversis Major: A Short History of the Educational Books Scheme* (London: Staples Press/British Red Cross, 1949)

Hynes, Samuel, *The Soldiers' Tale: Bearing Witness to Modern War* (London: Pimlico, 1998)

Lamb, Richard, *War In Italy 1943–1945: A Brutal Story* (London: John Murray, 1993)

Longden, Sean, *To the Victor the Spoils: D-Day to VE Day, The Reality behind the Heroism* (Moreton in the Marsh, Glos.: Arris Publishing, 2004)

MacKenzie, S. P., *The Colditz Myth: British and Commonwealth Prisoners of War in Nazi Germany* (Oxford: Oxford University Press, 2004)

Mason, W. Wynne, *Prisoners of War* (Wellington, NZ: War History Branch, Dept of Internal Affairs, 1954)

Maughan, Barton, *Tobruk and El Alamein: Australia in the War 1939–45* (Canberra: Australian War Memorial, 1966)

Moore, Bob, and Fedorowich, Kent (eds.), *Prisoners of War and their Captors in World War II* (Oxford: Berg, 1996)

Murphy, Sean, *Letting the Side Down: British Traitors of the Second World War* (Stroud, Glos.: Sutton Publishing, 2003)

Nichol, John, and Rennell, Tony, *The Last Escape: The Untold Story of Allied Prisoners of War in Germany 1944–45* (London: Penguin, 2003)

Prisoners of War: Armies and Other Land Forces of the British Empire 1939–1945 (Suffolk: J. B. Hayward & Son/IWM, 1990; first published London: HMSO, 1945)

Prisoners of War: British Army 1939–1945 (Suffolk: J. B. Hayward & Son/IWM, 1990; first published London: HMSO, 1945)

Prisoners of War: Naval and Air Forces of Great Britain and the Empire 1939–1945 (Suffolk: J. B. Hayward & Son/IWM, 1990; first published London: HMSO, 1945)

Reid, Pat, and Michael, Maurice, *Prisoners of War* (London: Chancellor Press, 2000)

Rolf, David, *Prisoners of the Reich: Germany's Captives 1939–1945* (London: Coronet, 1989)

Shoemaker, Lloyd R., *The Story of MIS-X, the Super-Secret US Agency behind World War II's Greatest Escapes* (New York: St Martin's Press, 1990)

Smith, Sydney, *'Wings' Day: The Man Who Led the RAF's Epic Battle in German Captivity* (London: Pan, 1970)

Somerville, Christopher, *Our War* (London: Weidenfield & Nicolson, 1998)

Thomas, Gabe, *Milag: Captives of the Kriegsmarine, Merchant Navy Prisoners of War 1939–45* (Alltwen, West Glamorgan: Milag Prisoner of War Association, n.d.)

Tickell, Jerrard, *Odette: The Story of a British Secret Agent* (London: Pan, 1955)

Toliver, Raymond F., *The Interrogator: The Story of Hans Scharff, Luftwaffe's Master Interrogator* (Fallbrook, Cal.: Aero Publishers, 1978)

Toye, Hugh, *The Springing Tiger: Subash Chandra Bose* (Bombay: Jaico Publishing, 1959)

Underhill, M. L., et al, *New Zealand Chaplains in the Second World War* (Wellington, NZ: War History Branch, Dept of Internal Affairs, 1950)

Vance, Jonathan F., *A Gallant Company: The Men of the Great Escape* (Pacifica, Cal.: Pacifica Press, 2001)

—— *Objects of Concern: Canadian Prisoners of War through the Twentieth Century* (Vancouver: UBC Press, 1994)

—— (ed.), *Encyclopedia of Prisoners of War and Internment* (Santa Barbara, Cal.: ABC-Clio, 2000)

Voukoutiotis, Vasilis, *Prisoners of War and the German High Command: The British and American Experience* (London and Basingstoke: Palgrave Macmillan, 2003)

Warren, C. E. T., and Benson, James, *The Broken Column: The Story of James Frederick Wilde's Adventures with the Italian Partisans* (London: Harrap, 1966)

Weale, Adrian, *Renegades: Hitler's Englishmen* (London: Pimlico, 2002)

ARTICLES

Absalom, Roger, '"Another crack at Jerry"? Australian Prisoners of War in Italy 1941–45', *Journal of the Australian War Memorial*, no. 14 (Apr. 1989)

—— 'The *Contadini* in Occupied Italy 1943–1945 and Prisoners on the Run', *Everyman's War*, no. 8 (winter 2003)

Alderton, E., 'Superior to Adversity', *Jack O'London's Weekly*, 1 June 1945

Brown, D. D., 'Hope Deferred: A Story of the Italian Armistice: 8 September 1943', *South African Military History Society Journal*, vol. 8, no. 3 (June 1990) – posted on www.samilitaryhistory.org – accessed Apr. 2005

Cochrane, A. L., 'Tuberculosis among Prisoners of War in Germany', *British Medical Journal*, 10 Nov. 1945

Connelly, Mark, and Miller, Walter, 'The BEF and the Issue of Surrender on the Western Front in 1940', *War in History*, vol. 11, no. 4 (Nov. 2004)

Davis, Gerald H., 'Prisoners of War in Twentieth-Century War Economies', *Journal of Contemporary History*, vol. 12, no. 4, (Oct. 1977)

Daymond, Emily, 'Music in Prisoner of War Camps', *R.C.M. Magazine*, vol. 41 (summer 1945)

Draper, Theodore, 'The Psychology of Surrender', *Infantry Journal*, vol. 57, no. 4 (Oct. 1945)

Engdahl, Brian, Dikel, Thomas N., Eberly, Raina, and Blank, Arthur, Jr., 'Posttraumatic Stress Disorder in a Community Sample of Former Prisoners of War: A Normative Response to Severe Trauma', *American Journal of Psychiatry*, 154(11) (1997), – posted on www.trauma-pages.com – accessed Apr. 2004

Ferguson, Niall, 'Prisoner Taking and Prisoner Killing in the Age of Total War: Towards a Political Economy of Military Defeat' *War in History*, vol. 11, no. 2 (Apr. 2004)

Gelber, Yoav, 'Palestinian POWs in German Captivity', *Yad Vashem Studies*, vol. 14 (1981)

Killingray, David, 'Africans and African Americans in Enemy Hands', in Bob Moore and Kent Fedorowich (eds.), *Prisoners of War and their Captors in World War II* (Oxford: Berg, 1996)

Liddle, Peter, and Whitehead, Ian, 'Not the Image but Reality: British POW Experience in Italian and German Camps', *Everyman's War*, no. 8 (winter 2003)

MacKenzie, S. P., 'The Shackling Crisis: A Case-Study in the Dynamics of Prisoner-of-War Diplomacy in the Second World War', *International History Review* vol. 17 (1995)

——'The Treatment of Prisoners of War in World War II', *The Journal of Modern History* , vol. 66, no. 3 (Sept. 1994)

Mallinson, W. P., and Warren, W., 'Repatriation: A Psychiatric Study of 100 Naval Ex-Prisoners of War', *British Medical Journal*, 8 Dec. 1945

Moore, Bob, 'Unruly Allies: British Problems with the French Treatment of Axis Prisoners of War 1943–1945', *War In History*, vol. 7, no. 2 (Apr. 2000)

——and Barbara Hately-Broad, 'Living on Hope and Onions: The Everyday Life of British Servicemen in Axis Captivity', *Everyman's War*, no. 8 (winter 2003)

Radford, R. A., 'The Economic Organisation of a P.O.W. Camp', in Paul A. Samuelson et al, *Readings in Economics*, 5th edn (New York: McGraw Hill, 1967); first published in *Economica*, vol. 12 (1945).

Read, David, 'Books in Prison: Reflections of a POW Chaplain', pts 1 and 2, *Chambers's Journal*, 9th Series, Oct., Nov. 1947

Rolf, David , '"Blind Bureaucracy": The British Government and POWs in German Captivity, 1939–45', in Bob Moore and Kent Fedorowich (eds.), *Prisoners of War and their Captors in World War II* (Oxford: Berg, 1996)

—— 'The Education of British Prisoners of War in German Captivity, 1939–1945', *History of Education*, vol. 18, no. 3 (Sept. 1989)

Rowe, Willis C., 'Ethics of Surrender' *Infantry Journal*, vol., 58, no. 4 (Apr. 1946)

'The Rüsselheim Death March', *After the Battle*, no. 57 (1987)

Shavit, David '"The Greatest Morale Factor next to the Red Army": Books and Libraries in American and British Prisoner of War Camps in Germany During World War II', *Libraries and Culture*, vol. 34, no. 2 (spring 1999)

'The "Special Treatment" of Jewish Prisoners of War', *The Wiener Library Bulletin*, vol., 18 no. 2 (Apr. 1964)

Vance, Jonathan F., 'The Politics of Camp Life: The Bargaining Process in Two German Prisoner of War Camps', *War and Society*, vol. 10 (May 1992)

—— 'The Trouble with Allies: Canada and the Negotiations of Prisoner War Exchanges', in Bob Moore and Kent Fedorowich (eds.), *Prisoners of War and their Captors in World War II* (Oxford: Berg, 1996)

Whiles, W. H.,'A Study of Neurosis among Repatriated Prisoners of War', *British Medical Journal*, 17 Nov. 1945

Wood, Richard, 'Music in P.O.W. Camps in Germany, 1940–1945', pts 1 and 2, in *Making Music*, May, June 1947

NEWSPAPERS AND MAGAZINES

The Camp, Daily Mail, Daily Telegraph, Guardian, Prisoner of War, Prisoner of War Bulletin, The Times, The Trentonian

Index

Index

POW refers to Allied prisoners unless stated otherwise.

Camps may be found listed either under their designation (e.g. Stalag Luft III) or their location (e.g. Sagan).

Camps in Germany and occupied territories are listed in Roman numerical order. Those in Italy carry a PG prefix.

INDEX

189, 194; Center compound
104, 124, 131, 175, 191, 198,
202, 228, 302; North compound
113, 114, 124, 174–5, 202; East
compound 124, 202; South
compound 175; escape attempts
255, 258, 259, 261, 264, 266,
269–72, 275
Sagan Golf Club 162–3
St Ives School (artists' community)
159
St Matthew Passion (J. S. Bach) 179
Saint-Nazaire: raid on 37–9, 44
Salonica (Frontstalag 183) 47, 48,
107, 159, 216
Sampson, Fr Francis L. 228, 230–1
San Francisco (magazine) 327
San Vittore (Milan): prison of 291
Sandbostel (Stalag XB; naval camp;
pre-1942) 44, 52, 78
sanitation 73, 91, 93
Sansom, Odette (aka 'Odette'; *later*
Churchill; *then* Hallowes) 21–3,
60–2, 89–90, 306–7, 326
Santos, Sergeant Ernest de los 263,
264
SAO (senior American officer) 123,
124–5
Sargent, Captain Roland L. 29–30
Sark (Channel Islands) 244
Sartre, Jean-Paul 94
SBO (senior British officer) 56,
123, 124
Scarborough, Fr Cyril 227–8
Scharff, Hanns Joachim 59
Schmidt, Paul 54
Schneider, Colonel 128
Schubin: Oflag 64 69, 82, 102–3,
127–8, 169, 187–8, 198, 301–2,
307; Oflag XXIB 81, 82, 125,
128–9, 259, 260, 266

Schuschnigg, Kurt von 305
Schuster, Herr (Gestapo agent) 111
Schweinfurt: raid on 29, 31, 57
Scouting for Boys (Baden-Powell) 185
Selby Wright, Very Revd Dr R.
('Radio Padre') 240
senior American officer (SAO) 56,
123, 124–5
senior British officer (SBO) 123,
124
Sestriere (Italian POW ship) 51
Seven Sonnets of Michelangelo
(Britten) 180
Sevigliano (PG 59) 167
sex 117–21
shackling of prisoners 244
Shanker, Sergeant Major ('Softie')
138
Sheely, Fr W. 13
Shepherd, Graham 292–3
Sherriff, RSM Sidney 132, 215
Shinn, Captain Roger L. 213; initial
capture 19–20, 23, 40–1; Stalag
XIIA 53, 109, 112, 206; Oflag 64
82, 99, 127–8, 187, 301; Stalag
XIIIC 139, 195, 209; liberation
and repatriation 307–8, 319;
aftermath 322, 326
Shinn, Carol 326
Shinn, Katherine 326
Shore, John 259–60
Shuttleworth, Lieutenant Colonel
286
Sidi Rezegh (North Africa) 12, 207
Signal (camp magazine; German
pub.) 193
Silone, Ignazio: *Fontamara* 185
Simonds, Lieutenant Colonel A. C.
283
Sinclair, Lieutenant Mike 256–7
Skanziklas, Sortiras 270–2

393